This Is BASIC

This Is BASIC

An Introduction to Computer Programming

Robert F. Sutherland

Bridgewater State College

Macmillan Publishing Company
NEW YORK

Collier Macmillan Publishers
LONDON

Macmillan Publishing Company
866 Third Avenue, New York, New York 10022

Collier Macmillan Canada, Inc.

Library of Congress Cataloging in Publication Data

Sutherland, Robert (Robert F.)
  This Is BASIC.

  Includes index.
  1. Basic (Computer program language)   I. Title.
II. Title: This is B.A.S.I.C.
QA76.73.B3S97   1984   001.64'24   83–907
ISBN 0–02–418370–9

Printing: 1 2 3 4 5 6 7 8   Year: 4 5 6 7 8 9 0 1 2

ISBN   0-02-418370-9

To Paula
and the clan:
Jeffrey
Andrew
Sara
Amy

The purpose of this text is to provide the reader with an introduction to computer programming. Anyone who is comfortable with elementary algebra has the necessary level of mathematical sophistication to complete this text. One of the prime requirements for computer programming is the ability to analyze a problem logically and construct a step-by-step solution. The text will assist the reader in this process. The BASIC programming language is the means used to introduce the reader to programming.

BASIC was developed at Dartmouth College in the early 1960's by John Kemeny and Thomas Kurtz. Since then it has become perhaps the most widely used programming language, and its popularity continues to increase. It is found on both large computer systems and small home computers. Its appeal is due primarily to its simplicity. BASIC is an uncluttered language and easy to learn.

It has been my experience that one of the most serious errors made by beginning programming students is the tendency to code a program at the terminal as it is being entered. Although this may be possible with simple programs, it is nevertheless a bad habit to acquire and will almost certainly lead to difficulty once the programs take on some complexity. Consequently, it is my belief that the student, even at the very beginning, should start the problem-solving process with at least a semi-formal problem analysis. Besides the writing of a program, the results of problem analysis are presented in one of three ways: an informal discussion of the solution to the problem; a more formal, step-by-step algorithm, and a flowchart. In this text, one, two, or sometimes all three methods are used.

Because of the interactive nature of BASIC, the INPUT statement has been introduced rather early (Chapter 6), followed fairly soon (Chapter 10) by the READ statement. Strings first appear in Chapter 7 and are integrated throughout the rest of the text. The topic of top-down programming is discussed in Chapter 14, although the technique is used earlier. Appendixes include uses and examples of system commands, data files, sorting, structured programming, and enhancements that may be found in different versions of BASIC. Appendix A may be read after the completion of Chapter 4. Appendix B, concerning BASIC data files, may be introduced after Chapter 10 has been completed. Since sorting requires the use of arrays, Chapter 13 should be completed before reading Appendix C. Sections D.1 through D.4 of Appendix D, which deal with structured programming constructs, require the completion of Chapter 9 in the text. Section D.5, which includes a discussion of the PRINT USING statement, will require a familiarity with the READ statement and so can be used after Chapter 10.

Problem-solving techniques and the necessary BASIC statements are presented through discussion and are illustrated by examples. The text includes over 190 examples.

There are over 325 exercises in the text, many with multiple parts. Several of the exercise sets are broken into two parts by three asterisks. The exercises above the asterisks can be done by everyone; those below are more complex and/or require a more extensive mathematics background to be meaningful. Solutions to many of the exercises are given in the back of the text.

An instructor's manual will be available that will include solutions to many additional problems.

BASIC is a very dynamic language. Since it was first introduced, there have appeared many "versions" of the language. They differ from one another in the extra features that they offer that may be available on one computer system but not on the next. The BASIC presented in this text corresponds to recommendations for a "minimal BASIC" proposed by the American National Standards Institute (ANSI) in their publication of 1978 (ANSI x3.60–1978) and/or to the recommendations, not yet published, by that same organization for a new set of guidelines for the BASIC language. Thus the BASIC shown in these pages should be able to be implemented on almost any computer. Several optional features are mentioned in the footnotes. In addition, since BASIC is used on different manufacturer's computers, the system commands for a particular computer may be different from the ones given in this text. For these two reasons it would be helpful, if not necessary, to consult with your instructor and/or the manuals for the computer you are using as you progress through this text.

To my students, who were the reason for a preliminary set of notes that became this text and whose suggestions helped to smooth some rough spots, I offer my sincere appreciation. Among the many people whom I want to thank are Joseph Chiccarelli, who helped to start it all; Walter Gleason, for his assistance at the very beginning of the development of this text; Robert Macek, Macmillan's computer science editor, for his help and guidance through this project; Joseph Martin, who class tested an early version of this text; and my colleagues at Bridgewater State College, for sharing their ideas. I wish to thank Henry Mailloux and Thomas Moore for their suggestions for the exercise sets and Donald Simpson, who found the time to read the entire manuscript. My thanks are extended to my reviewers Walter J. Briggs (University of Montana), James H. Buxton (Tidewater Community College), Richard M. Gilman

(University of Hartford), Patrick Lamont (Western Illinois University) and Roy L. McCormick (Ball State University) for their constructive criticisms and valuable suggestions.

To Patricia Shea, many thanks for the ability to read my writing and marginal notes and turn them into a readable manuscript.

Finally, "thank you" to my wife Paula for her patience and for the countless hours of proofreading at the kitchen table.

ROBERT F. SUTHERLAND
Bridgewater, Massachusetts

CONTENTS

1

1

Introduction

1.1	What Can Computers Do for You?	1
1.2	Computer Components	2
1.3	Computers: Large and Small	7
1.4	The Language of Computer Instruction	11
1.5	Time Sharing	12

2

2

Problem Solving

2.1	An Overview	14
2.2	Introduction to Flowcharts	15

3

3

Arithmetic in the Computer

3.1	BASIC Variables	25
3.2	Arithmetic	26
3.3	Evaluating Expressions	27

4

4

Entering a Program

4.1	The Terminal	31
4.2	On-Line	32
4.3	Your First Program	33
4.4	The END Statement	33

4.5   The LET Statement   34
4.6   The PRINT Statement   35
4.7   The RUN Command   35
4.8   The LIST Command   35
4.9   System Commands   36
4.10   Another Program—A Further Use of PRINT   36

5

5

5.1   An Example   40   **Editing and Errors**
5.2   Typing Lines Out of Order   41
5.3   Choice of Line Numbers   41
5.4   Eliminating a Line from Your Program   42
5.5   Changing Characters   42
5.6   Error Messages   44

6

6

6.1   An Example of Unnecessary Labor   47   **Conversing with the**
6.2   The INPUT Statement   47   **Computer**
6.3   When to Use INPUT Instead of LET   48
6.4   More on INPUT   49
6.5   PRINT with INPUT   49
6.6   A Last Look   50

7

7

7.1   PRINT   56   **More on PRINT**
7.2   The TAB Feature   59   **and LET**
7.3   A Closer Look at LET   62
7.4   Memory Diagrams   64
7.5   An Introduction to Strings   67

8

8

8.1   "Straight-Line" Programs   72   **Beginning Loops**
8.2   Detailed Flowcharts   72
8.3   Conditional Transfer   74
8.4   Relations   75
8.5   The Flowcharting Symbol   76
8.6   Loops   78

8.7   Stopping a Program   81

8.8   The REM Statement   82

8.9   Ingredients of a Loop   84

8.10   Memory Diagrams for Loops   92

8.11   Strings Used with IF-THEN   94

9

9

9.1   A Look Back   100

9.2   The GOTO Statement   103

9.3   The "Problem" with GOTO   111

9.4   The STOP Statement   114

9.5   Nested IFs   115

9.6   Another Form of IF-THEN   120

9.7   A Further Look at Strings   121

9.8   Counting   123

9.9   Summing   127

9.10   Large and Small Numbers   131

9.11   The ON-GOTO Statement   134

**More on Transfers
and Looping**

10

10

10.1   Three Apparently Different Programs   142

10.2   The Data Stack   143

10.3   The General Forms   145

10.4   The Flowcharting Symbol for READ   146

10.5   Strings with READ   148

10.6   Examples   150

10.7   End of Data Indicator   154

10.8   Finding the Largest Value in a Set of Numbers   158

10.9   RESTORE   158

**The READ
Statement**

11

11

11.1   The SQR Function   169

11.2   The ABS Function   171

11.3   The INT Function   173

11.4   Additional Mathematics Functions   182

11.5   User-Defined Functions   182

11.6   String Functions   185

Functions

12

Counting Loops: The Easy Way

12

12.1	An Example Done Two Ways	192
12.2	The General Form of FOR-NEXT	195
12.3	Flowcharting the FOR-NEXT	203
12.4	Nested FORs	208

13

One-Dimensional Arrays

13

13.1	Subscripted Variables in Mathematics and BASIC	226
13.2	Some Examples	228
13.3	The DIM Statement	232
13.4	Subscripted String Variables	241

14

Subroutines

14

14.1	GOSUB-RETURN	254
14.2	The Flowcharting Symbols	260
14.3	Modules and Top-Down Programming	262

15

Two-Dimensional Arrays

15

15.1	Warehouse Inventory	279
15.2	Double Subscripted Variables in Mathematics and BASIC	280
15.3	The DIM Statement Used with Two Subscripts	284

16

The Random Number Generator

16

16.1	The Built-in Function, RND	305
16.2	Random Numbers Over Any Range	306
16.3	Random Integers	308
16.4	Simulation and Games	310

Appendix A   Terminal Use and Some System Commands   325

A.1	Log-in	325
A.2	Storing a Program	328
A.3	Accessing a Stored Program	329
A.4	Changing a Permanent Program	330
A.5	Log-off	330
A.6	Some Extras	331

Appendix B Files   332

Appendix C Sorting   342

    C.1 A Simple Sorting Algorithm   342
    C.2 The Bubble Sort   347

Appendix D Structured Programs and Enhanced BASIC   352

    D.1 Structured Programming   352
    D.2 Sequence   352
    D.3 Selection   352
    D.4 Repetition   357
    D.5 Enhanced BASICs   359

Appendix E Answers to Selected Exercises   373

Index   443

1 Introduction

This book is about computers. More specifically, it will show you how to instruct (or program) a computer to do a variety of tasks. The computer is ushering in a new age that will undoubtedly have as great an impact on modern life as the industrial revolution did in years past. The industrial revolution was based on using machines to extend one's physical powers; the computer gives one a tool to extend one's mental powers.

After receiving very specific instructions on how to perform certain jobs, a computer can execute these instructions over and over again at an incredibly high speed. By combining various jobs that the computer has learned to perform, complex jobs can be undertaken. In this book we will instruct the computer by using a computer "language" called BASIC (Beginner's All-purpose Symbolic Instruction Code), which employs a small group of English words to control the computer.

A computer can be programmed to perform a variety of tasks. Business applications of computers include preparing bills for customers and paychecks for employees as well as many other important record-keeping and accounting functions. Scientific and engineering applications include using computers to perform many complex mathematical calculations. But these jobs, which people traditionally link to computers, are only the tip of the iceberg when it comes to the potential uses of computers.

Today computers are being used to study such philosophical questions as "How do people (and computers) learn?" and "What is intelligence?" Computers are being used to control robots, which may someday operate our factories. Computers can answer your phone, teach you how to fly a plane, improve your chess game, translate languages, and even compose poetry or music. Computers may not do all these things well, but their capabilities are advancing every day. Moreover, as their prices fall, computers are being built into everything from automobiles to kitchen appliances. Today the only limitation to the potential uses of computers is your imagination.

1

As you read this book, give free rein to your imagination. When you think of new uses for computers or new programming ideas, jot them down. As you progress through this book and your programming ability increases, many of your ideas may become reality. Your ideas may help you to join the growing ranks of computer pioneers who have added so much to the quality and enjoyment of our lives.

1.2 Computer Components

There are basically two types of computers: one is called *analog* and the other *digital*. Both perform calculations of some sort, but they differ in the way that they perform them. The analog computer essentially does its calculations by means of measuring. An example of an analog device (not a computer by any means) is the speedometer in your car. It shows you the results of its calculations (how fast your car is traveling as a result of measuring the speed of the rotation of a wheel). On the other hand, a digital computer does its calculations by means of counting. The abacus (Figure 1.1) is an example of a digital calculating device. The results of the calculations are seen by counting the appropriate beads on the wire frame. Since it is the digital type of computer that is most widely used, that is the type we will consider.

A digital computer can be thought of as being composed of five main parts. Figure 1.2 indicates this makeup.

We will look at each of the five parts in the paragraphs that follow.

Input. One of the most common input devices is a typewriter-style keyboard. You enter instructions and data by typing it in through the keyboard. To help you keep track of the information you are entering, the information entered is frequently displayed on a visual display unit or, as it is also called, a cathode ray tube (CRT), which resembles a television screen. A keyboard and a CRT are shown in Figure 1.3. Other

FIGURE 1.1. An abacus. (Courtesy of IBM.)

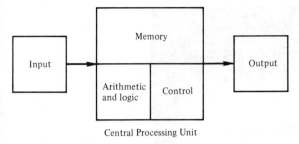

FIGURE 1.2. Diagram of a digital computer.

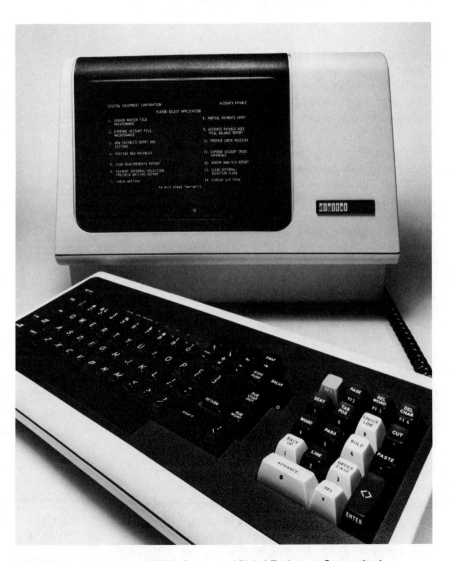

FIGURE 1.3. Keyboard and CRT. (Courtesy of Digital Equipment Corporation.)

FIGURE 1.4. A paper printing device. (Courtesy of Leading Edge Products, Inc.)

input devices may cause the information to be printed on paper rather than on a visual display unit. A paper printing unit is shown in Figure 1.4.

Another common input device is a card reader (shown in Figure 1.5), which takes the familiar punched cards and translates the information on the cards for the computer.

The function of input for a computer can be compared with the way in which we humans receive information about the world around us. We have learned to make use of our five senses of sight, hearing, smell, taste, and touch. The most common form of input to a computer is the keyboard, which in fact is a form of the sense of touch. You may have seen other methods of computer input based on this sense of touch in electronic games that use "joy sticks" and game paddles. An even newer development is the use of touch-sensitive screens that allow you to place your finger on a section of a video display screen and the computer can sense which portion of the screen your hand has touched. The computer may have been programmed to display expanded information on the topic that is located on the area of the screen you have touched.

Our sense of sight has been imitated by computers that can "read" product bar codes (UPC codes) found on packaged goods at the local supermarket. Smoke detectors and noise detectors used in burglar alarm systems can also be linked to computers, giving them a limited version of the senses of hearing and smell.

Optical character recognition (OCR) input devices allow computers to read human printing. Current developments in computer voice recognition have the capability to permit us to dictate a letter and have the computer automatically write out the text as we speak the words. Although this book concentrates on using the keyboard for input to the computer, it is interesting to stay abreast of developments in other forms of input.

Whatever the particular device available to you, in this text we will refer to it as a *terminal.*

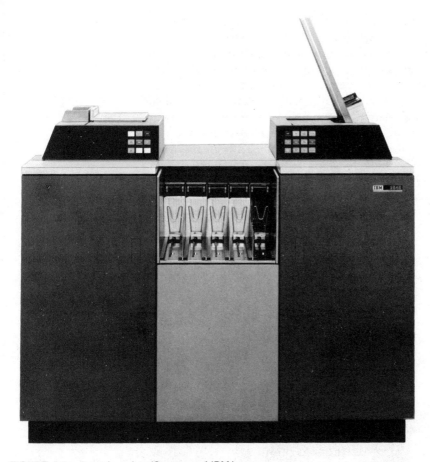

FIGURE 1.5. A card reader. (Courtesy of IBM.)

Central Processing Unit. This part, usually called the CPU, is really the computer itself. A large part of the CPU is made up of the memory unit where instructions and data can be stored. The arithmetic and logic section is where the computer performs its calculations and makes its decisions. Finally, the "control" portion of the CPU is the place where the machine does just what the label says it does—it controls. This part of the computer manages what happens in the other parts of the computer system. For example, control might first require that instructions and data be supplied from the input device. Then, using the instructions and data, "control" might cause some calculations to be done by the arithmetic section. The results of the calculations might then be stored back in memory—all being directed by the control section. If, in fact, the computer had performed some calculations and had stored the results, the computer would be wiser than we are, since it would have the answer to the problem (now stored in memory) and we would not know what it is. We now need a way of displaying the answer to the person who needs it.

Output. An output device is a means of displaying the results of the calculations the computer has performed. (Results displayed on an out-

put device can be other than numeric, as we shall soon see.) Control
will direct the results to be displayed on the output device. Very likely,
the output device you will use will be the same device that displayed
the information as you entered it from the input unit—namely, the CRT
or printer. Another common output device is a *line printer* that produces
an entire line of output at a time, in contrast to a CRT or terminal
printer, which displays one character at a time. (Such output devices
are called *serial printers*.) A line printer is shown in Figure 1.6.

Although the output produced by computers is usually in the form
of bodies of text or numeric results, meaningful output can be displayed
for certain users in numerous other forms.

Using a *plotter* (shown in Figure 1.7), data can be displayed in graph
form. Some line printers and plotters can make use of different colors

FIGURE 1.6.   A line printer. (Courtesy of Digital Equipment Corporation.)

FIGURE 1.7. A plotter. (Courtesy of Houston Instruments, a division of Bausch and Lomb.)

to produce attractive, eye-catching output. Color output is a standard feature of home video games that use a television set as its output device. Scientists and engineers frequently use programs that produce three-dimensional video line drawings (Figure 1.8) of objects that can be moved and rotated for further examination.

Computers are also able to generate sound that resembles the human voice. Sometimes when you dial a telephone number that has been disconnected, the "voice" on the other end of the line telling you about the disconnection is actually a computer-generated voice imitator. Recently, voice and music synthesizers have become available with home computers and video game systems.

The combination of an input device, a CPU, and an output device is frequently referred to as a "computer system," a "system," or merely a "computer"; the system you will work with will fit this description.

1.3 Computers: Large and Small

The year 1946 saw the completion of the first electronic digital computer—ENIAC (electronic numeric integrator and calculator). Its electronics consisted of over 18,000 vacuum tubes, it covered approximately 15,000 square feet of floor space, and it weighed 30 tons. It could perform over 200 multiplications in a single second and cost more than $400,000. Since then the appearance, performance, and cost of computers have undergone dramatic changes.

The CPU of a large computing system is sometimes called a *mainframe.* A mainframe is capable of processing large amounts of data at extremely high speeds, storing large quantities of data in its memory, and supporting many input and output devices. The users of main frames require large, fast, sophisticated computers to meet their needs. The price of a large computing system can easily reach $1 million or more.

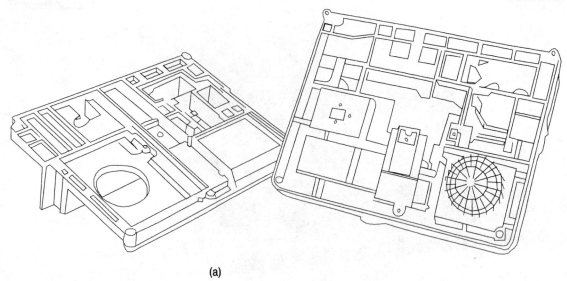

(a)

FIGURE 1.8. Three-dimensional video line drawings. (Courtesy of Houston Instruments, a division of Bausch and Lomb.)

A *minicomputer* can be thought of as a smaller version of a mainframe. It is usually a physically smaller machine, has less memory, and processes data less quickly. A minicomputer will usually be able to support several input and output devices but significantly less than that of a mainframe. As the physical size of mainframes decreases and improved technology increases the capabilities of minicomputers, the distinction between the two types of systems is becoming less obvious. However, since the prices for minicomputers start at $15,000 to $20,000, the price difference is still easy to see.

In the late 1960s and early 1970s, an incredible breakthrough in electronics resulted in the creation of tiny pieces of silicone (called *chips*) that could contain thousands of electronic components. A chip is approximately ¼ inch square—smaller than a fingernail—and due to improving technology can hold almost 100,000 components. Some chips can be purchased for less than $20.

A *microprocessor* is a single chip that acts as the arithmetic and logic unit as well as the control unit of a CPU. A microprocessor is the "computer" that is found in automobiles, appliances, and home video games. When one or more additional chips are added to the microprocessor as well as input and output units, the result is called a *microcomputer.*

One particular type of microcomputer is the *home computer* or *personal computer,* a fairly recent arrival in the computer marketplace. These computers are small and fairly inexpensive yet powerful enough to satisfy the needs of a homeowner, a student engaged in technical or scientific work, or even the owner or manager of a small business. The personal computer is appearing more and more frequently in elementary and high schools as well as being widely used in higher education. (A recent survey showed that there was at least one computer in over 25 percent of all elementary and secondary schools in the United States.) Three personal computers are shown in Figures 1.9, 1.10, and 1.11.

(b)

FIGURE 1.9. Commodore 64. (Courtesy of Commodore Business Machines.)

FIGURE 1.10. Radio Shack personal computer. (Courtesy of Tandy Corp.)

FIGURE 1.11. IBM PC. (Courtesy of IBM.)

The number of personal computers in use today exceeds 1 million and is growing dramatically. Prices for a personal computer range from less than $100 to $3,000, and the power of one of today's personal computers is far greater than that of ENIAC.

The computer language that you will be learning in this text can be used with most, if not all, of the personal computers available for purchase.

1.4 The Language of Computer Instruction

How does a computer understand an instruction such as "print"? A computer is an electronic machine and only "knows" or can sense whether or not electricity is passing through its circuits. Each circuit in a computer can be thought of as "on" (if there is current passing through it) or "off" (if there is no current). The computer is made so that when a collection of circuits has a certain arrangement of "ons" and "offs," the computer will cause something to be printed. A computer "understands" sequences of "ons" and "offs" in its circuitry. The language of a computer, then, is a collection of instructions, each of which is a sequence of "ons" and "offs." These instructions comprise what is called *machine language*. A person would write a machine language instruction by writing a collection of 1's and 0's that correspond to "ons" and "offs," respectively. A machine language is said to be written in *binary*, since it is composed solely of 1's and 0's. (The binary number system uses only 1's and 0's for its digits.)

A computer language that uses familiar words such as "print" or "read" is called a *high-level language*. However, since a computer understands only machine language, the words of a high-level language must be translated into machine language. The translation is done by something called a *compiler*. A compiler takes a word written in a high-level language and translates it into a set of machine language instructions that can be executed by the computer.

A *computer program* may be described as a sequence of instructions, written in a language understandable by a computer and given to a computer to solve a problem or perform a task. If the program is written in a high-level language, the program is called a *source program*. The compiler translates the source program into a machine language program called an *object program*. The object program is then executed by the computer.

Many small computers use an *interpreter* instead of a compiler to translate high-level instructions into machine language. The interpreter translates a single instruction into machine language, executes it, continues on to the next single instruction, translates and executes it, and proceeds in this manner through all the instructions. A compiler translates all the instructions into machine language and then executes the resulting object program.

Computer *hardware* refers to the actual physical machinery. Computer *software* generally refers to the programs, processes, and documentation associated with a computer system. This may include manuals written by the manufacturer of a particular computer and even textbooks used for study or reference. Input and output devices are part of the computer's hardware. Interpreters and compilers are part of the software of a computer since they are actual programs that reside in the computer's memory while a particular high-level language is being used.

The first major high-level programming language, called FORTRAN, was developed in 1957. It was, and still is today, a language primarily intended for scientific applications. Many other high-level languages quickly followed. COBOL is the name of a language that is used chiefly in business applications. The language studied in this book, BASIC, is considered a general-purpose programming language.

1.5 Time Sharing

Many of you as you proceed through this text will be using the computer on a *time-sharing* basis. Time sharing is a means by which a computer can service several users at virtually the same time. For example, suppose that ten people, using ten separate terminals, are connected to the computer at the same time. The computer might allocate one one hundredth of a second to each user. So the first person has the use of the computer for one one hundredth of a second, and then the computer moves on to the next user for another one one hundredth of a second, and so on. By the time the computer comes back to the first user, only one tenth of a second has elapsed. It would seem to each user that he or she has exclusive use of the computer, when, in reality, the ten users are sharing the computer's time.

FIGURE 1.12.   A personal computer system connected to a modem (*mo*dulator–*dem*odulator). (Courtesy of Epson.)

Because of the incredible speed at which computers operate, hundreds, not tens, of users can time-share on most large computers. These users need not be located near the computer, but instead, their terminals may be connected through telephone lines to the computer located many miles away. Sometimes the connection is made via a line that connects the terminal directly to the computer, but frequently the connection is made through a *data set* or *modem* that is attached to the terminal and that accepts a telephone receiver (see Figure 1.12). Modems can be purchased for personal computers so that they can be tied into a mainframe.

A system or *network* of small computers (including personal computers) or terminals can be connected to a mainframe to share data and communicate with each other.

Whatever type of a computer you will be using, you are now ready to learn how to use it.

2

Problem Solving

The computer is a piece of electronic equipment that has been designed by people whose background and training are extensive in mathematics and engineering. This does not mean that we need a lot of training in math or engineering to communicate effectively with and instruct a computer. It does mean, however, that we must be able to approach a problem in a logical way, since the computer is made to operate according to a well-defined set of instructions and in a very specific manner.

2.1 An Overview

The road from being given a problem to its solution by a computer has several steps. These steps are

1. Problem definition.
2. Analysis of problem.
3. Flowchart.
4. Coding of the program.
5. Input of the program into the computer.
6. Execution of the program (and correction of it afterward, if necessary).

Before we go any further, recall what the word *program* (or *computer program*) means. *A program is a sequence of instructions given to a computer to solve a problem.* Now that we see the relation between a program and a problem, let's consider the first step in the process—the problem definition. All we mean here is that the problem must be given to the person who is to solve it in a clear and precise manner. The problem statement may be verbal or written. Clearly, in this text, the problems will be in writing.

The second step, analyzing the problem, refers to the activity you will undertake shortly after you have received the statement of the problem. You will begin by making sure that the problem is clear and precise to you. If it is not, you go back to the person who made the assignment and ask enough questions until the problem becomes clear and precise. You then start to think about a way or ways to solve the problem. It may be that several occur to you to solve the problem. Decide on one. You should decide on what variables will be needed, what they will stand for, and how they will be used. (Variables are used to stand for various quantities that your program processes.) Some variables may be used for input, some for computations, and some for output. Some variables will likely be used for two or even all three of these purposes. You might write down some steps to follow to arrive at a solution. One or more of these steps may involve using a formula. You must think how the problem solution is related to the computer—its power and its restrictions. The end result of your analysis should be a step-by-step procedure that you will instruct the computer to follow to solve the problem. Such a step-by-step procedure is called an *algorithm.* The construction of the algorithm is perhaps the most important part of the problem solution.

A *flowchart* is merely a sketch or diagram of your algorithm. It eliminates much of the wording in your algorithm and replaces it with certain symbols that can easily be translated into computer instructions.

By *coding* we mean the actual writing of the instructions in a particular computer language for our program.

To *enter the program,* we will type it in at a terminal.

Finally, we will type in an instruction to tell the computer to *execute the program,* that is, to solve the problem. What can very likely happen, especially at first, is that, instead of the solution to your problem, your output will consist of one or more messages printed by the computer telling you that you have made some errors. These errors are most likely due to faulty typing, but they may also be due to the incorrect use of an instruction. You then correct your errors and execute the program again. (This time, it is hoped, it will work. If not, keep correcting your errors until it does.)

Errors in a computer program are called *bugs.* The process of correcting errors is called *debugging.* This last sequence of activities, executing the program and correcting errors, is referred to as *testing and debugging.*

2.2 Introduction to Flowcharts

The remainder of this chapter deals primarily with analyzing some problems, writing algorithms, and drawing flowcharts of the algorithms. Figure 2.1 gives some commonly used flowcharting symbols.

The terminal symbol, an oval, is used to indicate the beginning and end of the flowchart.

The rectangle is the symbol used when we wish to assign a value to a variable. The value may be a constant or the result of a calculation.

The symbol used for output is supposed to look like a sheet of paper hastily torn from a terminal or printer (hence the uneven bottom edge!).

The flowcharting symbols are connected by flow arrows that you follow when reading a flowchart. Note that between the bottom two symbols the arrow has been replaced by a straight line—this is called a flow line, and it is perfectly correct to use a line instead of an arrow (as

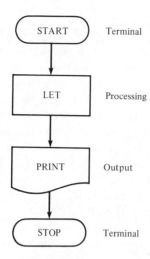

FIGURE 2.1.

long as we follow the convention that, if a flow line is used instead of a flow arrow, the flow should be from top to bottom or from left to right). The symbols used in flowcharting can be easily and neatly drawn by using a *flowcharting template,* a piece of plastic with holes cut out that are the necessary shapes. A picture of a template is shown in Figure 2.2.

The word "LET" appears in the processing symbol, and the word "PRINT" is found inside the output symbol. These words will be actual statements in the language we will study and so actually should not appear inside the symbols. (A flowchart should be, as much as possible, "language independent"; that is, the flowchart should show you how to solve a problem no matter what particular computer language you are using. Thus a flowchart should include no specific words from a

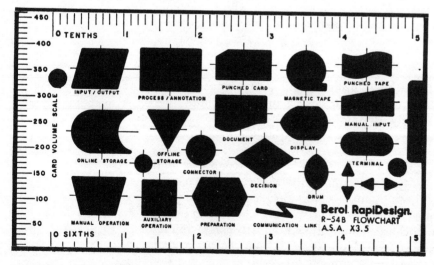

FIGURE 2.2. A flowcharting template. (Courtesy of Rapid Design.)

specific language.) However, for a little while at least, we will continue
to use words within the symbols so that you can more quickly associate
the symbols and their meanings.

Let us consider a flowcharting example.

EXAMPLE 2.1.   A car travels at a rate of 35 miles per hour for 4 hours.
We wish to calculate and print the distance the car has traveled. (This
is the problem statement.)

Our analysis includes the use of the formula for the distance traveled
by a moving object, $D = R \times T$, where D is distance, R is the rate of
speed, and T is the time traveled. The formula immediately shows us
that we need to use three variables: R (which will be assigned the value
35), T (to be given the value 4), and D (whose value will be assigned
by using the formula). Once the value of D is calculated, it will be printed
out. This analysis yields the more compact algorithm:

1. Assign 35 to R.
2. Assign 4 to T.
3. Assign to D the value calculated by the formula $D = R \times T$.
4. Print the value of D.

The algorithm then leads to the flowchart in Figure 2.3.

As we have pointed out before, to read a flowchart, find the

(START) symbol and from there follow the flow arrows until the

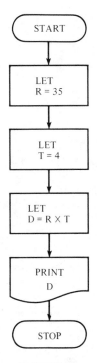

FIGURE 2.3.

STOP) symbol is reached. Whenever possible, draw a flowchart so that it is read from top to bottom. To assist you in drawing neat, readable flowcharts, use a flowcharting template.

Let us consider another problem, analyze it, develop an algorithm, and draw a flowchart.

EXAMPLE 2.2. Calculate and print the area of a circle whose radius is 7.

We see that the problem is very much like the previous one. We have a formula to use: $A = \pi R^2$, where A stands for area and R is the radius. The symbol π represents a number that we will approximate by 3.14. We will use the English letter P to stand for the Greek letter π, so the value 3.14 will have to be assigned to P. The algorithm to use, then, is

1. Let R have the value 7.
2. Let P have the value 3.14.
3. Let A be calculated using the formula $A = PR^2$.
4. Print A.

Notice that the wording in this algorithm differs somewhat from that of the previous algorithm. This is not important. What is important is that the correct sequence of steps is specified and the wording, no matter how it is phrased, describes the activity correctly.

From the algorithm, we get the flowchart in Figure 2.4.

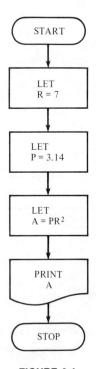

FIGURE 2.4.

EXAMPLE 2.3. A homeowner wishes to fence in a vegetable garden. The garden is rectangular in shape and measures 55 feet by 25 feet. Fencing costs $3 per foot. The flowchart should calculate and print the amount of fencing needed and the total cost for the fence.

The amount of fencing needed is equal to the perimeter of the rectangle, which can be calculated by the formula $P = 2 \times (L + W)$, where L is the length of the garden and W its width. The cost of the fence can be found by multiplying the perimeter by 3, the per foot cost of the fence. In addition to the three variables P, L, and W, we will need a variable for the cost of the fence. Call that variable C. An algorithm and flowchart are shown in Figure 2.5.

1. Let L be 55.
2. Let W be 25.
3. Calculate P by the formula $P = 2 \times (L + W)$.
4. Calculate C by $C = P \times 3$.
5. Print P.
6. Print C.

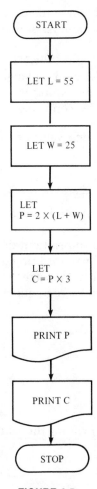

FIGURE 2.5.

If the program derived from the flowchart in Figure 2.5 were coded, entered, and executed (all correctly, we presume), the output displayed on the terminal would be the two numbers

160
480

If we were presented with the output

160
480

it may not be clear which number refers to the cost of the fence and which refers to the total amount of fencing. This illustrates the need for labeling our output. The output from a computer program should always include some sort of labeling—words or phrases that clearly describe what the numbers stand for. The next example will illustrate how this can be done.

EXAMPLE 2.4.   A flowchart is to be drawn for the problem of the previous example with the additional requirements that each number should be labeled.

First notice that in Figure 2.6 the words "LET" and "PRINT" are missing. It has already been stated that a flowchart should be language independent, so the removal of the two words is something we want to do. The symbols without the words should not be confusing, since

□   is to be used solely for processing (assigning values to variables) and ▱ will only be used for printing.

We also see the symbol ▱ "TOTAL FENCING" . This is the symbol that makes the last two flowcharts different. This symbol is used to print out the label "TOTAL FENCING" before the value of the perimeter is printed. So in general, to indicate on a flowchart that you wish a message (word, phrase, or even sentence) printed, you enclose the message in quotation marks and write it inside the output symbol.

The output for this problem would be

TOTAL FENCING
    160
COST
    480

You should note the important difference between printing the value of a variable and printing out some message. The symbol ▱ X

means print the *value* of the variable X (it is, of course, assumed that

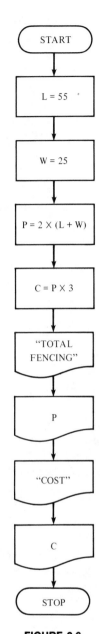

FIGURE 2.6.

X has already been assigned some value). On the other hand, to print the *letter* "X" (a sort of message!), the symbol would be used.

EXAMPLE 2.5. The population of a town has been growing at a rate of 12% over each 5-year period. The population today is 14,572. We want to know what the population will be 5 years from now.

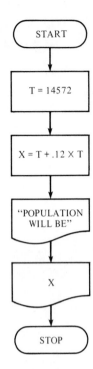

FIGURE 2.7.

To solve this problem, 12% of the current population must be calculated. When this result is added to the current population, the future
population will be obtained. The variable T will be assigned the value
14,572. The variable X will stand for the population in 5 years. X will
be calculated by adding T and .12 × T (.12 is the decimal representation
of 12%). X will then be printed, preceded by a label. The preceding
analysis gives the flowchart in Figure 2.7.

You should note that in the second processing symbol the assignment
statement X = T + .12 × T can be thought of as the "formula" needed
to calculate X. In some problems you will be able to use well-known
formulas; in others you will have to develop your own.

Write a brief analysis and draw flowcharts for Exercises 1 through 8.

EXERCISES

1 A worker is paid $5.34 per hour. Calculate and print the worker's weekly
pay for a 37.5-hour workweek.

2 A salesperson for a certain company receives a 14% commission of the
total sales. Calculate and print the amount of commission on sales of $2,782.

3 Janet Langone intends to install wall-to-wall carpeting in her living room.
The room is rectangular and measures 6 yards by 5.2 yards. The carpet costs
$12.95 per square yard. Calculate and print the area of the living room floor
(the formula is $a = l \times w$) and the cost for the carpeting. Each value should
be printed with a label.

4 A television that usually sells for $425 is on sale at a 20% discount. Calculate
and print the sale price of the TV. The price should be labeled.

5 The Fitch family is moving to another town and will rent a truck to make the move. The rental will be $16.50 per hour plus $1.25 per mile. It will take 9 hours to complete the move and the Fitch's new home is 23 miles away. Find out how much the move will cost the Fitch family.

6 The diameter of a circle is 5. Calculate and print the value of the circumference (the formula is $c = \pi d$).

7 The area of a triangle is ½ × base × height. Calculate and print the area of a triangle that has 15 as its base and 4 as its height. The value of the area should be labeled.

8 The formula used to calculate the hypotenuse of a right triangle is $h = \sqrt{x^2 + y^2}$, where x and y are the lengths of the sides of the triangle. Calculate and print the hypotenuse, labeled, of a triangle with sides 12 and 5.

9 What would be printed out by the computer if it executed the program that corresponded to the flowchart in Figure 2.8?

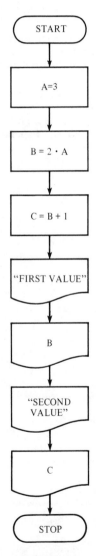

FIGURE 2.8.

Draw flowcharts for Exercises 10 through 16.

10 The radius of a certain circle is 11.2. Print out the values of the radius, diameter, circumference, and area. All four values should be preceded by a label.

11 The retail price of an appliance is $437. On sale, it is discounted by 12%. Print out, with labels, the retail price, the *amount* of the discount, and the sale price (after discount).

12 A baseball player has 123 hits in 416 times at bat. Print out the number of "at bats," the number of hits, and the batting average. Each should be preceded by a label. (The batting average is the number of hits divided by the number of "at bats.")

13 The price of a sports car this year is $14,386. Next year the price will increase by 9%. Find and print the *amount* of the increase and next year's price. Both quantities should be labeled.

14 The Chip Calculator Company employs 80 people. Of this total, 60% are employed in the early shift, 30% in the evening shift, and the remaining 10% in the night shift. Find the number of employees in each shift and print these results. The results should be labeled.

15 Fiberglass insulation is on sale at $4.23 per roll. A consumer purchases 17 rolls. The purchase is subject to a 6% sales tax. Calculate and print the amount spent before the sales tax, the amount of sales tax, and the total amount spent. Three values should be printed with labels.

16 Ms. Holmes earns a monthly salary of $1,524. Of this amount, 14% is taken by taxes and 5% is deducted for her retirement plan. Each month she must also pay $163 for her car, $275 for rent, $380 for groceries, and $155 for utilities. Find and print her monthly expenses and the amount of spendable income left over. Both amounts should be labeled.

As you have learned, the computer language you will study is called BASIC (Beginner's All-purpose Symbolic Instruction Code). Don't let the name frighten you. BASIC is probably the easiest computer language to learn, and once you do learn it, you should find it easier to learn other computer languages.

In the next chapter we will begin to write BASIC programs, but first, there are two other topics that must be discussed.

3.1 BASIC Variables

In the chapter on flowcharts we saw variables being used. For example, in one flowchart, the variable T was used for time; in another, C was a variable that stood for cost. What, then, are the variables that are allowed in BASIC?

A *variable* that can be used for the BASIC language is simply any letter of the alphabet or any letter followed by a *single* digit.[1]

For example, the following are "legal" BASIC variables.

A   X   B4   YØ

The symbol Ø following the Y is a zero, not the letter "oh." Since we will have to make the distinction between zero and "oh," from now on we will write Ø for zero and 0 for "oh."

The following are "illegal" BASIC variables.

1A   H2Ø   4

1A is not legal because it does not begin with a letter, H2Ø has too many characters, and 4 is a constant and not a variable.

---

[1] This description of a variable is that given by minimal BASIC. Many versions of BASIC allow more characters to be used. However, we will follow this convention in this text.

A variable, as it is used in computer programming, is the name of a location or address in the computer's memory. The datum that is stored in that memory address is the value of the variable that names the address. More will be said about this in the next chapter.

The second topic is arithmetic. We need to know what kind of arithmetic the computer will do for us, what symbols are used, and how the arithmetic is done.

BASIC allows five arithmetic operations: addition, subtraction, multiplication, division, and exponentiation (raising to a power). The table following shows the five operations, the symbol of arithmetic that is usually used, the symbol that BASIC uses for the operation, and examples from algebra with the same example written in BASIC.

Operation	Arithmetic Symbol	BASIC Symbol	Example from Algebra	Same Example in BASIC
Addition	$+$	$+$	$x + 3$	X+3
Subtraction	$-$	$-$	$a - b$	A−B
Multiplication	$\cdot$ or $\times$ or juxtaposition	$*$	$7 \cdot y$ or $7 \times y$ or $7y$	7*Y
Division	$\div$ or $/$	$/$	$t \div 8$	T/8
Exponentiation	None	$\uparrow$	5^2	5↑2

Some points should be noted about the contents of the table.

1. In the top line, we see the algebraic example $x + 3$ and the corresponding X+3 in BASIC. When you type in a program from a terminal, usually only capital letters will be used. Some terminals allow lowercase letters, but for this text we will use only capital letters.
2. The * is a symbol that *must* be used whenever you want to multiply two quantities. Even though it is perfectly permissible in algebra to omit a multiplication symbol (as in $7y$), this is *never* allowed in BASIC (you must always use 7*Y).
3. The division of T by 8 will be typed T/8; all the symbols should be on the same line—you should not try to make it look like $\frac{T}{8}$.
4. The upward-pointing arrow (↑) is the symbol for exponentiation (although some versions of BASIC use the double asterisk, **, and some allow both ↑ and **). It should be noted that some terminals only display the "head" of the arrow (that is, ˆ). Don't worry. Both will work.

All that remains is to find out how the computer evaluates an expression such as $3\uparrow2+4*(-3)-1$ (by "expression" we mean a combination of variables and/or constants connected by the arithmetic operations).

**3.3 Evaluating
Expressions**

The computer evaluates an expression by following the rules of algebra for evaluating an algebraic expression.[1] So first the machine searches the expression for a set of parentheses and, if found, evaluates whatever is inside. Next, the computer looks for the operation of exponentiation. If it finds that operation, it performs that calculation. The next type of simplification done is that of multiplication or division, and the final simplification done by the computer is addition or subtraction. You should note that, just as in algebra, two operation symbols may not appear consecutively unless one is enclosed within parentheses. For example, $3-+X$ is not legal.

You might rightly ask what happens if an expression to be evaluated has both multiplication and division. Which operation should be done first? The final rule that governs the evaluation of expressions is that, when faced with both operations of multiplication and division, or with both the operations of addition and subtraction, or perhaps an expression that has the same operations appearing more than once, the process to follow is to simplify going from *left to right.*

To summarize, the order to be followed when evaluating an expression is

1. Simplification within parentheses (if a set of parentheses contains one or more additional sets of parentheses, the simplification is done from the innermost set outward).
2. Exponentiation.
3. Multiplication and division (left to right).
4. Addition and subtraction (left to right).

A few examples should help to clarify these procedures.

EXAMPLE 3.1. Evaluate $4+(2*3)$.

We note the parentheses in the expression, so we calculate the $2*3$ first, getting 6. We may now think of the problem as looking like $4+6$. Since the only operation to be performed is addition, we do it and get the final result 10. Thus $4+(2*3)=1\emptyset$.

EXAMPLE 3.2. Evaluate $4+2*3$.

This example is the same as the last one except that the parentheses are omitted. Let's see what effect, if any, the omission has.

Since there are no parentheses, we now look for the exponentiation operation ($\uparrow$). There is none. Next we seek multiplication or division.

---

[1] One possible exception concerns the evaluation of an expression such as $-3\uparrow2$. Most computers follow the rules of algebra and square 3 first (getting 9) and then apply the unary operation of negation, giving the result -9. However, some computers may give 9 as the final result. Check yours.

There is a multiplication: 2*3. We perform this calculation and add 4 to the result to get the final answer, 10. Thus 4+2*3=1Ø.

This was the same result as the first example. Does this mean that parentheses are unneeded when writing expressions? Evaluation of (4+2)*3 should quickly show that the answer is no. Why then do 4+(2*3) and 4+2*3 have the same value? With 4+2*3, the operation of multiplication, according to the rules we stated earlier, must be performed before addition. But when considering 4+(2*3), the rules say that whatever is inside the parentheses must be done first—but what is inside is multiplication!.

As a safe rule, when you are *writing* expressions (whether in algebra or BASIC), do not hesitate to use parentheses, as long as you are using them correctly.

As an example, consider the two expressions

$$\frac{AB}{C}$$

and

$$\frac{A + B}{C}.$$

The first of these expressions is correctly written in BASIC as (A*B)/C, but you should observe that the parentheses are not needed. Without parentheses, the expression would be A*B/C, and since * and / are on the same level of evaluation, multiplication (the leftmost operation) is done before division. On the other hand, parentheses are necessary when writing

$$\frac{A + B}{C}$$

as (A+B)/C.

EXAMPLE 3.3. Evaluate 16−(6*2)/3.

$$
\begin{aligned}
16-(6*2)/3 &= 16-12/3 && \text{parentheses} \\
&= 16-4 && \text{division} \\
&= 12 && \text{subtraction}
\end{aligned}
$$

EXAMPLE 3.4. Evaluate 2↑4+16/4−1Ø*2.

$$
\begin{aligned}
2\uparrow4+16/4-1\emptyset*2 &= 16+16/4-1\emptyset*2 && \text{exponentiation} \\
&= 16+4-1\emptyset*2 && \text{division (left to right)} \\
&= 16+4-2\emptyset && \text{multiplication} \\
&= 2\emptyset-2\emptyset && \text{addition (left to right)} \\
&= \emptyset && \text{subtraction}
\end{aligned}
$$

EXAMPLE 3.5. Evaluate $(5+24/3)-3\uparrow2+7$.

$$
\begin{aligned}
(5+24/3)-3\uparrow2+7 &= (5+8)-3\uparrow2+7 && \text{parentheses, division} \\
&= 13-3\uparrow2+7 && \text{parentheses} \\
&= 13-9+7 && \text{exponentiation} \\
&= 4+7 && \text{subtraction (left to right)} \\
&= 11 && \text{addition}
\end{aligned}
$$

EXAMPLE 3.6. Evaluate $2*(6+(9-5)\uparrow3)-1$.

$$
\begin{aligned}
2*(6+(9-5)\uparrow3)-1 &= 2*(6+4\uparrow3)-1 && \text{inside parentheses} \\
&= 2*(6+64)-1 && \text{exponentiation, parentheses} \\
&= 2*70-1 && \text{parentheses} \\
&= 140-1 && \text{multiplication} \\
&= 139 && \text{subtraction}
\end{aligned}
$$

EXAMPLE 3.7. If $A=6$ and $B=2$, evaluate $A*4/3*B$.
If an expression contains variables, the very first thing to do is to substitute the numeric value for the variables and then continue as usual.

$$
\begin{aligned}
A*4/3*B &= 6*4/3*2 && \text{substitution} \\
&= 24/3*2 && \text{multiplication (left to right)} \\
&= 8*2 && \text{division (left to right)} \\
&= 16 && \text{multiplication}
\end{aligned}
$$

EXAMPLE 3.8. Find the value of $2*X\uparrow Y-4/Z$ when $X=3$, $Y=2$, and $Z = 8$.

$$
\begin{aligned}
2*X\uparrow Y-4/Z &= 2*3\uparrow2-4/8 && \text{substitution} \\
&= 2*9-4/8 && \text{exponentiation} \\
&= 18-4/8 && \text{multiplication (left to right)} \\
&= 18-.5 && \text{division} \\
&= 17.5 && \text{subtraction}
\end{aligned}
$$

EXERCISES

1 Which of the following can be used as a variable in BASIC?
a. X1   b. 23   c. F   d. AØ   e. −B   f. HI
g. D1Ø   h. J8   i. 5M

2 Identify the expressions that are valid in BASIC and correct those that are not valid.
a. A+2.3   b. 7X+1   c. 3+Z/Y   d. 5+(5)
e. M*(−7/J1)   f. A + −4   g. C(D+E)   h. 3Y↑2   i. 6↑−2

3 Evaluate the following.
a. 2+7*3   b. 4*6−1   c. 5+(−11)   d. 4↑2
e. −7*7   f. 5+2↑3*6   g. 12/4*3   h. 12/(4*3)
i. 12/(2+4)   j. 12/2+4   k. 12/(2+4)/2
l. 15+(3↑2+6/3)−(14−4)*2−1Ø   m. 2*(1↑3/4)/(1/2)

4 For A=2, B=3, X=−4, and Y=1, evaluate the following.
a. $A*X + B$ b. $(X{\uparrow}A)/(B+Y)$ c. $(B/A+Y)*X$
d. $Y{-}A{\uparrow}B$ e. $A+B/A+B$

5 Write the following algebraic expressions in BASIC.
a. $R \times T$ b. $2 \times (L + W)$ c. PR^2 d. $a^2 - 3x + 2y$
e. $x \div (y + z)$ f. $\frac{1}{3}pr^3$ g. $(x \div y) + z$ h. $ax^2 + bx + c$

i. $b^2 - 4ac$ j. $\frac{x}{y} \cdot z$ k. $\frac{p}{q} \cdot \frac{r}{s}$

l. $(x^2 + 4xy) \div (x \div 2y)$ m. $\frac{a + b}{c + d}$ n. $\frac{ab}{cd}$

6 How many different variables are there?

***

7 Find the value of $(10{\uparrow}2+5{\uparrow}2){\uparrow}(1/3)$.

8 Write the following algebraic expressions in BASIC.

a. $\sqrt{x}$ b. $\sqrt{r + s}$ c. $\sqrt{\frac{2a}{b}}$ d. $\sqrt{r} \div \sqrt{s}$

e. $\sqrt[3]{t - 100}$ f. $\sqrt{b^2 - 4ac}$

4.1 The Terminal

We are now ready to give our programs to the computer. This is done by typing the program on a terminal keyboard that is connected to the computer. The picture at the opening of this chapter is a keyboard of a typical terminal. You should carefully look over the keyboard of your terminal noting where such important symbols as ↑, *, (, and) are to be found.

Also notice the key labeled RETURN, which appears at the right-hand end of the second row of keys. The use of the RETURN key is very important and we will use ® to represent it. When you see ®, it means that the RETURN key is to be pressed. A little later on, the purpose of the RETURN key will be explained.

Let's go back for a moment and look at the flowchart of Example 2.4 that was used to calculate and print the amount of fencing needed to enclose a garden and the cost of the fence.

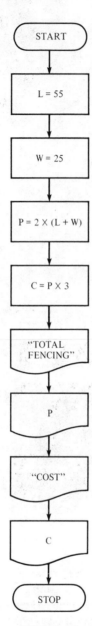

START

L = 55

W = 25

P = 2 × (L + W)

C = P × 3

"TOTAL
FENCING"

P

"COST"

C

STOP

FIGURE 4.1

The flowchart we used is shown in Figure 4.1.

We will now see the program that corresponds to the flowchart and how it is to be typed into the computer.

4.2 On-Line

Once you are seated at a terminal, you must get "connected" to the computer (once you are connected, this is called being "on-line"). There are many different ways to get on-line, depending on the kind of terminal and the kind of computer you are using. What is described in the paragraphs that follow is a very general method (another method is described in Appendix A). However, your instructor will describe the way that you must use to get connected with your particular computer.

On the terminal there is a power switch, frequently labeled OFF-ON. Put the switch in the ON position. You are now connected to the computer. (Your terminal may have another switch labeled LOCAL-LINE. If so, turn this to LINE.) Once you are on-line, you are ready to type in your program.

4.3 Your First Program

Assuming that you make no typing errors, the entry of the program should look like this:

```
10 LET L=55®
20 LET W=25®
30 LET P=2*(L+W)®
40 LET C=P*3®
50 PRINT "TOTAL FENCING"®
60 PRINT P®
70 PRINT "COST"®
80 PRINT C®
90 END®
```

Now let us take a close look at the program. A first glance shows that each line of the program starts with a number. These numbers are called *line numbers,* and each line or statement in a BASIC program must begin with a line number. The line numbers are used by the computer to establish the order in which the instructions are to be carried out: first, line 10 is to be performed by the computer, then line 20, then line 30, and so on. The computer always begins to execute the program beginning at the smallest line number and proceeding, at least for now, in increasing order. You can also see that the line numbers we use begin with 10 and increase by 10's. This pattern is not absolutely necessary, but for a while we will continue to follow it.

Next we notice that each line ends with ®; that is, after typing our entire line, we must finish the line by pressing the RETURN key. Pressing the RETURN key indicates that all the characters just typed (letters, numbers, special characters such as commas and semicolons, and even blanks) are to be considered by the computer as a single unit of information—in this case, a single instruction. Each instruction, then, is completed by pressing the RETURN key.

4.4 The END Statement

Next we shift our attention to line 90. The BASIC statement is END. In each program you write, the END statement must appear exactly once. It must be the last statement in your program; that is, the END statement must be preceded by the largest line number you use in your program.

4.5 The LET Statement

The statement LET appears four times in the program. We have already seen this word used in connection with our flowcharting. It was used with the processing symbol, the rectangle, and is used to assign a value to a variable. A LET statement must be used as follows. First, there must be a line number. Next, the word LET must appear. Following this, the variable to be defined (that is, to be assigned a value) must be given, followed by an equal sign (=) and finally some expression.

What we have just said describes the *general form* of a LET statement, that is, the way every LET statement must be written.

The *general form of a LET statement* is

line number   LET variable = expression or constant

In line 1Ø we see LET L=55. L is the variable to be assigned a value and 55 is the value that is given to L. You should note that the variable that is being assigned a value must *always* appear to the *left* of the equal sign. For example, it would be incorrect to write line 1Ø as LET 55=L.

In Chapter 3 it was stated that a variable was the name of a memory address and the contents of that address (datum) was the value of the variable. Considering LET L=55, when we say that the variable L was assigned the value 55, we mean that the number 55 is stored in a particular memory location that the program labels L. This can be visualized by a box labeled or named L containing the number 55 as shown.

```
+------+
|  55  |
+------+

   L
```

Both lines 3Ø and 4Ø are examples of variables being assigned values using expressions (in contrast to line 1Ø, where the variable L is assigned a value using the constant number 55). When a LET statement uses an expression to assign a value to a variable, the computer first evaluates the expression (simplifies it to a single number) and then assigns that single value to the variable on the left of the equal sign. To illustrate, let us consider line 3Ø. It was pointed out earlier that a computer executes a program beginning with the smallest line number and then proceeds to the next highest line number. Thus, when the computer reaches line 3Ø, both lines 1Ø and 2Ø have been executed so that L and W have numeric values. The machine now uses these values in the expression 2*(L+W) and calculates the number 160. This value, 160, is assigned to the variable P. You should remember that when a variable is to be assigned a value using an expression, all the variables *in the expression* must already have been given values.

Suppose, for example, that we had written

```
1Ø LET L=55
2Ø LET P=2*(L+W)
3Ø LET W=25
```

The variable in line 20 would not take on the required value, because at line 20, where the expression 2*(L+W) is being calculated, the variable W in the expression has not yet been given a value. So we can see that the order in which we write the statements in a program is crucial—but this is exactly what was meant when we said that a computer program was a *sequence* of instructions. You must do more than write down a set of correct instructions; they must also be written in the correct *order*.

4.6 The PRINT Statement

Finally, the output statement, PRINT, appears in lines 50, 60, 70, and 80. It is used in two different ways. In line 50, the statement

PRINT "TOTAL FENCING"

is used to print the *phrase* TOTAL FENCING. Thus whenever we want a word, phrase, or sentence printed on the terminal, we merely enclose the word, phrase, or sentence in quotation marks and precede it with a line number and the statement PRINT.

In line 60, the PRINT statement is used to print out the *value of a variable*. Recall again that PRINT P means "print the *value* of P" just as it did using the flowcharts. Thus to instruct the computer to print the value of a variable, you must type the line number followed by PRINT and then the variable.

4.7 The RUN Command

When we considered this problem as a flowchart in Chapter 2, it was pointed out that execution of the program would cause the output

```
TOTAL FENCING
    160
COST
    540
```

The command to cause the computer to execute your program is RUN. So after you have correctly typed in the entire program, you would then type RUN ® (don't forget to press RETURN!).

4.8 The LIST Command

If you now type LIST ®, a copy of your program will be printed on the terminal. Thus,

```
LIST ®

10 LET L=55
20 LET W=25
30 LET P=2*(L+W)
40 LET C=P*3
```

```
5Ø PRINT "TOTAL FENCING"
6Ø PRINT P
7Ø PRINT "COST"
8Ø PRINT C
9Ø END
```

RUN will cause your program to be executed, whereas LIST will cause a copy of your program to be typed out for you. Also, after you have typed LIST or RUN and the computer has completed the command, it will type READY.[1] [This is the computer's way of telling you that it has carried out your command (LIST or RUN) and is now "ready" for you to do something else.] Thus when you execute this program what you will see printed on the terminal is

```
RUN

TOTAL FENCING
 16Ø
COST
 48Ø

READY
```

4.9 System Commands

This is a good time to point out the difference between statements such as 8Ø PRINT C and commands such as RUN. The differences are significant but easy to understand and recognize.

A statement, for example, PRINT, is actually part of the vocabulary of the BASIC programming language, whereas the command RUN is not. RUN is an example of what is called a *system command*[2] or operating command. Essentially, a system command tells the computer what to do with your program (e.g., RUN it or LIST it). The language statement is part of your program and so is part of the sequence of steps that will solve your problem for you. The simplest way to tell the difference between a system command and a language statement is to notice that a system command does not begin with a line number, whereas a language statement in a program does. Some additional system commands may be found in Appendix A.

4.10 Another Program—A Further Use of PRINT

We will conclude this chapter by considering another example that illustrates another way in which the PRINT statement can be used.

---

[1] This response may differ somewhat from machine to machine.

[2] System commands are peculiar to the particular computer you are using. Different computer manufacturers may use different commands to accomplish the same result. For example, to execute a program, it may be necessary to type the system command GO rather than RUN.

EXAMPLE 4.1. A rectangular billboard is to be painted a solid color prior to the installation of an advertisement. The billboard is 25 feet long and 18 feet high. A gallon of paint will cover 375 square feet. A program is to be written that will print out the dimensions of the billboard, calculate and print the area to be painted, and finally find and print the number of gallons of paint needed for the job. All values should be labeled.

The area of a rectangle is obtained by the formula $a = l \times w$. An algorithm to solve this problem is

1. Assign 25 to L, the length.
2. Assign 18 to W, the width (or height).
3. Print L and W with labels.
4. Calculate the area A by L × W.
5. Print A with a label.
6. Calculate G, the number of gallons needed, by dividing A by 375.
7. Print G with a label.

Let us look at the program together with its output; then we will discuss the PRINT statements that were used to produce the output.

```
10 LET L=25
20 LET W=18
30 PRINT "LENGTH","HEIGHT"
40 PRINT L,W
50 LET A=L*W
60 PRINT "AREA IS",A
70 LET G=A/375
80 PRINT "NUMBER OF GALLONS NEEDED IS";G
90 END

RUN

LENGTH              HEIGHT
 25                  18
AREA IS             450
NUMBER OF GALLONS NEEDED IS 1.2

READY
```

It should be clear that the output of the program produces the required results. From line 30, we see that the PRINT statement can be used to print more than one word or phrase per line. Line 40 shows that the value of more than one variable can be printed on the same line. Notice that both these lines uses a comma between the items that are to be printed on the same line. Notice also that the words LENGTH and HEIGHT are printed out, separated by quite a few spaces. This is how the comma works in connection with the PRINT statement—placing commas between items to be printed will cause them to be printed on the same line separated quite a bit from each other.

The last two lines of output are caused by lines 60 and 80 in the program:

60 PRINT "AREA IS",A

and

80 PRINT "NUMBER OF GALLONS NEEDED IS";G

First, observe that a PRINT statement can be used to print *both* a phrase and the value of a variable. Again we see that these two items appear on the same line in the output. Because of the comma used in line 60, the two output items are separated. However, note that in the output caused by line 80 the phrase NUMBER OF GALLONS NEEDED IS appears close to the value of G, 1.2.

In line 80 a semicolon is used instead of a comma. The semicolon is used between items that are to appear on the same line of output but that, when printed, will appear rather close to each other.

The flow charting symbol to use for 30 is `"LENGTH", "HEIGHT"` and for line

80 `"NUMBER OF GALLONS NEEDED IS"; G`

---

1 Write a LET statement that
  a. assigns the value 7 to X.
  b. assigns to A the sum of B and C.
  c. assigns the expression $3M + 3N$ to Q.
  d. assigns to D the expression $G^2 + H^2$.
  e. assigns to M the expression $\dfrac{Y2-Y1}{X2-X1}$.

2 Write a PRINT statement that will
  a. print out the value of the variable Y.
  b. print out the phrase "your result is".
  c. print out the word "volume" and the value of V on the same line, closely spaced.
  d. print out the phrase "the surface area is" and the value of S on the same line, separated by quite a bit of spacing.

3 *Carefully* enter, RUN, and LIST the program.

```
10 LET C=4
20 LET E=3
30 PRINT "THIS IS CHAPTER"
40 PRINT C
50 PRINT "AND EXERCISE NUMBER"
60 PRINT E
70 END
```

4 What, if anything, is wrong with the following statements?
  a. LET X=2
  b. 180 PRINT A MESSAGE
  c. 100 END
  d. 215 LET X2=2X
  e. 317 LET X3=3*X
  f. 119 PRINT "PRINT"

5 Given the following program, show what its output would be, including the approximate spacing between output items.

```
100 LET X=3
110 LET Y=7
120 PRINT "X"
130 PRINT "Y"
140 PRINT X
150 PRINT Y
160 PRINT "X AND Y"
170 PRINT X;"AND";Y
180 PRINT "X","AND","Y"
190 PRINT X,"AND",Y
200 END
```

6 Refer to the flowchart of example 2.5. Code the program from the flowchart. Carefully type the program, LIST it, and RUN it.

7 Write the program from the flowchart you drew for Exercise 3 in Chapter 2. Enter it, LIST it, and RUN it.

8 At a terminal, get "on-line," type LIST, and see what happens. Then type RUN and see what happens.

9 Suppose the side of a square is 5. Write a program that prints the words "side," "perimeter," and "area" on a single line and below these words the three corresponding values. (You should draw a flowchart first.)

10 Refer to Chapter 2, Exercise 15. Write the program, enter it, LIST it, and RUN it.

11 Refer to Chapter 2, Exercise 16. Write the program, enter it, LIST it, and RUN it.

12 How could you change the program of Exercise 3 so that the values of C and E are printed on the same line as their respective descriptions?

13 Type and RUN the following program. Notice the output.

```
10 LET A=2
20 LET B=3
30 LET C=4
40 LET D=A+B
50 LET E=B↑A
60 LET F=C-D
70 PRINT A,B,C,D,E,F
80 END
```

5.1 An Example

In the last chapter it was assumed that you typed in your program without committing any typing errors. In practice you will very likely make a number of such errors. It will be the aim of this chapter to show you ways of correcting these errors. This is usually referred to as *editing* your program and will be best illustrated by considering some examples. We will use as our sample the program from Section 4.3 that dealt with fencing in a garden.

EXAMPLE 5.1.   The coding for the program you wish to enter is

```
10 LET L=55
20 LET W=25
30 LET P=2*(L+W)
40 LET C=P*3
50 PRINT "TOTAL FENCING"
60 PRINT P
70 PRINT "COST"
80 PRINT C
90 END
```

Suppose that you began typing in the program and you typed

```
10 LET L=55 ®
20 LET W=26 ®
```

At this moment, having entered line 20 incorrectly, you see your mistake (you typed a 6 instead of the required 5). To correct this error, you merely *retype the entire line correctly.* So you then type

```
20 LET W=25 ®
```

What has happened? It seems that you now have two line 20's. But what actually occurs is that this last version of line 20 completely replaces the first version you typed in! This technique can always be used to correct mistakes in your program; that is, after you have entered the incorrect line (by pressing ®), you merely type it over again correctly (don't forget to type in the line number, too).

5.2 Typing Lines Out of Order

EXAMPLE 5.2.   You have typed the following lines:

```
10 LET  L=55  ®
20 LET  W=25  ®
40 LET  C=P*3  ®
```

Now you see that line 30 has been accidentally left out. This omission is easily corrected by just typing

```
30 LET  P=2*(L+W)  ®
```

Since you used 30 as your line number, the computer understands you to mean that this last line should go between lines 20 and 40, and the computer will put it there. To check this for yourself, type LIST ®, and you will see

```
10 LET  L=55
20 LET  W=25
30 LET  P=2*(L+W)
40 LET  C=P*3
```

READY

Line 30 is included in the program just where it should be!

5.3 Choice of Line Numbers

A comment needs to be made at this time about the use of line numbers. You have been starting each program with line number 10 and have been adding 10 for each successive line number. This is not actually necessary. The line numbers that you can use for your program will depend upon the particular computer you are using, but most computers will allow you at least the numbers from 1 to 2000 for your line numbers (some machines allow line numbers as high as 99999). So why have we been using 10, 20, 30, and so on for our line numbers?

The chief reason that we do not use consecutive line numbers is so that we will have extra lines available to us in case we need them. This kind of a situation could arise if, after we typed in our program, we realized that we needed another line to make our program work correctly. For example, suppose that our program used lines 10, 20, 30, 40, and 50, and the program did not work because we had left out a line between our first two instructions (that is, between lines 1Ø and 2Ø). We could easily correct this difficulty by entering the needed instruction as line 15 (or 13 or 18 or any number between 1Ø and 2Ø). Notice that this insertion would not have been possible if we had originally used consecutive line numbers such as 1, 2, 3, 4, and 5 or 25, 26, 27, 28, and 29. So when you write your programs, be sure to leave "space" between your lines so that you can insert other lines if necessary.

5.4 Eliminating a Line from Your Program

EXAMPLE 5.3. Someone has typed in the following:

```
25 PRINT "FIRST LINE OF OUTPUT"
5Ø PRINT "THIS LINE WILL VANISH"
75 PRINT "SECOND OUTPUT LINE"
1ØØ PRINT "LAST LINE"
5Ø
125 END
```

If you typed RUN, the program would print out

```
FIRST LINE OF OUTPUT
SECOND OUTPUT LINE
LAST LINE
```

and if you typed LIST, the computer would give

```
25 PRINT "FIRST LINE OF OUTPUT"
75 PRINT "SECOND OUTPUT LINE"
1ØØ PRINT "LAST LINE"
125 END
```

Line 5Ø has disappeared! This was caused by the typing of "5Ø" after line 1ØØ in the original typing session. What happened was that a second line 5Ø was typed in (thus replacing the original line 5Ø), and no instruction was included in this latest line (that is, the new line 5Ø was an empty or blank line). The effect then is that line 5Ø has been eliminated from the program. So to eliminate a line from your program, merely type the line number and press the RETURN key.[1]

5.5 Changing Characters

The following example shows you how you can correct an error if you notice the error *before* you have entered the line (by pressing RETURN). (The first example that we look at in this chapter shows how to correct an error *after* it was entered.)

[1] As a general rule, be sure to press Ⓡ *immediately* after typing the line number. With some computers, if you type the line number, type a blank and then press Ⓡ, the line (with only the blank "character") will remain in your program.

EXAMPLE 5.4. You intended to type in the line 4∅ LET X=2, and when you had typed 4∅ LEY, you noticed that you had accidentally pressed the Y key instead of the T key. To correct this error, you press the RUBOUT key.

When you do this, a ← will be printed by the terminal. This means that the last character you typed (the Y) has been eliminated. The line on the terminal now looks like 4∅ LEY←. You merely continue typing the rest of the line correctly beginning with the letter T. So if you make no more typing errors, the line should be

    4∅ LEY←T X=2 ®

If you now LIST the lines you have typed in, you will see your problem line as

    4∅ LET X=2

Three points should be noted about this technique. First, the way in which a character is eliminated and the way in which the elimination is indicated may differ from computer to computer or even terminal to terminal. The procedure indicated (and the one that will also be used in Example 5.5) is used on some systems, but not all. The precise process for you to use can be found by referring to a manual for the equipment you are using or by asking your instructor. On most CRTs, the "←" will not be shown, but instead the cursor (the equivalent of the printhead on a printing terminal) will move back to the left one space each time you press RUBOUT. Instead of using RUBOUT, your computer may require that you press a key labeled BACKSPACE or perhaps ERASE. *You should check the requirement of the equipment you are using in this regard.*

Second, you may erase more than a single character by repeated uses of RUBOUT.

Finally, blanks are considered characters, so they may also have to be eliminated in your corrections.

EXAMPLE 5.5. We now illustrate these last two points. You have typed

    65 PRIMT A

and have discovered your error and have not yet pressed RETURN. To make your corrections you press RUBOUT four times (the first time to eliminate the A, the second to eliminate the blank, the third time for the T, and the fourth time for the M). You then complete the line correctly. So your typing line will be

    65 PRIMT A←←←←←NT A ®

When you type LIST, line 65 will be listed as

    65 PRINT A

Finally, we point out that to correct the error of this example, it might have been easier to press RETURN and retype the entire line—but such decisions will be yours to make as you are entering your programs.

5.6 Error Messages

Even though you know how to correct typing errors, other errors may occur that are due to your program and will be indicated to you by the computer. The computer will usually print an "error message" and tell you at what line in your program it occurred.

EXAMPLE 5.6

LIST

100 LET A=3
150 LET B=A↑2
200 END
250 PRINT A,B

READY

RUN

END NOT LAST AT LINE 200

READY

When you read the error message and look at the LIST of your program, it should be clear what the meaning of the error message is: the END statement, which is found in line 200, is not the last statement in your program. One way to correct this problem would be to type

200 ®
300 END ®

EXAMPLE 5.7

10 LET 5=J
20 PRINT J
30 END

RUN

ILLEGAL STATEMENT AT LINE 10

READY

The correct form to be used is

```
10 LET  J=5
```

and so you would type it in and RUN the program.

Examples 5.6 and 5.7 have illustrated *syntax errors.* A syntax error is caused when the syntactical (or grammatical) rules for the language are not followed precisely. In Example 5.6, the END statement was not the last statement in the program, as is required by BASIC. An incorrect form of the assignment statement caused the error in Example 5.7. This points out why care should be taken in coding BASIC statements—the structure of the coded statement must correspond to the general form of that type of statement. Syntax errors are found by the compiler as it translates the program into machine code. Syntax errors occur before execution and actually prevent execution of the program.

Even if your program contains no syntax errors, another kind of error may occur while the program is being RUN. These are called *execution errors* or *run-time errors.*

EXAMPLE 5.8. The program

```
10 LET  X=5
20 LET  Y=0
30 PRINT  X,Y
40 LET  Z=X/Y
50 PRINT  Z
60 END
```

contains no syntax errors, yet, when it is run, it produces

```
RUN

  5                     0
DIVISION BY  ZERO AT  LINE  40

READY
```

Generally, syntax errors are fairly easy to correct. Even though the execution error in Example 5.8 is obvious, execution errors are usually caused by faulty logic and are frequently difficult to determine.

In addition to error diagnostics issued by the BASIC compiler, your computer will print error messages if you enter faulty system commands. For example, if you had typed

```
RUM ®
```

instead of RUN, you might get

```
ILLEGAL  COMMAND

READY
```

There are many other error messages[2] that can be printed out by the computer, but they are too numerous to list here. They will be quite explicit, and you will learn quickly how to understand them and use them to correct your errors.

Finally, your computer will likely have an editing program of some kind. Such a program can be used to make changes in your BASIC program in ways different from those described in this chapter. As editing programs differ significantly from computer to computer, no attempt will be made to describe them. However, since they are valuable tools for editing your programs, you should become acquainted with the one used with your system.

---

1 How do you delete a line from your program?
For Exercises 2, 3, and 4, suppose that you have found the following lines on a terminal. If you typed LIST after each, what would the computer print?

2

```
20 PRINT "OVER"
10 PRINT "NOT"
40 END
30 PRINT "YET"
```

3

```
10 LET X=0
20 30←—LET A=4
30 LET F←G=X+A
40 PRINTF←F
50 END
```

4

```
RU←—15 PRINT "START"
25 LET R=2..7←—7
35 PRINT "MIDDLE"
45 LET S=4
55 LET T=3.1←—
65 PRINT "FINISH"
45 LET W←—W=3*R
75 PRINT T,W
85 EMD
35
```

---

[2] The error messages shown in the examples may not be printed word for word by your computer, but, however they are phrased, they will mean the same.

6.1 An Example of Unnecessary Labor

The following program calculates and prints, with a label, the area of a circle whose radius is 7.

```
10 LET R=7
20 LET P=3.14
30 LET A=P*R↑2
40 PRINT "AREA"
50 PRINT A
60 END
```

Suppose that you had just typed this program, executed it, and obtained the correct result. You now wish to find the area of a circle whose radius is 15.2. Do you need to type an entire new program to accomplish what you want to do? Certainly not! The only item that needs to be changed is the value of the radius that is defined in line 10; we have already seen that if a "new" line 10 is entered, it will replace the earlier version. Thus all that is necessary is to type

```
10 LET R=15.2
```

and RUN. If now you wish to calculate the area of a circle having radius 95.02, you merely type another line 10 that uses 95.02 as the value for R. Thus the ability to replace "old" lines with newly typed ones is certainly a time saver—we don't have to retype the entire program, only the line or lines that need to be changed. However, even this small amount of typing can be eliminated.

6.2 The INPUT Statement

A better way to write the program is to use the INPUT statement in place of the LET in line 10. If we do, the program will look like

```
10 INPUT R
20 LET P=3.14
30 LET A=P*R↑2
40 PRINT "AREA"
50 PRINT A
60 END
```

The first statement to be executed is, of course, the INPUT in line 10. When this happens, the machine prints a question mark (?) and waits for you to respond. You respond by typing in a number and pressing RETURN. The number you typed is the value that is assigned to the variable *R*. Then the machine continues in the same way as it has done before. A RUN of the program would look like

RUN

? 7   ← Here you type 7 ®
AREA
 153.86

READY

Now if you wanted to use the same program only with radius 10.1, all you need to do is type RUN and enter the value 10.1 in response to the "?".

RUN

? 10.1
AREA
 320.311

READY

Now each time you wish to find the area of a circle of any radius, merely RUN the program and type in the radius.

6.3 When to Use INPUT Instead of LET

INPUT is also used to assign a value to a variable. In response to the "?", when the user types a value and presses RETURN, that value is stored in the memory address named by the variable following the IN-PUT statement. Since LET and INPUT are both used to assign values to variables, you might wonder if there is a better time to use one statement rather than the other. The answer is yes. The program we just looked at is a good example. In it we use an INPUT to define a value for the radius *R* and a LET with the variable *P*. Since the value of P will always be the same each time we run the program, the LET is used. However, since the value for the radius is likely to be different each time we use the program, we use the INPUT command so that we can supply a value of R during the execution. You might also note that the value of A also changes each time a new radius is given, but you should also observe that the value of A is *calculated* by an expression and so would not be input. In general, if a value or values are likely to change each time a program is executed, the values should be assigned to the variables by using an INPUT statement in your program. On the other hand, if a variable always has the same value no matter how many times the program is run, use a LET to give the variable a value.

6.4 More on INPUT

Let's see another program that uses the INPUT statement.

EXAMPLE 6.1. This is a program to calculate the amount of interest obtained by investing a certain amount of money at a given interest rate for one year.

The program will use the formula $I = P \cdot R$, where I is the interest, P is the amount of money invested (the principal), and R is the rate of interest (in a decimal form, for instance, 2% is .02). Since both the principal and interest may change from RUN to RUN, both these values should be supplied using INPUT. As soon as the two values have been entered, the interest is calculated using the formula, and finally the value of the interest is printed. A program to do this task is the following.

```
10 INPUT P
20 INPUT R
30 LET I=P*R
40 PRINT "INTEREST=";I
50 END
```

Then a sample run might be

```
RUN

? 200
? .05
INTEREST= 10

READY
```

6.5 PRINT with INPUT

Even though the preceding program works, and even though it is technically correct, there is still a problem with it. After you type RUN, the first thing that happens is that the machine prints a ? and then waits for you to type a number. But when you see the ?, are you certain of what the program is requesting? Is it a length of a rectangle that is to be typed in? Is it a radius? Is it a principal? A rate? Unless you already know exactly what the computer is asking for, you might type in an incorrect value. Or look at it this way. Suppose that you have written a program for a friend to use and suppose that the first statement in the program is an INPUT. When your friend runs the program, will he or she know what the computer wants when it prints the question mark?

A good programming habit to develop is to precede INPUT statements with one or more PRINT statements that describe what is to be typed in by the person who is using the program.[1] So, to achieve this result, we would add two lines such as the following to the last program.

```
5 PRINT "PLEASE ENTER PRINCIPAL"
15 PRINT "PLEASE ENTER INTEREST RATE"
```

Now a run of the program is more easily understood.

```
RUN

PLEASE ENTER PRINCIPAL
? 200
PLEASE ENTER INTEREST RATE
? .05
INTEREST= 10

READY
```

Finally it should be noted that the addition of the lines below would aid the usability of the program even more (in fact, might even be necessary).

```
16 PRINT "THIS NUMBER SHOULD BE ENTERED AS A DECIMAL"
17 PRINT "FOR EXAMPLE 2 PER CENT SHOULD BE .02"
```

6.6 A Last Look

We know that if we want three values to be assigned to the variables A, B, and C, we can use three separate INPUT statements. It is also possible to do this with a single INPUT statement:

```
100 INPUT A,B,C
```

All the variables follow the INPUT statement, *separated by commas.*

When the computer executes line 100, it prints a single ? and waits for you to respond. You should respond by typing three values *on the same line, separated by commas.*

---

[1] Some versions of BASIC allow the PRINT and INPUT to be combined into a single statement. For example, the two lines

```
100 PRINT "WHAT IS THE COST"
110 INPUT C
```

might be combined as

```
100 INPUT "WHAT IS THE COST";C
```

The *general form of the INPUT statement* is

line number   INPUT   variable

or

line number   INPUT   a collection of variables separated by commas

EXAMPLE 6.2. Here is the interest program again.

```
19 PRINT "ENTER PRINCIPAL AND INTEREST RATE SEPARATED BY A COMMA."
29 INPUT P,R
39 LET I=P*R
49 PRINT "INTEREST=";I
59 END
```

RUN

```
ENTER PRINCIPAL AND INTEREST RATE SEPARATED BY A COMMA
? 200,.05
INTEREST= 10
```

READY

EXAMPLE 6.3. Your company, which sells computer terminals, pays its sales representatives a salary of $700 per month plus $85 for each terminal sold in that month. Write a program that asks for the number of terminals sold and then calculates and prints the monthly salary.

We will let S stand for the salary (so S will have the value 700 to begin with). We will let N be the number of terminals sold (the value of N will be supplied by the user). Then N will be multiplied by 85 and this result will be added to S giving the total salary, which will be printed. A program follows.

```
10 LET S=700
20 PRINT "HOW MANY TERMINALS SOLD THIS MONTH"
30 INPUT N
40 LET S=S+N*85
50 PRINT "MONTHLY SALARY IS";S
60 END
```

Before a few RUNs are shown, consider lines 10 and 40. In line 10, S is initially assigned the value 700. Recall that line 10 causes the value 700 to be entered into a memory location named S. Line 40, being a LET statement, causes a value to be entered into a memory location— in this case, the memory location named S, since S is the variable name that immediately follows LET. To find out what value will be entered into S, the expression to the right of the = must be *first* evaluated. The expression is the sum of the *original* value of S (700) plus any extra money due to the sale of terminals. The new value is to be entered into the memory location S, replacing the value that had been there.

When line 1Ø is executed, the memory location S should be visualized as

$$\boxed{700}$$
S

If one terminal were sold, the expression S+N*85 would have value 785, and so after the execution of line 4Ø, we would have

$$\boxed{785}$$
S

You should note that if a program uses a variable, say, *S*, there will be only one memory location named S that the program refers to. At any given time during program execution, a memory location can contain only a single value. Finally, observe that in both lines 1Ø and 4Ø the variable S has the same meaning—salary.

```
RUN

HOW MANY TTY'S SOLD THIS MONTH
? 1Ø
MONTHLY SALARY IS   155Ø

READY

RUN

HOW MANY TTY'S SOLD THIS MONTH
? Ø
MONTHLY SALARY IS   7ØØ

READY

RUN

HOW MANY TTY'S SOLD THIS MONTH
? 3
MONTHLY SALARY IS   955

READY
```

Since you should analyze and flowchart all your problems before coding them and since many will involve the INPUT statement, you need

to know what symbol to use. The symbol is [   ] . This symbol

will be used exclusively to stand for the INPUT statement, and thus you do not need to write the word "input" within the symbol, only the variables whose values are to be supplied. For example, the flow-chart equivalent of INPUT X,Y,Z would be

X, Y, Z

---

1 Find and correct the errors in the following program.

```
    PRINT "DOUBLE TROUBLE"
110 PRINT
114 PRINT "ENTER AN INTEGER
119 INPUT Z
125 "THANK YOU"
132 PRINT "NOW ENTER TWO MORE"
140 INPUT Y;X
150 LET Z2=2Z
160 LET 2Y=2*Y
170 LET X=X+X
191 PRINT "DOUBLE","DOUBLE","DOUBLE"
204 PRINT Z2,Y2,X
210 PRINT AND MORE
226 INPUT J=0
233 PRINT,J
```

For Exercises 2 through 6, write programs to perform the following tasks. Be sure that some kind of explanation is given to the user before the user must supply a value.

2 The user should supply the diameter of a circle, and the program should print out the radius. Run the program using 12, 3.5, .01, and 500 as values of the diameter. (The radius is one half the diameter.)

3 The user should supply a length, in feet, and the program should convert the length to inches and print out the length in inches. For values to use, try 3, 1, 43, and .5.

4 The program should convert a length in feet (supplied by the user) to yards. Run the program for the values 6, 1, 120, and 22.5.

5 The program should convert liters to quarts. Use 2, .46, and 1.75. (One liter is 1.06 quarts.)

6 The program should convert inches to centimeters. Use 6, 15.2, .78, 1, and .4. (One inch is 2.54 centimeters.)

7 The pressure exerted by water at the bottom of a cylindrically shaped container is 62.4 times the depth of the water (in feet). The user should supply the depth and then print the pressure. For values, try 4 (the depth of many private swimming pools), 7.5, 8, .5, and 12.

8 The Bob Dartmouth Car Rental Agency charges $12.95 per day plus $.16 per mile. Draw a flowchart and write a program so that the user (an employee of the agency) can enter the number of days and the number of miles and the program will print out the amount due. For data, try

Days	Miles
5	270
2	100
1	125
1.5	75
3	630

9 Suppose that the rate of exchange between British pounds and U.S. dollars is $1.00 is worth £.43. Write a program to accept an amount in U.S. dollars and print the equivalent in pounds. RUN the program using 200, 450, 835, and 1,219.

10 Write a program that asks the user to enter the number of miles the user's car has been driven in a year and the rate of gasoline consumption. The program should then calculate and print the number of gallons of gasoline used in a year.

11 Draw a flowchart and write a program for the following. The user should enter two numbers: the first should be the price of a purchase and the second the sales tax rate. The total price, labeled, should then be printed. Try your program with the values

Purchase Price	Sales Tax
$ 10.95	5%
173.28	4
5.55	2
101.20	3.5

12 A company's profit is equal to the amount of its sales minus its operating costs. The user should enter the sales and operating costs, and then the program should calculate and print the profit. For data, try

Sales	Costs
$ 54,783	$49,114
168,402	98,477
62,582	61,493
75,885	76,462

13 The formula for interest in Example 6.1 was a simplified version of the formula $I = PRT$, where T is the total amount of time, in years, that the money was invested. Write the program where the user enters the principal, rate, and time and then the interest is calculated and printed. For data, use

Principal	Rate	Time
$ 250	6.5%	2
1,000	7	5
725	7.25	4.5
12,000	11.82	.5

14 Flowchart and code a program for the following. In a certain mathematics course, the grade for a marking period depends on the average of three tests and one examination. Have the program request the three test grades. When this is done, the exam grade should be requested. Finally, the average of these four grades should be calculated and printed. For grades, use

Test Grades	Examination Grade
72, 81, 83	95
88, 92, 96	82
90, 73, 85	88

15 Suppose that the teacher of the mathematics course in Exercise 14 changed the way in which the average will be computed. The average of the three tests will be one grade, and this will be averaged with the examination grade to produce the grade for the marking period. Run the program with the same data given in Exercise 14.

16 Another variation of grading is to have the single exam score count as two test grades. Program this variation and use the data from Exercise 14.

17 Students are frequently heard to complain about school—how terrible it is to do all that work. An interesting program is one that would tell a student how many *hours* he or she has spent in school. We suppose that a school year consists of 180 days, that a school day begins at 8:30 A.M. and ends at 2:30 P.M., that half an hour is given for lunch, and that there is a 15-minute break each day. So the number of hours worked in school each day is 5.25. Write a program to ask the user for the last grade completed, and then calculate and print the number of hours worked in school.

18 A more up-to-date version of the program in Exercise 17 could be written if, in addition to the last grade completed, the user is asked to supply the number of weeks that have been completed in the current school year (also, how many days have been completed and perhaps even how many days has the user been absent).

19 The interest on a loan taken for a short amount of time (usually numbered in days) is frequently calculated in one of two ways. For an *ordinary interest loan,* a year is considered 360 days; for an *exact interest loan,* a year contains 365 days (or 366 days in a leap year). For such loans, the value to use for T in the formula $I = P \cdot R \cdot T$ is the number of days the loan is for divided by the number of days in that year. Write a program that calculates and prints the amount of interest due on a loan, using both methods of calculating interests. The user should enter the amount of the loan, the rate of interest, and the number of days the loan is for. Try your program using these numbers:

Loan	Rate	Days
$ 500	11%	60
2,200	9½	30
4,000	15	120

20 The user should supply the perimeter of a square. The program should calculate and print the length of a side and the area. Each should be labeled. RUN the program using 24, 18, 15, and 2.76.

* * *

21 The radius of a sphere should be entered from the terminal. Then its volume and surface area should be printed. Use 6, 7, 14, 1, and .3.

22 Two angles of a triangle are to be entered from the terminal. The third angle should be calculated and printed. For the two angles, use 30 and 40, 80 and 60, 155 and 10, 45 and 45, 60 and 60, and 105 and 75.

23 A linear equation of the form $AX + B = C$ should be solved. The user should supply the values of A, B, and C, and the program should print the solution in the form $X = $. The equations to be solved are

   a. $3X + 2 = 14$ c. $2X + 9 = 7$
   b. $7X - 5 = 51$ d. $-5X + 3 = -18$

24 The sum s of the squares of the integers from 1 to n is given by the formula

$$s = \frac{n(n + 1)(2n + 1)}{6}$$

Write a program in which the value of n is entered from the terminal and the value of s is calculated and printed.

In this chapter we continue to look at the PRINT and LET statements. We have already seen the PRINT used to print out the value of a variable (for example, 200 PRINT X), print a message (50 PRINT "HELLO"), or print a combination of the two (120 PRINT "ANSWER IS";Y). PRINT can also be used to print the value of an expression or print a constant.

EXAMPLE 7.1

```
10 LET  X=3
20 LET  Y=4
30 LET  Z=2*X+Y
40 PRINT  "X","Y","Z"
50 PRINT  X,Y,Z
60 PRINT
70 PRINT  "X+Y=";X+Y
80 PRINT  200
90 END
```

The new uses of PRINT appear in lines 60, 70, and 80. As you can see in the RUN of the program that follows, the PRINT in line 60 causes a line to be skipped. What is actually happening is that when line 60 is executed, a blank is printed (which, of course, we can't see) so that the effect is a skipped line. In line 70, following the message X+Y=, the *value* of the *expression* X+Y is printed. The computer first calculates the value of X+Y and then prints it out. Last, the constant 200 is printed out from the statement in line 80. The output for this program is

```
X                      Y                    Z
 3                     4                     10

X+Y=   7
  200
```

In Example 4.1 we saw the comma and semicolon used with the PRINT statement to give spacing to our output items. The general observation was that a comma between output items caused them to be printed on the same line, usually with several spaces between them, whereas a semicolon between items caused them to be printed close together. The comma and the semicolon are called *print control characters.* In this section, we shall see more precisely how the print control characters work as well as look at a BASIC feature to give additional preciseness to our output. To do this, we must first understand how the computer measures an output line.

For purposes of discussion, let us assume that our terminal can print 75 characters on a single line. The computer divides these 75 printing positions into five print "zones," each zone containing 15 print positions. (The number of print positions that can be used on a single line varies from one system to the next. For example, a machine that uses 72 print positions per line might use four zones of 15 characters each while the last zone contains only 12 positions.) This zoning, for a 75-position line, is as follows:

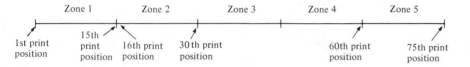

The comma, as a print control character, is directly related to the five zones. If a number or a text is to be printed and is *preceded* by a comma (as B is, in the statement PRINT A,B), it will be printed at the beginning of the next empty print zone.

EXAMPLE 7.2

```
1Ø PRINT "12345678901234567890"
2Ø PRINT "FIRST ZONE","SECOND ZONE"
3Ø END

RUN

1234567890123456789Ø
FIRST ZONE      SECOND ZONE

READY
```

The 20 digits printed by line 1Ø are for reference only—so that you may clearly see the print zones being accessed by the use of the comma. The F (in the word FIRST) is printed in the first print position, while the S (in SECOND) is printed in the sixteenth print position (the first print position of zone 2).

When the value of a variable or of an expression is printed, there is always a print position left for a sign (in case the value is negative). If the value is positive, a blank will be printed instead of a "+" sign.

EXAMPLE 7.3

```
20 PRINT "12345678901234567890"
30 LET A=5
40 LET B=-2
50 PRINT A,B
60 END
```

RUN

```
12345678901234567890
  5                    -2
```

READY

The value of A,5, is printed in the second position because A is positive. The blank preceding the 5 is the sign position. The value of B,−2, is printed in the first position of the second zone, position 16. Note that the "−" sign is in position 16.

EXAMPLE 7.4

```
10 PRINT "12345678901234567890"
20 LET N1=7
30 LET N2=9
40 LET N3=N1*N2
50 PRINT "THEIR PRODUCT IS",N3
60 END
```

RUN

```
12345678901234567890
THEIR PRODUCT IS                63
```

READY

Since the message (including blanks) is more than 15 characters long, the value of N3 will be printed at the beginning of the *next* empty zone. Zone 2 is not empty—it contains the letter S. Thus 63 must be printed in zone 3.

When the comma is used to print numbers, a maximum of five values can be printed on a single line.

EXAMPLE 7.5

```
10 LET A=3
15 LET B=5
20 LET C=8
25 LET D=11
30 LET E=-2
35 LET F=1
40 LET G=9
```

```
45 PRINT A,B,C,D,E,F,G
50 END
```

RUN

```
3               5               8               11              -2
1               9
```

READY

When all five print zones have been printed in and there is still more output to be printed, the computer will automatically move to the first print zone in the next line and continue from there.

Normally when the semicolon is used as a print control character between expressions or between an expression and a message, a space is printed between the output items. (With the semicolon, also, a space is used for the sign of the expression.) When two different texts are printed with a semicolon between them, there is *no* spacing between them (unless the programmer specifically includes a space in one of the messages, as seen in line 15 of Example 7.6).

EXAMPLE 7.6

```
10 PRINT "FIRST";"SECOND"
15 PRINT "CLOSE ";"TOGETHER"
20 LET U=23
25 LET V=489
30 LET W=-4
35 LET X=17
40 LET Y=6915
45 LET Z=88
50 PRINT U;V;W;X;Y;Z
55 END
```

RUN

```
FIRSTSECOND
CLOSE TOGETHER
 23   489  -4   17   6915   88
```

READY

7.2 The TAB Feature

The previous examples show that the use of the comma gives the programmer a great deal of ability in setting up the output from a program. The semicolon allows more than five values to be printed on a line, but, so far, there is no way to control exactly where those values will be printed.

TAB is a function that is used with the PRINT statement to allow the program to print results precisely in predetermined locations across the page. Recall that a line of output contains 75 print positions. Each of these positions is numbered from 1 to 75.[1]

Zone 1

Print position 1   Print position 15   Print position 75

Consider the program in Example 7.7.

EXAMPLE 7.7

```
20 PRINT "12345678901234567890"
30 PRINT TAB(4); "HELLO"
40 PRINT TAB(7); "THERE"
50 END

RUN

12345678901234567890
   HELLO
      THERE

READY
```

Line 20 is used only for reference. The execution of line 30 causes the message HELLO to be printed beginning in print position 4. This positioning is controlled by TAB(4). It tells the computer to move (or tab) out to the fourth print position and begin printing there. Similarly, line 40 tells the computer to begin printing in position 7.

Several TABs may be used with a single PRINT statement. This is illustrated in the following BASIC line.

```
10 PRINT TAB(5); "NAME"; TAB(20); "ADDRESS"; TAB(40); "TELEPHONE NO."
```

There is a "rule of thumb" to follow when using more than one TAB with a single PRINT. A semicolon should follow each TAB and also follow each item (except the last) that is to be output. (Some computers may treat this guideline rather liberally, but you will be safe if you follow it.)

Most computers require that tabbing proceeds from left to right. This statement, for example,

```
500 PRINT TAB(50); C; TAB(20); D
```

would not produce the apparent positioning for C and D (since a few computers do allow tabbing from right to left, you should try something like line 500 on yours).

---

[1] Some versions of BASIC number the positions from 0 to 74 instead of 1 to 75.

Suppose that we have three variables A, B, and C with values 2, 7, and 4 respectively. By now we know that if, in a program, we had

```
100 PRINT A
110 PRINT B
120 PRINT C
```

the three values would be printed on three separate lines:

```
2
7
4
```

So three distinct PRINT statements would produce three separate lines of output. However, if we had

```
230 PRINT A;B;C
```

we would get

```
2   7   4
```

namely, a single PRINT with three output items connected by print control characters will cause the three items to be printed on the same line. The same result would be accomplished by the following three lines.

```
360 PRINT A;
370 PRINT B;
380 PRINT C
```

The semicolons at the end of lines 360 and 370 override the machine's tendency to cause a new line of output for each PRINT statement. Line 360 may be thought as saying "print the value of A but do not go to the next line; rather, *whatever* is to be printed next (in this case, the value of B) should remain on the same line and be printed close to (because of the semicolon) the value of A." Line 370 makes a similar statement. This feature will be shown in the next example.

TAB would be needed if your problem called for more than five items to be printed on a single line, cleanly spaced (for five items or less the comma can generally produce the desired result).

EXAMPLE 7.8. This program requires six columns of output.

```
10 LET A=8
20 LET B=4
30 PRINT TAB(5);"A";TAB(15);"B";TAB(25);"A+B";TAB(35);"A-B";
40 PRINT TAB(45);"AXB";TAB(55);"A/B"
50 PRINT TAB(5);A;TAB(15);B;TAB(25);A+B;TAB(35);A-B;TAB(45);A*B;
60 PRINT TAB(55);A/B
70 END
```

RUN

A	B	A+B	A−B	AXB	A/B
8	4	12	4	32	2

READY

Line 30 begins the typing of six column headings. The physical limita-tion of the terminal prevented the last two headings from being typed at line 30. Line 30 ended with a semicolon, and the remaining two headings were coded in line 40. Something similar was done in lines 50 and 60.

7.3 A Closer Look at LET

Recall that a statement such as LET B=3*X+1 was executed by the machine doing two things: first, the expression on the right of the equal sign is evaluated, and, second, this value is assigned to the variable on the left of the equal sign.

Let us take a simple program and follow the values of the variables that are used in the program. The technique we will use is to draw a table next to the program, and we will *include in the table a column for each variable in the program.* So suppose our program is

```
10 LET X=2
20 LET Y=5
30 LET Z=3*X−Y
40 END
```

(a rather unexciting program!). Since there are three variables used (X, Y, and Z) our table will have three columns, one labeled X, one Y, and one Z. (Shortly, we will add another column to our table.) Now the program, together with the table we made, appears as

	X	Y	Z
10 LET X=2			
20 LET Y=5			
30 LET Z=3*X−Y			

40 END

Each of the boxes in the table refers to a memory address whose name is the variable that appears at the top of that column.

We now proceed through the program *just as the computer would.* As each LET is encountered (executed), we will enter the appropriate value in a particular box. The first line to be executed is line 10, which assigns the value 2 to the variable X. When this has been done the program/table should look like

	X	Y	Z
1Ø LET X=2	2		
2Ø LET Y=5			
3Ø LET Z=3*X−Y			

40 END

A 2 has been entered in the column under X, in the row of the table that corresponds to line 1Ø. What you should also note and readily understand is that no other entry is to be made in the table at this moment since *only the variable X has been assigned a value.*

Now line 2Ø is the next to be executed, and it deals *only with Y.* The value of X has not been affected—it is still the same. So

	X	Y	Z
1Ø LET X=2	2		
2Ø LET Y=5	2	5	
3Ø LET Z=3*X−Y			

4Ø END

Finally in line 3Ø, the expression 3*X−Y is evaluated to be 1, and the 1 is assigned to Z. So the program/table at the end of the program looks like

	X	Y	Z
1Ø LET X=2	2		
2Ø LET Y=5	2	5	
3Ø LET Z=3*X−Y	2	5	1

4Ø END

Let's move on to a program that is a little more significant.

```
15 LET X=12
25 LET Y=4
35 LET X=X/2
45 LET Y=Y*5
55 END
```

It should be clear that the program/table at the completion of line 25 would be

	X	Y
15 LET X=12	12	
25 LET Y=4	12	4

But what happens at line 35? If we follow the way a LET statement is evaluated (as was described earlier), *first* the expression X/2 is evaluated. Since the value of X is 12, the value of X/2 is 6. This value is *then* assigned to the variable following the word LET; that is, 6 is assigned to X. So the value of X (and the contents of the memory address X) is changed. Thus,

	X	Y
35 LET X=X/2	6	4

The next line shows that Y is changed similarly. So the entire program/table is

	X	Y
15 LET X=12	12	
25 LET Y=4	12	4
35 LET X=X/2	6	4
45 LET Y=Y*5	6	2Ø
55 END		

7.4 Memory Diagrams

The table that you draw next to the program is called a *memory diagram* because it shows what values are stored in the computer's memory for the variables you have in your program. Also, it shows how these values are changed as your program is executed.

Actually, in addition to columns for the variables in the memory diagram, there is usually one more column. This column is labeled "output" and is necessary because any program that does something even remotely significant will have one or more output statements.

EXAMPLE 7.9. What does the computer print when it executes the following program?

```
1ØØ LET G=3
2ØØ LET H=-2
3ØØ LET I=5*G+H
4ØØ PRINT G,H,I
5ØØ LET G=7
6ØØ PRINT G;H;I
7ØØ END
```

A memory diagram, including a column for output, is a good way of answering the question. The entries in the diagram for the first three lines of the program should be obvious.

	G	H	I	output
1ØØ LET G=3	3			
2ØØ LET H=−2	3	−2		
3ØØ LET I=5*G+H	3	−2	13	

For line 4ØØ, we merely enter the values to be printed in the output column together with the punctuation (commas) that was used with the PRINT command.

4ØØ PRINT G,H,I	3	−2	13	3,−2,13

Now what happens when line 5ØØ is executed? Notice that G is being given a value, 7. *No other variable is being assigned a value in line 5ØØ, so only the value of G is changed.* The line of the memory diagram at this line then is

5ØØ LET G=7	7	−2	13	

Two points should be noted about this. First, there is no entry in the output column. This is because line 5ØØ does not create any output; in a memory diagram, output should be entered only when there is an output command. Second, notice that the value of I has not changed. You might think that the value of I should be 33 since in line 3ØØ I=5*G+H and now G equals 7. But we have already said that the computer executes a program *according to the order of line numbers.* When we reach line 5ØØ, line 3ØØ has already been executed—we do not return to line 3ØØ to calculate a new value for I. In line 5ØØ, *only* G is being given a new value. Thus for line 6ØØ we see

6ØØ PRINT G;H;I	7	−2	13	7;−2;13

Finally, to answer the question (what is the output?), note that the output is contained in the last column of the memory diagram. However, you should also note that the punctuation will not actually appear in the output generated by the computer (the command PRINT G,H,I will cause the values of G, H, and I to be printed on a single line, and the commas are used *only* for the *spacing* of the output). The punctuation is included in the output column solely to tell us about the spacing of the output. Your answer to the original question should be

3   −2   13
7 −2   13

The process of examining what a program does, line by line, is called
tracing a program. Tracing can be used, as was done earlier, to find
the output of a program, but it is used more significantly in debugging
a program of its logical errors. A memory diagram is a convenient aid
to tracing.

Consider the statement LET X=X+1. At first glance, the statement
may appear meaningless (certainly as a statement in algebra, it is unsolva-
ble). However, by now we know that the LET statement, even though
it seems to include an equation, is an assignment statement—it assigns
a value to a variable. If we were tracing a program that included the
steps

    205 LET X=4
    210 LET X=X+1

then the memory diagram for line 205 would be

                            X
| 205 LET X=4 | 4 |

Line 210 again assigns a value to X. The value to be assigned is calculated
from the expression to the right of the equal sign: X+1. But what value
does X have in this expression? From the previous statement, line 205,
X has the value 4. The new value of X is to be the old value of X
plus 1. So

                          X
| 205 LET X=4 | 4 |
| 210 LET X=X+1 | 5 |

Thus the value of X at line 210 would be 5.

EXAMPLE 7.10

    10 LET A=2
    20 LET B=3
    30 LET C=A*B
    40 PRINT A,B,C
    50 LET A=A+1
    60 LET B=4*B
    70 LET C=A+B
    80 PRINT A,B,C
    90 END

A trace would produce this part of a memory diagram:

	A	B	C	output
4Ø PRINT A,B,C	2	3	6	2,3,6

Line 5Ø shows that the value of A is changed (it becomes a 3) and the value of B is changed in line 6Ø (it becomes a 12). Finally, in line 7Ø, a new value is computed for C and that new value is based upon the new values of A and B (since line 7Ø is executed *after* lines 5Ø and 6Ø)! The memory diagram from line 5Ø would look like

	A	B	C	output
5Ø LET A=A+1	3	3	6	
6Ø LET B=4*B	3	12	6	
7Ø LET C=A+B	3	12	15	
8Ø PRINT A,B,C	3	12	15	3,12,15

7.5 An Introduction to Strings

The variables that have been used up to now are sometimes called "numeric" variables because the values that are assigned to them are numbers. The numbers themselves are often called numeric constants to distinguish them from another kind of constant that appears in BASIC.

The word "alphanumeric" refers to a collection of letters (alpha) and/or numbers (numeric). A *string constant* is a collection of alphanumeric characters that frequently can also contain special characters such as blanks, commas, question marks, and so on. String constants often are found within quotation marks. We have already been using such string constants—our output messages and labels. String constants contained within quotation marks are called *quoted text.*

String constants are the "values" that are assigned to string variables. Since string constants differ from numeric constants, a different kind of variable is needed for them. A *string variable* is a letter followed by a $.

EXAMPLE 7.11. A$ and Y$ are examples of string variables. Note that there are 26 string variables: A$ through Z$.

EXAMPLE 7.12. This is an illustration of strings with LET and PRINT.

```
1Ø LET A$="PROGRAMMING"
2Ø LET B$="IS FUN."
3Ø PRINT A$
4Ø PRINT B$
5Ø PRINT A$,B$
6Ø PRINT A$;B$
7Ø END

RUN
```

```
PROGRAMMING
IS FUN.
PROGRAMMING       IS FUN.
PROGRAMMINGIS FUN.
```

READY

Line 1Ø shows how a string constant is assigned to a string variable using LET—the string constant must be within quotation marks. As with numbers, when a LET is executed, a value is entered into a named memory location. Line 1Ø puts the value PROGRAMMING into the memory location named A\$. Line 2Ø shows that a string constant need not be a single word. It may be a phrase or an entire sentence. The PRINT statements work as expected with perhaps one exception. Line 6Ø uses the semicolon to print the value of the two string variables. You should note that there is no space printed between the end of A\$ and the beginning of B\$. At least one blank *will* be printed if you use a semicolon between a numeric variable and quoted text or between two numeric variables. This has been illustrated in the examples in the previous chapters. If you use a semicolon between two string variables and you want a space printed between them, you must include the space in one of the string constants that is assigned to one of the string variables.

If this was the case, line 1Ø should be coded as

```
1Ø LET A$="PROGRAMMING "
```

or line 2Ø as

```
2Ø LET B$=" IS FUN."
```

String constants may be used without quotation marks when entered in response to an INPUT statement.

EXAMPLE 7.13.   The following shows INPUT with strings:

```
1Ø PRINT "WHAT IS YOUR NAME";
2Ø INPUT N$
3Ø PRINT
4Ø PRINT "I'M GLAD TO MEET YOU ";N$
5Ø END
```

RUN

```
WHAT IS YOUR NAME ? JAMES T. KIRK

I'M GLAD TO MEET YOU JAMES T. KIRK
```

READY

Notice that in line 4Ø the last character in the quoted text is a blank.

There are various possible restrictions on nonquoted string constants. For example, your system may require that a nonquoted string *not* begin with a character such as a plus sign or comma. (You should consult your instructor or computer manual on this.)

Some circumstances may require that a string constant that is to be input be enclosed in quotes.

EXAMPLE 7.14

```
100 PRINT "ENTER PLACE OF BIRTH"
125 INPUT P$
```

If the user were to type BOSTON, MASS., the computer would interpret this response as two strings BOSTON and MASS. because of the comma between them. Here quotation works are necessary and the correct response would be "BOSTON, MASS." If the program later caused the value of P$ to be printed, the output would be BOSTON, MASS.

The quotation marks are required for input, but they do not appear in the output.

What will be printed by the programs in Exercises 1 through 6?

1

```
10 LET C=4
20 LET D=3*C+1
30 PRINT D
40 END
```

2

```
15 LET R=7
30 LET S=2+9
45 PRINT R,S
60 LET T=R+S-1
75 PRINT R;S;T
90 END
```

3

```
1004 LET V=3
1044 PRINT V
1444 LET V=V+2
4444 PRINT V
5555 END
```

4

```
100 LET B=6
200 LET B=B*2
300 LET B=B-1
400 PRINT B
500 END
```

5

```
10 PRINT "3030303030300"
20 LET N=5
30 PRINT "VALUE"
40 PRINT N
50 PRINT TAB(3);"VALUE"
60 PRINT TAB(6);N
70 PRINT TAB(1);N;TAB(5);N
80 END
```

6

```
10 PRINT TAB(15);"START"
20 PRINT TAB(10);"BACK";
30 PRINT TAB(14);"ING"
40 PRINT TAB(5);"UP"
50 END
```

7

```
10 LET R$="ROMEO"
20 LET A$="AND"
30 LET J$="JULIET"
40 PRINT R$;TAB(10);A$;TAB(20);J$
50 PRINT J$
60 PRINT TAB(5);A$
70 PRINT TAB(10);R$
80 END
```

8 What, if anything, is wrong with the following statements?
   a. LET T+3=T   e. 190 PRINT A,B;TAB(10);C
   b. 21 LET Z=Z+Z   f. 100 LET N$=43
   c. PRINT P=P+Q   g. 150 LET J=J$
   d. 220 PRINT;TAB(3);J

Trace the programs in Exercises 9 through 11 by drawing a memory diagram
for each program and using it to describe the *exact* output of the programs.

9

```
102 LET N1=1
104 LET N2=3
106 PRINT "FIRST","SECOND"
108 PRINT N1,N2
110 LET N3=4*(N1+N2)
112 PRINT "NEXT"
114 PRINT N3
116 PRINT "ALL",N1;N2;N3
118 END
```

10

```
301 PRINT "VALUES"
302 LET A=5
303 LET B=2
304 LET C=A↑B
305 PRINT C;A;B
306 LET B=B+4
```

```
307 PRINT C,A,B
308 PRINT "CHANGES"
309 LET A=A-1
310 LET B=2*B
311 LET C=A*(B-1)
312 PRINT A,B;C
313 END
```

11

```
10 LET X=0
20 LET X=X+1
30 LET Y=X+1
40 LET X=X+Y
50 LET Y=Y*X
60 LET Z=(X+1)*(Y-1)
70 PRINT X,Y,Z
80 END
```

12 Suppose that the value 3 is supplied first for X, 5 for Y, and 7 for X the second time. Show what will be displayed when the program is executed.

```
500 LET A=3
510 INPUT X
520 LET B=A*X
530 PRINT A,B,X
540 LET A=A↑2-1
550 INPUT Y
560 LET B=B+1
570 INPUT X
580 LET C=A+B+X+Y
590 PRINT A,B,C,X,Y
600 END
```

13 Tell what the following program does.

```
10 PRINT "FIRST","SECOND"
15 LET X=4
20 LET Y=9
25 PRINT X,Y
30 LET Z=X
35 LET X=Y
40 LET Y=Z
45 PRINT X,Y
50 PRINT "ALL"
55 PRINT X;Y;Z
60 END
```

14 Write a program with only two lines whose output is the average of the values 7, 2, 3, and 5.

15 Write a program, using TAB, that produces the following output.

```
0123456789
    * * * * *
    *       *
    *       *
    *       *
    * * * * *
```

All the programs you have seen or written so far had something in common. This commonality can be most easily seen by looking at their flowcharts. Each flowchart is drawn in a single direction, from top to bottom. Hence each flowchart resembles, in a very general sense, a straight line. For this reason, we call the programs that correspond to such flowcharts *straight-line programs.* For the most part, straight-line programs tend to be rather uninteresting and tiresome (especially when compared with the programs you will be doing later on). Nevertheless before we leave the realm of straight-line programs, we will use one to illustrate a rather important technique.

We now consider one last example of a straight-line program.

EXAMPLE 8.1. Write a program that has the user type in a length, in feet, and have the machine convert the feet to meters and print the result.

Since the *user* is to supply a value, this means that the INPUT statement will be used in the program (preceded, of course, by a PRINT). The conversion from feet to meters is accomplished by using the formula $M = .305f$. A flowchart that solves the problem is shown in Figure 8.1.

This is an example of a detailed flowchart. By a detailed flowchart we mean a flowchart whose parts may be assigned line numbers and directly from this numbered flowchart the program can be coded. (So if you can draw a detailed flowchart for a problem, you can consider your program as written!) Suppose that we decide to number the flowchart with line numbers beginning with 100 using increments of 50.

Since you read the flowchart beginning at (START) and following the flow lines, this is the way we will number each symbol. The completed, detailed flowchart, then, is shown in Figure 8.2.

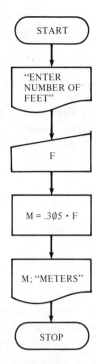

FIGURE 8.1.

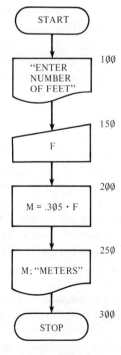

FIGURE 8.2.

Notice that the (START) is not numbered. Its purpose is merely to indicate where to begin to read the flowchart. However (STOP) is numbered because it will correspond to the END statement in our program. The program can be coded directly from the detailed flowchart because each flowcharting symbol stands for a particular BASIC statement and each symbol is numbered. Immediately then the program is

```
100 PRINT "ENTER NUMBER OF FEET"
150 INPUT F
200 LET M=.305*F
250 PRINT M;"METERS"
300 END
```

8.3 Conditional Transfer

As you know by now, the computer executes a program *in sequence* according to the line numbers used. However, BASIC allows the programmer to break out of the sequence and cause control of the program to jump or transfer to another part of the program.

One of BASIC's transfer statements is the "IF-THEN" statement. It looks like

line number   IF   condition   THEN   line number

The first line number tells where in the program the "IF-THEN" statement is located. The way the statement works is simple: if the "condition" between the words IF and THEN is true, transfer is immediately made to the line number following THEN and the program continues from there; if the "condition" is false, *no* transfer is made, the program continuing in its usual sequence.

An example of an IF-THEN statement is

```
120 IF X=9 THEN 250
```

The condition appears between the words IF and THEN: $X=9$. Suppose that the program that includes the IF-THEN statements uses line numbers that change by 10's. When line 120 is executed, the computer evaluates the condition $X=9$. If it is true, transfer is made to line 250, and the statement there is executed next. The program would then continue in sequence, namely, 260, 270, and so on. However if $X=9$ is false, no transfer is made. Instead the normal sequence of execution is followed, that is, 130, 140, and so on.

These are the kinds of decisions that the computer can make: whether certain conditions such as $X=9$ are true or false. The result of the decision can possibly cause the computer to transfer out of the normal execution sequence. For this reason, the IF-THEN is called a *conditional transfer statement.*

To be more specific, the "condition" in the conditional transfer is "expression relation expression."

The *general form of the IF-THEN* is

line number   IF   expression   relation   expression   THEN   line number

The relation used in the illustration of the last section was "equals," and the symbol used was the familiar =. There are six different relations that can be used in the condition of an IF-THEN. They are listed as follows:

Relation	Mathematics Symbol	BASIC Symbol
Is equal to	$=$	$=$
Is less than	$<$	$<$
Is greater than	$>$	$>$
Is less than or equal to	$\leq$	$<=$
Is greater than or equal to	$\geq$	$>=$
Is not equal to	$\neq$	$<>$

You can see that the last three symbols in BASIC differ from the mathematical notation. Most terminals do not contain a single key with the symbol "$\leq$" on it. So BASIC uses two symbols (in order) that correspond to the relational phrase "is less than or equal to" (in order). Obviously the same thing is done for "is greater than or equal to." Now, if you read the BASIC symbol "$<>$", you could say "is less than or greater than"—and this certainly means the same as "is not equal to"!

EXAMPLE 8.2. Suppose that a program uses line numbers that begin with 1Ø and uses increments of 1Ø's.

1. If, in the program, there is a line

7Ø IF A=2.7 THEN 22Ø

transfer will be made from line 7Ø to line 22Ø if the value of A is 2.7. If A is any other value, the line which will be executed after line 7Ø is line 8Ø (the next line in sequence).
2. The program also includes

13Ø IF C↑2>B↑2 THEN 1ØØ

The computer calculates the values of C^2 and B^2, and if C^2 is greater than B^2, the execution of the program will transfer to line 1ØØ; if C^2 is less than or equal to B^2 (not "greater than"), the program will continue on to line 14Ø.
3. If 32Ø IF M=M+3 THEN 4Ø is a line in the program, transfer will *never* be made from 32Ø to 4Ø since the condition is always false (perhaps it was only a typing error!).

Let's look at a simple example that uses an IF-THEN.

EXAMPLE 8.3. Two numbers are to be entered from the terminal. If their product is less than 100, the program should merely end. However, if the product is *not* less than 100, the word "BIG" should be printed and then the program end.

```
10 PRINT "ENTER TWO NUMBERS"
20 INPUT A,B
30 IF A*B<100 THEN 50
40 PRINT "BIG"
50 END
```

Suppose an execution of this program started with

```
ENTER TWO NUMBERS
? 5, 7
```

The value of A has been entered as 5 and B as 7. Their product is 35, so that the condition in line 30 (A*B<100) is true. Since the condition is true, the computer transfers to line 50 (skipping line 40) and the program ends.

Consider another RUN.

```
ENTER TWO NUMBERS
? 10, 12
```

Now the product is 120, so "A*B<100" is false. Transfer is not made to line 50; instead, line 40 is executed next, printing the word BIG. Finally following line 40, line 50 is executed and the program stops.

8.5 The Flowcharting Symbol

The flowcharting symbol that corresponds to the IF-THEN statement is called a *decision symbol* and is diamond shaped:  The decision symbol is entered via a flow arrow at one of the points, usually the top. Within the diamond you write the condition that is to be evaluated by the computer. The part of a flowchart for line 30 of Example 8.2 would be

The condition within the diamond is either true or false, and something is to be done if it is true while something else will be done if the condition is false. Thus, two flow arrows must lead out from the diamond. One flow arrow will be labeled "True" and the other "False."

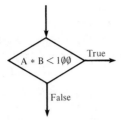

Each of these lines leading out of the diamond is called a *branch,* and consequently a transfer statement is frequently called a *branching statement.*

It is usually easier to think of the condition as a question. The condition "A*B<1ØØ" then becomes the question "Is A times B less than 1ØØ?" The answer to the question is either "Yes" (which is like "true") or "No" (like "false"). The flowchart symbolism becomes

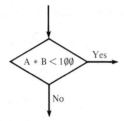

The "Yes-No" labeling will be followed in this text.

The complete detailed flowchart for the program of Example 8.3 is shown in Figure 8.3.

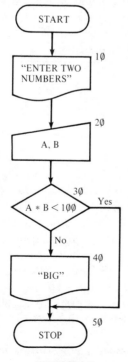

FIGURE 8.3.

The ability to transfer out of sequence allows the repetition of one or more statements with a minimum of coding. To see this, we will consider the problem of printing the first ten counting numbers. One program to do this could start as follows:

```
10 LET A=1
20 PRINT A
30 LET B=2
40 PRINT B
     .
     .
     .
```

One reason for the unsuitability of this program is the use of ten different variables: A, B, C, and so on. Were the problem to print the first 50 counting numbers, the coding would be brutal. Another approach might be to use only one variable:

```
10 LET I=1
20 PRINT I
30 LET I=I+1
40 PRINT I
     .
     .
     .
```

Notice that the statements PRINT I and LET I=I+1 are being executed over and over. By using a conditional transfer, we can cause these two statements to be repeatedly executed without the necessity of coding them more than once. The following program does just that:

```
10 LET I=1
20 PRINT I
30 LET I=I+1
40 IF I<=10 THEN 20
50 END
```

The first time line 20 is executed, I has the value 1, and this number is printed. At line 30, the value of I is increased by 1, becoming 2. Line 40 asks the question, "Is the value of I less than or equal to 10?" Since the answer is "Yes," a transfer is made to line 20 (the line number following the word THEN), which causes the value of I, 2, to be printed. Line 30 is again executed, giving I the value 3. The pattern repeats. Later, at line 30, I becomes 10. The question "I<=10?" still is answered "Yes," and so a jump is again made to line 20, printing a 10. Now at line 30, I becomes 11. The question of line 40 is answered "No," so transfer is *not* made to line 20. Execution continues to line 50 where the program halts.

The detailed flowchart corresponding to the program is shown in Figure 8.4.

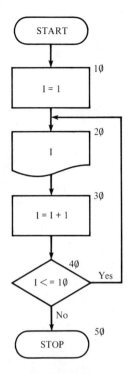

FIGURE 8.4.

Each time the "Yes" branch is followed, the PRINT I and LET I=I+1 statements are executed. A *loop* is a statement or collection of statements that is automatically repeated in a program. The word "loop" describes the almost "circular" configuration of statements and flow arrows connecting them. One of the most powerful aspects of the computer is its ability to perform calculations with incredible speed (and, of course, accuracy). Looping is a programming activity that makes use of this aspect.

EXAMPLE 8.4. You deposit $250 in a bank that pays an annual interest rate of 7%. At the end of the year, you leave the interest along with the original amount in the account. This *total* gains 7% interest during the second year. Each year you allow the money plus whatever interest it has earned to remain in the account. Of course, you wish to know how your money is "growing" each year in the bank.

At a first glance, the problem seems very complicated. However there is a formula that can be used that makes the problem easy. The formula is

$$C = P(1 + R)^N$$

and is frequently called a *compound interest formula*. P is the amount of money you first put into the account (P is the principal). R is the rate of interest your money earns. R should be expressed as a decimal in the formula. N is the number of years your money is left in the account.

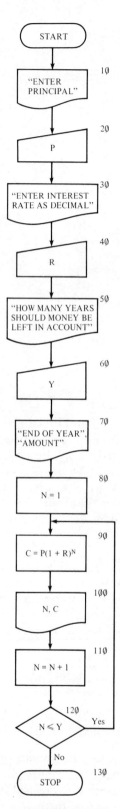

FIGURE 8.5.

C is the amount you are really interested in—the *total* amount that is in the account after a certain number (N) of years.

To make the program more interesting (and more usable), we will have the user supply the principal, the rate, and the number of years (Y) the money is to stay in the account. To see how the money grows each year, we will let N range from 1 to Y. Each time N takes on one of these values, another value of C will be calculated, and the values of N and C will be printed next to each other in two columns. The two columns will have headings. Figure 8.5 illustrates our algorithm.

Consider the decision symbol, which has been assigned the line number 120. How would we code this? Since a decision symbol is coded as an IF-THEN and since number 120 corresponds to the decision in the flowchart, our coding, in part, would be

```
120 IF    THEN
```

Between the IF and THEN is written the condition, coded in BASIC, found within the diamond. Thus

```
120 IF  N<=Y  THEN
```

A line number is to be written after THEN. To find what line number, merely follow the "Yes" branch. The "Yes" branch loops back to a part of the flowchart that leads to 90. The number 90 is the one to use. The complete coding is

```
120 IF  N<=Y  THEN 90
```

The rest of the coding will be left as an exercise. A RUN of the program showing several years and corresponding amounts is as follows:

```
RUN

ENTER PRINCIPAL
? 250
ENTER INTEREST RATE AS A DECIMAL
? .07
HOW MANY YEARS SHOULD MONEY BE LEFT IN ACCOUNT
? 30
END OF YEAR    AMOUNT
1                267.5
2                286.225
3                306.261
4                327.699
.                .
.                .
.                .
```

8.7 Stopping a Program

If the compound interest program of the last section were executed using 100 for the number of years, the output might take considerable time to complete. Suppose that while the output is being displayed, the user decides that he does not care to see any more output; that is, the output should be stopped. It is very simple to do this. Just press the ESC (for "escape") key.[1] The computer will print a message such as TERMINATED, stop the output, and print READY. To illustrate,

```
RUN

ENTER PRINCIPAL
? 250
ENTER INTEREST RATE AS A DECIMAL
? .07
HOW MANY YEARS SHOULD MONEY BE LEFT IN ACCOUNT
? 100
END OF YEAR      AMOUNT
   1               267.5
   2               286.225
   3               306.261
   4               327.699
   5               350.638
   6               37-TERMINATED-     ← here the user pressed ESC


READY
```

The ability to transfer and, in particular, to loop certainly makes programs more interesting and useful. The problems that can now be solved and the programs written to solve them are also more complicated. When you write a program you really have two tasks: The first is to solve the problem; the second is to write a program that is both readable and maintainable. The two are not independent—in fact, they are closely related.

A program can be considered *readable* if someone, not necessarily the original programmer, who knows the statement of the problem and who also knows the particular computer language in which the program is written can examine a listing of the program and follow the sequence of logic used to solve the problem.

To be *maintainable* means that a program can be easily modified by someone other than the original programmer. It should be obvious that readability is really a prerequisite for maintainability.

In this section we shall consider readability. Actually, we have already been using one tool to aid the readability of a program. In the very first flowcharting example (Example 2.1), which dealt with distance, rate, and time, we used the variables D for distance, R for rate, and T for time. Of course, this was an obvious choice, since the formula required in the problem used those letters. The point is that choosing particular variable names that can be identified quickly with the quantity for which

8.8 The REM Statement

---

[1] This procedure will vary from computer to computer. On some systems, the BREAK key is used instead of ESC; on others, holding down the CONTROL key while pressing the T key will work. Check your own system.

they are being used aids readability. Many programs do not use formulas as such, so how do we choose a good (readable) variable name? Suppose that a program were to use a variable to stand for a sum. Would M or S be a better variable name to use? If a program involved calculating two quotients, Q1 and Q2 would be suitable and readable.

Another tool for the readability of programs is the use of the REM statement. REM is an abbreviation of REMARK.

The *general form of the* REM *statement* is

line number   REM   anything you want to write

The reason that you can follow REM with anything you would like is that REM is a *nonexecutable* statement—that is, when the machine encounters a REM statement in your program, it ignores the REM and continues on to the next statement in sequence. However, since it is part of your program, it will appear when you list your program.

REMs can and should be used in many different ways within a program. It is a common practice to start programs with a REM that gives a brief description or title to a program. For example,

10 REM PROGRAM TO FIND AREA OF RECTANGLE

or merely

10 REM AREA OF RECTANGLE

Another REM that is frequently found near the beginning of a program gives the name of the person who originally created the program. Information such as this is put into a program to make it more easily maintained. For instance, suppose that a person is using a program originally created by someone else. If the person using the program finds something in it that he or she cannot understand, it might be possible to contact the originator of the program for clarification.

In addition to the choice of particular variable names to represent specific quantities, REMs are used in programs to describe explicitly the meanings of variables. For example,

30 REM P IS SELLING PRICE OF ITEM
40 REM T IS AMOUNT OF TAX ON ITEM
50 REM C IS FINAL COST OF ITEM

Frequently REMs are put into programs, usually near the beginning, to describe *briefly* the algorithm or process used in the program to solve the problem:

100 REM P WILL BE MULTIPLIED BY TAX RATE, .06, GIVING TAX T
110 REM FINAL COST C IS SUM OF P AND T

It is customary to put REMs of the type described in the preceding paragraphs at or near the beginning of a program so that when reading the program a person can get a quick overview of what is to follow. Other REMs may be inserted between program statements when they (the REMs) are used to clarify a statement or statements whose function may be somewhat obscure.

A last note about REMs is that they should never be used to describe the obvious. For example,

```
100 REM SET X EQUAL TO ZERO
110 LET X=0
```

EXAMPLE 8.5. To illustrate some of these ideas, let's look at the beginning of the program for compound interest that was presented in Section 8.6. For this example, we will choose line numbers starting at 100 and changing by 10's.

```
100 REM COMPOUND INTEREST PROGRAM
110 REM
120 REM PROGRAMMED BY JULIA THOMPSON
130 REM
140 REM ********** VARIABLES **********
150 REM   P: PRINCIPAL (AMOUNT INVESTED)
160 REM   R: INTEREST RATE (A DECIMAL)
170 REM   Y: NUMBER OF YEARS MONEY LEFT IN ACCOUNT
180 REM   N: PARTICULAR YEAR NUMBER
190 REM   C: TOTAL AMOUNT IN ACCOUNT
200 REM *****************************
210 REM
220 REM   P,R AND Y WILL BE SUPPLIED BY USER
230 REM   LOOP FROM N=1 THROUGH N=Y
240 REM   IN LOOP 1) C WILL BE CALCULATED BY
250 REM   C=P(1+R)↑N, 2) N AND C WILL BE
260 REM   PRINTED, 3) N WILL BE INCREASED AND
270 REM   CHECKED AGAINST Y
280 REM
290   (executable statements begin here)
```

The REMs (with nothing following them) in lines 110, 130, 210, and 280 are used to visually separate the various parts. Some programmers prefer to "highlight" some sections of their programs (as seen in lines 140 and 200) by repeated printings of the same character.

Most of the remaining programs in this text will not be quite as elaborate in their REMs as the preceding example. The reader, nevertheless, should get into the habit of including effective and pertinent REMs in all programs.

A final observation about REMs. It is not unusual to find application programs written in BASIC whose coding is made up of as much as 20% REMs.

8.9 Ingredients of a Loop

EXAMPLE 8.6. A farmer has a field that measures 45 feet long and 32 feet wide. He wishes to enlarge the field until the area of the new field is double (or slightly more) than that of the current field. He plans to expand the field by increasing the width 2 feet for every 1 foot the length is increased. A program is to be written that will tell the farmer the dimensions of the new field.

An algorithm for the program is

1. Assign 45 to L and 32 to W.
2. Calculate the original area A1 by A1 = L×W.
3. Print out the length, width, and area of the current field.
4. Increase L by 1.
5. Increase W by 2.
6. Calculate the new area A2.
7. If A2<2*A1 go back to step 4; otherwise, continue on to step 8.
8. Print the length, width and area of the new field.

From the algorithm a detailed flowchart, shown in Figure 8.6, is drawn.

Before we look at the coding, the line numbers on the flowchart should be noted. Increments of 50's are used to give plenty of room to insert REMs into the code. Generally, REMs are not included in a flowchart. The only exception is the kind of REM that will be embedded in the program to describe or clarify how a statement is used. The

flowcharting symbol for a REM is ⌐‾‾‾‾‾ with the REM coding in-

side. This symbol is connected to the rest of the flowchart by a series of dashes; for example,

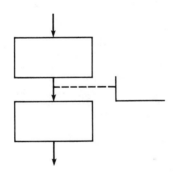

The coding for the program follows.

```
100 REM DOUBLING AREA OF FIELD
110 REM L IS LENGTH, W IS WIDTH
120 REM A1 IS ORIGINAL AREA
130 REM A2 IS NEW AREA CALCULATED WHEN
140 REM L IS INCREASED BY 1, W BY 2
150 REM INCREASING WILL CONTINUE UNTIL
160 REM A2 IS DOUBLE (OR MORE) A1
200 LET L=45
250 LET W=32
300 LET A1=L*W
350 PRINT "CURRENT FIELD"
400 PRINT "LENGTH","WIDTH","AREA"
450 PRINT L,W,A1
```

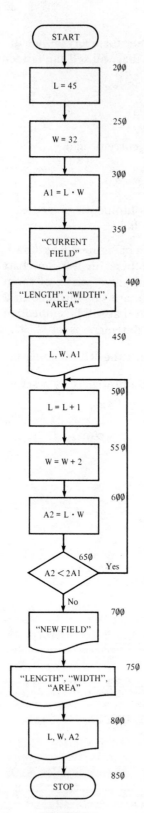

FIGURE 8.6.

```
5ØØ LET  L=L+1
55Ø LET  W=W+2
6ØØ LET  A2=L*W
65Ø IF  A2<2*A1  THEN  5ØØ
7ØØ PRINT  "NEW  FIELD"
75Ø PRINT  "LENGTH" , "WIDTH" , "AREA"
8ØØ PRINT  L , W , A2
85Ø END
```

The execution is

RUN

CURRENT FIELD

LENGTH	WIDTH	AREA
45	32	144Ø

NEW FIELD

LENGTH	WIDTH	AREA
56	54	3Ø24

READY

We wish to focus our attention on the loop in this program and then loops in general. What made the loop possible was the conditional transfer statement of line 65Ø. It is this statement that regulates the flow of control: whether to continue through the loop again or to exit from the loop and go on with the rest of the program. It should be clear that this must be the case with any loop; namely, there must be a transfer statement that directs the flow back through the loop or directs it to continue in the usual sequence through what remains in the program.

The branching of a transfer statement is due to the condition between IF and THEN. In the example, the condition is "A2<2*A1". As many times as this condition is evaluated and found to be true, a transfer is made back to line 5ØØ and the looping continues. Once the condition becomes false, the looping stops. (Truth or falsity is not critical—a program could have a loop that is executed as long as a condition is false and when the condition becomes true the loop is exited.) We see that the condition of an IF-THEN must eventually change from true to false or from false to true.

The condition in the example is A2<2*A1. This condition is true several times and eventually becomes false. How does the condition change from true to false? The value of 2*A1 is calculated in line 3ØØ and from that point on remains fixed. On the other hand, the value of A2 changes because it is the product of L and W within the loop where L and W each change. We see that it is the changing of A2's values that eventually causes the condition to become false and then the loop to be exited. The variable that causes the condition in a transfer statement to change from true to false or from false to true (and thus causing the loop to be re-entered or exited) is called the *control variable* for the loop. The control variable for the last example is A2.

We can now describe what goes into any loop—its "ingredients."

1. There must be a condition (in a transfer statement) that uses a control variable.
2. The control variable must be given its first value (this is called *initializing*) before the condition is checked. A2 is initialized at line 600 the *first* time that line 600 is executed.
3. The control variable must be changed so that eventually the condition will change from true to false, or vice versa. The control variable A2 is changed *each* time line 600 is executed.

EXAMPLE 8.7.   Look back to the flowchart of Example 8.4. The control variable is N. Its initial value is 1. It changes by being increased by 1. The condition is "$N \leq Y$".

EXAMPLE 8.8.   The program in Section 8.6 first introduced loops. Its control variable is I. I is initialized to 1 and is increased by 1. The condition is "$I <= 10$".

The loops mentioned in Example 8.7 and 8.8 are special types of loops called *counting loops.* This name is given because the purpose of the control variable is to count how many times the loop is being executed. In one program, I counted from 1 to 10; in the other, N counted from 1 to Y. The loop in the farmer's field program is not a counting loop. The control variable, A2, represents an area and does not do counting.

Consider the following program segment (part of a program) from Example 8.6.

```
400 PRINT "LENGTH","WIDTH","AREA"
450 PRINT L,W,A1
500 LET L=L+1
550 LET W=W+2
600 LET A2=L*W
650 IF A2<2*A1 THEN 500
```

The loop consists of lines 500, 550, 600, and 650. To aid the readability of the program, it is customary to indent all the statements of the loop except the transfer statement. Thus it is easy to see the statements that are repeatedly executed. Using this convention, the segment just given would be written

```
400 PRINT "LENGTH","WIDTH","AREA"
450 PRINT L,W,A1
500     LET L=L+1
550     LET W=W+2
600     LET A2=L*W
650 IF A2<2*A1 THEN 500
```

Let's look at two more problems involving loops, one of which will involve a counting loop.

EXAMPLE 8.9. The method of payment for a car bought and financed through the Pulcher Car Company is as follows: the first payment is 25% of the total amount and each following payment is 25% of the balance as long as the balance is $100 or more. When the balance slips below $100, that balance becomes the last payment. The program should print each payment as well as the current balance.

As you analyze a problem, you should look to see if the solution involves repetition. If so, you should then think of a loop. There is certainly repetition involved in this problem, namely, the calculation and printing of the monthly payment due and the new balance. How does the repetition stop? The problem statement tells us that the repetition is to stop when the new balance is less than $100 (or, equivalently, the repetition is to continue while the balance is $100 or more). Thus the condition in the loop does not depend on a counting result and so the loop is not a counting loop.

We will have the user enter the total amount to be financed and so an algorithm for this problem is

1. Print a message to the user.
2. Have the user supply the total amount T.
3. Print column headings for payment and balance.
4. Calculate a payment P.
5. Calculate the new balance T.
6. Print P and T.
7. If T>=1ØØ, go back to step 4; otherwise, continue to step 8.
8. Print the final payment T and the final balance Ø.

Note that in step 5, the new balance is named T, which is the same variable used for the total amount. This is reasonable since the total amount is actually the original balance. Step 8 says to print T as the final payment. The value of the balance when step 8 is reached is less than $100 and so becomes the final payment. At step 8, the final payment is made so that the balance is 0. The program and a RUN follow.

```
100 REM PULCHER CAR COMPANY
110 REM PAYMENT SCHEDULE
120 REM MONTHLY PAYMENT IS 25% OF BALANCE
130 REM UNTIL BALANCE FALLS BELOW $100
140 PRINT "ENTER TOTAL AMOUNT"
150 INPUT T
160 PRINT
170 PRINT "PAYMENT" , "BALANCE"
180    LET P=.25*T
190    LET T=T-P
200    PRINT P,T
210    IF T>=100 THEN 180
220    PRINT T,0
230    END
```

RUN

ENTER TOTAL AMOUNT
? 1000
PAYMENT   BALANCE
 250   750
 187.5   562.5
 140.625   421.875
 105.469   316.406
 79.1016   237.305
 59.3262   177.979
 44.4946   133.484
 33.371   100.113
 25.0282   75.0847
 75.0847   0

READY

EXAMPLE 8.10. The Deca Company employs ten workers, each of whom is paid an hourly wage. A program is to be written that requests, for each worker, the number of hours worked and the hourly rate of pay. The program should calculate and print the workers' gross salary.

There is clearly repetition involved in this problem: the activities for a single worker (entering the number of hours worked and the hourly rate of pay and the calculation and printing of the gross pay) are repeated for all ten employees. The loop is a counting loop.

A flowchart is shown in Figure 8.7; program listing and execution are as follows.


```
100 REM DECA COMPANY PAYROLL
110 REM TEN EMPLOYEES
120 REM GROSS SALARY=HOURS WORKED X PAY RATE
130 LET W=1
140    PRINT "ENTER HOURS AND PAY RATE"
150    INPUT H,P
160    LET S= H*P
170    PRINT "GROSS PAY";S
180    LET W= W+1
190 IF W<=10 THEN 140
200 END
```

RUN

ENTER HOURS AND PAY RATE
? 40,5.25
GROSS PAY 210
ENTER HOURS AND PAY RATE
? 35,6.50
GROSS PAY 227.5
ENTER HOURS AND PAY RATE
? 37.5,4.75
GROSS PAY 178.125
ENTER HOURS AND PAY RATE
? 40,6.00
GROSS PAY 240
ENTER HOURS AND PAY RATE
? 15,7.70
GROSS PAY 115.5
ENTER HOURS AND PAY RATE
? 28,8.65
GROSS PAY 242.2
ENTER HOURS AND PAY RATE
? 40,7.89
GROSS PAY 315.6
ENTER HOURS AND PAY RATE
? 12,4.15
GROSS PAY 49.8
ENTER HOURS AND PAY RATE
? 39,5.62
GROSS PAY 219.18
ENTER HOURS AND PAY RATE
? 40,9.10
GROSS PAY 364

READY

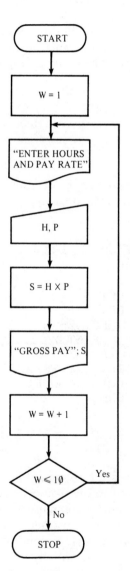

FIGURE 8.7.

One way of dealing with a problem that involves a counting loop is to identify the activities that are to be repeated and then to construct the loop around them. In Example 8.10, the statements to be repeated are

```
140    PRINT "ENTER HOURS AND PAY RATE"
150    INPUT H,P
160    LET S=H*P
170    PRINT "GROSS PAY";S
```

This is the solution to the problem for one worker, so to repeat it for ten workers, we enclose these statements with other statements that will cause the counting loop to be executed ten times:

```
130 LET W=1
180    LET W=W+1
190 IF W<=10 THEN 140
```

A modified memory diagram can be used to trace a program that includes a transfer statement.

8.10 Memory Diagrams for Loops

EXAMPLE 8.11. Use a memory diagram to find the output from the program

```
100 LET X=9
110 LET Y=6
120    LET Z=X+Y
130    PRINT Z
140    LET X=X-2
150 IF X>=Y THEN 120
160 PRINT "DONE"
170 END
```

Besides the columns for each variable and for output, two columns are added to the memory diagram: at the left of the memory diagram, there will be a column used to show the line number of the statement being executed; just before the output column, there will be a column whose heading is the condition in the IF-THEN statement. In this latter column will be written either "True" or "False" (depending on the condition) on the line corresponding to the IF-THEN condition. For the preceding program the memory diagram would begin

line no.	X	Y	Z	X ≥ Y	output
100	9				
110	9	6			
120	9	6	15		
130	9	6	15		15
140	7	6	15		
150	7	6	15	true	

The bottom line shows "true" in the condition since the value of X (7) *is* bigger than or equal to Y (6). We know that when the condition of an IF-THEN statement is true, control is transferred to the statement whose line number follows THEN—in this case line 120. So the memory diagram continues:

line no.	X	Y	Z	X ≥ Y	output
100	9				
110	9	6			
120	9	6	15		
130	6	6	15		15
140	7	6	15		
150	7	6	15	true	
120	7	6	13		
130	7	6	13		13
140	5	6	13		
150	5	6	13	false	

The condition of line 150 is now false, so no transfer is made; control continues to the next line in sequence, line 160, and then the program ends.

The completed memory diagram is

line no.	X	Y	Z	X ≥ Y	output
100	9				
110	9	6			
120	9	6	15		
130	9	6	15		15
140	7	6	15		
150	7	6	15	true	
120	7	6	13		
130	7	6	13		13
140	5	6	13		
150	5	6	13	false	
160	5	6	13		DONE

and the output is

    15
    13
    DONE

The condition checked by an IF-THEN statement may include comparison of strings. String variables may be compared with string constants and with other string variables. When a string variable is compared with a string constant, the constant must be contained within quotation marks.

8.11 Strings Used with IF-THEN

EXAMPLE 8.12. A store arrives at the retail price of an item by adding to the wholesale price a percentage of that wholesale price. A program is to be written for the store that finds the retail price for one or more items.

Since the wholesale price of items will differ from item to item and the store will likely use a different percentage rate for different items, these two values will be supplied from the terminal. The retail price will then be calculated and printed. Since the program is to be written so as to allow more than a single item to be processed, the user will be asked whether or not there are any more items. If so, the wholesale price and percent of increase will again be requested (re-enter the loop); if not, the program will print a message and then stop.

```
100 REM RETAIL PRICE CALCULATIONS
110 REM W IS WHOLESALE PRICE
120 REM P IS RATE OF MARK-UP
130 REM R IS RETAIL PRICE
140   PRINT "ENTER WHOLESALE PRICE"
150   INPUT W
160   PRINT "ENTER PERCENT OF INCREASE AS DECIMAL"
170   INPUT P
180   LET R=W+P*W
190   PRINT "RETAIL PRICE:"; R
200   PRINT "IS THERE ANOTHER ITEM";
210   INPUT A$
220   PRINT
230 IF A$="YES" THEN 140
240 PRINT "PROCESSING COMPLETE."
250 END

RUN

ENTER WHOLESALE PRICE
? 78
ENTER PERCENT OF INCREASE AS DECIMAL
? .10
RETAIL PRICE 85.8
IS THERE ANOTHER ITEM? YES

ENTER WHOLESALE PRICE
? 356.23
ENTER PERCENT OF INCREASE AS DECIMAL
? .33
RETAIL PRICE 473.786
IS THERE ANOTHER ITEM? NO

PROCESSING COMPLETE.

READY
```

The value of the string variable A$ is entered at line 210 and is compared with the quoted string constant YES at line 230. If they are equal the loop is re-entered; if not, the loop is exited.

BASIC is frequently referred to as a "conversational" computer language. This is because BASIC allows a user to interact with a program (using the INPUT statement); by using conversationlike words ("yes", for example), the operator is able to "converse" with and even control the actions of a program.

When two string variables are compared in an IF-THEN, neither should be in quotation marks. A statement such as

```
220 IF A$<>B$ THEN 500
```

is a legal statement comparing two string variables. Comparisons of strings using relations other than "=" and "<>" will be dealt with in later chapters.

1 What is meant by a "straight-line" program?

2 What is meant by a "detailed" flowchart?

3 What, if anything, is wrong with the following statements?
  a. 100 IF X IS EQUAL TO Y THEN 70
  b. 420 IF N+6 THEN 10
  c. IF A=B THEN 95
  d. 335 IF X+1<Y−2 THEN 150
  e. 15 IF C≠0 THEN 55
  f. 110 IF B↑2<=C THEN 500
  g. 185 IF G$=EXIT THEN 295
  h. 120 IF Y$<>Z$ THEN 800

4 A program has been written that uses line numbers that begin with 25 and change by 25's. Among others, the program uses variables A, B, C, X$ and Y$ whose values are 7, −2, 3, GOOD, and BAD, respectively. (Assume that these values do not change during the program.) The following are some conditional transfer lines. Tell which line will be executed after the conditional transfer and explain your answer.
  a. 150 IF A>=7 THEN 775
  b. 1225 IF B<C THEN 100
  c. 1475 IF C↑2<A THEN 2000
  d. 600 IF 2*A<>B*C−8 THEN 1550
  e. 950 IF M+1>M THEN 1075
  f. 1725 IF X$<>Y$ THEN 500
  g. 1550 IF Y$="POOR" THEN 1900

5 For each of the following program segments, identify the control variable, the transfer condition and rewrite the segment with proper indentation. Which loops, if any, are counting loops?
  a.

```
140 LET M=11
150 LET B=5
160 LET Y=2
170 PRINT B,Y
180 LET B=B+1
190 LET Y=Y+2
200 IF B+Y<M THEN 170
```

  b.

```
210 LET F=1
220 PRINT "ENTER VALUE"
230 INPUT X
240 PRINT "SQUARE IS",X↑2
250 LET F=F+1
260 IF F<=7 THEN 220
```

  c.

```
415 PRINT "ENTER TWO WORDS"
420 INPUT A$,B$
425 IF A$<>B$ THEN 415
430 PRINT "MATCH"
```

  d.

```
100 LET X=0
110 LET C=2
120 PRINT "TYPE IN A NUMBER"
```

```
130 INPUT Y
140 PRINT X*Y
150 LET X=X-1
160 LET C=C+2
170 IF C<=18 THEN 120
```

6 What is the output for each of the following programs?

a.

```
11 LET C=0
21 PRINT "RECORDING"
31    LET C=C+1
41     PRINT "ERROR";C
51 IF C<5 THEN 31
61 END
```

b.

```
10 LET X=1
20    PRINT "GOING"
30    LET X=X+1
40 IF X=2 THEN 20
50 PRINT "GONE"
60 END
```

c.

```
10 PRINT "N1","N2"
20 PRINT
30 LET N=5
40 LET M=6
50    PRINT N,M
60    LET N=N+2
70 IF N<15 THEN 50
80 LET M=N+1
90 PRINT N,M
100 END
```

d.

```
100 PRINT "BEGIN"
110 LET X=9
120 LET Y=4
130    PRINT "CONTINUE"
140    LET X=X+1
150    LET Y=Y+2
160 IF Y<=X THEN 130
170 PRINT X,Y
180 PRINT "STOP"
190 END
```

7 For this program, a list of values is to be supplied, one value at a time, in response to the INPUT statement (be careful, all the values might not be needed). What is the output?

```
10 LET T=0
20 LET X=7
30    PRINT "ENTER A NUMBER"
40    INPUT Y
```

```
50    IF Y<0 THEN 30
60    LET T=T+1
70 IF X<>Y THEN 30
80 PRINT "DONE";T
90 END
```

The list: 4, −1, 0, 3, 6, 9, −2, 6, 7, 8, 0, −1, 5, 7, 3

8 Refer to the description of Exercise 7 and tell what the output of the following program is.

```
100 LET A$="BALL"
110 LET I=0
120    INPUT B$
130    LET I=I+1
140    IF B$=A$ THEN 120
150    PRINT B$;A$
160 IF I<=4 THEN 120
170 END
```

The list: BASE, BALL, GUM, FOOT, BALL, BASKET, BEARING, ODD

9 Enter the program and note the appearance of its output. Do you know why the output looks as it does?

```
10 LET N=3
20 LET X=5.7
30 LET A=N*X
40 PRINT X;A,
50 LET X=X+.4
60 IF X<62.1 THEN 30
70 END
```

10 For parts (a) and (b) of this exercise, detail the flowcharts on p. 99, using line numbers starting at 100 and changing by 10's, and then code the program from the flowchart.

11 Code the program of Example 8.4. Run it using the values

Principal	Interest Rate
500	4%
100	5.5
1,000	6.75
2,000	11.7

12 Find out how much money the Indians would have today if they had invested the sum that they had received for the sale of Manhattan Island. Assume an interest rate of 4.5% (Manhattan Island was purchased in 1626 for the equivalent of $24.)

13 Write a program to print the whole numbers from 1 to 50 along with their doubles and squares. The output should be in the form of a three-column table where the number is printed in the first column, the double of the number in the second column, and the square of the number in the third.

14 The population of Northfork is increasing at a rate of 4.1% per year. Assuming that the growth rate stays the same each year, find the population of Northfork in 25 years.

　　a. Write the program so that each year's population is printed.

　　b. Write the program so that only the population at the end of 25 years is printed.

[10(a)]   [10(b)]

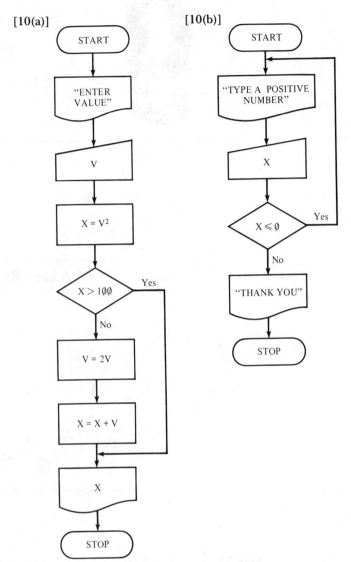

15 Write a program to do the following. Assign, as initial values, 8 and 5 to N1 and N2, respectively. Their product is to be calculated and printed. Then N1 is to be incremented by 3 and N2 by 4. Their product is to be calculated and printed. This activity, incrementing and printing, is to be continued until the product exceeds 20,000, at which time the value of the product should be printed as well as the number of products that have been calculated.

* * *

16 The user should supply two numbers. If they are equal, the word EQUAL should be printed; otherwise, the phrase NOT EQUAL should be printed.

17 Louis is standing on a cliff that is 350 feet high. The cliff is at the very edge of a lake. Louis drops a rock over the edge of the cliff. Write a program that prints, at 1-second intervals, the time since the rock was dropped, the speed of the rock, and the distance of the rock from the surface of the lake. When the rock hits the lake, the word SPLASH should be printed. For this problem, if t stands for time (in seconds), the speed of the falling rock is the product $a \times t$ and the distance the rock has fallen from the top is given by $.5 \times a \times t^2$, where a is the acceleration due to gravity ($a = 32$).

The programs in Chapter 8 that involved a transfer shared a common design. In terms of a flowchart, they looked like

9.1 A Look Back

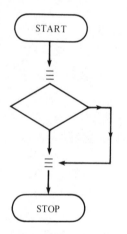

or

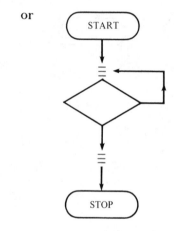

FIGURE 9.1.

FIGURE 9.2.

In particular, the programs that used loops resembled the design of Figure 9.2, where the conditional transfer that determined whether to re-enter the loop or to exit from the loop is located at the "bottom" of the loop. Not all loops copy this design, as can be seen by the problem in Example 9.1.

EXAMPLE 9.1. An investor wants to write a program that will provide her with some information before she invests her money. She plans to invest $2500 but has several different options that vary by the length of time the money must be invested and the interest rate that applies to her investment.

A program is to be written where the investor can supply the length of time and the interest rate. If the time entered is 0 or less, the program should print JOB COMPLETE and end. Otherwise, the amount of interest should be calculated using the formula $I = P \times R \times T$ and printed, and the investor should be asked to enter another time and interest rate.

A flowchart would begin as shown in Figure 9.3.

Since the problem wants to allow the user to be able to enter additional information after the interest has been printed, there must be a transfer back to the statement that asks the user to enter the time. Thus, we draw a flow arrow back to that output symbol. (See Figure 9.4.)

It is clear that a transfer is made from the output symbol at the

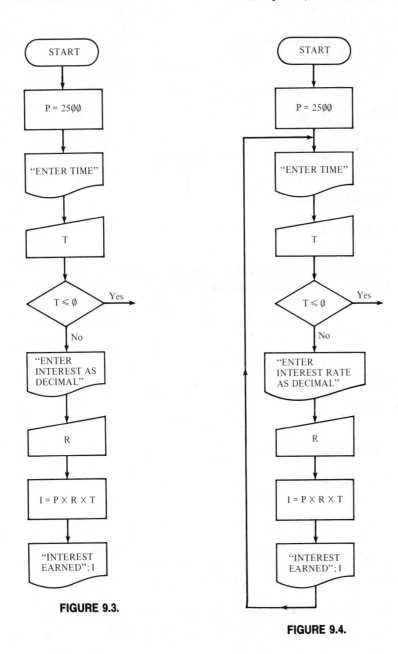

FIGURE 9.3.

FIGURE 9.4.

bottom to one near the top. This is not a conditional transfer (there is no diamond symbol at the bottom) but rather an unconditional transfer.

The loop created by this unconditional transfer will be repeated until the user enters a value for T that is 0 or less, at which time the condition "T ≤ Ø" will be true and a transfer will be made to an output statement and the flowchart will stop. The completed flowchart is shown in Figure 9.5.

The program corresponding to this flowchart is

```
100 REM  INTEREST  PROGRAM
110 REM  $2500  WILL  BE  INVESTED
120 REM  FOR  LENGTH  OF  TIME  T  AND
130 REM  AT  INTEREST  RATE  R
140 REM
150 LET  P=2500
160    PRINT  "ENTER  TIME"
170    INPUT  T
180    IF  T=<Ø  THEN  240
190    PRINT  "ENTER  INTEREST  RATE  AS  DECIMAL"
200    INPUT  R
210    LET  I=P*R*T
220    PRINT  "INTEREST  EARNED"; I
230 GOTO  160
240 PRINT  "JOB  COMPLETE"
250 END
```

The unconditional transfer statement is found in line 23Ø. It causes the program to loop back to statement 16Ø. A sample RUN is

```
RUN

ENTER  TIME
?  2
ENTER  INTEREST  RATE  AS  A  DECIMAL
?  .Ø7
INTEREST  EARNED  35Ø
ENTER  TIME
?  3.5
ENTER  INTEREST  RATE  AS  A  DECIMAL
?  .115
INTEREST  EARNED  1ØØ6.25
ENTER  TIME
?  Ø
JOB  COMPLETE

READY
```

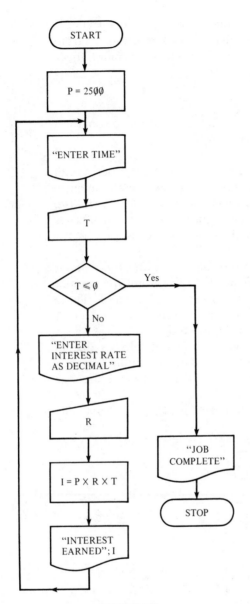

FIGURE 9.5.

9.2 The GOTO Statement

BASIC's unconditional transfer statement is GOTO.
　The *general form of the GOTO statement* is

line number　GOTO　line number

　When executed, the GOTO will cause an immediate transfer of control
to the line number that follows GOTO. In the program of Example
9.1, we saw

230 GOTO 160

Each time line 23Ø was executed, a transfer was made to line 16Ø.

Looking back at the flowchart we see that a flow line brings us from 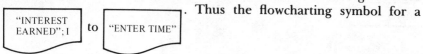. Thus the flowcharting symbol for a

GOTO statement will be a flow line. Let's now look at more programs that involve the use of an unconditional transfer.

EXAMPLE 9.2. A salesperson is paid a base salary of $725 per month plus a commission that depends on the amount of sales for that month. If sales are $4000 or more, the commission is 5% of the sales; otherwise, it is 2%. A program is to be written that requests the amount of sales and then calculates and prints the commission earned as well as the total salary for the month.

The base salary, B, will be assigned the value 725, and the amount of sales, A, will be entered from the terminal. At this point the amount of sales is checked so that the commission can be calculated. These are two possible calculations (for the different commission rates). A partial flowchart would be that shown in Figure 9.6.

What is to be done next? The problem statement tells us that in either case the commission is to be printed. The two branches then come together at the output statement which prints the commission and its label. (See Figure 9.7.)

The flowchart is completed by calculating and printing the total salary S. (See Figure 9.8.)

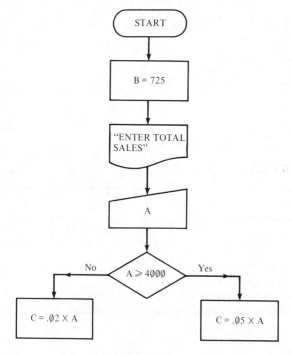

FIGURE 9.6.

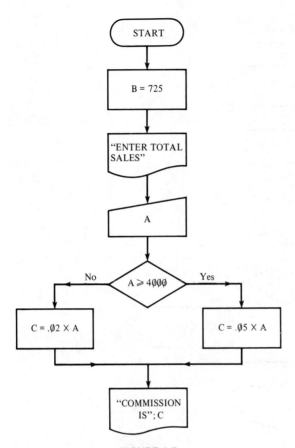

FIGURE 9.7.

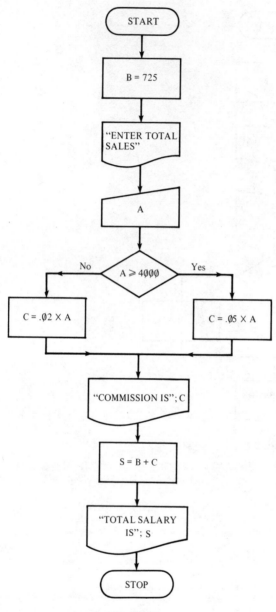

FIGURE 9.8.

The program and several RUNs follow.

```
100 REM PROGRAM TO COMPUTE SALESPERSON'S TOTAL SALARY
110 REM TOTAL SALARY IS BASE SALARY PLUS COMMISSION
120 REM COMMISSION DEPENDS UPON TOTAL SALES
130 REM IF TOTAL SALES>=$4000 COMMISSION IS 5%
140 REM OTHERWISE COMMISSION IS 2%
150 REM
160 LET B=725
170 PRINT "ENTER TOTAL SALES"
180 INPUT A
190 IF A>=4000 THEN 220
200 LET C=.02*A
210 GOTO 230
220 LET C=.05*A
230 PRINT "COMMISSION IS";C
240 LET S=B+C
250 PRINT "TOTAL SALARY IS";S
260 END
```

RUN

```
ENTER TOTAL SALES
? 3500
COMMISSION IS 70
TOTAL SALARY IS 795
```

READY

RUN

```
ENTER TOTAL SALES
? 5178.35
COMMISSION IS 258.918
TOTAL SALARY IS 983.918
```

READY

RUN

```
ENTER TOTAL SALES
? 4000
COMMISSION IS 200
TOTAL SALARY IS 925
```

READY

The previous flowchart displays an important design that you should try to follow when flowcharting solutions to problems. It is referred to as a *two-way selection* design, and it looks like the chart in Figure 9.9.

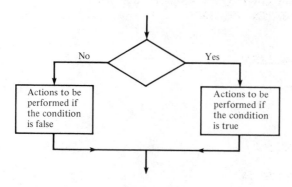

FIGURE 9.9.

Depending on the truth or falsity of the condition in the decision symbol, one of two possible sets of computer activities is to take place. No matter what set of actions is performed, control eventually reaches a common point in the flow chart and continues from there. In the previous example, depending on whether or not the value of A was greater than or equal to 4000, the value of C was calculated by multiplying A by .02 or by .05. In any case the flow of control always reached the output statement, which printed the value of C.

The coding for this particular segment was

```
190 IF A>=4000 THEN 220
200 LET C=.02*A
210 GOTO 230
220 LET C=.05*A
230 PRINT "COMMISSION IS";C
```

You should note both the conditional and unconditional transfer statements.

If we draw a flowchart that uses the two-way selection design, how could we detail the flowchart? To illustrate, suppose that a part of our flowchart looked like the chart in Figure 9.10.

The flowcharting symbols are empty because here the point we are considering is the numbering of the symbols and not what they contain.

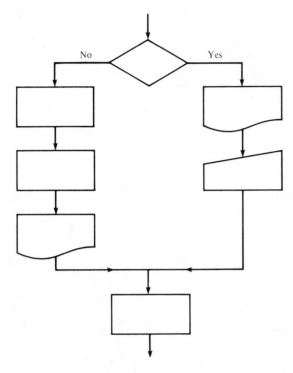

FIGURE 9.10.

Let's assume that the line numbers we are using change by 10's and that the decision symbol has just been assigned line number 210. Because of the way the IF-THEN statement works, the next line number, 220, must be used along the "no" branch. Additionally, once we assign 220 to the first rectangle on the "no" branch, we follow the flow of control through the next two symbols, the rectangle and output symbol. The partially detailed flowchart is shown in Figure 9.11.

Now what we want to do is to transfer to the rectangle at the bottom, which means that a GOTO is needed. The flowcharting symbol for a GOTO is a flow line, and so we label the line coming out of 240 (the output symbol) as 250. (See Figure 9.12.)

This completes the detailing of the "no" branch, and we now turn to the "yes" branch. We begin by numbering the output symbol with 260 and continue with 270 for the input symbol and 280 for the processing symbol at the bottom.

From the detailed flowchart of Figure 9.13 we should be able to go directly to code. The coding for lines 210 and 250 are of particular interest. Line 210 is an IF-THEN statement, and since the "yes" branch leads to the symbol labeled 260, the code (except for the condition) for line 210 is

```
210 IF    THEN 260
```

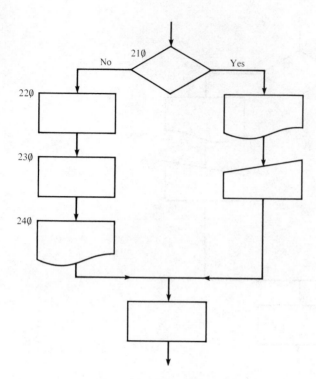

FIGURE 9.11.

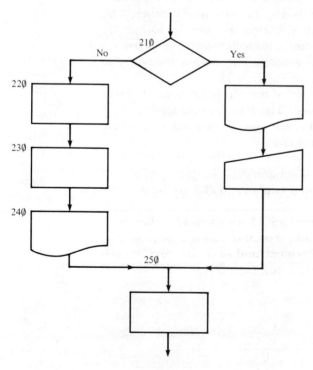

FIGURE 9.12.

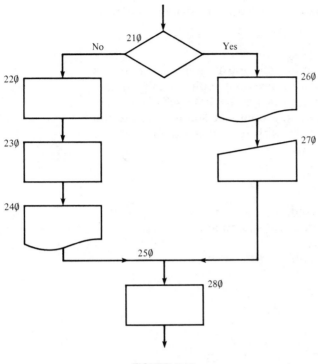

FIGURE 9.13.

Line 25Ø is coded from a flow arrow and thus is a GOTO statement. But to what is the transfer made? Following the flow we are led to the rectangle numbered 28Ø. The code for 25Ø is

    25Ø GOTO 28Ø

9.3 The "Problem" with GOTO

In recent years, there has been considerable discussion, sometimes rather heated, about the GOTO statement. The discussions have taken place not only at the academic level by teachers of programming but also at the application level by professional programmers. A major emphasis today is that programs be written in such a way that they can be easily read and understood. Readability has been briefly discussed in Chapter 8.

It should be clear that the flow of logic of a straight-line program is easy to follow. Complexity enters with the transfer statements, making it more difficult to understand the logical flow. The more transfers that are needed for a program, the more difficult it is to follow the logic for a solution to the problem. However, many problems are, by their nature, complex and will involve several transfers for their solution. Our goal is to make a program (or flow chart) as readable and as understandable *as possible.* Since more transfers mean more complexity, one way in which to achieve our goal is to try to minimize the number of transfer statements in a program. To illustrate, consider the following simple example.

EXAMPLE 9.3. A magazine distributor sells most of his subscriptions through telephone contacts. He hires several people to call random households attempting to sell subscriptions. If a worker sells more than $800 worth of subscriptions in a week, a bonus of $95 is added to the worker's base pay, which is $150. We wish to find the total pay for a worker.

An algorithm for this problem is

1. Set base pay, P, to 150.
2. Request total of subscriptions sold, S.
3. If S>800, transfer to step 5; otherwise, continue to step 4.
4. Transfer to output at step 6.
5. Calculate new pay by adding bonus of $95 (P=P+95).
6. Print P.

From this algorithm, we write the program.

```
100 LET P=150
110 PRINT "ENTER SUBSCRIPTION TOTAL"
120 INPUT S
130 IF S>800 THEN 150
140 GOTO 160
150 LET P=P+95
160 PRINT "SALARY IS";P
170 END
```

The two transfer statements are found in lines 130 and 140. A program to do the same job but one that uses only one transfer statement is

```
200 LET P=150
210 PRINT "ENTER SUBSCRIPTION TOTAL"
220 INPUT S
230 IF S<=800 THEN 250
240 LET P=P+95
250 PRINT "SALARY IS";P
260 END
```

It was stated earlier that we would try to minimize the number of transfer statements. As shown in the last two programs, it would be more precise to say that *we will attempt to minimize the number of GOTOs.*

In the first version of the program, we employed two transfer statements, one of them being a GOTO. In the second version, only one transfer was needed. The method used to enable us to do this was to use *opposite* or *complementary relations.* For example, the relation that is the opposite of "=" is "<>". The following table shows the six BASIC relations and their opposites.

Relation	Opposite Relation
=	<>
<>	=
>	<=
<	>=
>=	<
<=	>

Instead of using the relation ">" followed immediately by a GOTO, we eliminated the GOTO and used the opposite relation "<=".

EXAMPLE 9.4. Two numbers, representing the length and width of a rectangle, are to be entered from the terminal. The program should determine if the rectangle in question is a square. If so, the word SQUARE should be printed, the area of the square calculated and printed, and then the program should stop. Otherwise the program should keep requesting two more numbers until a square is found.

L and W will be the variables used for length and width, respectively, and A will stand for area. An algorithm is

1. Request L and W.
2. If L=W then transfer to step 4; otherwise, continue to step 3.
3. Transfer to step 1.
4. Print word SQUARE.
5. Calculate and print A.

In steps 2 and 3, we see a conditional transfer followed immediately by an unconditional transfer. Here is a situation where the two transfer statements can be replaced by one transfer statement.

1. Request L and W.
2. If L≠W, transfer to step 1; otherwise, continue to step 3.
3. Print word SQUARE.
4. Calculate and print A.

Programs corresponding to each algorithm are the following:

```
10 REM TWO TRANSFERS
20 PRINT "ENTER LENGTH AND WIDTH
30 INPUT L,W
40 IF L=W THEN 60
50 GOTO 20
60 PRINT "SQUARE"
70 LET A=L*W
80 PRINT "AREA IS";A
90 END
```

```
10 REM ONE TRANSFER
20 PRINT "ENTER LENGTH AND WIDTH"
30 INPUT L,W
40 IF L<>W THEN 20
50 PRINT "SQUARE"
60 LET A=L*W
70 PRINT "AREA IS";A
80 END
```

Which program should you use? Which program is the "better" program? No definite answer can be given to either of these two questions. On one hand you realize that many GOTOs in a program can make the program difficult to read, and so you should try to minimize the number of GOTOs in a program. For this reason you might choose the program on the right. On the other hand, the problem statement talks about what to do if the rectangle *is* a square, namely, if the length equals the width. So you might choose a condition that expresses this ("IF L=W" in the program on the left). You must make the decision as to which program would make the most sense to a person reading it—namely, what, in your opinion, makes the program more easily read. You might want to write the program on the right because it does not contain a GOTO statement but feel that the condition "L<>W" might be somewhat unclear. In this case you could add the following REMS to help clarify the condition.

```
32 REM RECTANGLE IS SQUARE IF L=W
34 REM SO NO SQUARE IF L<>W
```

The final decision will be yours. You must strive to make programs understandable.

9.4 The STOP Statement

In certain cases BASIC's STOP statement can be used instead of a GOTO since STOP is equivalent to "GOTO the END statement" (at whatever line END is found).

The *general form of the STOP statement* is

line number   STOP

When the STOP statement is executed, execution of the program is terminated.[1]

EXAMPLE 9.5. The user will be asked to type in a non-zero value until one has been typed in. Then the output will be only a single word: POSITIVE or NEGATIVE, depending on the value typed in.

The flowchart for the problem is shown in Figure 9.14.

We have seen this structure before and know that the code would be

```
10    PRINT "ENTER A NON-ZERO VALUE"
20    INPUT X
30 IF X=0 THEN 10
40 IF X>0 THEN 70
50 PRINT "NEGATIVE"
60 GOTO 80
70 PRINT "POSITIVE"
80 END
```

Since line 60 causes a transfer to the END statement, it could be coded as 60 STOP

---

[1] Some versions of BASIC will terminate the program and print a diagnostic such as

BREAK IN 220

(220 being the line number of the STOP statement). Except when used as a debugging aid, it is not desirable to end a program with such a diagnostic, and in these cases, the equivalent GOTO should be used.

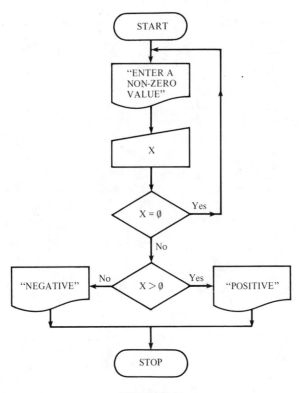

FIGURE 9.14.

Frequently a problem will require one or more conditions to be checked, depending on the result of an earlier condition. Such a collection of conditional transfer statements is frequently referred to as *nested IFs*.

9.5 Nested IFs

EXAMPLE 9.6. Aquarius Community College uses the following schedule to determine the total cost for a student enrolled in the college.

A student who does not live within the state is charged $75 per credit. A resident of the state is charged $60 per credit for 1 to 15 credits and $50 per credit for any credits over 15. A program is to be written to calculate and print the bill for a student.

An algorithm is

1. Request number of credits, C, and whether state resident.
2. If state resident, transfer to step 5.
3. Calculate bill, B, by B=C×75.
4. Transfer to step 10.
5. If C>15 then transfer to step 8.
6. Calculate B by B=C×6∅.
7. Transfer to step 10.
8. Calculate extra credits, X, beyond 15 by X=C−15.
9. Calculate B by B=(15×6∅)+(X×5∅).
10. Print B.

This is the flowchart as shown in Figure 9.15.

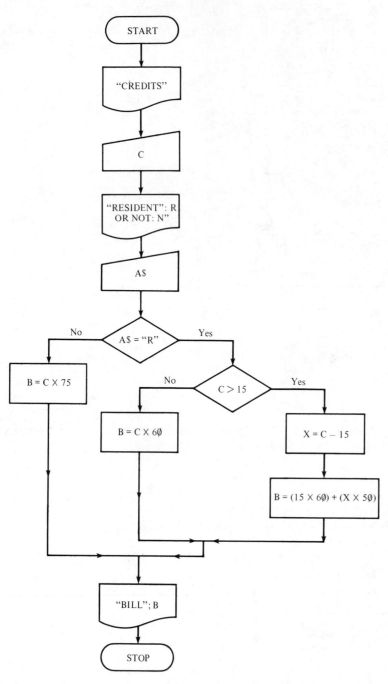

FIGURE 9.15.

This is the program:

```
100 REM AQUARIUS FINANCIAL PROGRAM
110 REM
120 REM CHARGES ARE:
130 REM     NON-RESIDENTS-$75/CREDIT
140 REM     RESIDENTS-$60/CREDIT FOR 1ST 15 CREDITS
150 REM             -$50/CREDIT FOR CREDITS OVER 15
160 REM
170 PRINT "HOW MANY CREDITS IS STUDENT ENROLLED FOR";
180 INPUT C
190 PRINT
200 PRINT "IF STUDENT IS RESIDENT OF STATE, ENTER LETTER R"
210 PRINT "OTHERWISE ENTER LETTER N."
220 INPUT A$
230 IF A$="R" THEN 260
240 LET B=C*75
250 GOTO 310
260 IF C>15 THEN 290
270 LET B=C*60
280 GOTO 310
290 LET X=C-15
300 LET B=(15*60)+(X*50)
310 PRINT
320 PRINT "STUDENT'S BILL IS $";B
330 END

RUN

HOW MANY CREDITS IS STUDENT ENROLLED FOR? 14

IF STUDENT IS RESIDENT OF STATE, ENTER LETTER R
OTHERWISE ENTER LETTER N.
? N

STUDENT'S BILL IS $ 1050

READY

RUN

HOW MANY CREDITS IS STUDENT ENROLLED FOR? 14

IF STUDENT IS RESIDENT OF STATE, ENTER LETTER R
OTHERWISE ENTER LETTER N.
? R

STUDENT'S BILL IS $ 840

READY

RUN

HOW MANY CREDITS IS STUDENT ENROLLED FOR? 17

IF STUDENT IS RESIDENT OF STATE, ENTER LETTER R
OTHERWISE ENTER LETTER N.
? R

STUDENT'S BILL IS $ 1000

READY
```

EXAMPLE 9.7. A company that lends money charges an interest rate of 1.25% per month on the unpaid balance of the loan. It also requires that each monthly payment be 5% of the balance and that a minimum monthly payment of $10 be made. Further, once the balance is less than $10, the entire balance must be paid. The company calculates the 1.25% *before* it calculates the payment that must be made. A program is to be written that asks the user for the amount of money to be borrowed and then prints out a table that displays the pertinent financial data for each month until the loan is paid. The table should be made up of three columns—the first showing the month number, the second showing the amount to be paid that month and the third showing the balance of the loan after the payment has been made.

Let's call the amount of the loan L (to be input). We will also use it as the unpaid balance. We will let M be the number of months (to start, it should be assigned the value l) and P the amount of payment. Each month, starting with the first, a new unpaid balance is calculated by adding 1.25% of the old balance to itself. The payment, P, is found by calculating 5% of this new balance. Remember that the company requires a minimum monthly payment of $10. So at this point, if the value of P is less than 10, we change it so that it becomes equal to 10 (the minimum payment). If we subtract P from the new balance we get the amount that still remains to be paid (another new balance!). These values will be calculated and printed using a loop. The only point that remains is to determine when to exit from the loop. If, at the place where we added 1.25% of the old balance to get a new balance, the new balance is less than or equal to 10, the loop should be left. Note, however, that even though we have exited from the loop, one more line of output is needed—that for the final payment.

Here is the program.

```
100 REM LOAN COMPANY PROGRAM
110 REM L IS UNPAID BALANCE.SO AT FIRST L IS AMOUNT OF LOAN
120 PRINT "HOW MUCH IS LOAN";
130 INPUT L
140 PRINT
150 PRINT "MONTH","PAYMENT","BALANCE"
160 REM M IS MONTH NUMBER
170 LET M=1
180 REM INTEREST ON LOAN IS 1.25% PER MONTH
190    LET L=L+.0125*L
200    REM IF UNPAID BALANCE L<=10, FULL PAYMENT MUST BE MADE
210    IF L<=10 THEN 350
220    REM MONTHLY PAYMENT, P, IS 5% OF LOAN
230    LET P=.05*L
240    REM MINIMUM MONTHLY PAYMENT IS 10
250    REM CHECK IF MONTHLY PAYMENT EXCEEDS MINIMUM
260    REM OTHERWISE MAKE PAYMENT EQUAL MINIMUM
270    IF P>=10 THEN 300
280    LET P=10
290    REM DEDUCT PAYMENT FROM BALANCE
300    LET L=L-P
```

```
310    PRINT M,P,L
320    REM ANOTHER MONTH OF PAYMENT
330    LET M=M+1
340 GO TO 190
350 PRINT M,L,0
360 END
```

The complexity of some problems may require more than two nested IFs.

EXAMPLE 9.8. A bank offers giftware for new savings accounts. If an account is opened with a deposit of $3000 or more, the gift is a camera; for $2000 or more (but less than $3000), a food blender; for $1000 or more (but less than $2000), a printing calculator. A flowchart to determine the gift is shown in Figure 9.16.
Note that additional STOP statements could be used in place of GOTOs.

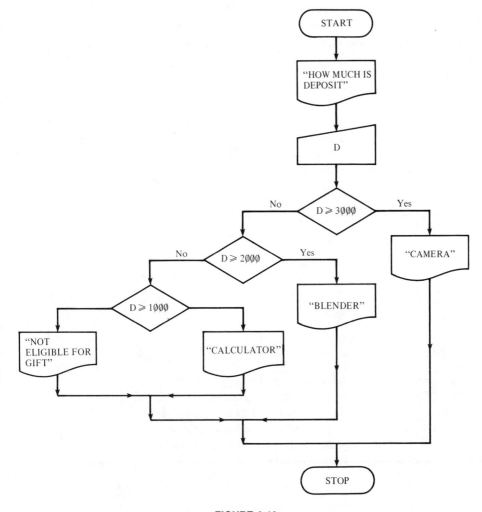

FIGURE 9.16.

The IF-THEN statement that has been used is referred to as a conditional *transfer* statement, since, when the condition is true, it causes a transfer or "jump" out of the usual sequence. There is a slightly different conditional statement whose general form is

9.6 Another Form of IF-THEN

line number   IF   condition   THEN   statement

As before, if the condition is false, execution continues on to the next line number in sequence. However, if the condition is true, the statement following THEN is executed, and execution continues to the next line number (unless, of course, the statement following THEN is a GOTO statement).

EXAMPLE 9.9. Let A and B have the values 5 and −2, respectively, and suppose the following statements are contained in a program whose line numbers differ by 10s'.

1. 140 IF A<=B THEN PRINT "MARGIN"

Since the condition is false, the next statement that will be executed is that in line 150.

2. 210 IF A+B>0 THEN LET N=A*B

Here the condition is true, so N is calculated and assigned the value −10. Once this has been done, control continues to the next line in sequence, line 220.

The flowcharting to illustrate this conditional statement is shown in Figure 9.17.

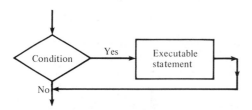

FIGURE 9.17.

EXAMPLE 9.10. Six students are applying for admission to their school's honor society. Three tests are given to the students, and if the average of the three tests exceeds 90, the student will be admitted.

The following program asks that the three scores be entered, then calculates the average, and if the average meets the requirement, prints a message to admit the student to the honor society.

```
100 REM HONOR SOCIETY ADMISSION PROGRAM FOR 6 STUDENTS
110 LET R=90
120 LET S=1
130    PRINT "ENTER THE THREE SCORES"
140    INPUT X,Y,Z
150    LET A=(X+Y+Z)/3
160    IF A>R THEN PRINT "ADMIT THIS STUDENT"
170    PRINT
180 LET S=S+1
190 IF S<=6 THEN 130
200 END

RUN

ENTER THE THREE SCORES
? 92,95,91
ADMIT THIS STUDENT

ENTER THE THREE SCORES
? 91,90,89

ENTER THE THREE SCORES
? 87,82,94

ENTER THE THREE SCORES
? 99,89,95
ADMIT THIS STUDENT

ENTER THE THREE SCORES
? 76,99,87

ENTER THE THREE SCORES
? 91,94,88
ADMIT THIS STUDENT

READY
```

9.7 A Further Look at Strings

In addition to the "equals" and "not equals" relations, strings may be compared by the "greater than" or "less than" relations. For example, PIPE<SMOKE is a true statement whereas APPLE >= CIDER is false. Each character on the terminal, number or otherwise, has a numeric code that is used by the computer. Comparisons are made on the basis of these numeric codes. For our purposes, the comparisons that will be made will involve only numbers, letters, and/or blanks. Many computer manufacturers have adopted a standard that designates that the numeric code for a blank (space) is less than the numeric code for any single digit and the numeric code for a digit is less than the numeric code for any letter.[2] (What the particular codes are is not important for us to know—only their relationships.) That standard will be assumed in this text. Thus, the ordering of single characters by their codes is blank $< \ldots < \emptyset < 1 < \ldots < 9 < \ldots < A < B < \ldots < Z$

Strings are compared character by character. For example,

ABEL<CAIN

since A<C. Also TWO>TOO because when the first character of each string is compared, they are found to be equal and so the comparison is done by the second characters: W>O. When the computer compares strings of different lengths, the computer adds enough blanks on the right of the shorter string to make it equal in length to the longer string and then compares the two strings character by character. Therefore ADAM<ADAMS. In terms of words, you can think of the ordering as an *alphabetic ordering*.

EXAMPLE 9.11. The user will enter a keyword and after that five more words. After each of the five words is entered, the program will tell if the word appears alphabetically before or after the keyword.

```
1000 REM ALPHABETIC COMPARISONS
1010 PRINT "ENTER YOUR KEYWORD"
1020 INPUT K$
1030 PRINT "TYPE IN A WORD IN RESPONSE TO EACH QUESTION MARK."
1040 PRINT
1050 LET W=1
1060    INPUT A$
1070    IF A$<K$ THEN 1100
1080    PRINT A$;" FOLLOWS ";K$
1090    GOTO 1110
1100    PRINT A$;" PRECEDES ";K$
1110    LET W=W+1
1120 IF W<=5 THEN 1060
1130 END


RUN


ENTER YOUR KEYWORD
? PROGRAM
TYPE IN A WORD IN RESPONSE TO EACH QUESTION MARK

? BOOK
BOOK PRECEDES PROGRAM
? WORM
WORM FOLLOWS PROGRAM
? TERMINAL
TERMINAL FOLLOWS PROGRAM
? PRO
PRO PRECEDES PROGRAM
? PROGRAMS
PROGRAMS FOLLOWS PROGRAM


READY
```

---

[2] Unfortunately, however, that standard is not followed by all manufacturers. Be sure that you find the numeric code ordering that is used on your computer.

The idea of counting has already been used in many of our looping programs. In this section, we will expand upon and generalize the topic of counting.

To discover how to instruct a computer to count, just think about how a person would go about counting a set of objects. The first object would be counted, then the second, the third, and so on. As each object is counted, the count changes: one, two, three, and so on. Observe that the count changes by one each time an object is counted. *So to do counting in a computer program, all we need is a variable that increases by one each time the object is counted.* One other detail completes the discussion of counting: the variable that will be doing the counting should be, at the start, set equal to zero as a beginning value (this is called *initializing the variable*) just in case there are no objects that can be counted. Hence, in a counting program, we would need a variable, say, C, for counting. Before any counting is done we would have a statement LET C=Ø, and when we encounter the object to be counted, we would have a statement LET C=C+1. A variable used to do counting is frequently called, for obvious reasons, a *counter*. The following problems illustrate the technique of counting.

EXAMPLE 9.12. Twelve words are to be entered, one at a time, from the terminal. The program should count how many of the words start with a letter in the first half of the alphabet (A to M).

Since the problem involves repetition, a loop will be used. The loop is a counting loop, so the control variable will be used for counting the number of times the loop is executed. It will be initialized to one. Another counter will be used to count the words that begin with one of the letters from A through M. This counter will be initialized to zero. (You should note that although both W and C are counter variables, they are given different initial values. W, the loop counter, is initialized to one because we will be repeating a set of instructions a certain, known number of times and in such cases the normal counting pattern begins with one. On the other hand, the word counter C is initialized to zero since it may happen that no words beginning with a letter from A through M are entered.)

An algorithm is

1. Initialize loop counter, W, to 1.
2. Initialize word counter, C, to Ø.
3. Request word, X$.
4. If X$ starts with a letter from A to M, increase C by 1.
5. Increase W by 1.
6. If W ≤ 12 go back to step 3; otherwise continue to step 7.
7. Print C.

The condition in step 4 can be expressed by

X$<"N"

and so the program is

```
100 REM COUNTING PROGRAM
110 REM W IS CONTROL VARIABLE FOR LOOP
120 REM C COUNTS WORDS IN FIRST HALF OF ALPHABET
130 LET W=1
140 LET C=0
150    PRINT "ENTER A WORD"
160    INPUT X$
170    IF X$<"N" THEN LET C=C+1
180    LET W=W+1
190 IF W<=12 THEN 150
200 PRINT C;"WORDS COME FROM FIRST HALF OF ALPHABET"
210 END

RUN

ENTER A WORD
? ALGORITHM
ENTER A WORD
? LOOP
ENTER A WORD
? TERMINAL
ENTER A WORD
? FLOWCHART
ENTER A WORD
? TEXT
ENTER A WORD
? OUTPUT
ENTER A WORD
? HARDWARE
ENTER A WORD
? DATA
ENTER A WORD
? PROGRAM
ENTER A WORD
? ASSIGN
ENTER A WORD
? STRING
ENTER A WORD
? COUNTER
 7 WORDS COME FROM FIRST HALF OF ALPHABET

READY
```

EXAMPLE 9.13. The Athenian Academy, a school renowned for its academic excellence, administers three comprehensive tests to each of its students at the end of each school year. As a result of these tests, certain students will be placed in accelerated classes during the next school year, while other students will not be allowed to return for another year. If the total score for the three tests is 280 or more, that student will be placed in an accelerated class. If the total score is less than 230, that student will not be allowed to return. To schedule classes correctly for the following year, the number of students to be enrolled in accelerated classes as well as the number of students not returning is needed. A program is to be written to perform this task.

The program will require two variables for counting: one for the number of students to be placed in accelerated classes (A) and one for the number of students who will not return (B). Both should be initialized to zero. The person using the program will enter three scores (we will use the variables S1, S2, and S3). The scores will be summed and the sum assigned to the variable S. The sum will then be checked. If S is greater than or equal to 280, the counter A will be increased by 1. If S is less than 230 the counter B will be increased. After either of these is done, we will go back and get another triple of scores. At the start of the program the user will be instructed to enter three "−1"s to terminate the counting and proceed to the output.

A flowchart is presented (see Figure 9.18), followed by some observations, the program, and a sample RUN.

Before looking at the program, some points about the flowchart should be noted:

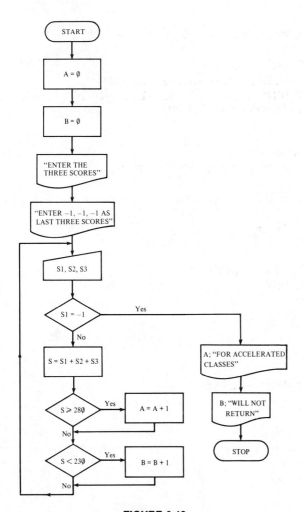

FIGURE 9.18.

1. The first decision checks to see if the value of S1 is −1. This is true when the user has entered the triple of numbers "−1,−1,−1" to indicate that all scores have been supplied. When this happens we transfer to output. Otherwise, we calculate the sum S and investigate its value. (It should be noted that although only the value of one of the input variables (S1) is checked, the user must enter three numbers to satisfy the INPUT request. Actually to indicate that no additional scores are to be entered, the user could enter *any* triple of values whose first entry is −1. Instructing the user to enter three of the same number merely makes it easy for the user. This aspect of making things as easy as possible for the user is sometimes referred to as writing a program that is "user-friendly.")
2. The next two decisions show the structure of the "IF-THEN statement" condition (the "yes" branch leading to a single statement and then the flow line leading back to the "no" branch) and so will be coded that way.
3. After the last condition has been checked an unconditional transfer leads back to the INPUT symbol.

Guided by the flowchart and adding some REMs, the program is written.

```
60 REM PROGRAM FOR ATHENIAN ACADEMY
70 REM A COUNTS STUDENTS FOR ACCELERATED CLASSES
80 REM B COUNTS STUDENTS WHO WILL NOT BE ALLOWED TO RETURN
90 REM DECISION BASED ON THREE TEST RESULTS
100 LET A=0
110 LET B=0
120 PRINT "ENTER THE THREE SCORES"
130 PRINT "ENTER -1,-1,-1 AS LAST THREE SCORES"
140    INPUT S1,S2,S3
150    IF S1=-1 THEN 200
160    LET S=S1+S2+S3
170    IF S>=280 THEN LET A=A+1
180    IF S<230 THEN LET B=B+1
190 GO TO 140
200 PRINT A;"FOR ACCELERATED CLASSES"
210 PRINT B;"WILL NOT RETURN"
220 END


RUN


ENTER THE THREE SCORES
ENTER -1,-1,-1 AS LAST THREE SCORES
? 78,98,87
? 55,67,76
? 87,86,84
? 90,90,97
? 85,87,98
? 76,78,79
? 88,85,82
? 87,89,76
? 98,97,90
```

```
? 80,80,81
? 75,76,72
? 76,70,72
? 87,85,89
? 78,79,79
? 80,84,85
? 79,83,84
? 87,83,84
? 76,90,97
? 97,90,91
? -1,-1,-1
  1 FOR ACCELERATED CLASSES
  3 WILL NOT RETURN

READY
```

You should finally note that the RUN of the program processes only 19 triples of numbers. The program will work, however, with many, many more—as long as the last triple entered is −1,−1,−1.

9.9 Summing

Summing, an important and frequently used computer activity, is a technique that is fairly easy to learn. Suppose that we wish to sum the column of figures

```
    2
    7
    3
 +  1
```

Most people would add the numbers the same way—the only possible difference being whether to add up from the bottom or down from the top. Let's start adding from the bottom and see what steps we go through.

First we add 3 and 1, giving a result of 4.

```
    2
    7
    3
 +  1   = 4
```

Next we add the previous result, 4, plus 7 giving 11.

```
    2
    7      = 11
    3
 +  1    4
```

Now we add the last result, 11, plus 2, giving 13.

$$
\begin{array}{r}
2 \\
7 \quad 11 \\
3 \\
+\ 1
\end{array} = 13
$$

Since there are no more values to be added, the final sum is 13.

$$
\begin{array}{r}
2 \\
7 \\
3 \\
+\ 1 \\
\hline
13
\end{array}
$$

Notice the sequence of partial results: 4, 11, 13. The last partial result was our final result. This is how people add. A sequence of partial or intermediate sums is calculated until a final sum is reached. Each intermediate sum is merely equal to the sum of the previous intermediate sum plus the next value to be added. So, if in writing a program, we want S to be the sum of our values and X is the variable given to our values, the statement that does the summing is simply

LET S=S+X

Notice what this statement is doing. It is assigning as the new value of S the quantity on the right of the =. But that quantity, S+X, is the sum of the previous value of S and the value to be added (X).

When writing programs that involve summing, you should get into the habit of initializing the sum to zero. Among other things this makes the adding of the first term easier. Let's consider some examples.

EXAMPLE 9.14. This is a program to add the numbers 4, 6, 8, 10, 12, and 14.

Since the set of numbers begins with 4 and continues to 14 in steps of 2, we can supply these values using a loop.

```
100 REM ADD NUMBERS 4,6,8,10,12,14
110 REM S WILL BE SUM; X VALUE TO BE ADDED
120 LET S=0
130 REM USE LOOP TO GET THESE VALUES
140 LET X=4
150    LET S=S+X
160    LET X=X+2
170 IF X<=14 THEN 150
180 PRINT "SUM IS";S
190 END
```

RUN

SUM IS 54

READY

The values to be summed could also be typed in, one at a time, from the terminal.

EXAMPLE 9.15. Pat pays for her purchases at the local service station by using her credit card. Write a program for Pat to sum each of her purchases and print the result.

Since the number of purchases may be different from one month to the next, before any summing is done, Pat should be asked how many purchases were made. This value can be used in the condition to determine whether or not to re-enter the summing loop.

```
200 REM T IS TOTAL OF PAT'S PURCHASES
210 LET T=0
220 PRINT "HOW MANY PURCHASES THIS MONTH";
230 INPUT N
240 PRINT
250 REM SUMMING LOOP
260 LET I=1
270    PRINT "ENTER PURCHASE AMOUNT"
280    INPUT A
290    LET T=T+A
300    LET I=I+1
310 IF I<=N THEN 270
320 PRINT
330 PRINT "THIS MONTH'S TOTAL IS";T
340 END
```

RUN

HOW MANY PURCHASES THIS MONTH? 7

ENTER PURCHASE AMOUNT
? 14.50
ENTER PURCHASE AMOUNT
? 12.00
ENTER PURCHASE AMOUNT
? 8.75
ENTER PURCHASE AMOUNT
? 15.31
ENTER PURCHASE AMOUNT
? 5.00
ENTER PURCHASE AMOUNT
? 10.00
ENTER PURCHASE AMOUNT
? 7.25

THIS MONTH'S TOTAL IS 72.81

READY

The summing done in the previous two examples might have been done just as easily with a hand calculator. The program of Example 9.16 processes a large number of values and so is better suited to computer solution. The technique is nevertheless the same as that just illustrated.

EXAMPLE 9.16. This is a program to sum the numbers 1, 4, 7, 10, . . . , 997.

The numbers in the set to be added go from 1 to 997, changing each time by 3. Thus,

```
100 LET S=0
110 LET K=1
120    LET S=S+K
130    LET K=K+3
140 IF K<=997 THEN 120
150 PRINT "SUM IS";S
160 END

RUN

SUM IS 166167

READY
```

Because of its importance and simplicity, we repeat the technique of summing.

1. A variable for the sum is initialized to zero.
2. A loop is entered, in which the values to be added are obtained. The summing statement in the loop looks like LET S=S+X, where S is the sum and X is the term to be added.
3. After the loop has been executed the required number of times, the value of S is the required sum.

9.10 Large and Small Numbers

EXAMPLE 9.17. We wish to print out the values of the integer powers of 5 (5^n) from $n = 0$ through $n = 9$.

The program is

```
100 REM POWERS OF 5
110 PRINT "EXPONENT",  "VALUE"
120 LET N=0
130    LET P=5↑N
140    PRINT N,P
150    LET N=N+1
160 IF N<=9 THEN 130
170 END
```

RUN

EXPONENT	VALUE
Ø	1
1	5
2	25
3	125
4	625
5	3125
6	15625
7	78125
8	39Ø625
9	1.95313E+6

READY

The appearance of the last number in the second column is new. What does it mean? It is the special way that BASIC uses to print numbers that are very large or very small. These "E-numbers" are the computer's way of writing a number in scientific notation.

To write a number in scientific notation means to write the number as a product of a whole number or decimal between 1 and 10 and an integral power of 10. Let's look at several examples.

EXAMPLE 9.18. In scientific notation, 123 is written as 1.23×10^2. Let's see what is necessary to do the change (of course, you first must observe that the two values are in fact, equal; that is, $123 = 1.23 \times 10^2$).

The decimal point in 123, as with any integer, is to the right of the units digit, the 3. In the change to scientific notation, the decimal point has been moved two places to the left. The number now looks like 1.23. The decimal point was moved in such a way that the number to its left (in this case, 1) is a single digit from 1 to 9. Moving the decimal point in such a way (two places to the left) is the same as dividing by 100. But the original number, 123, cannot be changed. So if we divide by 100, we must also multiply by 100. But 100 is 10^2, a power of 10. Thus 1.23×10^2 is a number written in scientific notation that is equal to the original number 123.

EXAMPLE 9.19. Written in scientific notation, $.00456 = 4.56 \times 10^{-3}$. You can see that the decimal point was moved *three* places to the *right* and that the exponent used with 10 was *negative three*. This occurs because the moving of the decimal point is the same as multiplying by 1000 (or by 10^3), and to balance this we must divide by 10^3, which is the same as multiplying by 10^{-3}.

Thus, to change a number to scientific notation,

1. Move the decimal point so that there is only one nonzero digit to the left of the decimal point.

2. Multiply the number you get in step 1 by a power of 10. The exponent is the number of places you had to move the decimal point to get the number in step 1. The sign of this exponent will be *positive* if you moved the decimal point to the *left;* it will be *negative* if you moved it to the *right.*

EXAMPLE 9.20. Write 85,623 in scientific notation.

The decimal point must be moved four places to the *left* (giving 8.5623). So in scientific notation $85,623 = 8.5623 \times 10^4$.

Example 9.21. Write 7,400,000 in scientific notation.

$7,400,000 = 7.4 \times 10^6$

Note that the zeroes following the 4 after moving the decimal point are insignificant and so are not written.

EXAMPLE 9.22. Write .00004129 in scientific notation.

$.00004129 = 4.129 \times 10^{-5}$

EXAMPLE 9.23. Change the number 3.02×10^3 (written in scientific notation) to its usual form.

The exponent of 10, a positive 3, says to move the decimal point three places to the right. Thus,

$3.02 \times 10^3 = 3020$

Note that since the decimal point must be moved three places and there are only two digits written (the 0 and the 2), we include another digit, 0, to complete the movement of the decimal point.

EXAMPLE 9.24. To change 4.621×10^{-2}, we move the decimal point to the left two places, giving .04621.

Now that you know how to change numbers to and from scientific notation, it is easy to understand the "E-numbers" of BASIC. The E merely stands for the 10 used in scientific notation, and the number following the E is the exponent that goes with the 10.

EXAMPLE 9.25

1.2603×10^3 is the same as 1.2603E+3.

EXAMPLE 9.26. Write 53,702 as an "E-number."

First we write 53,702 in scientific notation: $53{,}702 = 5.3702 \times 10^4$. Finally we change 10^4 to E+4 and write $53{,}702 = 5.3702E{+}4$.

Returning to the numbers that were printed by our program, we saw 1.95313E+6. We know now that this means

$$1.95313E{+}6 = 1.95313 \times 10^6$$
$$= 1{,}953{,}130$$

A very important point should be noted here about numbers that are printed using the E. Numbers that are printed this way may not be exact! They very likely will be only approximations. For example, the exact value of 5^9 is 1,953,125 while the computer printed out this value as 1.95313E+6, which, we see, is 1,953,130. The reason this happens is that any computer is built in such a way that it only can print out a certain number of digits. When a number is too large to be printed out in its entirety, it is changed to E-form and then printed out. However, with the E-form, there is a restriction on the number of digits that can be used (in our example, that number is 6; other computers may use more or less). When the actual number of digits in the value to be printed is more than the number of digits that the machine can print, the number will be rounded off and then printed.

So to print 1953125 using only six digits, the number goes through the following changes:

$$1953125 = 1.953125 \times 10^6 \quad \text{(change to scientific notation)}$$
$$= 1.95313 \times 10^6 \quad \text{(rounding)}$$
$$= 1.95313E{+}6 \quad \text{(change to E-form)}$$

In summary, you will occasionally write programs that will produce numeric output written in E-notation. These numbers are numbers written in the computer's version of scientific notation. To see what these numbers look like in their usual form, follow the steps given in Figure 9.19 (an example is included for illustration).

The number	2.703E+2
1. Write the E and the number following it as a multiplication of a power of 10.	2.703×10^2
2. The power of 10 tells you how many places the decimal point must be moved (in the example, two).	
3. If the exponent is *positive* (as it is in the example), move the decimal point to the *right*. If the exponent is *negative*, move the decimal point to the *left*.	2.703×10^2
4. Drop the multiplication by the power of 10.	270.3

FIGURE 9.19

The IF-THEN is a conditional transfer statement that transfers control to one of *two* statements in the program. BASIC contains a *multiple-branch transfer statement* that allows transfer to one of *many* statements in the program. This statement is the ON-GOTO statement. Consider the following programming line

9.11 The ON-GOTO Statement

```
275 ON T GOTO 20,50,135,50,85
```

When the statement is executed, the computer uses the value of T to determine to which line transfer will be made.

If T = 1, the transfer is to line number 20
        (the *first* line number following GOTO).
If T = 2, the transfer is to line number 50
        (the *second* line number following GOTO).
If T = 3, transfer to line number 135
        (the *third* after GOTO).
If T = 4, transfer to line number 50
        (the *fourth*).
If T = 5, transfer to line number 85
        (the *fifth*).

The *general form of the ON-GOTO* is

line number   ON   numeric expression   GOTO line 1, line 2, . . . , line k.

The expression is evaluated, and if it is not already an integer, the computer rounds the value of the expression to the nearest integer.[3] If there are k line numbers following GOTO, the value of the expression (rounded, if necessary) must be one of the integers from 1 to k inclusive, or else an error is generated.[4] If the expression does lie from 1 to k, a transfer is made. Control is transferred to the first line number following GOTO if the value of the expression is 1, to the second line number listed if the value is 2, and so on, up to a possible transfer to the kth line number listed after GOTO if the value of the expression is equal to k.

EXAMPLE 9.27. Property in a certain town is divided into four categories. Each of the four categories has a different tax rate. The tax rate for property in category 1 is 14%, 18% for category 2, 11% for category 3, and 9% for category 4. Write a program where the user supplies the value of the property and the category number that applies to the property. The program should then calculate and print the amount of tax to be paid on that property.

The amount of tax to be paid depends upon the category, and since

---

[3] Some versions of BASIC truncate instead of round.
[4] Some versions of BASIC do not treat this as an error but merely continue on to the next line number in sequence.

the categories are numbered with consecutive integers beginning with 1, this is an ideal situation to use the ON-GOTO statement.

```
100 REM REAL ESTATE TAX CALCULATION
110 PRINT "WHAT IS THE PROPERTY VALUE";
120 INPUT V
130 PRINT
140 PRINT "WHAT IS THE TAX CATEGORY";
150 INPUT C
160 PRINT
170 REM MULTIPLE TRANSFER
180 ON C GOTO 190,220,250,280
190 REM TAX FOR CATEGORY 1 IS 14 PERCENT
200 LET T=.14*V
210 GOTO 300
220 REM TAX FOR CATEGORY 2 IS 18 PERCENT
230 LET T=.18*V
240 GOTO 300
250 REM TAX FOR CATEGORY 3 IS 11 PERCENT
260 LET T=.11*V
270 GOTO 300
280 REM TAX FOR CATEGORY 4 IS 9 PERCENT
290 LET T=.09*V
300 PRINT "TAX BILL IS";T
310 END
```

EXERCISES

1 What, if anything, is wrong with the following statements?
  a. 175 GOTO END
  b. STOP
  c. 500 GOTO 500
  d. 808 ON X↑2+4 GOTO 20,400,10,280
  e. 95 IF X$<ANSWER THEN "WRONG"
  f. 250 ON T$ GOTO 100,40,100,290

2 Suppose that the line numbers in a program are incremented by 10's and that the program begins with

```
10 LET X$="GOOD"
20 LET Y$="BAD"
30 LET Z$="AVERAGE"
```

When the following lines are executed, what is the *next* line to be executed?
  a. 100 IF X$=Y$ THEN 350
  b. 170 IF Z$<=Y$ THEN 80
  c. 250 IF X$<="GREAT" THEN 700
  d. 360 IF Y$>"BADLY" THEN 500

3 Liz is now 10 years old and her uncle, Jim, is 30. Write a program that uses a loop to find out in how many years Liz's age will be half that of her uncle's.

4 The population of the town of Yorkville is 14,326 and is increasing at the rate of 3.2% each year. Find the least number of years until the population is double (or more) what it is today.

5 Write a program which will produce ten lines of output that begin like

ECHO Ø	15	1
ECHO 1	15	2
ECHO 2	15	4
ECHO 3	15	8

6 Modify the program of Example 9.7 so that a fourth column shows the interest paid that month.

7 Samantha wants to invest some money. What interest rate would be needed in order that Samantha's money is doubled in ten years? Use the formula $C = P(1 + R)^N$ where the interest rates to check should start at 6% and be increased each time by .01%.

8 A number is to be entered. The user is then asked whether the square or the cube of the number is to be printed. When the indicated number has been output, the user should be given the choice to halt or to do the same thing again.

9 A baby-sitter charges $1.25 per hour up to midnight and $1.75 per hour after midnight. Enter the starting time and ending time of the baby-sitter's job and print the amount to be paid. You should use a 24-hour clock (e.g., 2 A.M. would be 2 but 2 P.M. would be 14 and 24 means midnight). Use the values

Start	Finish
19	23
19	1
17	3
18	24

10 A publishing company has agreed to pay an author royalties according to the following schedule. For the first 5000 copies, the royalties are 12% of the total sales. However, if more than 5000 copies are sold, the royalties are 14% of all copies sold over 5000 plus the royalties earned on the first 5000 copies. Write a program for the publishing company to determine how much the author must be paid. The cost of a single book and the total number of books sold are to be input. RUN your program using the data

Cost	Number of Copies
$5.25	2500
6.95	4800
9.32	3650
8.24	4825
8.24	5175
8.02	7500

11 Two numbers are to be entered from the terminal. *Without actually multiplying them* the program should determine if their product is positive, negative, or zero. When the program has been written, try it using 5 and 7, 2.4 and −4, 0 and 15, −1 and −3, −6.2 and 11.1, and 77 and 0.

12 A building supply company calculates a customer's bill by using the following plan:
   a. If the bill is less than $50, no discount is given.
   b. If the bill is less than $200 but $50 or more, a 7% discount is given.
   c. For $200 or more an 11% discount is given.

The bill should be entered by the user and the final charge calculated and printed. Then the user should be asked if another bill is to be computed. If it is, do so; if not, the word "finished" should be printed and the program should halt.

Use the following as data for the customer's bill:
a. $99.98   b. $100   c. $35   d. $200   e. $375   f. $50

13 Hibrough Prep School gives only three grades: "unsatisfactory," "satisfactory," and "commendable." A grade is based on the average of four tests. If the average is less than 55, the grade given is "unsatisfactory"; "commendable" is given for an average of 85 or above. The four test grades should be supplied from the terminal. The output should show the average as well as the "word grade."

For data, you could use
a. 57,95,82,88   b. 96,98,84,89   c. 75,40,53,55

14 The Clayton Bank and Trust requires a down payment on a home mortgage according to the following schedule.

20% of the selling price up to and including $30,000
30% of the next $20,000
50% of any remaining amount

However the bank will not give a mortgage on a house selling for more than $75,000. Write a program for the bank that calculates and prints the required down payment and the amount that must be financed by the mortgage. The selling price should be entered from the terminal. For selling prices try $54,900, $36,000, $29,800, and $83,000.

15 The annual tax to be paid by the Braintree Painting Company is computed by the following schedule. (Suppose P is the profit earned by the company.)
  a. If $P \leq 0$, no tax.
  b. If $0 < P \leq \$15,000$, tax is 20% of the profit.
  c. If $\$15,000 < P \leq \$40,000$, tax is 20% of the first $15,000 plus 35% of the amount over $15,000.
  d. If $P > \$40,000$, the tax is 20% of the first $15,000, 35% of the next $25,000, and 50% of any amount remaining.

A program is to be written for the company. The total annual income should be entered from the terminal and then the total annual expenses. The profit should be then calculated and printed. Finally, the amount of taxes to be paid should be calculated and printed. A detailed flowchart should first be drawn and then the program written and run using

Income	Expenses
$15,200	$ 9800
3550	4295
11,590	3860
25,000	1000
48,300	12,860
65,945	14,020

16 Write a program to calculate and print the following sums.
  a. $2 + 4 + 6 + \cdots + 98 + 100$
  b. $10 + 20 + 30 + \cdots + 990 + 1000$
  c. $(-7) + (-5) + (-3) + \cdots + 119 + 121$
  d. $1 + 4 + 9 + \cdots + 81 + 100$

17. Positive and negative numbers are to be entered from the terminal one at a time until a 0 is entered. When the 0 has been entered, the program should display how many negative numbers had been entered and also the sum of the positive values. Try your program with the numbers 4, −7, 15, −1, −2, 8, 1, and 0, then with 1, 2, 3, 11, and 0, and finally with −2, −6, −3, and 0.

18 Write each of the numbers, given in E-form, in its usual form.

a. 7.2834E+2   e. 6.200598E+4
b. 4.35E+0   f. 4.832E−1
c. 8.1011E+4   g. 2.00304E−8
d. 3.091E−4   h. 5.55E−5

19 For each number given, first change it to scientific notation and then write it in E-notation, supposing that you can use a maximum of six digits.

a. 34,095   e. 11.000217
b. 110,247   f. 6348.2873
c. 763.512   g. 1,000,000
d. .0438621   h. .00004321798

20 A ball that is dropped from some height h will bounce back to one half its original height (and then, of course, drop again and bounce again, and on and on). Write a program that asks the user to supply the original height of the ball and then calculates and prints all the succeeding heights for the first 20 bounces. For the heights to be entered, try

a. 1000   c. 10
b. 100   d. 3

21 The speed of light is 186,000 miles per second. Write a program to find out how far an object, traveling at the speed of light, would go if it traveled for 12 hours; for 24 hours.

22 Given the programming statement

```
220 ON 3*X-5 GO TO 35,90,410,280
```

to what line number will transfer be made if

a. $X = 3$?
b. $X = 2$?
c. $X = 5$?

23 Write a sequence of statements (not an entire program) beginning at line 175 that

a. Gets a value (X) from the user (you may assume X is an integer)
b. Transfers to line 230 if $X = 2$ or $X = 5$
c. Transfers to line 405 if $X = 3$
d. Transfers to line 100 if $X = 4$
e. Transfers to line 20 if X is any other value.

24 Write a program that asks the user to supply a number and then asks which of the following should be printed:

a. The double of the number
b. The triple of the number
c. The square of the number
d. The cube of the number

Of course, once the user elects one of the four options, it should be carried out.

Execute your program with the following:

−7, double
5, cube
−3, square
100, triple

* * *

25 The user should type in three numbers (A, B, C) and the program should determine whether the third (C) is the hypotenuse of a right triangle, whose legs are the first two values (A and B). Depending on the result, an appropriate message should be printed. (The condition to check is whether $C^2 = A^2 + B^2$). Some values to supply are

A	B	C
3	4	5
6	7	10
12	5	13
5.2	3.7	40.73
2.03	7.1	54.54
1.001	1.1	2.212

26 Three lengths (call them S1, S2, and S3) will form the sides of some triangle if *each* side is less than the sum of the other two (that is, if S1 < S2 + S3, if S2 < S1 + S3, and if S3 < S1 + S2). A program is to be written that determines whether three values typed at the terminal could form the sides of a triangle. Depending on the result, either the word *yes* or the word *no* should be printed.

Try your program using the data

S1	S2	S3
6	4	1
1	2	3
2	4	5
8	5	3

27 An angle should be supplied from the terminal. Suppose that X is the angle. If $0 < X < 180$ the program should determine if the angle is acute, right or obtuse and an appropriate message printed. Otherwise the message OUT OF RANGE should be printed.

Try your program by entering as X values 45, 0, 90, 180, 178, 1, 180, and 89.9.

28 A famous number sequence is the Fibonacci sequence. Its first two terms are 1 and 1. Each succeeding term is the sum of the previous two terms.

Write a program to print the ratios of each pair of successive terms, for the first 30 terms, of the Fibonacci sequence. Your output should look like

TERMS	RATIO
1 AND 1	1
1 AND 2	2
2 AND 3	1.5
3 AND 5	1.666667
—	—
—	—
—	—

29 The user should supply the measure of an angle (in degrees) that is less than 360° and greater than or equal to 0°. If the angle measures 0°, 90°, 180°, or 270°, the message "quadrantal angle" should be printed. Otherwise the program should print the quadrant in which the angle lies and its reference angle. For this program use the angles 30°, 270°, 110°, 0°, 180°, 225°, and 350°.

30 Draw a flowchart that finds and prints the largest of three values that are entered from the terminal.

31. The constants A, B and C for the linear inequality $AX + B < C$ should be supplied from the terminal. The solution should be printed as $X <$ _____ or $X >$ _____ . Use the program to solve the given inequalities

$3X + 5 < 17$ $2X - 1 < 9$

$7X + 2 < -19$ $4X - 3 < 15$

$-5X + 1 < 36$ $-9X - 4 < -13$

32 Division of positive integers can be thought of as repeated subtractions. Perform the given divisions by this method. The quotient, together with the remainder, should be printed. If the remainder is 0, it should not be printed. The divisions are

a. $24 \div 4$	c. $65 \div 9$	e. $91 \div 7$
b. $110 \div 11$	d. $157 \div 3$	f. $6389 \div 17$

33 Two numbers are to be entered from the terminal. They represent the coordinates of a point in the plane. The program should determine if the point lies on an axis or, if not, in which quadrant it lies. For example, if the point were $(-2, 5)$, the output should be

THE POINT (-2,5) IS IN QUADRANT 2

and if the point were $(7, 0)$ the output should be

THE POINT (7,Ø) IS ON AN AXIS.

Data for your program could include the points $(-2, 5)$, $(7, 0)$, $(1, 1)$, $(-1, 0)$, $(-4, -3)$, $(0, 0)$, $(0, 2)$, $(7, -2)$, $(0, -8)$.

34 A linear equation has form $AX + BY = C$. The user should enter the constants A, B, and C. The output should be the slope of the line and the two intercepts, printed under the headings

SLOPE,X INTERCEPT,Y INTERCEPT.

If the line is vertical, the word NONE should be printed under slope. RUN your program for the lines

$3x + 2y = 7$	$x - y = 1$
$5x + 3y = 0$	$2y = -9$
$x = 6$	$-7x + 2y = 4$
$x = 0$	$y = 0$

35 An interval is to be divided into a number of subintervals of equal length. The user should enter the end points of the original interval and the required number of subintervals. The program should then print the endpoints of each subinterval. For data you might try

Left End Point	Right End Point	Number of Subintervals
0	5	5
−2	3	10
.1	.2	20
0	1	25

36 Rick is 35 years old and works for a company that has no retirement plan. He plans to retire when he is 65 and is starting a savings account for that purpose. The savings account pays a simple annual interest rate. Rick plans to deposit $250 at the start of each year. Write a program for Rick to show him how much money is in the savings account at the end of each year from now until he retires.

37 Refer back to Exercise 10 which dealt with royalties payment. Now the author has been given a choice of payments. The first option is 8% on all books sold up to 4000 and 18% on all copies more than 4000. The other option is a constant 15% on all books sold. Write a program for the author to determine how many books will have to be sold before the royalties from the first method exceeds the royalties from the second method. A flowchart should be drawn first. For the price of the book use $5.00.

38 A word is to be typed in from the terminal. After that, words are to be entered, one at a time, as long as they are in alphabetical order. When the alphabetic order is not maintained, the phrase "out of sequence" should be printed. Run your program with the words a, certain, number, of, questions, seem, to, arise.

39 Write a program for the Creampuff Auto Agency, a new car dealership. The program should print out an itemized bill for a customer who has just purchased a new car. A possible discount (at the discretion of the sales manager) of not more than 12% of the "window sticker" price is available. A sales tax of 4% of the selling price must be added on. Finally, a shipping charge must be included. The amount of the shipping charge depends upon the city where the car was manufactured. If the car was manufactured in Detroit, a charge of $42.87 is made; if the car was made in Harrisburg, the shipping charge is $36.05. The program should

a. Request the "window sticker" price of the car (if the amount is less than $3500, a message saying that there must be a mistake—the price is too low—should be printed and again a request for the price should be made).

b. Ask for the discount rate (if more than 12%, a mistake has been made).

c. Find out where the car was manufactured.

d. Calculate the discount (money), the selling price, the amount of sales tax and the total price.

e. Skip a few lines.

f. Print a bill similar to the one shown below.

```
STICKER PRICE:        $
DISCOUNT RATE:
DISCOUNT:             $
SELLING PRICE:        $
SALES TAX:            $
SHIPPING:             $

***TOTAL PRICE***     $
```

Try your program with

Sticker Price	Discount Rate	City
$4,115	7%	Detroit
7,339	9	Harrisburg
5,286	14	Detroit

(This will have to be re-entered—use 4%)

6,590	0	Detroit
2,500	5	Harrisburg

(This will have to be re-entered—use $4,500)

9,275	11	Harrisburg

10

Prior to this chapter, two statements have been used to assign values to variables. These two statements are LET and INPUT. The third and last statement of BASIC that assigns a value to a variable is READ. Actually, a READ statement alone is useless (and, in fact, would produce an error message) because another statement is needed to hold the information to be processed by the READ. That second statement is a DATA statement. With this brief and admittedly sketchy introduction, let's look at some simple programs that use these two new statements.

Consider the following program.

10.1 Three Apparently Different Programs

```
10 READ A
20 READ B
30 READ C
40 PRINT A;B;C
50 DATA 3
60 DATA 12
70 DATA 7
80 END
```

Although the READ has not been explained, you should be able to make a good guess at what the output would be. There are three separate READs and three separate DATA statements, and each of these DATA statements contains a single number. If you guessed that since A is the first variable to be READ (past tense!) and 3 is the first number in a DATA line and so 3 is assigned to A, your guess would be correct. Similarly, 12 would be assigned to B and 7 to C. Thus the output would be

```
3   12   7
```

Now look at the following program and try to guess its output:

```
11 READ A,B,C
22 PRINT A;B;C
33 DATA 3,12,7
44 END
```

There is a single READ followed by three variables, and there is a single DATA followed by three numbers. Because of this apparent correspondence between the variables and the DATA values, you might guess that this program works like the last one. That is correct, and so, of course, the output would be

```
3   12   7
```

With both the previous programs, there seemed to be a matching between variables in READ statements and values in DATA statements. That matching appeared obvious in the ways the programs were typed; the first program had three separate READs together with three separate DATAs; the second had a single READ with three variables and a single DATA with three values. The next does not show any such matching.

```
10 READ A
20 READ B,C
30 PRINT A;B;C
40 DATA 3,12
50 DATA 7
60 END
```

The first READ uses only a single variable, while the first DATA contains two values. The second READ references two variables, but the second DATA contains only one value. Nevertheless, the program works exactly the same way as the first two (that is, A=3, B=12, C=7) and produces the same output. To see why this is so, we now consider how the READ/DATA works.

10.2 The Data Stack

When the computer executes a program that contains READs and DATAs, the first thing it does is to collect *all* the values from *all* the DATA statements. This collection of data may be thought of as being in a column or *stack*. Thus the data stack from each of the three programs we considered would be the same, namely,

```
3
12
7
```

Associated with a data stack is something called a *pointer*. We shall view the pointer as an arrow that *points at the value to be assigned to the next variable when it is read*. At the beginning of a program, the pointer is always found at the top of the data stack. At the start of any of the three programs, the data stack looks like this:

```
3 ←——
12
7
```

Figure 10.1 shows the first program and the appearance of the data stack as the three READs are executed. (The appearance of the data stack *before* the first READ is executed was shown.)

Program	After line 10	After line 20	After line 30
10 READ A	3	3	3
20 READ B	12 ←	12	12
30 READ C	7	7 ←	7
40 PRINT A;B;C			←
50 DATA 3	A has been given	B is equal to 12	The value of C is
60 DATA 12	the value 3. The	(A is still 3),	read as 7 and
70 DATA 7	pointer has	and the	the pointer
80 END	dropped to 12,	pointer drops.	drops down
	the next value		and off the
	to be used.		stack since
			there are no
			more data
			values.

FIGURE 10.1.

The same idea applies if more than one variable is to be defined by a single READ statement. This was the case in the second and third programs. Suppose, for example, a line read 100 READ X,Y. Then when line 100 is executed, *two* values are used from the stack. The first value is assigned to X and the second to Y. In this case the pointer moves *two* places down the stack.

EXAMPLE 10.1.   What is the output from the program?

```
2 LET I=1
3    READ A
5    PRINT A
7    LET I=I+1
11 IF I<=3 THEN 3
13   READ B,C
17 PRINT A,B,C
19 DATA 7,8,9,0,1,2
23 END
```

Our data stack consists of six values. A loop is executed three times. In the loop, a value for A is read and printed. The first time through the loop, A has the value 7. The second time the loop is executed, A is assigned the new value 8 and the last time through A=9. So just prior to the execution of line 11 the pointer is at the 0. Now two values are read, the first for B and the second for C. After line 13, the data stack looks like this:

```
7
8
9
Ø
1
2 ◄──
```

After line 13 comes the last PRINT statement and then the program ends. So the output would be

RUN

```
7   ◄──  the value of A the first time through the loop
8   ◄──  A, the second time through
9   ◄──  the third value A takes on
9        Ø              1   ◄──   from line 17
```

READY

You might be wondering about the last value in the data stack, 2. Even though the data stack contains six values, the program only reads five. This is not unusual. The sixth data value is just not processed. The opposite situation is more critical. If your DATA lines contain fewer values than will be required by the READs in your program, the pointer will move off the bottom of the stack before all the READs are executed. When a READ is executed and there are no data available, an error message such as

OUT OF DATA

will be printed and your program will be terminated.

10.3 The General Forms

The *general form of the READ statement* is

line number   READ variable or list of variables separated by commas

and the *general form of DATA* is

line number   DATA constant or constants separated by commas

You should observe that there is no special matching between the number of READ statements and the number of DATA statements. A single READ may refer to one or more DATA statements (see the program in Figure 10.2), or many READs may be served by a single DATA line (see Figure 10.3). The general form just shown may be somewhat

```
10 READ G,H,I          5  READ X,Y           100 DATA 9,11
20 PRINT G*(H+I)      15  READ P,Q           200 READ X
30 DATA 7             25  PRINT X+Y,P*Q      300 DATA 3,5
40 DATA 3,-2          35  DATA 1,8,-3,4      400 READ Y,Z,Q
50 END                45  END                500 PRINT X,Y,Z,Q
                                             600 END
```

FIGURE 10.2.	**FIGURE 10.3.**	**FIGURE 10.4.**

misleading in that it seems to imply that the DATA statement must follow the READ statement in a program (as the earlier programs were written). However, this is not the case. Since the computer first gathers *all* the data into a data stack, the data may appear *anywhere* in the program (see Figure 10.4). Nevertheless, there is a good reason why the convention to *put all data just before the END statement* is used. If all the data are collected in one place in the program and your program is not working properly so that you have to debug it, it will be easier to find the data being processed if they are all in one place.

10.4 The Flowcharting Symbol for READ

A parallelogram, ⟱, is the flowcharting symbol that will be used for READ.[1] We will use no symbol for the DATA statement, but when reading or writing a flowchart that uses a READ, we will always assume that there will be data supplied for the program.

EXAMPLE 10.2.   Each month the Albatross Insurance Company evaluates applicants for employment. Each applicant must take a written examination (0 to 50 possible points), meet with the company psychologist who prepares a psychological profile (0 to 10 possible points), and be interviewed by someone in the personnel department who also makes a report (0 to 10 points). Based upon the results of these evaluations, an applicant is told that no position is available or is told to return to the company for further interviews. If the applicant scores 35 or more on the written examination and a combined total on the two interviews that is greater than 14, the applicant should be asked to return; otherwise, no position is available for the applicant.

The information for each applicant will be typed into a DATA line. The data will consist of four numbers: an identification number, the score on the written examination, the score on the psychological profile, and the score on the personnel interview. For simplicity we will assume

---

[1] Some texts use the parallelogram as the symbol for INPUT also (in fact, some use it for all I/O—that is, for PRINT also). However since the methods for supplying the data differ—typed externally with INPUT, internally for READ—we choose to use different symbols.

that 100 applicants are screened each month. A flowchart using the

symbol follows.

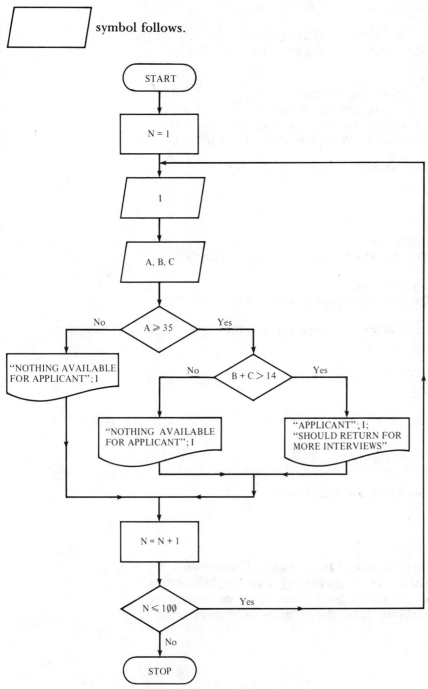

FIGURE 10.5.

The following program, with several sample data sets, is obtained from the flowchart shown in Figure 10.5.

```
100 REM ALBATROSS INSURANCE COMPANY
110 REM PRELIMINARY EVALUATION OF JOB APPLICANTS
120 REM
130 REM INFORMATION FOR EACH APPLICANT IS FOUND ON
140 REM DATA LINES AND IS ENTERED IN THE FORM
150 REM DATA I
160 REM DATA A,B,C
170 REM WHERE I = APPLICANT CODE NUMBER
180 REM        A = SCORE ON WRITTEN EXAM
190 REM        B = SCORE ON PSYCHOLOGICAL PROFILE
200 REM        C = SCORE ON PERSONNEL REPORT
210 REM
220 REM PROGRAM PROCESSES 100 APPLICANTS
230 REM
240 LET N=1
250    READ I
260    READ A,B,C
270    IF A>=35 THEN 300
280    PRINT "NOTHING AVAILABLE FOR APPLICANT";I
290    GOTO 340
300    IF B+C>14 THEN 330
310    PRINT "NOTHING AVAILABLE FOR APPLICANT";I
320    GOTO 340
330    PRINT "APPLICANT";I;"SHOULD RETURN FOR MORE INTERVIEWS."
340    PRINT
350    LET N=N+1
360 IF N<=100 THEN 250
370 DATA 323
375 DATA 44,9,6
380 DATA 514
385 DATA 32,8,7
390 DATA 473
395 DATA 38,9,7
     .
     .            (The rest of the data would appear here.)
     .
     .
2000 END
```

REMs of the type shown in lines 130 through 200 are commonly used and aid both readability and maintainability. You should note that the setup of the data in the DATA lines is not required because of the way the data stack works but helps the program to be more understandable.

10.5 Strings with READ

We have seen string constants assigned to string variables by using the LET statement and the INPUT statement. This section illustrates the processing of strings using the READ statement.

EXAMPLE 10.3. The following uses READ with strings.

```
100 LET N=1
110   READ A$,G
120   PRINT A$;"'S GRADE IS";G
130   LET N=N+1
140 IF N<=5 THEN 110
150 DATA TOM,62
160 DATA MARY,97
170 DATA BETH,75
180 DATA DICK,84
190 DATA HARRY,92
200 END

RUN

TOM'S GRADE IS 62
MARY'S GRADE IS 97
BETH'S GRADE IS 75
DICK'S GRADE IS 84
HARRY'S GRADE IS 92

READY
```

The READ statement on line 110 requires that a string constant and a numeric constant (in that order) be supplied from the data stack. But the data stack is constructed from the five DATA lines, each containing a pair of values. So the data stack for the program is

```
TOM
62
MARY
97
BETH
75
DICK
84
HARRY
92
```

Each pair of values in the data stack is a string constant followed by a numeric constant. The string constants in the DATA lines are not quoted and, in general, need not be unless some special circumstance requires it. One such circumstance is a string with a comma embedded in it—this has already been illustrated in Example 7.14.

Another instance is when the string constant begins with a blank. Leading blanks in unquoted string constants are ignored by the computer.

EXAMPLE 10.4

```
100 PRINT "ENTER THE NAME"
110 INPUT R$
120 PRINT
```

```
13Ø READ C$,D$
14Ø PRINT C$;D$;R$
15Ø DATA BONNIE
16Ø DATA " PRINCE"
17Ø END
```

RUN

ENTER THE NAME
? SS

BONNIE PRINCESS

READY

The space after BONNIE is due to the blank preceding the P in PRINCE in the *quoted* string constant in line 15Ø. However, the string SS is printed immediately after the string PRINCE. Now look at another RUN.

RUN

ENTER THE NAME
? " CHARLIE"

BONNIE PRINCE CHARLIE

READY

The word CHARLIE is separated from PRINCE because a *blank* begins the *quoted* string constant typed at the terminal.

We now look at several examples of programs that use READ/DATA.

10.6 Examples

EXAMPLE 10.5. Determine the output from the following program.

```
1Ø READ A,B
2Ø LET T=A
3Ø     READ C
4Ø     PRINT C,
5Ø     LET T=T+1
6Ø IF T<=B THEN 3Ø
7Ø DATA 2,4,5,6,8
8Ø END
```

The program begins by READing values for A and B. So A is 2 and B is 4. These values are used as the first and last values of a loop determined by the variable T. The loop is executed three times

(T=2,3,4). The statements within the loop are READ and PRINT. So the output is

RUN

5　　　　　　　　6　　　　　　　8

READY

EXAMPLE 10.6.　A small credit company has given credit to 15 people. Each of the 15 people is identified by a code number. A program is to be written for the credit company. The customer code number is to be entered from the terminal. The program should then print the amount of credit given to that customer.

The program will include 15 DATA lines. Each line will contain two numbers. The first will be the customer code number and the second will be the amount of credit. A number (N) will be typed in at the terminal. A loop will then be entered that will be executed at most 15 times. In the loop two numbers (C1 and C2) are READ. C1 refers to the customer number; C2 refers to the credit amount. If the customer number typed at the terminal is the same as the customer number in the data (that is, if N=C1), the credit amount C2 is printed out. However, there is the possibility that the number from the terminal will not match any of the customer numbers in the data. This will occur if the loop has been repeated 15 times and no match (N=C1) has been found. If this does occur an appropriate message should be printed.

```
110 REM CREDIT CHECK PROGRAM
120 PRINT "WHAT IS CUSTOMER NUMBER";
130 INPUT N
140 PRINT
150 LET T=1
160 REM C1 IS DATA CUSTOMER NUMBER
170 REM C2 IS CUSTOMER CREDIT
180    READ C1,C2
190    REM CHECK FOR MATCH
200    IF N=C1 THEN 260
210    LET T=T+1
220 IF T<=15 THEN 180
230 REM IF LOOP COMPLETED, NO MATCH
240 PRINT "CUSTOMER NUMBER NOT FOUND"
250 STOP
260 PRINT "CREDIT IS";C2
270 DATA 304,575
271 DATA 58,358.30
272 DATA 1449,2500
273 DATA 536,823.75
274 DATA 99,1421.77
275 DATA 183,15.15
276 DATA 621,463.25
277 DATA 1563,1008
278 DATA 34,88.10
```

```
279 DATA 243,49
280 DATA 11,1213.14
281 DATA 777,1109
282 DATA 76,17
283 DATA 802,960
284 DATA 14,816.60
300 END

RUN

WHAT IS CUSTOMER NUMBER? 621

CREDIT IS 463.25

READY

RUN

WHAT IS CUSTOMER NUMBER? 883

CUSTOMER NUMBER NOT FOUND

READY
```

EXAMPLE 10.7.   A store is having an "end-of-the-year" sale and a program is to be written that produces the sale information. For simplicity, we shall assume that the store carries only ten items. Each of the ten items will be discounted by 20% or 45% or not discounted at all. For each of the ten items, the information to be entered into DATA lines is

name of item, retail price, sale code

The sale code is a D (a discontinued item that will be discounted by 45% of the retail price), an S (sale item; 20% discount), or an R (no discount—ordinary retail price still in effect). The program should print the name of the item, its retail price and its sale price.

An algorithm might be

1. Print out column headings.
2. Do steps 3 through 11 ten times.
3. Read name of item (N$), retail price (P), and sale code (C$).
4. If no discount on item, transfer to step 10; otherwise, continue to step 5.
5. If item is discontinued, transfer to step 8; otherwise, continue to step 6.
6. Calculate a 20% discount and assign sale price to S (i.e., $S = P - .20 \times P$).
7. Go to step 11.
8. Calculate a 45% discount by $S = P - .45 \times P$.
9. Go to step 11.
10. Set sale price equal to retail price ($S = P$).
11. Print N$, P, S.

And the program is

```
100 REM END OF YEAR SALE
110 REM DATA IS OF THE FORM:
120 REM ITEM NAME, RETAIL PRICE, SALE CODE
130 REM
140 REM IF CODE=D, DISCOUNT IS 45%
150 REM IF CODE=S, DISCOUNT IS 20%
160 REM IF CODE=R, NO DISCOUNT
170 REM
180 PRINT "ITEM","RETAIL PRICE","SALE PRICE"
190 PRINT
200 LET I=1
210    READ N$,P,C$
220    IF C$="R" THEN 280
230    IF C$="D" THEN 260
240    LET S=P-.20*P
250    GOTO 290
260    LET S=P-.45*P
270    GOTO 290
280    LET S=P
290    PRINT N$,P,S
300    PRINT
310    LET I=I+1
320 IF I<=10 THEN 210
330 DATA STOVE,249.50,S
340 DATA GLOBE,35,D
350 DATA BOOKCASE,36.95,R
360 DATA LAMP,25.99,D
370 DATA RUG,109.29,S
380 DATA WATCH,89.20,S
390 DATA RADIO,45.10,S
400 DATA WOK,19.95,R
410 DATA TOASTER,17.75,S
420 DATA GLOVES,4.85,D
500 END
```

RUN

ITEM	RETAIL PRICE	SALE PRICE
STOVE	249.5	199.6
GLOBE	35	19.25
BOOKCASE	36.95	36.95
LAMP	25.99	14.2945
RUG	109.29	87.432
WATCH	89.2	71.36
RADIO	45.1	36.08
WOK	19.95	19.95
TOASTER	17.75	14.2
GLOVES	4.85	2.6675

READY

We know that LET, INPUT, and READ are all used to assign values to variables—to supply the numbers or data to the computer for processing. READ is like INPUT in that these statements should be used to supply numbers that will likely change from one RUN of the program to the next. READ is like LET in that they both define their values from *within* the program (as opposed to INPUT, which gets its values from *outside* the program, that is, from the user). So when values are likely to change, the programmer must make a decision whether to use INPUT or READ. A general guideline is to use READ when *many* numbers are to be processed; INPUT if there are just a few. (Remember, however, that in textbooks examples and exercises rarely use massive amounts of data.)

To find the average of a set of values, you first add all the values and then divide the sum by the number of values in the set. We will now consider three programs, each of which is written to calculate an average. The three programs differ because of the different number of values they must process.

10.7 End of Data Indicator

EXAMPLE 10.8.   A program is to be written that will average 100 values.
Since this program will always process *exactly* 100 pieces of data, a loop that is executed 100 times will be used. In the loop, a number will be read and summed. When the loop has been completed, the sum will be divided by 100 to obtain the average.

```
10 LET  S=0
20 LET  L=1
30     READ X
40     LET S=S+X
50     LET L=L+1
60 IF L<=100 THEN 30
70 LET A=S/100
80 PRINT "THE AVERAGE IS";A
90 DATA . . .
    —
    —                          (The 100 pieces of data are typed in
    —                          lines starting at 90.)
200 END
```

The restriction on the program in Example 10.8, due to its being able to average exactly 100 values, no more, no less, makes the program hardly usable. The program would be much more effective if it could average a different number of values each time. The method shown in Example 10.9 holds for the averaging of different numbers of values.

EXAMPLE 10.9.   A program is to be written to calculate the average of a set of values assuming that the number of values in the set is known.
All the values to be averaged are typed into DATA lines at the bottom

of the program. The number of values to be averaged (which we assumed was known) is typed into a DATA line by itself and prior to the values to be averaged. The program then reads how many values are to be averaged (we'll call it N) and sums them in a loop that will be executed N times. The average is then calculated and printed. For purposes of illustration, we will find the average of the six values 11, 4, 7, 2, 9, and 3.

```
200 REM A MORE GENERAL AVERAGING PROGRAM
210 REM S IS SUM: L COUNTS THROUGH LOOP
220 REM A IS AVERAGE: X IS TERM TO BE ADDED
230 REM N IS NUMBER OF VALUES TO BE AVERAGED
240 LET S=0
250 LET L=1
260 READ N
270    READ X
280    LET S=S+X
290    LET L=L+1
300 IF L<=N THEN 270
310 LET A=S/N
320 PRINT "THE AVERAGE IS";A
330 REM NEXT LINE CONTAINS THE NUMBER OF VALUES
340 DATA 6
350 REM NEXT LINE(S) CONTAIN THE VALUES
360 DATA 11,4,7,2,9,3
500 END
```

The data stack from this program would look like

```
6
11
4
7
2
9
3
```

The purpose of the first number in the stack is to indicate how many values follow—that is, the first number is used to control how many times the "reading and summing" loop is executed.

It is also possible to find the average of a set of values when we do *not* know how many values there are. To do this, we add an extra data item *after* the values to be averaged; the extra data item will then appear at the *bottom* of the data stack. This number that appears at the bottom of the data stack is called an *end of data indicator,* an end of data tag, or simply an *eod tag.* The eod tag is not meant to be processed; its purpose is to indicate that the bottom of the data stack has been reached and that no more reading should be done.

EXAMPLE 10.10. A large amount of data is collected. Its average is to be calculated and printed. The number of data items is unknown. Since the number of values is not fixed (as in Example 10.8) or even known (Example 10.9), an eod tag must be used. Values will be read, one at a time, from DATA lines. As long as the value is not the eod tag, it will be summed and counted (this will tell us how many values there are and will be the number we divide by to get the average). Once the eod tag is read, transfer will be made to a statement that will calculate the average. Finally, there will be an output statement displaying the number of values processed and their average.

```
100 REM AVERAGING WITH AN EOD TAG
110 REM X IS TERM, S IS SUM OF TERMS
120 REM K COUNTS THE TERMS
130 REM A IS THEIR AVERAGE
140 REM THE NUMBER 99999 IS EOD TAG
150 LET S=0
160 LET K=0
170 READ X
180 REM CHECK FOR EOD
190 IF X=99999 THEN 250
200    REM SUM, COUNT, READ NEXT DATUM AND CONTINUE LOOP
210    LET S=S+X
220    LET K=K+1
230    READ X
240 GOTO 190
250 LET A=S/K
260 PRINT "THE AVERAGE OF THE";K;"VALUES IS";A
270 REM DATA STARTS HERE
280 DATA . . .
   .
   .
   .
498 REM EOD TAG ON NEXT LINE
499 DATA 99999
500 END
```

An observation should be made about the eod tag, 99999. *The most critical consideration about an eod tag is that it be a value that does not appear in any of the other DATA statements;* that is, it must not be one of the significant pieces of data to be processed. The assumption made in Example 10.10 is that we would *not* find the number 99999 in the set of values whose average we want. One way of choosing an eod tag is to make the eod tag a number that is very close to either the largest or smallest number that your computer can handle. For example, if your computer could process numbers between -10^{12} and 10^{12}, a good choice for an eod tag would be 10^{11}. In such a case, lines 190 and 499 of the previous program would be changed to

```
190 IF X=1E+11 THEN 250
499 DATA 1E+11
```

Actually we have previously used eod tags in several programs. If you look back at Example 9.1, you'll notice that if the user entered a zero or a negative number the program would halt. Zero or any negative number works as an eod tag in the sense that, when entered, it signals that no more significant data are to be supplied.

An eod tag need not be a number—it need only be a value that will not occur in the processing of the significant data.

EXAMPLE 10.11.   The following is an inventory program. The data for the program are of the form

product code, wholesale unit price, number of units

where the product code is a letter followed by one or more digits. For each product the program will print the three data items as well as the total cash value of the inventory for that particular product.

Since the product code is not numeric, it will be read using a string variable. For our eod tag, we will use a string constant that does not fit the description of a product code (i.e., that is *not* a letter followed by one or more digits). We use the word DONE as our eod tag.

```
100 REM INVENTORY-EOD STRING
110 PRINT "CODE","UNIT PRICE","NUMBER","VALUE"
120 PRINT
130 READ C$
140 IF C$="DONE" THEN STOP
150    READ P,N
160    LET V=P*N
170    PRINT C$,P,N,V
180    READ C$
190 GOTO 140
200 DATA B211,9.72,14
210 DATA XJ349,51.25,18
 .
 .
 .
499 DATA DONE
500 END
```

Since only the product code is read before a check for more data is made, it is sufficient to have the last line contain only one data item, the eod tag. However if the READ statements were combined into

READ C$,P,N

the last DATA line would have to contain three values, say,

DATA DONE,0,0

because three values must be read *before* the check for the eod tag is made.

A task that is frequently employed is that of selecting from a set of data its largest value. An algorithm to solve this problem is the following. We will assume that there are N values typed into DATA lines.

1. Read the first number and call it L. (We will assume that L is the largest value until a larger one is found.)
2. Perform steps (a) through (c) $N - 1$ times.
   a. Read a number, call it X.
   b. Compare L and X. If X is bigger than L, assign the value of X to L (so L still contains the largest value encountered thus far).
   c. Return to step a).
3. Print the value of L.

By performing step 2 $N - 1$ times, all the data values are processed (one value was processed in step 1). Each time a number is read, it is compared with the current, largest value. If the number read is bigger, it becomes the largest value; if not, the reading and comparing continues. A flowchart is shown in Figure 10.6 and after it a program and RUN using 20 data values.

```
100 REM FINDING LARGEST VALUE
110 REM 20 NUMBERS USED
120 READ L
130 LET I=1
140    READ X
150    IF X>L THEN LET L=X
160    LET I=I+1
170 IF I<=19 THEN 140
180 PRINT "LARGEST VALUE IS";L
190 DATA 4,7,0,3,8,9,7,12,4,10
200 DATA 1,2,2,5,6,11,9,6,0,3
210 END

RUN

LARGEST VALUE IS  12

READY
```

Minor modification can be made to the program so that the smallest value can be found. It is also possible to make modifications so that alphabetically the first or last word from a list can be determined. These ideas will be treated in the exercises.

10.9 RESTORE

We have seen that as values from a data stack are assigned to variables by a READ statement, the pointer moves down the stack. Thus any values in the stack that are above the pointer cannot be used again. However, there may occur a situation where the data are needed again. The RESTORE statement can be used to do this.

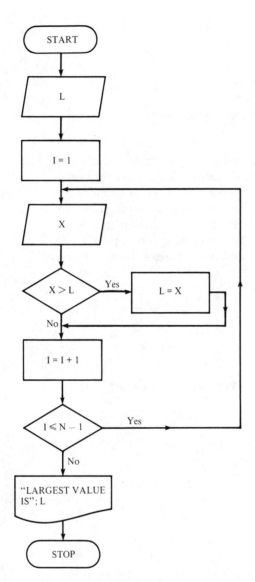

FIGURE 10.6.

The *general form of the RESTORE statement* is

line number   RESTORE

When a RESTORE statement is executed, the pointer immediately moves back to the top of the data stack (and points again at the first piece of data in the stack). Let's look at a program that uses RESTORE.

EXAMPLE 10.12. Discuss the status of the data stack and show the output from

```
11 READ A,B
21 PRINT A+B
```

```
31 RESTORE
41 READ X
51 PRINT X↑2
61 RESTORE
71 READ P,Q,R
81 PRINT P*Q*R
91 DATA 3,2,-1
101 END
```

After line 11 is executed, A=3, B=2, and the data stack is as shown in
Figure 10.7. Line 21 causes output. Line 31 causes the pointer to return ·
to the top of the stack, as shown in Figure 10.8. Line 41 causes a value
to be read and assigned to X. Since the pointer is at the top of the
stack, 3 is assigned to X and the pointer drops, as shown in Figure
10.9. Execution of line 61 causes the data stack to again appear as in
Figure 10.8. Line 71 reads three values and hence causes the data stack
configuration of Figure 10.10.

3	3 ←	3	3
2	2	2 ←	2
-1 ←	-1	-1	-1
			←

FIGURE 10.7.   FIGURE 10.8.   FIGURE 10.9.   FIGURE 10.10.

Thus when we execute the program we get

```
RUN

5
9
-6

READY
```

EXAMPLE 10.13.   Twenty customers of a bank have special savings accounts. The bank wants to know the average amount in the accounts
and how many of the accounts are above the average.

Twenty pieces of data (an amount for each of the accounts) must
be included in the program. The data must be read, summed, and averaged. At this point, all the data have been processed, so to be able to
count how many pieces of data are greater than the average, the data
must be RESTOREd. When this has been done, the data can again be
read, checked against the average, and the counter increased when appropriate. Of course, the program will create output—the average savings amount and the value of the counter. The program and a RUN
follow.

```
100 REM SPECIAL ACCOUNTS PROGRAM
110 LET S=0
120 LET I=1
```

```
130    READ Z
140    LET S=S+Z
150    LET I=I+1
160 IF I<=20 THEN 130
170 LET A=S/20
180 PRINT "ACCOUNT AVERAGE IS";A
190 REM RESTORE FOR COUNTING
200 RESTORE
210 LET N=0
220 LET I=1
230    READ Z
240     IF Z>A THEN LET N=N+1
250    LET I=I+1
260 IF I<=20 THEN 230
270 PRINT "NUMBER OF ACCOUNTS ABOVE AVERAGE IS";N
280 DATA 1556,3721.40,5000,212.55
290 DATA 4665,980.43,8883.25,1000
300 DATA 7399.20,427.33,4566,2500
310 DATA 1250,1890,1300,57.25
320 DATA 999.99,1001,304.72,1123
400 END

RUN

ACCOUNT AVERAGE IS 2441.86
NUMBER OF ACCOUNTS ABOVE AVERAGE IS 7

READY
```

The program that follows illustrates RESTORE and uses a string eod tag.

EXAMPLE 10.14. This program was written for the registrar of a small college (currently it has only three students!). For each student in the college, there is a DATA line that includes the student's name and the current overall average. Following the students' data there is an eod tag—the word DONE followed by the number zero. The registrar should be able to enter a student's name, and if the student's name is contained in the program's data, the student's average should be printed. If the student's name entered from the terminal does not match any of the data in the program, an appropriate message should be printed. In either case, the registrar should be asked if another name will be entered and, depending on the response, appropriate action taken.

```
100 REM NAME SEARCH
110    PRINT "PLEASE ENTER NAME"
120    INPUT N$
130    PRINT
140    REM READ STUDENT NAME AND AVERAGE
150    READ A$,G
160    REM IF NAME READ IS EOD TAG THEN NAME
170    REM ENTERED IS NOT IN DATA LINES
```

```
180    IF A$="DONE" THEN 230
190    REM IF NO MATCH THEN READ MORE DATA
200    IF A$<>N$ THEN 150
210    PRINT "CUMULATIVE AVERAGE FOR ";N$;" IS";G
220    GOTO 240
230    PRINT N$;" NOT FOUND."
240    PRINT
250    PRINT "DO YOU WANT TO CHECK ANOTHER NAME?"
260    PRINT "ANSWER YES OR NO."
270    INPUT X$
280    PRINT
290    RESTORE
300 IF X$="YES" THEN 110
310 PRINT "END OF RUN"
320 DATA ISAAC NEWTON,73.4
330 DATA ALFRED E. NEWMAN,95
340 DATA SNOOPY,99.9
350 DATA DONE,0
500 END
```

The RESTORE statement occurs in line 290 before the registrar's response is checked even though strictly the data need not be restored unless the response is "yes." The coding of the RESTORE statement after the registrar's response would lead to an unnecessary GOTO and distract from the flow of the program.

```
RUN

PLEASE ENTER NAME.
? SNOOPY

CUMULATIVE AVERAGE FOR SNOOPY IS 99.9

DO YOU WISH TO CHECK ANOTHER NAME?
ANSWER YES OR NO.
? YES

PLEASE ENTER NAME.
? SANTA

SANTA NOT FOUND.

DO YOU WISH TO CHECK ANOTHER NAME?
ANSWER YES OR NO.
? YES

PLEASE ENTER NAME.

? ALFRED NEWMAN

ALFRED NEWMAN NOT FOUND.
```

DO YOU WISH TO CHECK ANOTHER NAME?
ANSWER YES OR NO.
? YES

PLEASE ENTER NAME.
? ALFRED E NEWMAN

ALFRED E NEWMAN NOT FOUND.

DO YOU WISH TO CHECK ANOTHER NAME?
ANSWER YES OR NO.
? YES

PLEASE ENTER NAME.
? ALFRED E. NEWMAN

CUMULATIVE AVERAGE FOR ALFRED E. NEWMAN IS 95

DO YOU WISH TO CHECK ANOTHER NAME?
ANSWER YES OR NO.
? NO

END OF RUN

READY

From the RUN of the program, you can see that, just as with numbers, to have strings considered equal, they must be identical (ALFRED E NEWMAN is not identical to ALFRED E. NEWMAN).

EXERCISES

1 What, if anything, is wrong with the following statements?
  a. 1Ø1 READ A
  b. 152 READ A,$B
  c. 2Ø2 READ,A,B
  d. 254 READ X Y
  e. 3Ø3 READ X;Y
  f. 356 DATA Ø;−2;−1
  g. 4Ø4 DATA ONE,1,WORD,2,"ONLY"
  h. 458 DATA 3,6,5
  i. 5Ø5 DATA 6.4,22/7,19
  j. 555 RESTORE 1Ø
  k. 6Ø6 RESTORE A,B
  l. 666 RESTORE

2 Determine the output from the following programs.
a.   b.

```
1Ø LET I=1
2Ø    READ X
3Ø    PRINT X,X↑2
4Ø    LET I=I+1
5Ø IF I<=5 THEN 2Ø
6Ø DATA 2,-3,Ø,4,1
7Ø END
```

```
1Ø READ J
2Ø LET I=2
3Ø    READ A,B
4Ø    PRINT A+B
5Ø    LET I=I+1
6Ø IF I<=J THEN 3Ø
7Ø DATA 4,6,8,-3
8Ø DATA 5,4,1,7,-2
9Ø END
```

c.

```
100 READ X$,Y$
110 READ X,Z$
120 LET Y=3*X
130 PRINT Y$,Z$
140 PRINT Y
150 PRINT X$,Z$
160 PRINT Y
170 PRINT Y$
180 DATA HAPPY,AMERICA,592,BIRTHDAY
190 END
```

f.

```
100 LET X=1
110     READ N$,H1
120     IF H1<=0 THEN 110
130     READ M$,H2
140     IF H1>H2 THEN 170
150     PRINT M$,N$
160     GOTO 180
170     PRINT N$,M$
180     LET X=X+1
190 IF X<=4 THEN 110
200 DATA HEIDI,1528,JOAN,1554
210 DATA TERRY,-1491,JACK,1202
220 DATA PHIL,1604,KEVIN,-1020
230 DATA SANDY,-1801,PAUL,1499
240 DATA SUE,-1585,RICK,1448
250 END
```

d.

```
10 READ M,N
20 PRINT M;N
30 LET P=M
40     READ L
50     PRINT L*(M+N)-P
60     LET P=P+1
70 IF P<=N THEN 40
80 DATA -1,2,4,1
90 END
```

g.

```
200 READ X
210 IF X=-99 THEN 290
220     READ Y
230     IF X=Y THEN PRINT "SQUARE";
240     PRINT X*Y
250     READ X
260 GOTO 210
270 DATA 3,-2,5,4,11,4,1,-99
280 DATA 4,3,3,8,6,6,-99
290 END
```

e.

```
10 READ C
20 READ X,Y,I,J
30 PRINT TAB(I);X;TAB(J);Y
40 LET C=C+1
50 IF C=3 THEN 80
60 IF C>=4 THEN 130
70 GOTO 20
80 RESTORE
90 GOTO 20
100 DATA 1,2,3,7,12
110 DATA -6,8,3,7,8
120 DATA 14,1,5
130 END
```

h.

```
500 READ X$
510 LET I=1
520     READ Y$,Z$
530     IF Y$=Z$ THEN PRINT X$
540     IF Y$<Z$ THEN 570
550     PRINT Y$
560     GOTO 580
570     PRINT Z$
580     LET I=I+1
590 IF I<=5 THEN 520
600 DATA SAME,CRAB,APPLE
610 DATA SMITH,SMYTH,BAT
620 DATA MAN,WOMAN,CHILD
630 DATA FLEECE,BARBER,SHOE
640 END
```

3 Modify the program of Example 10.11 so that the total number of all inventory items is printed along with the total value of the entire inventory.

4 Write an algorithm or draw a flowchart for the following problem. Twenty pairs of numbers are to be read from DATA lines. As they are read, they are to be printed out together with their product. The sum of the 20 products is to be calculated and printed.

5 Write a program from what you did in Exercise 4. For your data try the numbers 7, 6, 2, −1, 3, 8, 11, 5, 20, 1, 8, −2, 0, 4, 13, 12, −7, 8, −2, and 5.

6 Write a program to
a. Read in 30 values, one at a time.
b. Count how many are positive.
c. Add the positive values.
d. Average the positive values.
The output should show the result of the count, the sum, and the average.

7 Twenty-five pairs of values are to be read in. Counts should be made as to how many times the two values are equal, how many times the first value is greater than the second, and how many times the second is greater than the first.

8 Write a program that calculates the sum of the positive values and the sum of the negative values that are all found in DATA lines. The total number of values, both positive and negative, is not known. Run your program using the values 7, −2, 3, 8, 9, 1, −1, −6, 3, 8, and 5.

9 The Springfield Shots, a hockey team, is planning an appreciation banquet for its most faithful fans. A fan who has purchased a season's ticket for ten years or more will be invited. The team has the information on all season's ticket holders stored in DATA lines. The information is recorded in the form

name, number

where "name" is a ticket holder's name and "number" is the number of years the person has bought a season's ticket. Write a program that prints out all the names of people who will be invited to the banquet and prints out the number of people invited.
Run your program using the following data.

Name	Number	Name	Number
James Orlean	9	Al Sideoff	5
Sam Breck	11	Rose Fahn	16
Joan Martin	14	Mike Arbour	7
Fred Fister	11	Fran Smith	10
Liz London	3	Don Smith	10
Rene Lavoie	18	Eric Guest	1

10 The Hawk Transport Company has been told that the weight of each of its items to be shipped must be given in kilograms. At present, the company has the weights only in pounds. The relation between the two units of weights is 1 pound = .454 kilograms. Listed here are 12 pairs of numbers—the first is an item number, the second is the weight of the item in pounds. Write a program for the Hawk Shipping Company that begins by printing out the company's name near the middle of the page. Then a three-column table should be printed; in the first column is the item number, in the second the weight of the item in pounds, and in the third the weight of the item in kilograms. The columns should have headings.

a. 52, 125
b. 3, 850
c. 98, 104
d. 35, 117.5
e. 11, 400
f. 15, 325
g. 12, 562.25
h. 27, 1024
i. 5, 3.75
j. 10, 100
k. 73, 688.5
l. 1, 2000

11 A small exclusive shop has given ten of its customers credit. The customers are identified by the numbers 1 through 10, and the credit amounts are listed in DATA lines in that respective sequence; that is, the *first* piece of data is the credit amount for customer 1. (Thus customer numbers are not needed in the DATA statements.) Write a program that requests the customer number and the amount that the customer wishes to charge. If the amount to be charged exceeds the credit amount, the credit amount should be printed out with a message that the customer does not have enough credit. Otherwise, a message should be printed indicating that there is sufficient credit and the new credit balance that is available after the charge has been applied to the old credit balance. Run the program three times. First, enter a charge that exceeds the credit; second, a charge less than the credit; and third, a charge that equals the credit. For your program you can use the lines

```
DATA 475.50,500,172.98,155,189.98
DATA 52.17,115.25,81.33,45,209.09
```

and enter a charge of $172.99 for customer 3, a charge of $25.04 for customer 6, and a charge of $189.98 for customer 5.

12 Change the program in Exercise 11 so that after the output is generated, the opportunity of processing another customer is possible. (You must assume that it is a *different* customer since, if not, a customer may have already altered his or her credit balance.)

13 The More Pictureframe Company pays its workers $40 per week plus a piecework rate, which is $8 for each frame made. Read the data given and use it to print pay reports for each person. Each DATA line is to contain the name of a worker and the number of picture frames that that worker has completed during the week. The output should show the worker's name, the number of frames made, and the weekly salary.

Name	Number	Name	Number
Sam Hampton	18	Jennifer Elder	17
Paul Whitman	15	John Manilla	16
Beverly Franc	16	Bridgett Middel	20
Armand Gambo	11	Kathy Rafferty	23
Marlene Schmidt	9	Eileen Laast	10
Lauria Temple	14	Thomas Edwards	7

14 A formula that is sometimes used to calculate the depreciation of an item is

$$d = \frac{2}{n} \cdot w$$

where d is the depreciation, n is the number of years of life of the item, and w is the worth of the item at the beginning of each year. For example, suppose that a home video recorder is bought new for $1,000 and that it has an expected life of five years. Then a table that might be printed for this item is

YEAR	DEPRECIATION	CURRENT VALUE
1	400	600
2	240	360
3	144	216
4	86.40	129.60
5	51.84	77.76

Write a program to read six sets of values from DATA lines. Each set contains three values. The first value is the description of a piece of equipment, the second is the number of years of life of the item, and the third is the initial cost of the item. A table similar to the one just given should be printed for each item. However, in addition, the description should be printed above the table, over the column labeled DEPRECIATION. For data use

Video recorder, 5, $1000
Electric typewriter, 7, $850
Stereo, 10, $300
Washing machine, 15, $425
Commercial oven, 4, $1500
Word processor, 12, $4800

15 Write a program that reads 20 words and prints any word that begins with a letter from D through S. Use the DATA lines

```
DATA BOOK,PROGRAM,"QUILT",MATH
DATA SUITCASE,PENCIL,NEST,"COMPUTER"
DATA "RADIUS",AREA,FLOWCHART,IGLOO
DATA" SWORD",NAP,MNEMONIC,OFFICE
DATA ALGORITHM,DATA,"END",NAME
```

16 For data use the 20 words found in the previous exercise to write two programs. The first should print the words that begin with the letter N. The second program should print the word that would appear first in an alphabetical listing and also print the word that would appear last in the listing.

＊ ＊ ＊

17 Modify the program of Exercise 13 so that the name of the least productive worker (the one who made the smallest number of frames) is printed out.

18 The More Pictureframe Company has decided to use an incentive payment plan for its piecework employees. The pay for an employee is still $40 per week plus an amount for each frame made. However, if a worker makes more than 11 frames, the rate paid *for each frame* is $10.50. (Otherwise the rate is still $8.) Run the program using the same data.

19 In addition to commercial and residential buildings, the Bog Realty Co. lists plots of vacant land. Each plot is rectangular in shape. The plots are listed in Bog's *Vacant Land Catalogue.* Associated with each plot of land is a catalogue number, the length and width of the plot, and the asking price for the land. The company has recently purchased a small computer and is presently trying to computerize as much of its activities as possible. You are to write a program relating to the vacant land aspect of the business. The program is to be used by Bog's realtors. The program should ask for the minimum square footage acceptable to the potential customer and the amount the customer is willing to pay. The program should then check the data that are included in the program (and that appear shortly) and print out any plots that fit the description entered from the terminal. What should be printed out, under headings, are the catalogue number, length of the plot, width, square footage, and the asking price. Experience has shown that money amounts in real estate dealings are frequently flexible. Thus if the asking price of the plot of land is no more than 10% more than the customer is willing to pay, that land should also be listed. The data for the program are in the form

catalogue number, length, width, asking price

For your data use

Number	Length	Width	Price
99	40	210	$ 3500
106	550	200	12,000
172	215	100	7250
283	300	90	5000
323	80	50	700
351	100	100	9800
417	625	370	14,600
499	210	450	11,500

RUN the program, using the input values

Square Footage	Price
8000	$ 3600
20,000	7000
95,000	13,500

20 An insurance company offers four different homeowner's policies. The difference among the four is the amount of deductible for the policy. One kind of policy uses a $25 deductible, a second has a $50 deductible, the third $100, and the fourth $200. Each policy is identified by number. A program is to be written that processes approved insurance claims. The policy number and the amount of the claim should be supplied from the terminal. The program should then read through the data (which are described later) and print out the result of the search. If the policy number is not found in the data, a message to that effect should be printed out. However, if the policy number is found, the amount of payment to be made by the insurance company (which is the claim minus the deductible) should be printed. Some data that you could use in your program are

```
DATA 354,1,628,1,533,4,609,3
DATA 588,2,634,4,123,3,901,2
DATA 981,2,419,4,512,3
```

The data should be considered in pairs: the first number is the policy number, the second indicates which of the four deductible categories refers to that policy. A 1 means $25 deductible, a 2 means $50, a 3 means $100, and a 4 means $200. Run the program entering from the terminal
   a. 588, 377
   b. 123, 105
   c. 492, 125
   d. 628, 35
(You might find the ON-GOTO useful for this problem.)

21 Modify the program of Exercise 20 so that if the claim is less than the deductible, an appropriate message will be printed. Run the program and enter 901 and 45.

In addition to the five basic arithmetic operations presented in Chapter 3, BASIC gives us the ability to obtain automatically other frequently needed results such as square roots. More generally, these results are obtained by using *functions*. To use a function means to instruct the computer to execute automatically a set of instructions (already part of the language) and obtain the result. Since the instructions that lead to the result are part of BASIC (and not something that you need to code), the functions are sometimes referred to as "built-in functions."

11.1 The SQR Function

As mentioned in the previous paragraph, calculating a square root is a fairly common operation. This is done in BASIC by using the function whose "name" is SQR. For example, if $X = 25$ and we want to calculate $\sqrt{X}$, this could be accomplished by the programming lines

```
7Ø LET  X=25
8Ø LET  Y=SQR(X)
```

Line 80 assigns a value to Y. The value is the result of the calculation done on the right of the equal sign. In line 80, that calculation is to find the square root of X. This is done by placing X within parentheses following SQR. The value that is found within the parentheses is called the *argument* of the function. An argument of a function can be an expression. Sometimes, however, the arguments of functions must satisfy certain conditions. The SQR function is one of these. To use SQR, its argument must not be negative or else the computer will print an error message.

For example, if a program contained the line

```
5Ø LET  B=SQR(-7)
```

when the computer tried to execute that line, the attempt to calculate the square root of a negative number would produce an error message such as

NEGATIVE ARGUMENT IN SQR AT LINE 50

and then stop execution of the program.

EXAMPLE 11.1. Two numbers are to be typed in. They represent the length and width of a rectangle. The length of a diagonal is to be calculated and printed.

Let L and W be the variables used for length and width and D the length of the diagonal. Then D is calculated using the formula

$$D = \sqrt{L^2 + W^2}$$

The program is

```
10 PRINT "ENTER LENGTH AND WIDTH"
20 INPUT L,W
30 LET D=SQR(L↑2+W↑2)
40 PRINT "LENGTH OF DIAGONAL IS";D
50 END
```

EXAMPLE 11.2. The numbers from 9 to 25 are to be printed out together with their squares and square roots. The output should be in table form so that each line of output shows a number, its square, and its square root. The three columns should each have a heading.

The program involves a loop using a variable (N) that starts at 9 and ends at 25. Each time a new value of N is calculated, N, N^2, and $\sqrt{N}$ should be printed. All that remains is to print out column headings before the loop is entered.

```
100 PRINT "NUMBER","SQUARE","SQUARE ROOT"
110 PRINT
120 LET N=9
130    PRINT N,N↑2,SQR(N)
140    LET N=N+1
150 IF N<=25 THEN 130
160 END
```

Note that the program contains a counting loop of sorts—where the "counting" starts at 9.

EXAMPLE 11.3. If (x_1, y_1) and (x_2, y_2) are the coordinates of two points in the plane, the distance between them is given by the formula $\sqrt{(x_2 - x_1)^2 + (y_2 - y_1)^2}$. The user should enter the coordinates of both points and then the distance should be calculated and printed.

```
1 PRINT "ENTER COORDINATES OF FIRST POINT"
11 INPUT X1,Y1
```

```
21 PRINT "ENTER COORDINATES OF SECOND POINT"
31 INPUT X2,Y2
41 PRINT
51 LET D=SQR((X2-X1)↑2+(Y2-Y1)↑2)
61 PRINT "THE DISTANCE BETWEEN THE POINTS IS";D
71 END
```

11.2 The ABS Function

ABS stands for "absolute value." When the absolute value of a positive number is evaluated, the result is the original number. The absolute value of zero equals zero. When the absolute value of a negative number is evaluated, the result is the negative of the original number. Since the original number was negative, the final result is positive. In other words, when dealing with a negative number, we may think of the absolute value as dropping the negative sign and returning a positive value.

EXAMPLE 11.4. ABS(6) = 6 (the positive argument is returned as the answer).

EXAMPLE 11.5. ABS(0)=0.

EXAMPLE 11.6. ABS(−3)=3 (the negative sign in front of the argument is dropped).

EXAMPLE 11.7. If $X = -2$ and $Y = 5$, then

```
ABS(3*X+Y) = ABS(3*(-2)+5)
           = ABS(-6+5)
           = ABS(-1)
           = 1
```

The standard mathematics notation for the absolute value of x is $|x|$. So the absolute value of 4 is mathematically written as $|4|$; in BASIC, it is ABS(4).

We can use ABS to tell if a number is within a certain range from a second fixed number. For instance, we know that 6 (the first number) is not more than three units away (the range) from the number 8 (the fixed number). This is readily seen on a number line.

Note that the absolute value of the difference of 6 and 8 is 2; that is, $|6 - 8| = 2$, which is less than 3.

The number 9 is within three units of 8.

and $|9 - 8| = 1$, which is less than 3.

However the graph

4 units

8 9 10 11 12

shows us that 12 is more

than three units away from 8 and $|12 - 8| = 4$, which is greater than 3.

So a number that is within three units away from 8 will be some number x such that $|x - 8| < 3$.

EXAMPLE 11.8. Five numbers are to be typed, one at a time, at the terminal. After each is typed, it is to be checked to see whether it is within 2.5 units of 4.7. If the value is within 2.5 units of 4.7, the message "within range" should be printed; otherwise, "out of range" should be printed.

```
110 LET  C=1
120    PRINT  "TYPE  IN  YOUR  NUMBER"
130    INPUT  X
140    REM  SEE  IF  X  IS  IN  RANGE
150    IF  ABS(X-4.7)<2.5  THEN  180
160    PRINT  "OUT  OF  RANGE"
170    GOTO  190
180    PRINT  "WITHIN  RANGE"
190    REM  INCREASE  COUNTER
200    LET  C=C+1
210    REM  SEE  IF  5TH  VALUE
220 IF  C<=5  THEN  120
230 END

RUN

TYPE  IN  YOUR  NUMBER
?  3.2
WITHIN  RANGE
TYPE  IN  YOUR  NUMBER
?  2.77
WITHIN  RANGE
TYPE  IN  YOUR  NUMBER
?  8
OUT  OF  RANGE
TYPE  IN  YOUR  NUMBER
?  4.7
WITHIN  RANGE
TYPE  IN  YOUR  NUMBER
?  .302
OUT  OF  RANGE

READY
```

EXAMPLE 11.9. The DATA lines for a program will contain a collection of positive and negative values representing deposits and withdrawals for a checking account. The program will print two columns—one for deposits and the other for withdrawals. Finally the total number of transactions will be printed.

Since the data are either positive or negative, 0 will be used as an eod tag.

```
100 PRINT "DEPOSIT","WITHDRAWAL"
110 PRINT
120 LET T=0
130 READ B
140 IF B=0 THEN 220
150    IF B>0 THEN 180
160    PRINT,ABS(B)
170    GOTO 190
180    PRINT B
190    LET T=T+1
200    READ B
210 GOTO 140
220 PRINT
230 PRINT "NUMBER OF TRANSACTIONS IS";T
240 DATA 17.55,-21.99,-1.25
250 DATA 19.42,-6.68,14.29
299 DATA 0
300 END
```

RUN

```
DEPOSIT           WITHDRAWAL

 17.55
                  21.99
                   1.25
 19.42
                   6.68
 14.29
```

NUMBER OF TRANSACTIONS IS 6

READY

The comma following PRINT in line 160 is used to print the value of ABS(B) in the second print zone. Some systems will not allow the comma to be used this way, and on such systems, the same result could be accomplished by enclosing a blank between quotation marks as the first output item, that is, 160 PRINT " ",ABS(B).

11.3 The INT Function

In BASIC, INT stands for a function that, in mathematics, is called the *greatest integer function*. When INT(X) is evaluated, the value that is returned is the *largest integer that is less than or equal to X (the argument)*.

EXAMPLE 11.10. INT(3.6) = 3, since 3 is the largest integer less than or equal to 3.6 (note that the "less than" part applies here).

EXAMPLE 11.11. INT(5) = 5, since 5 is the largest integer that is less than or equal to 5 (the "equal to" applies here).

EXAMPLE 11.12. INT(.73) = 0.

EXAMPLE 11.13. INT(−2.2) = −3. Notice that the answer here is *not* −2 since INT gives a number that must be *less than* or equal to the argument and −2 is *not* less than −2.2.

Where can the INT function be of use? It happens that it can be used in quite a number of instances. For one thing it can be used to determine whether or not a particular number is an integer. Look at the following table. In the first column, a list of integers is given, and in the second the INT of these values is shown. Numbers that are not integers are given in the third column and the fourth column shows the corresponding INT values.

N	INT(N)	N	INT(N)
3	3	5.3	5
16	16	−8.01	−9
−4	−4	2.073	2
7	7	6.998	6

What should be clear after only a short glance is that whenever N is an integer, N equals INT(N), and if N is not an integer, N and INT(N) are not equal! Furthermore, the converse is true: that is, if N equals INT(N), then N is an integer; if N does not equal INT(N), then N is not an integer. Let's now see this used in a simple program.

EXAMPLE 11.14. A program is to be written that asks the user to supply a number and then tells the user what kind of a number was typed in (integer or "mixed").

```
10 PRINT "TYPE IN A NUMBER"
20 INPUT X
30 REM CHECK IF X IS INTEGER
40 IF X=INT(X) THEN 70
50 PRINT "YOUR NUMBER IS MIXED."
60 STOP
70 PRINT "YOUR NUMBER IS AN INTEGER"
80 END
```

By considering a second table we can discover another use of INT.

B	B/2	INT(B/2)
2	1	1
3	1.5	1
4	2	2
5	2.5	2
6	3	3
7	3.5	3
−4	−2	−2
−5	−2.5	−3

What you should notice in the table is that for every number B that is divisible by 2 (an even number), B/2 and INT(B/2) are equal. On the other hand, if B is odd, B/2 $\neq$ INT(B/2). So to see if a number B is divisible by 2

1. Form the quotient B/2.
2. Take the INT of the quotient in step 1—that is INT(B/2).
3. If the two values are equal (B/2=INT(B/2)) the number B is evenly divisible by 2; otherwise, 2 does not divide B evenly.

This result is immediately extendable for division by *any* number (except 0, of course). As an example, consider the following.

EXAMPLE 11.15.   The user is to type in positive integers, one at a time. The program should count the number of integers typed in that are divisible by 5. When a nonpositive integer is typed in, the program should print out the results of the counting and stop.

```
510 LET C=0
520 PRINT "TYPE IN A POSITIVE INTEGER"
530 INPUT I
540 REM CHECK FOR POSITIVE OR NOT
550 REM IF NOT, TRANSFER TO OUTPUT
560 IF I<=0 THEN 660
570    REM CHECK TO SEE IF 5 DIVIDES I
580    REM IF 5 DOES NOT DIVIDE I, RETURN TO INPUT
590    IF I/5<>INT(I/5) THEN 630
600    REM SINCE 5 DIVIDES I, INCREASE COUNTER
610    REM AND REQUEST ANOTHER VALUE
620    LET C=C+1
630    PRINT "TYPE IN A POSITIVE INTEGER"
640    INPUT I
650 GOTO 560
660 PRINT C;"VALUES WERE DIVISIBLE BY 5"
670 END

RUN

TYPE IN A POSITIVE INTEGER
? 6
TYPE IN A POSITIVE INTEGER
? 10
TYPE IN A POSITIVE INTEGER
? 25
TYPE IN A POSITIVE INTEGER
? 14
TYPE IN A POSITIVE INTEGER
? 3
TYPE IN A POSITIVE INTEGER
? 0
 2 VALUES WERE DIVISIBLE BY 5

READY
```

EXAMPLE 11.16.   Several thousand (the exact number is unknown) numeric test results have been collected and typed into data lines. The sum of the results is to be found. It is speculated that as the sum accumulates, a pattern to the intermediate sums can be observed. To verify the speculation, the intermediate sums for each 100 terms is to be printed (that is, the sum of the first 100 terms, the first 200 terms, the first 300 terms, etc.).

A count must be kept of the number of terms processed to print out the intermediate sums. When the count reaches a number that is evenly divisible by 100, an intermediate sum will be printed.

```
100 REM PRINTING SUMS OF EVERY 100 TERMS
110 REM EOD TAG IS -999
120 PRINT "INTERMEDIATE SUMS"
130 LET S=0
140 LET C=0
150 READ X
160 IF X=-999 THEN 230
170   LET S=S+X
180   LET C=C+1
190   REM CHECK FOR DIVISIBILITY BY 100
200   IF C/100=INT(C/100) THEN PRINT S
210   READ X
220 GOTO 160
230 PRINT "FINAL SUM=";S
240 DATA . .
 .
  . 
 .
998 DATA -999
999 END
```

Many of the programs of previous chapters have dealt with monetary problems, but their outputs frequently displayed amounts with three or four digits to the right of the decimal point. This "awkwardness" of output can be considerably bettered by the use of the INT function.

Suppose that A and B are variables that stand for amounts of money and that the values of A and B have been calculated to be 16.2143 and 21.437, respectively. Clearly, these numbers do not appear to be "dollars and cents" amounts. To be so represented, A should be 16.21 and B should be 21.44, namely, the original values of A and B should be rounded to the hundredths (cents) place. The step-by-step procedure to do this is as follows:

1. Original values   A=16.2143
                              B=21.437

2. Multiply by 100   100*A=1621.43
                              100*B=2143.7

3. Add .5   100*A+.5=1621.93
                              100*B+.5=2144.2

4. Apply INT function   INT(100*A+.5)=1621
                             INT(100*B+.5)=2144

5. Divide by 100   INT(100*A+.5)/100=16.21
                             INT(100*A+.5)/100=21.44

Thus to round a decimal number X to the nearest hundredths (or, in other words, to round a dollar amount X to the nearest cent), we would use the expression

    INT(100*X+.5)/100

It should be noted that by rounding numbers we arrive at a result that is an approximation to our original value. The value of A was 16.2143, and when rounded it became 16.21, which is not *exactly* the same as the original value. This is one of the reasons why, when paying for an item on installments, the final payment is sometimes slightly different from the others.

EXAMPLE 11.17.   In this case, $1000 is to be paid back in 24 payments. We will calculate a single monthly payment by dividing $1000 by 24 and rounding this result to the nearest cent. We then multiply the rounded value by 23 and subtract this result from $1000, giving the final payment.

```
10 LET B=1000
20 LET M=24
30 LET P=B/24
40 LET P=INT(100*P+.5)/100
50 PRINT "FIRST 23 PAYMENTS AT $";P
60 LET F=B-23*P
70 PRINT "24TH PAYMENT IS $";F
80 END

RUN

FIRST 23 PAYMENTS AT $ 41.67
24TH PAYMENT IS $ 41.59

READY
```

EXAMPLE 11.18.   Workalot Junior College gives five different grades for its courses. They are A, B, C, D, and F. F is a failing grade; A is the highest passing grade, and D is the lowest. Professor Cleary, of the Mathematics Department, calculates a numerical average for each of his students. This average is the average of three examination grades. He converts the numerical average into a letter grade by using the following conversion table.

If M is a student's numerical average, then

if $M \geq 90$, the letter grade is A
if $80 \leq M < 90$, the letter grade is B

if $70 \leq M < 80$, the letter grade is C

if $60 \leq M < 70$, the letter grade is D

if $M < 60$, the letter grade is F

The program should read the student's name and three examination grades and then calculate and print both the numeric average and the letter grade. This activity should continue until the eod tag (EOD, Ø, Ø, Ø) is reached.

First, the program will read and print the name and three grades. Then the average will be calculated and printed. Next a decision must be made: which of the five letters will be printed? A transfer to one of five PRINT statements will be made depending on the value of the average. A sequence of IF-THEN statements, like the one following, would certainly be sufficient. (M stands for the average.)

```
IF  M≥9Ø  THEN        ◄───────────   transfer to print the letter A
IF  M≥8Ø  THEN        ◄───────────   transfer to print B
IF  M≥7Ø  THEN        ◄───────────   print C
IF  M≥6Ø  THEN        ◄───────────   print D
PRINT  "FINAL  GRADE  IS          F"
```

However, instead of the sequence of IF-THENs, we wish to use an ON-GOTO to accomplish the multiple branching. The obvious difficulty we face is that the averages that the computer calculates very likely will not be integers, and even if they were, there are far too many possible values to make the ON-GOTO economical to use. However, the average can be modified so that its use with ON-GOTO is feasible. Let's suppose that we have calculated an average of 83.24. If we divide this number by 10, we get 8.324. Now if we apply the INT function to this last value, the result is 8—an integer! Consider the following table. In the first column are some numbers that possibly could be averages. The second column shows the result of the INT function applied to the number in the first column divided by 10.

M	INT(M/1Ø)
96.8	9
83.24	8
77.9	7
70	7
61.02	6
55	5
43.1	4
38.44	3
26.03	2
15.6	1
9.2	0

Notice that the possible values for INT (M/1Ø) are 0, 1, 2, 3, 4, 5, 6, 7, 8, and 9.

These values *cannot* be used with ON-GOTO since ON-GOTO will not work if one of the possible values is 0. But if we add 1 to each of these values (namely, we use the expression INT(M/1Ø)+1), we get the integers 1 to 10 and so we *can* use the ON-GOTO. A program to perform the task for Professor Cleary is given next.

```
200 REM PROF. CLEARY'S GRADE CONVERSION PROGRAM
210 REM N$ IS STUDENT'S NAME
220 REM A,B,C ARE EXAMINATION GRADES
230 REM M IS NUMERICAL AVERAGE
240 READ N$,A,B,C
250 IF N$="EOD" THEN 999
260    PRINT N$
270    PRINT "EXAMS:";A;B;C
280    LET M=(A+B+C)/3
290    PRINT "SEMESTER AVERAGE:";M
300    REM CONVERT GRADE AND USE ON-GOTO
310    ON INT(M/10)+1 GOTO 320,320,320,320,320,320,340,360,380,400
320    PRINT "SEMESTER GRADE: F"
330    GOTO 410
340    PRINT "SEMESTER GRADE: D"
350    GOTO 410
360    PRINT "SEMESTER GRADE: C"
370    GOTO 410
380    PRINT "SEMESTER GRADE: B"
390    GOTO 410
400    PRINT "SEMESTER GRADE: A"
410    PRINT
420    PRINT
430    READ N$,A,B,C
440 GOTO 250
450 DATA MATILDA ADAMS,92,86,88
455 DATA JUAN CARLOS,58,65,61
460 DATA HERBERT CARY,100,91,90
465 DATA AMELIA DODD,42,51,48
    .    .
    .    .
    .    .
510 DATA TOBIAS TYNE,71,80,75
998 DATA EOD,0,0,0
999 END

RUN

MATILDA ADAMS
EXAMS: 92 86 88
SEMESTER AVERAGE: 88.6667
SEMESTER GRADE: B

JUAN CARLOS
EXAMS: 58 65 61
SEMESTER AVERAGE: 61.3333
SEMESTER GRADE: D

HERBERT CAREY
EXAMS: 100 91 90
SEMESTER AVERAGE: 93.6667
SEMESTER GRADE: A
```

```
AMELIA DODD
EXAMS:  42  51  48
SEMESTER AVERAGE:  47
SEMESTER GRADE:  F

  .
  .

TOBIAS TYNE
EXAMS:  71  80  75
SEMESTER AVERAGE:  75.3333
SEMESTER GRADE:  C

READY
```

You should notice that the possibility of a student's having an average of 100 is not considered (if $M = 100$, INT($M/10$)+1 = 11 and an error will be generated). If you think that this would be possible, a line such as

```
295 IF M=100 THEN 400
```

should be included or an additional "400" at the end of line 310.

EXAMPLE 11.19. A program to determine if a number N, entered from the terminal, is a prime number.

Recall that a number is a prime if it is greater than 1 and its only divisors are itself and 1 (or, equivalently, a number is not a prime if there is some other number besides itself or 1 that divides it).

Once the value of N is typed in, how can we determine if N is a prime? One method is to attempt to divide N by each of the numbers from 2 through $N - 1$. If any one of these numbers divides N, then N is not a prime. However if none of the numbers from 2 through $N - 1$ divides N, we may conclude that N is a prime.

Although the method just outlined certainly works, it can be made more efficient because it is not necessary to check all the numbers from 2 through $N - 1$. It turns out that the trial division need only continue up to the square root of N—that is, we will attempt to divide N by the numbers from 2 through $\sqrt{N}$. A flowchart (see Figure 11.1) and program follow.

```
100 REM PRIME NUMBER CHECK
110 PRINT "ENTER YOUR NUMBER"
120 INPUT N
130 LET D=2
140 IF D<=SQR(N) THEN 170
150 PRINT N;"IS PRIME"
160 STOP
170 IF N/D=INT(N/D) THEN 200
180 LET D=D+1
190 GOTO 140
200 PRINT N;"IS NOT PRIME"
210 END

RUN
```

ENTER YOUR NUMBER
? 91
 91 IS NOT A PRIME NUMBER

READY

RUN

ENTER YOUR NUMBER
? 1Ø1
 1Ø1 IS A PRIME NUMBER

READY

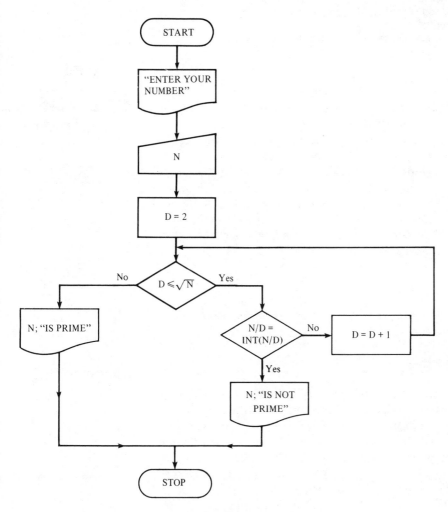

FIGURE 11.1

In addition to SQR, INT, and ABS, BASIC has quite a few other built-in functions. Since we will not use them (except in some optional problems at the end of this chapter for those readers who are familiar with them), we will list only the most common ones. Your particular version of BASIC may very likely have others available so it would be to your advantage to inquire about them.

11.4 Additional Mathematics Functions

Function	Description
SGN(X)	Returns a 1, 0, or −1: if X is positive, SGN(X)=1; if X is zero, SGN(X)=0; if X is negative, SGN(X)=−1
SIN(X)	sine of X, X measured in radians
COS(X)	cosine of X, X measured in radians
TAN(X)	tangent of X, X measured in radians
ATN(X)	arctangent of X, $-\pi/2 \leq ATN(X) \leq \pi/2$
LOG(X)	natural log of X (i.e., ln X), X > 0
EXP(X)	exponential, e^x
RND(X)	random number generator (discussed in Chapter 16)

11.5 User Defined Functions

We continue the discussion of functions with a special category of functions—those defined by the programmer. These are *not* built into the computer but, rather, are built into a particular program. In spite of the numerous built-in functions, very likely the programmer would like to be able to use other functions. They might fall into the realm of algebra or calculus or they might be "application" functions. For example, it might be convenient if there were a function that changed degrees Fahrenheit to degrees Celsius. There is no such built-in function, but the programmer can easily design his or her own for a particular program. The formula that makes this conversion is

$$C = 5/9(F - 32)$$

At the very beginning of a program that will use this, you would write the equation as a function as

```
5  DEF  FNC(F)=5/9*(F-32)
```

The first three letters, DEF, indicate that a function is to be defined. Following this is found the "name" of the function (the "name" of the square root function is SQR). The name of a user-defined function (for that is what they are called—even though "programmer-defined function" might be better) must be three letters long and the first two of these three letters must be FN. The third letter in the name is chosen by the user. Usually the letter used is the single letter that appears by itself on one side of the equation that is being used (this is why we chose C). Following the name, in parentheses, is the variable that is the argument of the function. The letter to use as the argument is the other letter of the formula. Hence our argument is F. Following this is an "=" sign and then finally the algebraic expression from the formula.

The function must be defined before it can be used, and this is the reason that the definition must be found at the beginning of the program.

EXAMPLE 11.20.   The following is a program that takes the values 10°, 20°, 30°, 40°, 50°, 60°, and 70° (Fahrenheit) and prints their equivalents in Celsius.

```
110 REM DEFINE FUNCTION
120 REM CHANGE FAHRENHEIT TO CELSIUS
130 DEF FNC(F)=5/9*(F-32)
140 PRINT "FAHRENHEIT", "CELSIUS"
150 REM FAHRENHEIT LOOP
160 LET F=10
170    PRINT F,FNC(F)
180    LET F=F+10
190 IF F<=70 THEN 170
200 END
```

RUN

FAHRENHEIT	CELSIUS
10	−12.2222
20	−6.66667
30	−1.11111
40	4.44444
50	10.
60	15.5556
70	21.1111

READY

Most algebra texts contain a section that has the student construct a table of values like the one shown at the right. Usually an equation is given that involves the variables x and y. The student takes a value of x, substitutes it into the equation, and gets a value of y. The x and y values are then entered into the table. Then another value of x is used, a value of y is calculated, and these two values are also placed in the table. This continues until all the given values of x have been used. The necessary calculations are frequently tedious at best, especially if the equation is rather complicated or if the values of x are not integers. This is an ideal situation for the computer to do its work.

EXAMPLE 11.21.   Suppose that we have the equation $y = 2x^3 - x^2 + 3x - 7$. We wish to print out a table of values for x and y where x takes on the values 3, 4, 5, 6, 7, 8, and 9.

We will describe the equation with a user-defined function. The values of x can be obtained using a loop.

```
100 REM USER FUNCTION
110 REM TABLE OF X AND Y VALUES
120 DEF FNY(X)=2*X↑3-X↑2+3*X-7
130 PRINT "X","Y"
140 PRINT "-","-"
150 PRINT
160 REM X VALUES ARE INTEGERS FROM 3 TO 9 INCLUSIVE
170 LET I=3
180    PRINT I,FNY(I)
190    LET I=I+1
200 IF I<=9 THEN 180
210 END
```

RUN

X	Y
3	47
4	117
5	233
6	407
7	651
8	977
9	1396

READY

You might wonder what happened to X in the program and how does the I enter into our considerations. The argument of the function when it is *used* need not be the same as the argument when the function is *defined*. The letter used for the argument when the function is defined indicates the variable that appears on the right-hand side of the "=" sign. However, when the function is being used in the program, the argument stands for a *number* that is to be substituted into the expression.

In the previous example, our function was to be evaluated using values ranging from 3 to 9. It should be clear that the same result would be obtained if our program had been written as

```
170 LET X=3                    170 LET B=3
180    PRINT X,FNY(X)    or     180    PRINT B,FNY(B)
190    LET X=X+1                190    LET B=B+1
200 IF X<=9 THEN 180           200 IF B<=9 THEN 180
```

The final point about user-defined functions concerns the expression on the right of the "=" sign. It may include built-in functions and also other user-defined functions.

EXAMPLE 11.22. 10 DEF FNZ(G) = INT(2.7 − 5*SQR(G)) is a valid user-defined function that is defined using the built-in functions INT and SQR.

EXAMPLE 11.23. A user-defined function to round a number to the hundredths place (see Example 11.17) is

```
10 DEF FNH(X)=INT(100*X+.5)/100
```

EXAMPLE 11.24

```
5 DEF FNA(T)=T↑2-1
15 DEF FNB(X)=X*FNA(X)
```

Line 15 defines the function FNB using the *previously defined* function FNA. Note that if the order of the definitions were reversed (that is, FNB defined in line 5 and FNA in line 15), FNB would *not* be well defined since *at line 5* FNA would be unknown.

11.6 String Functions

In addition to numeric functions, described in the preceding sections, many computers also offer several functions that work on strings. Four common ones are described next along with a string operation.

The *length* of a string constant is the number of characters in the string. For example, the length of the string THELMA'S is 8. The function LEN(A$) returns the length of its string argument. The argument may be either a string constant or variable.

EXAMPLE 11.25

```
100 REM COUNTING CHARACTERS
110 PRINT "STRING";TAB(20);"NUMBER OF CHARACTERS"
120 PRINT
130 LET I=1
140    READ X$
150    PRINT X$;TAB(27);LEN(X$)
160    LET I=I+1
170 IF I<=5 THEN 140
180 DATA WORDS, CALCULATOR
190 DATA TWO
200 DATA "LONG JOHN SILVER"
210 DATA ALPHABET
220 END

RUN

STRING                  NUMBER OF CHARACTERS

WORDS                   5
CALCULATOR              10
TWO                     3
LONG JOHN SILVER        16
ALPHABET                8

READY
```

Observe that the two blanks in the quoted string LONG JOHN SILVER were counted.

A *substring* is part of a string. Substrings may be examined or even extracted from strings by the use of one of the three string functions LEFT\$, RIGHT\$, or MID\$.

The *general form of the LEFT\$ function* is

```
LEFT$(X$,I)
```

which returns the first I characters of the string X\$.

To illustrate, consider this small program:

```
10 LET X$="PROGRAMMING"
20 LET Y$=LEFT$(X$,7)
30 PRINT Y$
40 END
```

In line 20 a substring of the string PROGRAMMING is created and is assigned to the string variable Y\$. Y\$ will be taken from the first seven characters of the string X\$. Thus

```
RUN

PROGRAM

READY
```

RIGHT\$ acts like LEFT\$ except that the right-hand end of the string is used.

The *general form of RIGHT\$* is

```
RIGHT$(X$,I)
```

and its evaluation returns the last I characters of X\$.

For example, execution of

```
10 LET X$="ENVELOPES"
20 LET Y$=RIGHT$(X$,6)
30 PRINT Y$
40 END
```

would be

```
RUN

ELOPES

READY
```

The *general form of the string function MID\$* is

```
MID$(X$,I,J)
```

The substring of X$ that results from applying MID$ is the substring beginning at the Ith character of X$ and is J characters long. This is illustrated in the program that follows.

```
10 LET X$="TARANTULA"
20 LET Y$=MID$(X$,4,3)
30 PRINT Y$
40 END

RUN

ANT

READY
```

EXAMPLE 11.26.   The user will type in his or her entire name and the program will then print the user's first name.

The entire name will be entered as the value of the string variable N$. The string will be examined, one character at a time, until a blank is found. A count, C, will be kept of the number of characters examined up to and including the blank. The substring formed by all the characters preceding the blank is the first name and so will be printed.

```
100 PRINT "PLEASE ENTER YOUR ENTIRE NAME"
110 INPUT N$
120 REM C COUNTS TO BLANK
130 LET C=1
140 IF MID$(N$,C,1)=" " THEN 170
150    LET C=C+1
160 GOTO 140
170 REM FIRST NAME IS C-1 LETTERS LONG
180 PRINT "YOUR FIRST NAME IS ";LEFT$(N$,C-1)
190 END

RUN

PLEASE ENTER YOUR ENTIRE NAME
? PAULA LOUISE SULLIVAN
YOUR FIRST NAME IS PAULA

READY

RUN

PLEASE ENTER YOUR ENTIRE NAME
? BAT MAN
YOUR FIRST NAME IS BAT

READY
```

Concatenation is an operation on strings that combines two or more strings into a single string. The symbol for concatenation is "&" (although many systems use "+").

EXAMPLE 11.27

```
10 LET A$="CULTURE"
20 LET B$="AGRI"
30 LET C$=B$&A$
40 PRINT C$
50 PRINT A$&"D"
60 END

RUN

AGRICULTURE
CULTURED

READY
```

1 If $X = 3$ and $Y = -5$, find the value of each of the following.
a. INT(X*Y−.3)
b. ABS(X+Y)
c. INT(1/2*(−X)*Y)
d. SQR(X↑2+16)
e. ABS(X↑2+Y↑2)
f. 5−2*INT(Y/X)
g. ABS(Y−X)+INT(X/Y)*SQR(Y↑2*(X+1))

2 If the sides of a right triangle are r and s, then the hypotenuse h is calculated by the formula $h = \sqrt{r^2 + s^2}$. Write the program that has the values of r and s supplied by the user and then calculates and prints the value of the hypotenuse. The output should be labeled. For values of r and s you could use 4 and 3, 7 and 5, 1 and 1, 5 and 12, 6 and 8, and 2.7 and 3.01.

3 A number is divisible by 6 if it is divisible by 2 and divisible by 3. Write a program where the user types in a number and the computer tells the user if the number is divisible by 2, by 3, and by 6. Supposing that the user typed in a 9, the output for the program should look something like

```
9 IS NOT DIVISIBLE BY 2
9 IS DIVISIBLE BY 3
9 IS NOT DIVISIBLE BY 6
```

After the output has been printed, the user should be allowed to try another number if the user wishes to. Try the program with the numbers 12, 15, 16, 0, 36, and 474.

4 A certain camera will give pictures of excellent clarity if the subject is exactly 12 feet from the camera. The clarity will be good if the subject is within 2.5 feet, on either side, of the 12-foot mark. Write a program such that the user should supply to the program the distance from camera to subject and the program should tell whether the picture's clarity will be good or bad.

5 The user should enter two numbers for a division problem. The first is the divisor, the second the dividend. The output should show the quotient and remainder (if any). For values, use

Divisor	Dividend
6	74
9	63
5	5
11	121
4	43
89	1652
47	89,116

6 Write a program to do the following. The program should request that the user enter an improper fraction—numerator first, then denominator. If the fraction is not improper, keep asking the user until one is entered. The program should then change the improper fraction to a mixed number. To make distinct the whole number part of the mixed number from its fraction part, a colon should be printed between the two. For example the mixed number 2 ⅚ should be printed 2:5/6. Try your program with the improper fractions ¹⅞, ⁵⁄₂, and ⁷⁷⁄₈.

7 Write a program that prints the first 30 prime numbers.

8 Write a program that prints all the prime numbers from 207 through 351.

9 Modify Example 11.9 so that the first DATA line contains a single number—the previous balance. The program should count the number of deposits and, separately, the number of withdrawals; the output should show a third column—the present balance. Have your program use $43.35 as the previous balance.

10 Refer to Example 11.17. When the single payment that is different from the others is greater than each other payment, the single payment is usually the first rather than the last, as shown in the example. Write a program to determine if the single payment is to be first or last and print out information similar to that of the example. The program should allow the user to enter the amount to be repaid and the number of payments. Try your program with

Amount	Number of Months
$1000	24
2500	48
3100	30
2000	18
2200	24

11 You know that to change from inches to feet, you divide the number of inches by 12. So, for example, 27 inches is 2.25 feet. It would be an easy matter to write a program to do this. A more interesting program would have the 27 inches printed out as 2 FEET 3 INCHES. The program you are to write should have the user supply the length in inches and the program should print out the length in feet and inches. Try your program using 27, 35, 61, 78, 63,362, and 12.

12 Write a program to do the following. The user is to type in a number. The number should be thought of as a time, measured in seconds. The program should convert the time to hours, minutes, and seconds and print the result. Try the program using 130, 4055, 78, and 16,254.

13 One of the benefits of working for the Endall Utilities Company is that the company pays for a life insurance policy for each employee. The amount of the policy is two and one-half times the annual salary of the employee. For simplicity, the amount of insurance will be correct to the next hundred-dollar amount. A program should be written that gets an employee's salary from the terminal, calculates two and one-half times it, corrects this amount by bringing it to the next highest hundred dollars, and prints out this amount as the value of the life insurance policy. As sample salaries, you could try $15,950, $13,142, $17,491, and $20,000.

14 If d is the distance in feet an object falls and t is the time in seconds it takes the object to fall that distance, the relationship between the two quantities is given by $d = 16t^2$. Write a program that uses a user-defined function to print a table of times and distances where the times to be used start at 0 and go up to 60 in steps of 5.

15 Write a user-defined function that rounds a decimal (a) to the nearest thousandth; (b) to the nearest tenth.

16 Modify Professor Cleary's program (Example 11.18) so that after all students have been processed, the program will also print out the number of A's earned as well as the number of B's, C's, D's, and F's. In addition, the percentage (rounded to the nearest tenth) of each grade should be printed.

17   Use the eod tag DONE and the data lines

```
DATA  LAMP, CAMERA, SCISSORS, TROPHY
DATA  LIGHT, CATAMARAN, PENCIL
DATA  TENT, CLOCK
```

in a program that reads each item and prints it out with an abbreviated description made of the first three letters.

18   Each DATA line in a collection contains a person's name and telephone number. For example,

```
DATA  JOSEPH MATTHEWS,  800-555-1212
```

Write a program that prints out the name and telephone number excluding the area code. You could try your program with the following lines:

```
DATA  HELEN KERL,  900-212-9175
DATA  LOUIS LUKI,  199-617-9100
DATA  LORRY COOMS,  447-053-1734
```

19   Write a program to count the number of three letter words in the sentence "The trophy was presented to the two men from Tay." (Enter each word as a separate piece of data on DATA lines.)

20   Write a program to print the first letter of each word in the sentence of the last exercise.

21   Use the data lines

```
DATA  JACOB WIRT, ERICA JOHNSON
DATA  PAUL SANDERS, MAURA GREENE
DATA  CARA TOOMIS, MARGARET SANDERS
DATA  PETER BUYERS
```

and write a program to print out each person's last name followed by the first intial.

22   Assuming that only a single blank separates words in a sentence, enter the sentence from Exercise 19 as a single data item on one DATA line and write a program to count the number of words in a sentence.

* * *

23   Write a program that has the user enter 45 values, one at a time, and that counts how many of the values end in a 0. (Hint: To end in a 0, a number must be evenly divisible by 10.)

24   The user should enter a positive integer and then the program should print the number of digits in the integer. Try 4327 and 831.

25   A positive integer should be entered and the sum of its digits printed out. Try 6552 and 98724.

26   A positive integer should be entered from the terminal. The output should be the expanded form of the number. For example, the number 4327 should be output as $4000 + 300 + 20 + 7$. For data use
a. 4327   b. 6552   c. 831   d. 98724

27   The following algorithm (called the "guess method") can be used to find the square root of a number.

a. Ask the user to supply a number N whose square root is sought.
b. Ask the user to take a guess G at the square root of N.
c. Calculate the quotient Q of N and G (Q = N/G).
d. If G and Q differ by a very small amount (say, less than .000001), then Q is at least a good approximation to $\sqrt{N}$ so transfer to step g; otherwise, continue to step e.
e. Average G and Q and assign this average to G.
f. Transfer to step c.
g. Print Q.
Write a program and RUN it using the values

N	G	N	G
a. 80	9	e. 115.3	11
b. 80	8	f. 115.3	10
c. 47.6	7	g. 115.3	19
d. 72.56	8	h. 552	make your own guess

28 You can check the accuracy of the "guess-method" algorithm against the SQR function merely by having the value of SQR(N) printed out after the usual output of the program. Do so.

29 Write and RUN a program that prints, on a single line, the values N,SQR(N),N↑.5,SQR(N)−N↑.5 for integer values of N from 1 to 25.

30 Write a program that employs a user-defined function to change an angle in degrees to an angle in radian measure. Use 3.14159 as the value for π. The program should print the angle, in both measurements. Convert the angles from 0° to 360° (inclusive) in steps of 10°.

31 The *greatest common divisor* (gcd) of two positive integers A and B is a positive integer G such that
a. A is divisible by G.
b. B is divisible by G.
c. G is the largest number that divides both A and B.
Write a program that calculates and prints the gcd of A and B that are supplied one at a time from the terminal. As A and B are entered, each should be checked to be sure it is positive and is an integer. (One way of finding the gcd of A and B is to note that it is the largest integer from 1 to the smaller of A and B inclusive, that divides both A and B.) Try your program with the following data.

A	B	A	B
16	10	24	−8
14	63	5	0
−2	10	12	60
25	16	12	66
3.9	1.3	12	67

32 Two positive integers A and B are called *relatively prime* if the gcd of A and B is 1. Change the last problem so that if the gcd of A and B is 1, a message saying that they are relatively prime is printed out.

A program that prints the squares of the first five positive odd integers is

12.1 An Example Done Two Ways

```
1Ø LET N=1
2Ø IF N>5 THEN 7Ø
3Ø    LET K=2*N-1
4Ø    PRINT K↑2
5Ø    LET N=N+1
6Ø GOTO 2Ø
7Ø END
```

Repeating the discussion of Section 8.9 regarding the "ingredients" of a loop, recall that

1. There must be a condition (in a transfer statement) that uses a control variable.
2. The control variable must be initialized before the condition is checked.
3. The control variable must be changed so that the loop will eventually be left.

The control variable in a counting loop is called a *counter* or *index*. In the program above, N is the index of the loop. It is initialized in line 1Ø and incremented (changed) in line 5Ø. The condition is found in the transfer statement of line 2Ø.

There is a pair of statements that can be used to write counting loops more easily. The same problem programmed using these two statements is as follows.

```
1Ø FOR N=1 TO 5
2Ø    LET K=2*N-1
3Ø    PRINT K↑2
4Ø NEXT N
5Ø END
```

The new BASIC statements are the FOR/NEXT pair and are used to write counting loops. The *body* of a FOR/NEXT loop is the collection of statements that are repeated. The body in the program above is made up of lines 2∅ and 3∅ and is indented as before.

The difference in the loops between the two programs is in the initializing and incrementing of the index of the loop and in the decision that must be made. All of this is taken care of for us in the FOR and the NEXT statements. Let's look at line 1∅ of the new program

```
1∅ FOR N=1 TO 5
```

First, the index of the loop is the variable that comes right after the word FOR (here it is N). Next, the index is initialized to the value that follows the = sign (so N is initialized to 1). The value following TO is the last value that N will have. (This sentence will be changed somewhat later on but for now it is valid.) Now the index is checked against the last value (1 is compared with 5) and as long as the value of the index does not exceed the last value (that is, is less than or equal to the last value) the body of the loop is entered. Otherwise transfer is made to the statement that immediately follows NEXT.

The NEXT statement may be thought of as that part of the loop where the index is incremented and after that a transfer is made back to the FOR statement so that another comparison can be made between the index and the last value.

We again look at the program and use it to illustrate what has just been said.

```
1∅ FOR N=1 TO 5
2∅    LET K=2*N−1
3∅    PRINT K↑2
4∅ NEXT N
5∅ END
```

Line 1∅ is executed and N becomes 1; the value of N is compared with 5 and is found to be less than 5. In line 2∅, K is calculated to be 1 (that is, $2*1-1$); the value of K^2 is printed in line 3∅. When the computer reaches line 4∅ (completing the first time through the loop), the value of N becomes 2; control transfers to line 1∅. N is now compared with 5, and since N does not exceed 5, the computer continues to line 2∅. This second time that line 2∅ is executed, the value of N is 2, so the value of K is calculated to be 3 (that is, $2*2-1$). Line 3∅ prints the current value of K. Line 4∅ increases N by 1 (so now N is 3) and goes back to line 1∅.

This pattern is followed until, at line 4∅, N becomes 5; transfer is made to line 1∅. The value of N is compared with 5, and since it is still not greater than 5, lines 2∅ and 3∅ are executed. N becomes 6 at line 4∅; transfer is made to line 1∅ where the value of N is found to exceed 5; transfer is then made to the line that follows NEXT—that is, line 5∅, the END statement, is executed and the program halts.

So a FOR/NEXT loop works in the following way:

1. The index is initialized in the FOR statement.
2. The index is checked against the value that follows the word TO.

a. If the index is greater than the value following TO, a transfer is made to the statement that comes after NEXT (that is, the body of the loop is not executed).

b. If the index is less than or equal to the value following TO, the statements between FOR and NEXT (the body of the loop) are executed.

3. At the NEXT statement, the index is incremented. Transfer then returns to the top of the loop (the FOR statement, in this description, to step 2) for the next comparison.

EXAMPLE 12.1. Print the numbers from 3 to 8 together with their squares and cubes.

```
 5 PRINT "NUMBER", "SQUARE", "CUBE"
15 PRINT
25 FOR I=3 TO 8
35    LET S=I↑2
45    LET C=I↑3
55    PRINT I,S,C
65 NEXT I
75 END
```

RUN

NUMBER	SQUARE	CUBE
3	9	27
4	16	64
5	25	125
6	36	216
7	49	343
8	64	512

READY

This example shows that the index of the loop need not begin at 1.

In the two FOR/NEXT examples we have seen, the index has performed two activities. It has served as a counter, and it has also been used as part of the calculations done in the body of the loop (the way in which K was calculated in the first example and the way in which S and C were in the second).

EXAMPLE 12.2. Four values will be read in, one at a time (we will assume, for simplicity, that they will be positive integers). After each value is read, the program should determine if that number is odd or even and print out an appropriate message.

Recall that to see if a number X is odd or even, we compare X/2 and INT(X/2). What you should recognize in this problem is that there is a repetition to be carried out. One task is to be repeated over and over. In our problem what is to be repeated is the reading of the number, the determination whether the number is even or odd, and the printing of a message. These steps need to be repeated four times. Thus, one way of solving the problem is first to write a program to solve the problem once and then to modify this by putting it inside a loop that is executed the required number of times.

First, we write a program to tell if a number is odd or even. A DATA line is omitted. The particular values would, of course, have to be entered to have the program work.

```
110 READ X
120 IF X/2=INT(X/2) THEN 150
130 PRINT X;"IS AN ODD NUMBER"
140 STOP
150 PRINT X;"IS AN EVEN NUMBER"
160 END
```

Now we want this to take place four times, so we "enclose" this program in a FOR/NEXT loop. We must not forget to eliminate the END statement from the program and to finish our new program with an END. The final change refers to line 140. Now we do not want the program to stop after printing "odd" but rather to continue and request another number of the user. Thus we write a transfer to the NEXT statement. The new program now looks like

```
100 FOR J=1 TO 4
110    READ X
120    IF X/2=INT(X/2) THEN 150
130    PRINT X;"IS AN ODD NUMBER"
140    GOTO 160
150    PRINT X;"IS AN EVEN NUMBER"
160 NEXT J
170 END
```

As a final observation, you should note that in this program the index of the loop, J, is being used only to count how many times the loop is being executed—it is not used in the body of the loop.

12.2 The General Form of FOR/NEXT

The *general form of the FOR/NEXT pair* is

line number FOR simple variable = expression TO expression STEP expression
.
.
.
line number NEXT simple variable

The dots between FOR and NEXT stand for the body of the loop.
The simple variable that follows FOR and NEXT must be the same in both places.
The expression following "=" is called the *initial value* of the index.

The expression following TO is called the *final value* of the index.
The expression following STEP is the *increment value* of the index.

As seen in the programs already written in this chapter, the STEP
value may be omitted if the increment is 1. Thus the next two lines
mean the same.

```
150 FOR T=5 TO 11
150 FOR T=5 TO 11 STEP 1
```

Notice the three *expressions* in the FOR statement. As long as the
expressions are defined, a statement such as

```
255 FOR V=A+1 TO 3*B STEP X
```

is perfectly admissable.

It can be said that each FOR/NEXT loop determines a set of numbers.
The numbers in this set are those values that the index of the loop
takes on as each pass through the loop is executed. For example, we
have seen that the statement

```
FOR N=1 TO 5
```

describes the set of values 1, 2, 3, 4, and 5 that are the different values
assigned to N as it goes through the loop five times.

EXAMPLE 12.3. A loop that begins with

```
FOR D=2 TO 17 STEP 3
```

describes the set of numbers 2, 5, 8, 11, 14, and 17. Since there are
six numbers listed, the loop will be executed six times.

Thus to find the values that will be given to the index of your loop,
begin with the initial value and keep adding the increment value—as
long as you do not exceed the final value.

The problem with which we began this chapter, namely, to print the
squares of the first five positive odd integers, could also now be done
as

```
10 FOR N=1 TO 9 STEP 2
20    PRINT N↑2
30 NEXT N
40 END
```

EXAMPLE 12.4. Consider the following program together with its run.

```
 7 FOR W=3 TO 16 STEP 2
17    PRINT W;
27 NEXT W
37 END
```

RUN

   3 5 7 9 11 13 15

READY

The final value of the index given in line 7 is 16, and yet the last value
the computer printed was 15. If you check the set of values that the
index assumes, you will get 3, 5, 7, 9, 11, 13, and 15. If we calculated
another value, it would have to be 17, and 17 *is larger than our final
value.* The index frequently takes on the final value, but sometimes not.
It is always the case, however, that the index can never exceed the final
value.

The word "exceed" in the last sentence may be somewhat misleading.
There was no restriction made about the expression that follows STEP.
Thus the expression could be a negative value. For instance, the state-
ment

   100 FOR Y=10 TO 3 STEP −1

is perfectly valid. But what does it mean? It means that the index Y
will begin at 10 and will *decrease* to 3 with an increment (or decrement!)
of −1. This could be described somewhat as "stepping backward." So
it may seem confusing, in this case, to say that Y can never exceed
the final value, 3. However, the meaning should be clear—the final value
is the value that may never be exceeded, whether exceeded means
"greater than" for a positive step value or "less than" for a negative
step value.

You must be certain when writing a FOR/NEXT counting loop that,
if the STEP value is *positive*, then the initial value should be *less than*
the final value and, conversely, if the initial value is less than the final
value, then the STEP must be positive. Equivalently, if the STEP is
negative, then the initial value should be *greater than* the final value and
conversely.

EXAMPLE 12.5.   What are the values of the index and how many times
will the loop be executed that begins with

   200 FOR I=22 TO 3 STEP −4

The values are calculated by beginning with 22 and *subtracting* 4, remem-
bering not to use values less than 3. So we get 22, 18, 14, 10, and 6
and the loop will be executed five times.

EXAMPLE 12.6.   This little program, illustrating STEP values, might
be used to launch missiles from Cape Kennedy or your backyard.

```
 5 FOR J=10 TO 0 STEP −1
15    PRINT J
25 NEXT J
35 PRINT "LIFT OFF"
45 END
```

The expression following STEP can also be a decimal value.

EXAMPLE 12.7

```
10 REM SQUARE ROOTS OF SOME DECIMALS
20 PRINT "NUMBER","SQUARE ROOT"
30 FOR A=.2 TO 1.2 STEP .05
40    PRINT A,SQR(A)
50 NEXT A
60 END

RUN
```

NUMBER	SQUARE ROOT
.2	.447214
.25	.5
.3	.547723
.35	.591608
.4	.632456
.45	.67082
.5	.707107
.55	.74162
.6	.774597
.65	.806226
.7	.83666
.75	.866025
.8	.894427
.85	.921954
.9	.948683
.95	.974679
1.	1.
1.05	1.0247
1.1	1.04881
1.15	1.07238
1.2	1.09545

READY

EXAMPLE 12.8. Your company employs 15 workers whose salaries are determined by an hourly rate of pay and the number of hours worked. A worker is paid time and a half for hours worked beyond 40. Each worker is identified by a number from 1 to 15. A program is to be written that identifies each worker by number and then asks for the hourly wage and the number of hours that person worked during the week. When this information has been supplied, two lines of output should be printed, the first line being the headings

REGULAR PAY OVERTIME OVERTIME PAY TOTAL PAY

and the second line being the corresponding numbers under these headings.

This program requires that a single activity be repeated 15 times, and so a way to solve this is to create the solution to the single situation and then enclose this solution in a loop.

This problem will be solved by considering the problem in parts, analyzing the parts, and writing the code for each part.

First, we see that we need two variables for input (hourly rate and numbers of hours worked) and four for output (which correspond to the output headings). Since a given worker may not receive pay for a particular week (perhaps due to an unpaid leave of absence), the four output variables should be initialized to zero. We could begin our coding

```
150 REM P IS REGULAR PAY, 01 IS OVERTIME HOURS
160 REM 02 IS OVERTIME PAY, T IS TOTAL PAY
170 REM INITIALIZE VARIABLES
180 LET P=0
182 LET 01=0
184 LET 02=0
186 LET T=0
190 PRINT "ENTER HOURLY RATE, NUMBER OF HOURS WORKED"
200 INPUT R,H
```

Next we check to see if there were any overtime hours worked and if so to calculate how many. If there is no overtime, we transfer to the calculation of the regular pay. If there is overtime pay, it is calculated by multiplying the number of hours worked on overtime by 1.5 times the hourly pay rate. Our coding continues.

```
210 CHECK FOR OVERTIME
220 IF H<=40 THEN 290
230 REM CALCULATE OVERTIME HOURS
240 LET 01=H-40
250 REM CALCULATE OVERTIME PAY
260 LET 02=01*(1.5*R)
270 REM FOR OVERTIME WORKER, RESET REGULAR PAY HOURS TO 40
280 LET H=40
290 REM CALCULATE REGULAR PAY
300 LET P=R*H
```

In line 260, the parentheses are unnecessary—they are put there only to emphasize that the overtime rate is 1.5 times the regular rate R. Notice also that regular pay should be calculated whether or not there is overtime pay. This is accomplished by transferring from line 220 to 290 if there is no overtime (H≤40) or by first calculating overtime pay and then regular pay (lines 240, 260, 280, and 300). Also, as the remark in line 270 indicates, the regular pay hours for a worker who has worked more than 40 hours needs to be reset to 40, or else that worker would receive, in addition to overtime pay, pay for that many hours (the original value of H) at the regular rate.

What remains to be done is to calculate total pay and print the results.

The total pay T is the sum of the regular pay P and the overtime pay
02. If there is no overtime (H≤40), transfer is made from line 220 to
line 290; and so the value of 02 is not recalculated in line 260 and
thus still is 0. In this case T=P+0, or T is merely the regular pay.
When these new programming lines are added to what we have done
before, we get

```
150 REM P IS REGULAR PAY, 01 IS OVERTIME HOURS
160 REM 02 IS OVERTIME PAY, T IS TOTAL PAY
170 REM INITIALIZE VARIABLES
180 LET P=0
182 LET 01=0
184 LET 02=0
186 LET T=0
190 PRINT "ENTER HOURLY RATE, NUMBER OF HOURS WORKED"
200 INPUT R,H
210 REM CHECK FOR OVERTIME
220 IF H<=40 THEN 290
230 REM CALCULATE OVERTIME HOURS
240 LET 01=H-40
250 REM CALCULATE OVERTIME PAY
260 LET 02=01*(1.5*R)
270 REM FOR OVERTIME WORKER, RESET REGULAR PAY HOURS TO 40
280 LET H=40
290 REM CALCULATE REGULAR PAY
300 LET P=R*H
310 REM CALCULATE TOTAL PAY
320 LET T=P+02
330 REM PRINT OUT RESULTS AFTER SKIPPING LINE
340 PRINT
350 PRINT "REGULAR PAY", "OVERTIME", "OVERTIME PAY", "TOTAL PAY"
360 PRINT P,01,02,T
```

These lines will constitute the body of a loop that must be executed
15 times—once for each worker. Thus we merely construct a loop around
the program and add an END statement.

```
100 FOR I=1 TO 15
370 NEXT I
380 END
```

One last detail needs to be added—the problem statement says that
the program should identify the workers by number. This is easily accomplished by including a statement, within the loop and at the beginning
of it, such as

```
110 PRINT "INFORMATION FOR WORKER";I
```

An indication of a RUN of the program follows.

RUN

INFORMATION FOR WORKER 1
ENTER HOURLY RATE, NUMBER OF HOURS WORKED
? 4.25,43

REGULAR PAY	OVERTIME	OVERTIME PAY	TOTAL PAY
170	3	19.125	189.125

INFORMATION FOR WORKER 2
ENTER HOURLY RATE, NUMBER OF HOURS WORKED
? 5.50,40

REGULAR PAY	OVERTIME	OVERTIME PAY	TOTAL PAY
220	0	0	220

INFORMATION FOR WORKER 3
ENTER HOURLY RATE, NUMBER OF HOURS WORKED
? 4.75,0

REGULAR PAY	OVERTIME	OVERTIME PAY	TOTAL PAY
0	0	0	0

INFORMATION FOR WORKER 4
ENTER HOURLY RATE, NUMBER OF HOURS WORKED
? 7.00,30

REGULAR PAY	OVERTIME	OVERTIME PAY	TOTAL PAY
210	0	0	210

INFORMATION FOR WORKER 5
ENTER HOURLY RATE, NUMBER OF HOURS WORKED
? 3.10,40

REGULAR PAY	OVERTIME	OVERTIME PAY	TOTAL PAY
124	0	0	124

INFORMATION FOR WORKER 6
ENTER HOURLY RATE, NUMBER OF HOURS WORKED
? 8.00,50

REGULAR PAY	OVERTIME	OVERTIME PAY	TOTAL PAY
320	10	120	440

.
.
.

INFORMATION FOR WORKER 15
ENTER HOURLY RATE, NUMBER OF HOURS WORKED
? 5.79,32.25

REGULAR PAY	OVERTIME	OVERTIME PAY	TOTAL PAY
186.728	0	0	186.728

READY

We conclude this example with two observations. Since we attempted
in line 340 to make the output somewhat orderly looking by separating
the input data from the output lines with a blank line and then when

we looked at the output, we saw that it was not quite so orderly looking, we could add a line

```
365 PRINT
```

to add another blank line between the output lines and the following line that begins with the word INFORMATION. This is clearly not a statement that affects the working of the program, but it makes the output more readable.

Second, if we look at the pay received by some of the workers (numbers 1 and 15, for example), we see that the number printed does not look like a money amount. Here we have an example of a program that could use the rounding-off technique shown in Chapter 11.

EXAMPLE 12.9. The label on a quart of paint says that the paint will cover approximately 120 square feet. A large circle is to be made in the middle of an athletic field and the paint is to be sprayed on the ground to cover the circle. The tool that is used to draw the circle is 4 feet long and can be extended in 6-inch lengths up to a maximum length of 8 feet. The length of the tool is the same as the radius of the circle. Find the radius of the largest circle that can be drawn with the tool and that can be covered with the paint.

At first reading, the problem may seem complicated, but it really isn't. In fact, it's chief purpose is to illustrate the idea of transferring out of a loop before the loop has been completed. We wish to calculate areas of circles with different radii, starting with radius 4 (the length of the tool) up to a maximum of 8 changing by .5 (since 6 inches is .5 feet). As long as the area calculated is less than 120, we go on and calculate a new area. If the area is 120 or more, then the paint will not cover the circle. When this happens the *previous value* of the radius will be the largest that can be used.

```
10 REM PAINTING A CIRCLE
20 LET P=22/7
30 REM LOOP FOR RADIUS VALUES
40 FOR R=4 to 8 STEP .5
50    LET A=P*R↑2
60    REM CHECK AREA FOR COVERAGE
70    IF A>=120 THEN 90
80 NEXT R
90 REM DECREASE RADIUS BY .5
100 LET R1=R-.5
110 PRINT "DRAW CIRCLE OF RADIUS";R1;"FEET"
120 END

RUN

DRAW A CIRCLE OF RADIUS 6 FEET

READY
```

We return to the program with which we began this chapter. It's purpose was to print the squares of the first five odd counting numbers. Shown next are the program and its detailed flowchart. (See Figure 12.1.)

12.3 Flowcharting the FOR/NEXT

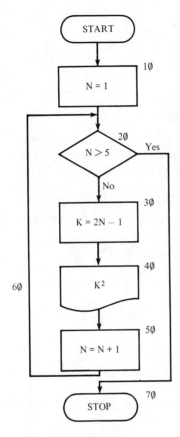

FIGURE 12.1.

```
10 LET N=1
20 IF N>5 THEN 70
30    LET K=2*N−1
40    PRINT K↑2
50    LET N=N+1
60 GO TO 20
70 END
```

When the program is written using a FOR/NEXT loop, it looks like

```
10 FOR N=1 TO 5
20    LET K=2*N−1
30    PRINT K↑2
40 NEXT N
50 END
```

Clearly, the coding of the program from the detailed flowchart gives us the first program and not the second. However, since using FOR/NEXT makes the writing of loops so easy, we need to have a symbol to use in a detailed flowchart.

The flowcharting symbol for FOR is ![FOR symbol]. It is merely the rectangle used for LET, divided into three parts. The flowchart equivalent of

FOR J=2 TO 87 STEP 5 is ![symbol with J=2, 87, 5]

Thus the index and initial value are placed in the upper triangle, the final value in the middle triangle, and the increment (STEP) in the lower triangle. (If the STEP value is 1, the lower triangle will be left blank and so correspond to the actual coding.)

Two flow lines will be drawn coming out of the right-hand side of the rectangle. One of the lines (the lower one) will lead to the body of the loop, while the other line will proceed to whatever else is to happen after the loop is finished. Thus for our program

```
1Ø FOR N=1 TO 5
2Ø    LET K=2*N−1
3Ø    PRINT K↑2
4Ø NEXT N
5Ø END
```

lines 1Ø, 2Ø, 3Ø, and 5Ø would be coded from Figure 12.2.

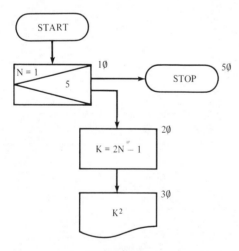

FIGURE 12.2.

The only line missing from the flowchart is 4Ø, which corresponds to the NEXT statement. But when the loop is being executed, we keep going between FOR and NEXT. Thus we will draw a flow line from the last statement in the body of the loop to the bottom of the FOR symbol; this line will be the flowcharting symbol for NEXT. The completed, detailed flowchart is shown in Figure 12.3.

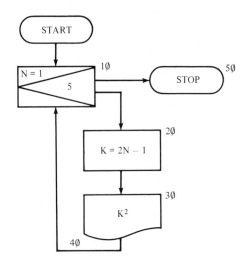

FIGURE 12.3.

EXAMPLE 12.10. Recently, gasoline has begun to be priced and sold by the liter rather than by the gallon. To assist the consumer, a program will be written to print a conversion table with three columns. The first column will show a figure in gallons (ranging from 5 to 25), the second column will show the equivalent amount in liters, and the third column will show the cost for that amount of gasoline. Before the table is printed, the user will be requested to enter the price per liter.

The conversion between gallons and liters will use the relationship 1 gallon = 3.79 liters. An algorithm for the problem is

1. Request price per liter, P.
2. Print column headings.
3. Repeat the following as gallons, G, change from 5 to 25.
   a. Calculate number of liters, L, by G × 3.79.
   b. Calculate cost, C, by L × P.
   c. Print G, L, C.

```
300 REM GALLONS - LITERS CONVERSION
310 REM
320 REM 1 GAL. = 3.79 LITERS
330 REM P IS PRICE OF GASOLINE PER LITER
340 REM G IS GALLONS : 5 TO 25
350 REM L IS EQUIVALENT IN LITERS
360 REM C IS COST FOR GASOLINE
370 REM FNR ROUNDS COST TO NEAREST CENT
380 REM
390 DEF FNR(X)=INT(100*X+.5)/100
400 PRINT "HOW MUCH DOES 1 LITER OF GASOLINE COST";
410 INPUT P
```

```
420 PRINT
430 PRINT
440 PRINT "GALLONS","LITERS","COST"
450 FOR G=5 TO 25
460    LET L=G*3.79
470    LET C=L*P
480    PRINT G,L,FNR(C)
490 NEXT G
500 END
```

RUN

HOW MUCH DOES 1 LITER OF GASOLINE COST? .385

GALLONS	LITERS	COST
5	18.95	7.3
6	22.74	8.75
7	26.53	10.21
8	30.32	11.67
9	34.11	13.13
10	37.9	14.59
11	41.69	16.05
12	45.48	17.51
13	49.27	18.97
14	53.06	20.43
15	56.85	21.89
16	60.64	23.35
17	64.43	24.81
18	68.22	26.26
19	72.01	27.72
20	75.8	29.18
21	79.59	30.64
22	83.38	32.1
23	87.17	33.56
24	90.96	35.02
25	94.75	36.48

READY

Several points should be made regarding the use of FOR/NEXT loops.

1. There should be a one-to-one correspondence between FOR statements and NEXT statements. In other words, for each FOR statement, there should be exactly one NEXT statement, and, conversely, for each NEXT statement in a program there should be exactly one FOR statement.
2. A FOR/NEXT loop may be left via a conditional transfer that is part of the body of the loop. For instance, the scheme shown here is valid.

```
        .
        .
        .
200 FOR  J=1  TO  20
        .
        .
        .
250     IF  K+I<J  THEN  550
        .
        .
        .
310 NEXT  J
```

3. Branching within the body of a loop, as shown, is allowed.

```
        .
        .
        .
100 FOR  A=2  TO  N
        .
        .
        .
160     READ  X
170     IF  X>A  THEN  210
        .
        .
        .
        .
250 NEXT  A
```

4. A loop should be entered only at the "top"—that is, at the FOR statement. A transfer, from outside a loop, should not be made to any statement of the loop but the FOR statement.

5. Transferring to a FOR statement generally will cause the loop to be begun. However, you should not transfer to a FOR statement from within the loop determined by that FOR statement. It could cause an infinite loop, and some systems do not allow such a transfer and will terminate the program with an error message. To skip statements within the body of the loop and continue with the next repetition of the loop, transfer to the NEXT statement, not the FOR statement.

6. After a loop has been completed by exiting through the NEXT statement, the value of the index is usually the terminal value plus the step value. However, this is not always the case. In the exercises, you will be directed to check how your system handles this situation. A general guideline is not to use the index of a loop, after the loop has been exited, unless the index has been specifically assigned a value.

7. A loop may contain another loop.

The following program tests the user about multiplication by 5. A count of the number of correct responses is kept. When the user answers incorrectly, the correct response is given.

12.4 Nested FORs

```
10 REM C COUNTS CORRECT ANSWERS
20 LET C=0
30 PRINT "MULTIPLICATION QUIZ"
40 PRINT
50 FOR F=1 TO 12
60    PRINT "HOW MUCH IS 5 TIMES";F
70    INPUT A
80    REM CHECK ANSWER
90    IF A=5*F THEN 130
100   REM PRINT OUT CORRECT ANSWER
110   PRINT "NO. 5 TIMES";F;"IS";5*F
120   GOTO 160
130   REM INCREASE COUNTER AND PRINT MESSAGE
140   LET C=C+1
150   PRINT "THAT IS CORRECT"
160   PRINT
170 NEXT F
180 PRINT "YOU ANSWERED";C;"QUESTIONS CORRECTLY"
190 END

RUN

MULTIPLICATION QUIZ

HOW MUCH IS 5 TIMES 1
? 5
THAT'S CORRECT

HOW MUCH IS 5 TIMES 2
? 10
THAT'S CORRECT

HOW MUCH IS 5 TIMES 3
? 14
NO. 5 TIMES 3 IS 15

HOW MUCH IS 5 TIMES 4
? 24
NO. 5 TIMES 4 IS 20

HOW MUCH IS 5 TIMES 5
? 25
THAT'S CORRECT

HOW MUCH IS 5 TIMES 6
? 30
THAT'S CORRECT
```

```
HOW MUCH IS 5 TIMES 7
? 45
NO. 5 TIMES 7 IS 35

HOW MUCH IS 5 TIMES 8
? 40
THAT'S CORRECT

HOW MUCH IS 5 TIMES 9
? 45
THAT'S CORRECT

HOW MUCH IS 5 TIMES 10
? 50
THAT'S CORRECT

HOW MUCH IS 5 TIMES 11
? 55
THAT'S CORRECT

HOW MUCH IS 5 TIMES 12
? 75
NO. 5 TIMES 12 IS 60

YOU ANSWERED 8 QUESTIONS CORRECTLY

READY
```

Part of the calculations done in this program includes multiplications by 5. In essence, they could be used to print the following multiplication table.

```
RUN

THE '5 TIMES' TABLE

5 × 1 = 5
5 × 2 = 10
5 × 3 = 15
5 × 4 = 20
5 × 5 = 25
5 × 6 = 30
5 × 7 = 35
5 × 8 = 40
5 × 9 = 45
5 × 10 = 50
5 × 11 = 55
5 × 12 = 60

READY
```

A program that creates this table follows.

```
10 PRINT "THE '5 TIMES' TABLE"
20 PRINT
30 LET I=5
40 FOR J=1 TO 12
50    PRINT I;"X";J;"=";I*J
60 NEXT J
70 END
```

Notice that if we wanted to get the "8 times" table, all that we would need to do is to change line 30.

EXAMPLE 12.11. We wish to write a program to print the table of multiplication facts shown.

$1 \times 1 = 1$
$1 \times 2 = 2$
$1 \times 3 = 3$
$1 \times 4 = 4$

$2 \times 1 = 2$
$2 \times 2 = 4$
$2 \times 3 = 6$
$2 \times 4 = 8$

$3 \times 1 = 3$
$3 \times 2 = 6$
$3 \times 3 = 9$
$3 \times 4 = 12$

Let's examine the two numbers surrounding the "×" symbol in each line.

In the first grouping, the first number (to the left of the "×") is always a 1, while the second number changes from 1 to 4. So this first grouping looks like a short table of multiplication by 1.

In the second grouping, the first number is always a 2, while the second number changes from 1 to 4 (as it did in the first grouping). The second grouping resembles multiplication by 2.

Similarly, the third grouping resembles a short table of multiplication by 3.

Notice that in each grouping the second number always goes from 1 to 4. So no matter what group we consider, we wish to have

```
225 FOR J=1 TO 4
250    LET K=I*J
275    PRINT I;"X";J;"=";K
300 NEXT J
```

Of course, the variable I does not yet have a value. But consider the table. For the first grouping, we would want I to be 1. For the second, I should equal 2; for the third, I should equal 3. So I is to take on the values 1, 2, and 3. As I takes on each of these values, the same activity is to happen—namely, lines 225 to 300 as shown. This means that we wish to construct a loop around these lines—a loop with I as its index and I changing from 1 to 2 to 3. We construct the loop and get

```
200 FOR I=1 TO 3
225    FOR J=1 TO 4
250       LET K=I*J
275       PRINT I;"X";J;"=";K
300    NEXT J
325 NEXT I
350 END
```

The body of the I loop contains another loop, the J loop. We have a loop within a loop. Loops within loops are called *nested loops*. Let's look at a RUN of the program.

RUN

```
1 X 1 = 1
1 X 2 = 2
1 X 3 = 3
1 X 4 = 4
2 X 1 = 2
2 X 2 = 4
2 X 3 = 6
2 X 4 = 8
3 X 1 = 3
3 X 2 = 6
3 X 3 = 9
3 X 4 = 12
```

This is not quite what we wanted. We wanted a space between the groupings. Since it is I that changes from one grouping to the next, all we need to do is to insert a PRINT after the J loop has been completed and before I changes. So

```
310 PRINT
```

will do the job.

READY

It is of interest to look at a flowchart that corresponds to this program. You should study it carefully to see that you understand it and how it describes the program. (See Figure 12.4.)

EXAMPLE 12.12. The City Machine Company will start producing microcomputers. Research has shown that the amount of profit that can be made is described by the equation

$$p = 9xy - y^3 - x$$

where p is the profit, x is the number of semiskilled technicians needed to assemble the microcomputers, and y is the number of skilled technicians needed to assemble and test the product. The company is willing to hire from two to five semiskilled technicians and from three to five skilled ones. Write a program for the City Machine Company that will show all the possible profits from the various combinations of hirings.

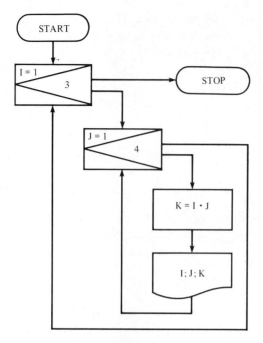

FIGURE 12.4.

We will use nested loops to produce all possible combinations of the number of semiskilled workers and the number of skilled workers. The outer loop will use the index X and will stand for the number of semiskilled technicians. X will vary from 2 to 5. Inside the X loop will be a Y loop which will stand for the number of skilled technicians. Y will vary from 3 to 5. Inside the Y loop, the formula will be evaluated, and then the values of X, Y, and the corresponding profit will be printed. The output will begin with labels for the three quantities. The program and a RUN follow.

```
100 REM CITY MACHINE CO. PROFIT PROGRAM
110 REM USING NESTED LOOPS
120 PRINT "SEMI-SKILLED","SKILLED","PROFIT"
130 REM X IS NUMBER OF SEMI-SKILLED TECHNICIANS
140 FOR X=2 TO 5
150    REM Y IS NUMBER OF SKILLED TECHNICIANS
160    FOR Y=3 TO 5
170       REM CALCULATE PROFIT, P, FROM EQUATION
180       LET P=9*X*Y-Y↑3-X
190       PRINT X,Y,P
200    NEXT Y
210 NEXT X
220 END
```

RUN

SEMISKILLED	SKILLED	PROFIT
2	3	25
2	4	6
2	5	-37
3	3	51
3	4	41
3	5	7
4	3	77
4	4	76
4	5	51
5	3	1Ø3
5	4	111
5	5	95

READY

By looking at this RUN, the City Machine Company will know exactly how many of each type of worker to hire to make its profit as large as possible.

Suppose we indicate a J loop by the diagram at the right. Suppose further that a program is to have more than one loop—for simplicity, there will be two loops: a J loop and a K loop. There are three possible configurations: separate or disjoint loops (Figure 12.5), nested loops (Figure 12.6), and overlapping loops (Figure 12.7).

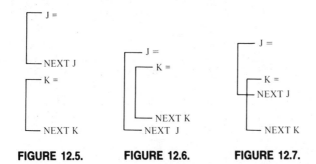

FIGURE 12.5.   FIGURE 12.6.   FIGURE 12.7.

The situation of Figure 12.7, overlapping loops, is never allowed. It will lead to an error message and the termination, by the computer, of your program.

EXAMPLE 12.13. For each of the eight salespeople your company employs a DATA line will contain the salesperson's name followed by five numbers that represent daily sales totals. The program that will process this data should print out the salesperson's name, the salesperson's weekly total, and the salesperson's daily average.

For a single salesperson, a loop will be used to read and sum the five daily totals. Since the processing for an individual is to be repeated

eight times (for the eight salespeople), another loop will be required.
An algorithm for this problem is

1. Print headings.
2. Repeat the following eight times.
   a. Set total, T, to Ø.
   b. Read a name, N$.
   c. Do the following as D goes from 1 to 5.
      (1) Read a daily sales amount, S.
      (2) Add S to T.
   d. Calculate daily average, A.
   e. Print N$, T, and A.

(Notice the two different ways a FOR loop is described in the algorithm.
The important thing is that your algorithm clearly describes the problem-
solving process.)

```
1000 REM WEEKLY TOTAL, DAILY AVERAGE
1010 REM NESTED LOOPS
1020 PRINT "NAME OF","WEEKLY","DAILY"
1030 PRINT "SALESPERSON","TOTAL","AVERAGE"
1040 PRINT
1050 FOR P=1 TO 8
1060    LET T=0
1070    READ N$
1080    FOR D=1 TO 5
1090       READ S
1100       LET T=T+S
1110    NEXT D
1120    LET A=T/5
1130    PRINT N$,T,A
1140 NEXT P
1150 DATA JOHN BROOKS,105.20,89.77,153.89,201.23,179.76
1160 DATA MONA ALVES,123.45,167.54,177.54,122.00,198.74
1170 DATA JANE O'TOOLE,99.99,95.16,200.15,210.88,221.00
1180 DATA HOLLY FORMET,157.65,115.29,173.20,158.84,56.73
1190 DATA ALICE BURGER,0,164.72,119.88,192.44,190.01
1200 DATA DAVID DUNN,183.94,172.88,204.15,273.15,0
1210 DATA KELLY BROWN,204.73,208.91,195.51,157.18,179.23
1220 DATA JERE WHITE,110.00,174.25,198.07,0,0
1230 END
```

RUN

NAME OF SALESPERSON	WEEKLY TOTAL	DAILY AVERAGE
JOHN BROOKS	729.85	145.97
MONA ALVES	789.27	157.854
JANE O'TOOLE	827.18	165.436
HOLLY FORMET	661.71	132.342
ALICE BURGER	667.05	133.41
DAVID DUNN	834.12	166.824

```
KELLY  BROWN      945.2           189.04
JERE  WHITE       482.32          96.464
```

READY

As was mentioned earlier, more than one loop can be contained within a first loop. For example, each of the configurations in Figures 12.8 and 12.9 is allowed.

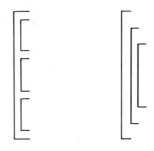

FIGURE 12.8.   **FIGURE 12.9.**

Example 12.14 shows a program using loops as described in Figure 12.9.

EXAMPLE 12.14.   The volume of a rectangular solid (e.g., a cardboard box) is calculated by the formula $v = l \cdot w \cdot h$, where v stands for volume, and l, w, and h are the length, width, and height, respectively. A program is to be written that calculates the volumes of a collection of rectangular solids. The lengths are to vary from 1 to 3, the widths from 2 to 5, and the heights from 4 to 5. The output should be in table form, with column headings.

```
10 REM VOLUMES USING NESTED LOOPS
20 PRINT "LENGTH","WIDTH","HEIGHT","VOLUME"
30 PRINT
40 REM L IS LENGTH;OUTSIDE LOOP
50 FOR L=1 TO 3
60    REM W IS WIDTH;MIDDLE LOOP
70    FOR W=2 TO 5
80      REM H IS HEIGHT;INSIDE LOOP
90      FOR H=4 TO 5
100        REM VOLUME FORMULA
110        LET V=L*W*H
120        PRINT L,W,H,V
130      NEXT H
140    NEXT W
150 NEXT L
160 END
```

RUN

LENGTH	WIDTH	HEIGHT	VOLUME
1	2	4	8
1	2	5	1Ø
1	3	4	12
1	3	5	15
1	4	4	16
1	4	5	2Ø
1	5	4	2Ø
1	5	5	25
2	2	4	16
2	2	5	2Ø
2	3	4	24
2	3	5	3Ø
.	.	.	.
.	.	.	.
.	.	.	.
3	5	4	6Ø
3	5	5	75

READY

In Chapter 7 it was stated that the argument of TAB can be an expression. The next example illustrates this.

EXAMPLE 12.15

```
1Ø REM LOOP WITH VARIABLE TAB
2Ø PRINT "1234567890"
3Ø FOR I=1 TO 5
4Ø    PRINT TAB(I);I↑2
5Ø NEXT I
6Ø END
```

RUN

```
1234567890
 1
   4
    9
      16
       25
```

READY

The first time through the loop I=1, so line 4Ø reads

```
PRINT TAB(1);1↑2
```

The computer is instructed to print the value of 1^2 starting in print position number 1, and this is exactly what happens—the blank for the *sign* of 1^2 is printed in the first print position. The same thing happens for 4, 9, 16, and 25.

TAB can be used to print designs.

EXAMPLE 12.16.   The following is a simple design using TAB.

```
100 PRINT "12345678901234567890"
110 PRINT TAB(12);"*"
120 FOR I=1 TO 4
130    PRINT TAB(12-I);"*";TAB(12+I);"*"
140 NEXT I
150 PRINT TAB(7);"***********"
160 FOR I=1 TO 3
170    PRINT TAB(11);"* *"
180 NEXT I
190 PRINT TAB(11);"***"
200 END
```

RUN

```
12345678901234567890

           *
         *   *
       *       *
      *         *
     *           *
    * * * * * * * * * *
         *   *
         *   *
         *   *
         * * *
```

READY

The 11 *'s that are produced by line 150 can be done in a different way that is frequently useful. We begin by printing a single * in position number 7 and ending the command with a semicolon so that there is no advance to the next line. We then code a *loop* to print ten *'s on the same line. Finally, after the loop a simple PRINT is included to cancel the effect of the semicolon and enable the computer to print on the next line. Thus line 150 could be *replaced* by

```
151 PRINT TAB(7);"*";
153 FOR J=1 TO 10
155    PRINT "*";
157 NEXT J
159 PRINT
```

Even though we are replacing a single programming line with five lines, we are letting the computer do the printing (and counting, also) for us.

EXAMPLE 12.17. A large computing service is planning to update its terminals. To help choose one of six possible replacements, the six have been rented for five days and have been made available for general use. The number of hours per day that each of the six terminals was used has been recorded. Write a program to display the daily use of each terminal as well as the total hours for each. A DATA line will contain the terminal model number (a three- or four-character code) and the five days' times. The output should be in table form.

The processing will consist of reading, printing, and adding. The tabular output will have to display seven columns: one for the terminal code, five for the daily number of hours, and one for the week's totals. Since there are more than five columns, a comma cannot be used between the output items.

To give the table a neat appearance, output items will be aligned by using the TAB feature. Some planning will be required to set up the output.

The terminal code is at most four characters long, and we will allow the first ten spaces on the output line for it. We will print each of the six numbers eight spaces from the previous number beginning in print position number 11. The printing positions to be used will be 11, 19, 27, 35, 43, and 51. These numbers have purposely been chosen so that their pattern can be easily described for use in a FOR loop. The loop will cause a TAB to each of these positions where an output item will be printed.

```
100 REM TERMINAL COMPARISONS
150 REM SIX TERMINALS FOR FIVE DAYS
200 FOR T=1 TO 6
250    LET S=0
300    READ C$
350    PRINT C$;
400    FOR X=11 TO 43 STEP 8
450       READ H
500       PRINT TAB(X);H;
550       LET S=S+H
600    NEXT X
650    PRINT TAB(51);S
700 NEXT T
750 DATA SAS3,5,6,5,7,4,5,7
800 DATA AJ2,6,5,7,7.25,4,3.6
850 DATA AL4,4,6,6,4,7.2,8.1
900 DATA JDS1,7,5,7.9,6.2,5.1,5.3
950 DATA PLC0,4.5,7.8,8.2,6.8,8.5
1000 DATA EXX0,2.5,7.5,6.2,5.1,4
1050 END
```

RUN

SAS3	5	6.5	7	4.5	7	30
AJ2	6.5	7	7.25	4	3.6	28.35
AL4	4	6	6.4	7.2	8.1	31.7

JDS1	7.5	7.9	6.2	5.1	5.3	32.
PLCØ	4.5	7.8	8.2	6.8	8.5	35.8
EXXØ	2.5	7.5	6.2	5.1	4	25.3

READY

Column headings could be provided by the following modifications.

```
15Ø READ A$
16Ø PRINT A$;
165 FOR I=11 TO 51 STEP 8
17Ø    READ A$
175    PRINT TAB(I);A$;
18Ø NEXT I
185 PRINT
19Ø PRINT
71Ø DATA MODEL,MON,TUE,WED,THUR,FRI,TOTAL
```

EXERCISES

1 What, if anything, is wrong with the following statements?
   a. 1ØØ FOR L=1−5
   b. 11Ø FOR J=7 TO 2
   c. 250 FØR A=3 TO 11
   d. 175 FOR K=D↑2 TO 1ØØ*F
   e. 22Ø FOR M=−2 TO 9
   f. 5ØØ FOR N=−2 TO −7
   g. 360 FOR J+1=5 TO 15

   h. 1ØØ FOR A=1 TO 6
      11Ø FOR B=2 TO 5
        −   −
        −   −
        −   −
      18Ø NEXT A
      19Ø NEXT B

2 For the listed FOR statements
   a. What is the index of the loop?
   b. What is the initial value?
   c. What is the final value?
   d. What is the set of values the index takes on as the loop is executed?
   e. How many times is the loop executed?
   i. FOR J=2 TO 7
   ii. FOR M=1 TO 11
   iii. FOR T=5 TO 15
   iv. FOR W1=−5 TO 15 STEP 2
   v. FOR X=7 TO 83 STEP 3
   vi. FOR D2=8 TO 3 STEP −1
   vii. FOR K=27 TO −4 STEP −2
   viii. FOR M=−2 TO −33 STEP −5

3 If $A = 3$ and $B = -4$, answer the questions asked in Exercise 2 using these FOR statements.
   i. FOR Y=A TO B STEP −1
   ii. FOR Z4=B TO A STEP 2
   iii. FOR I=B TO 12 STEP A−1
   iv. FOR F9=A−B TO B−A STEP A+B

4 For the set of values given, write a FOR statement whose index takes on each value in the set using the order of the numbers as shown.

a. 1, 2, 3, 4, 5
b. 9, 10, 11, 12, 13, 14
c. 7, 9, 11, 13, 15, 17, 19
d. −2, −1, 0, 1, 2, 3
e. 5, 10, 15, . . . , 95

f. −11, −7, −3, . . . , 17
g. 16, 13, 10, 7, 4, 1
h. 150, 140, 130, . . . , 60
i. 81, 79, 77, . . . , −13
j. −5, −11, −17, . . . , −59

5 Find the output from each program listed.

a.

```
105 FOR J=1 TO 4
110    PRINT J↑2
115 NEXT J
120 END
```

e.

```
10 FOR H=1 TO 6
20    IF H<=4 THEN 40
30    PRINT "GOING"
40 NEXT H
50 PRINT "GONE"
60 END
```

b.

```
10 FOR S1=3 TO 8
20    LET S2=2*S1
30    LET S3=S2-3
40    PRINT S1,S2,S3
50 NEXT S1
60 END
```

f.

```
10 LET N=1
20 FOR J=1 TO 4
30    PRINT TAB(2*N-1);N+5
40    LET N=N+2
50 NEXT J
60 END
```

c.

```
10 FOR N=-3 TO -7 STEP -2
20    PRINT N+4
30 NEXT N
40 END
```

g.

```
10 LET A=2
15 LET B=8
20 FOR I=1 TO 6
25    IF I/2=INT(I/2) THEN 40
30    PRINT TAB(A);I
35    GOTO 45
40    PRINT TAB(B);I
45 NEXT I
50 PRINT TAB(B-A);A*B-5
55 END
```

d.

```
5 FOR D=.3 TO 1.6 STEP .3
10    LET X=D*.2
15    PRINT X,
20 NEXT D
25 END
```

h. To check the value of the index after completion of a loop, enter the program of Exercise 5a, add the line

```
118 PRINT J
```

and run the program.

6 What are the line numbers of the statements that constitute the body of loops found in the programs of Exercise 5?

7 Write a program using a FOR/NEXT loop that causes the even numbers from 6 to 22 inclusive, together with their squares, to be printed out.

8 Write programs using FOR/NEXT loops to find the following sums:

a. 1 + 3 + 5 + 7 + 9 + 11
b. 4 + 7 + 10 + . . . + 40
c. 17 + 13 + 9 + . . . + (−7) + (−11)
d. 5 + 10 + 15 + . . . + 200

9 A program is to be written that calculates and prints the average of six values that are entered from the terminal. Do any of the programs given perform this task? If not, explain why not.

a.

```
10 LET S=Ø
20 INPUT X
30 LET C=1
40 IF C>=6 THEN 90
50    INPUT X
60    LET S=S+X
70    LET C=C+1
80 GO TO 40
90 LET A=S/6
100 PRINT "AVERAGE=";A
110 END
```

c.

```
10 LET S=Ø
20 FOR C=1 TO 6
30    INPUT X
40    LET S=(S+X)/6
50 NEXT C
60 PRINT "AVERAGE=";S
70 END
```

b.

```
10 LET S=Ø
20 FOR C=1 TO 6
30    INPUT X
40    LET S=S+X
50 NEXT C
60 LET A=S/6
70 PRINT "AVERAGE=";A
80 END
```

d.

```
10 LET C=Ø
20 LET S=Ø
30    INPUT X
40    LET S=S+X
50    LET C=C+1
60 IF C<=5 THEN 30
70 LET S=S/C
80 PRINT "AVERAGE=";S
90 END
```

10   Write a program that prints out, in the form of a two-column table, relationships between speeds measured in miles per hour and in feet per second. The first column of the table should show miles per hour from 0 to 60 in increments of 5. The second column should show the corresponding speeds in feet per second.

11   Write a program that gets a number X from the terminal and then calculates X^{10} *without using exponents.*

12   Modify the program of Example 12.12 so that, after the table is printed, the number of semiskilled and the number of skilled workers that will produce maximum profit is also printed.

13   Modify the program of Example 12.17 so that the output also prints out the model that was used the least.

14   The formula $C = P(1 + R)^N$, used in Chapter 8, is actually a simplified version, of the formula $C = P(1 + R/T)^{NT}$, where T is the number of times the interest is compounded each year. For this problem, suppose that the principal is $500 and that the interest rate is 5.5%. Show, in table form, the amount accumulated for varying compounding schemes. The values of T to use are 1, 2, 3, 4, 6, and 12. Let the values of N go from 1 to 25 in steps of 3.

15   A radio station was searching for a publicity gimmick it could use to increase the number of its listeners. One suggestion that was made was to have a money giveaway. The station would have a certain amount of money in a "daily jackpot." The radio station would telephone someone at home and if that person knew the amount in the jackpot, that person would win it. The amount in the jackpot should be different from the day before, and to keep listeners' attention, the amount should increase each day. One suggestion for the amount of money was to start with 50 cents on the first day, and for each day after, the amount in the jackpot would be double the amount of the previous day. Assume a 30-day month and write a program that would show how much money would be in the jackpot each day. Your output should be in two columns, the first being labeled "DAY" and the second "JACKPOT". You should first draw a flowchart for the problem.

16   Write a program that prints out the integers from 10 to 99 inclusive, and on the same line as the integer, the sum of the digits of the integer should be printed. You should use nested loops to generate the digits of the number: one loop for the first digit and one for the second.

17 The Numbercrunch Computer Company wishes to employ J & A Consulting for a job that is expected to last 30 days. Numbercrunch offers J & A a fee of $1200 per day. J & A makes the following counteroffer: the salary for the first day is 1 cent ($.01), 2 cents on the second day, 4 cents on the third, and so on, each day doubling the salary of the previous day. Write a program that shows, in table form, the comparative money flow from each payment method. The first column should show the day number, the second should show the total amount accumulated by the computer company method, the third should show the amount being paid to J & A (by J & A's method) that day, and the fourth should show the total amount accumulated (by J & A's method). The output should look something like this:

DAY	NUMBERCRUNCH TOTAL	J & A DAILY	J & A TOTAL
1	1200	.01	.01
2	2400	.02	.03
–	–	–	–
–	–	–	–
–	–	–	–

18 A piece of cardboard is .01 inches thick. It is to be folded in half 15 times in succession. Obviously each fold will produce a thickness that is twice as thick as the previous one. Print out the thickness of the cardboard after each fold from 1 to 15 inclusive. Have the thickness labeled with the appropriate physical dimension—that is, begin with "inches" and change to "feet" if necessary.

19 Write a program that finds the *smallest* value of a set of 25 numbers. The numbers should be read from DATA lines (make up your own). After each of the first 24 numbers is read, the value of the current, smallest value should be printed. After the last value is read, the message "the absolute minimum is" should be printed along with the least value.

20 Write a program that prints a row of 30 X's starting at print position number 15.

21 Write a program that prints a rectangle of X's with ten rows. Each row should contain 30 X's and start at print position 15 (see Exercise 20).

22 Write programs to print out the following designs.

a.   b.   c.

```
* * * * * *           * * * * * *           XXXXXXXXX
*         *                    *                  SHIFT
*         *                      *                SHIFT
*         *                        *              SHIFT
* * * * * *                          *            SHIFT
                                       *          SHIFT
                            * * * * * *

              * * *
```

23 The Volunteer Marching Band, from Liberty, Pennsylvania, has been invited to take part in a national competition in Denver, Colorado. Members of the band, together with the managers, total 95 people. It is expected that some relatives and friends will want to attend the competition. The band has contacted a charter airline company that will supply a 175-seat airplane. If the plane is filled, the charge for the round trip is $165 per person. However, for each unfilled seat, the airline charges an extra $7.50. The total charge for the unfilled seats is divided equally among the passengers and is added to their cost. Write a program that displays each passenger's cost as the number of unfilled seats decrease from 80 to 0.

24 At the end of each term, Mrs. Samuelson, principal of Ferndale High School, requests a report on each subject. The report should show the subject, the total number of grades given in the subject, and the percentage of those grades that were passing grades. A program should be written to perform this task. The data for each subject is in three parts: the subject, the number of passing grades, and the number of failing grades. Test your program with the data given. You should use an eod tag. The percentage figure should be rounded to the nearest hundredth.

Subject	Pass	Fail
General Math	95	65
Literature	112	32
Programming	75	25
History	125	12
Chemistry	50	30
Algebra II	93	31
French	84	7
Accounting	64	11
Composition	134	29

25 A meteorology class had a project to find the average weekly temperature for each week of each month. These temperatures were then to be averaged to give a monthly average. The information for a given month is typed into a single DATA line. A DATA line might look like

    DATA MARCH,5,36.7,40,1,33.8,43.9,48.7

where the first item is the month, the second item is the number of weeks in that month, and the remaining values are the average weekly temperatures. Write a program that reads the data and prints the month and the average temperature for that month.

The data that were compiled by the meterology class were typed in the order in which they were gathered. So, as you can see from the data given, the months are not in the correct order. For the program, disregard this difficulty. The data collected were

    MARCH,5,36.7,40.1,33.8,43.9,48.7
    APRIL,4,47.3,45.2,50.6,56.2
    AUGUST,4,82.3,91.4,88.1,87.5
    NOVEMBER,4,53.2,49.8,43.7,41.9
    SEPTEMBER,5,82.1,75.6,72.1,68.4,62.3
    JANUARY,5,32.4,30.6,38.4,33.1,32.1
    JULY,5,78.1,72.4,77.3,79.2,77.5
    DECEMBER,4,40.6,42.4,35.8,34.1
    JUNE,4,68.3,71.2,70.3,75.5
    OCTOBER,4,65.1,59.2,58.6,52.9
    FEBRUARY,4,28.4,26.5,23.2,29.9
    MAY,4,58.3,50.2,60.7,63.0

26 The output from Exercise 25 would be much nicer if it were printed in the usual order of months: January to December. Modify the program of Exercise 25 to do this. (Suggestion: Just before each DATA line that you used, type another DATA line that contains only a single number—a number that corresponds to the month. For instance, if you had

440 DATA SEPTEMBER,etc.
450 DATA JANUARY,etc.

you would add

435 DATA 9
445 DATA 1

Now check these new data values with the index of your loop.)

27 Write a program to produce the following output. Your program should use the line

DATA A,B,C,D,E

A
BB
CCC
DDDD
EEEEE

28 Use the same DATA statement as Exercise 27 and write a program to produce

A
AB
ABC
ABCD
ABCDE

29 One way to approximate the value of π is to use the formula for $\pi/2$:

$$\pi/2 = \frac{2}{1} \cdot \frac{2}{3} \cdot \frac{4}{3} \cdot \frac{4}{5} \cdot \frac{6}{5} \cdot \frac{6}{7} \cdot \frac{8}{7} \cdots$$

This formula uses an infinite number of terms. We will use only a small, finite number, say, 15. Since the formula gives a value for $\pi/2$, if we double that value, we will get a value for π. Write a program to approximate π by this method. All 15 successive approximations should be printed.

30 Another approximation for π can be obtained by using the formula

$$\pi/4 = 1 - \frac{1}{3} + \frac{1}{5} - \frac{1}{7} + \frac{1}{9} - \cdots$$

Use 20 terms and print out all 20 approximations.

31 Refer to the cardboard folding problem (Exercise 18). Change it in the following way. The user should be allowed to enter the number of folds to be made. In addition to "inches" and "feet," the program should convert the thickness to "miles" if necessary. Run the program three times: for 9 folds, 15 folds, and 30 folds.

32 Modify the output of the program in Exercise 31 so that if a thickness in feet were printed, it would be instead changed to feet and inches and then printed. For example, instead of printing "4.25 FEET", the program should print "4 FEET 3 INCHES". A similar modification should change miles to miles, feet, and inches. Run the program for the same three values.

33 If a person pays back in full an installment loan before the final payment is due, he is due a refund on the unearned interest on the loan. A common method of calculating this refund is called the *rule of 78*. The name of the method comes from a hypothetical situation of a 12-month loan. The sum $1 + 2 + 3 + \cdots + 11 + 12$ equals 78. If the loan is for 12 months, the interest in the first month is 12/78 of the total amount of interest due. The interest due in the second month is 11/78 of the total. This pattern continues until the amount of interest which is paid in the final (twelfth) month is one seventy-eighth of the total.

a. Write a program that has the user supply the total amount of interest due and then have the program print out a table that shows the number of the payment (1 through 12) and the amount of interest due in that month. Run the program several times using for interest the values 156, 316, 908.38, and 1,500.

b. If the loan is for more than one year, a similar method of repayment is used. For example, if the loan is for three years, 36 monthly payments will have to be made. The denominator of each of the 36 fractions is the sum of the numbers 1, 2, . . . , 36—namely, 666. The interest payments would be 36/666 of the interest, 35/666 of the interest, and so on. The program should request of the user the total amount of interest and the number of monthly payments. The output should be in the form mentioned in part (a). (You will find it helpful to use the formula $s = n(n + 1)/2$, where n is the total number of payments and s is the sum $1 + 2 + 3 + \cdots + n$.) For data try

Number of Payments	Total Interest
12	$ 908.36
24	3566.48
30	562.25
60	2322.18

34 Several polynomial functions are listed here. Approximate where the graph of each function crosses the x axis by finding two consecutive x values such that the corresponding function values differ in sign. A set of x values to be used with each function is given.

Function	x Values
a. $f(x) = 4x^2 - 8x - 21$	$-5, -4, -3, \ldots, 4, 5$
b. $f(x) = x^2 - x$	$-1, -.9, -.8, \ldots, 1.3, 1.4$
c. $f(x) = x^3 + x^2 - 8x - 1$	-5 to 4 with steps of 1
d. $f(x) = x^3 + x^2 - 8x - 1$	-5 to 4 with steps of .5

One-Dimensional Arrays

The variables that have been used so far in this text are called simple variables. Simple numeric variables were introduced in Chapter 3 and simple string variables in Chapter 7. By the way each type was described, there are 286 simple numeric variables and 26 simple string variables.[1] These numbers have certainly been adequate for any of the programs we have had to write. In fact we have been able to *process* large numbers of data items using only a single simple variable (recall the averaging of an unknown number of values). However the number of values *stored* during any program's execution has been small. To store, say, 100 values would require the use of 100 different variables, and it is not hard to see how cumbersome that would be. In this chapter, we will begin an easy way to accomplish this task. In addition, there are certain problems, even of a fairly simple nature, that can be at least awkward if we are limited to the use of simple variables. For instance, a program to count 6 different kinds of objects can certainly be written using only simple variables. How about counting 20 different objects? Yes, it still can be done with simple variables, but usually not easily. In this chapter we shall see a way to do a job like this simply. A program used to calculate the retirement pay of an employee might need to refer to a table containing retirement data. Such processing will also be discussed in this chapter.

13.1 Subscripted Variables in Mathematics and BASIC

Suppose that we have the four values 15, 29, 23, and 34 that we wish to assign to variables. In mathematics we could do something like

$$a = 15$$
$$b = 29$$
$$c = 23$$
$$d = 34$$

[1] Versions of BASIC that define variable names differently will have a different number of simple variables available.

Similarly, these four values could be assigned to the variables A, B, C, and D by using a LET, INPUT or READ. If it were done by a READ, we would have statements like

```
100 READ A,B,C,D
110 DATA 15,29,23,34
```

Instead of using *a*, *b*, *c*, and *d* as the variable names, the assigning of the four values could have been done by

$$x_1 = 15$$
$$x_2 = 29$$
$$x_3 = 23$$
$$x_4 = 34$$

where x_1 (read "*x* sub one"), x_2, x_3, and x_4 are *subscripted variables* and the number written in the lower right-hand corner beside each *x* is called its *subscript*.

The numbers 15, 29, 23, and 34 may be thought of as a collection whose *first* value is 15 (and so will be assigned to the variable whose subscript is 1), second value is 29, third is 23, and fourth is 34. It is easier to name 25 variables using subscripted variables (x_1, x_2, . . . , x_{25}) than it is to use simple variables (*a*, *b*, . . . , *y*), and it is much easier when you want to name 65 variables: x_1, x_2, . . . , x_{65}; with simple variables, how would you do it?

In BASIC, subscripting is accomplished by enclosing the subscript in parentheses following the letter. Thus the mathematical subscripted variable x_1 would be written in BASIC as X(1). It should be noted that X1 and X(1) are different *kinds* of variables: the first is a simple variable, while the second is a subscripted variable. The importance of the distinction will shortly be made clear.

The following two programs will accomplish exactly the same thing.

```
10 READ A,B,C,D          10 READ X(1),X(2),X(3),X(4)
20 PRINT A,B,C,D         20 PRINT X(1),X(2),X(3),X(4)
30 DATA 15,29,23,34      30 DATA 15,29,23,34
40 END                   40 END
```

It is certainly clear that less typing would be involved in the first program than in the second. So why bother about subscripted variables? The versatility of subscripted variables lies in the fact that *their subscripts may be variables*. So the four values could be read in and printed, using a loop, as in the following program.

```
5 FOR I=1 TO 4
15  READ X(I)
25  PRINT X(I),
35 NEXT I
45 DATA 15,29,23,34
55 END
```

The first time through the loop the variable that is read and printed is $X(1)$, since $I=1$. The second time through the loop, $X(2)$ is processed; the third time it is $X(3)$, and the fourth time it is $X(4)$. This is an example of a very important concept that should be remembered when you are reading or debugging a program that uses subscripted variables—at any given place in a program, the subscript is a *number* and *not a letter*. In the program just given, the subscript is a variable I that takes on a different *value* each time through the loop.

The power of the subscripted variable should be easily seen when you consider how easy it would be to write a program to read and print the values of 65 subscripted variables as opposed to a program that used 65 simple variables.

A collection of singly subscripted variables is called a *one-dimensional array* or sometimes a *list*. $X(1)$, $X(2)$, $X(3)$, and $X(4)$ comprise an array. The *name* of the array is the common letter shared by all the subscripted variables, and each subscripted variable is called an *element* of the array. X is the name of an array, and $X(1)$, $X(2)$, $X(3)$, and $X(4)$ are its elements. As mentioned earlier, the subscript indicates the position of the particular element in the array. The subscript 3 indicates that $X(3)$ is the third element in the array X. (The subscripts in no way indicate the relationship between the values of the subscripted variables, but only indicate *where* in the array the value appears.)

Since an array is a collection of variables, it may also be thought of as a collection of memory locations. Each element of an array—that is, each subscripted variable—is an individual memory location. If X is the array with elements $X(1)$, $X(2)$, $X(3)$, and $X(4)$, we may envision a part of the computer's memory as

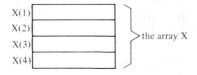

The preceding observations about arrays and their elements will be seen and expanded upon in the following examples.

EXAMPLE 13.1

13.2 Some Examples

```
101 FOR I=1 TO 7
111    READ A(I)
121 NEXT I
131 PRINT A(6),A(2),A(5)
141 DATA 4,9,0,8,7,-2,1
151 END

RUN

-2              9              7

READY
```

The program uses seven subscripted variables A(1), A(2), . . . , A(7), and after the loop has been executed we would have in memory

A(1)	4
A(2)	9
A(3)	$\emptyset$
A(4)	8
A(5)	7
A(6)	-2
A(7)	1

array A

Line 131 causes the values of three elements of A to be printed—these elements are referenced by their subscripts.

EXAMPLE 13.2. Here are two programs that add five numbers and print the sum.

```
10 LET A=0                10 LET A=0
15 FOR N=1 TO 5           15 FOR N=1 TO 5
20    READ B              20    READ B(N)
25    LET A=A+B           25    LET A=A+B(N)
30 NEXT N                 30 NEXT N
35 PRINT "SUM IS";A       35 PRINT "SUM IS";A
40 DATA 7,2,-3,1,4        40 DATA 7,2,-3,1,4
45 END                    45 END
```

Each program will produce exactly the same output:

RUN

SUM IS 11

READY

Although the output produced is the same, a significant difference between the programs appears in the way the data is read in. The first program uses only one variable (the *simple* variable B); the second program uses five *subscripted* variables B(1), B(2), B(3), B(4), and B(5). If the data were needed for additional processing, in the first program it would be necessary to RESTORE, READ again, and process while in the second program, *since all the values are stored in memory* processing could occur immediately without RESTOREing and additional READing.

EXAMPLE 13.3. A program is to be written that calculates and prints the average of nine values, read from DATA lines, and prints out those values that are less than the average.

This program is very much like the savings accounts problem of Example 10.13. However, since we will use subscripted variables in this program, once the values have been read, they are stored in memory and can be processed a second time (for the comparison with the average and the printing).

```
100 REM SUBSCRIPTED VARIABLES IN PROGRAM
110 REM TO AVERAGE AND PRINT VALUES BELOW AVERAGE
120 LET S=0
130 FOR K=1 TO 9
140    READ N(K)
150    LET S=S+N(K)
160 NEXT K
170 LET A=S/9
180 PRINT "THE AVERAGE IS";A
190 PRINT
200 PRINT "THE NUMBERS BELOW THE AVERAGE ARE"
210 FOR J=1 TO 9
220    IF N(J)>=A THEN 240
230    PRINT N(J)
240 NEXT J
250 DATA 45,87.9,23.6,122,76.7,44.4,60.1,89,6.34
260 END

RUN

THE AVERAGE IS 61.6711

THE NUMBERS BELOW THE AVERAGE ARE
 45
 23.6
 44.4
 60.1
 6.34

READY
```

The index of the first loop is K—yet J was used as the index of the second loop. This causes absolutely no problems since a subscript should always be viewed as a number. It makes no difference if the *number* is the *value* of the variable K or the variable J.

EXAMPLE 13.4. A survey was taken to find out which of six toothpastes tasted best. Samples of each toothpaste were sent to hundreds of college dormitories. The toothpaste tubes were labeled with only one of the numbers 1, 2, 3, 4, 5, or 6 and so the raw data from the survey are a collection of 1's, 2's, 3's, 4's, 5's, and 6's. A program is to be written to process the survey results that are entered on DATA lines. The number 0 is placed after all the survey data as an eod tag. The program should count the number of people who favored toothpaste number 1, the number who favored number 2, and so on. The output should show the total number of people surveyed and then, in table form, the toothpaste number, the number of people who preferred that toothpaste, and what percentage of the total that number is.
The problem is essentially a counting one (and was briefly mentioned

at the start of this chapter). Six different objects (the numbers 1 to 6) are to be counted and so six different counting variables are needed. We might choose C1, C2, C3, C4, C5, and C6. A rough algorithm might be

1. Initialize all counters to $\emptyset$.
2. Read a number N.
3. If N=$\emptyset$ transfer to step 7.
4. Check N against the numbers 1 through 6 and increase the appropriate counter by 1.
5. Read a number N.
6. Transfer to step 3.
7. Add the six counters, call the sum S.
8. Print S.
9. Print the numbers 1 through 6, the values of the six counters and the corresponding percentages.

Step 4 could be accomplished by something like the sequence

```
IF N=1 THEN LET C1=C1+1
IF N=2 THEN LET C2=C2+1
IF N=3 THEN LET C3=C3+1
IF N=4 THEN LET C4=C4+1
IF N=5 THEN LET C5=C5+1
IF N=6 THEN LET C6=C6+1
```

or by the use of an ON-GOTO statement. However, instead of using the simple variables C1 through C6 as our counters, we will use the subscripted variables C(1), C(2), . . . , C(6) to do the counting. C(1) will count the 1's, C(2) the 2's, and so on. If N is the variable used to read a data value, then the value of N will be one of the numbers 1, 2, 3, 4, 5, or 6. *So C(N) is the counter for the particular value of N.* After a value of N is read, we increase C(N) by 1—there is no need for conditional statements nor transfer statements.

The summing of the six counters specified in step 7 can be done with a loop similar to that of Example 13.2.

The output of the table (step 9) can be easily accomplished with a loop because of our use of subscripted variables.

All these ideas are incorporated in the program that follows.

```
100 REM  TOOTHPASTE  SURVEY  RESULTS
110 REM  SIX  BRANDS  (NUMBERED  1  -  6)  TESTED
120 REM
130 REM  EOD  TAG  IS  Ø
140 REM
150 REM  ARRAY  C  USED  FOR  SIX  COUNTERS
160 REM
170 REM  INITIALIZE  ALL  COUNTERS
180 FOR  I=1  TO  6
190    LET  C(I)=Ø
200 NEXT  I
210 READ  N
```

```
220 IF N=Ø THEN 26Ø
230    LET C(N)=C(N)+1
240    READ N
250 GOTO 220
260 REM S IS TOTAL PEOPLE SURVEYED - SUM OF COUNTERS
270 LET S=Ø
280 FOR I=1 TO 6
290    LET S=S+C(I)
300 NEXT I
310 PRINT S;"PEOPLE WERE SURVEYED."
320 PRINT
330 REM P IS PERCENTAGE OF TOTAL
340 PRINT "NUMBER", "PREFERRED BY", "PERCENTAGE"
350 FOR I=1 TO 6
360    LET P=C(I)/S*100
370    PRINT I,C(I),P
380 NEXT I
390 DATA 1,5,4,3,6,2,2,4,5,4,2,1
391 DATA 3,5,3,2,4,4,5,6,1,3
392 DATA 4,5,4,3,6,4,2,4,1
393 DATA 2,3,5,1,1,1,6,4
394 DATA 1,6,6,2,6
395 DATA 1,5,2
398 DATA Ø
399 END

RUN

  47 PEOPLE WERE SURVEYED
```

NUMBER	PREFERRED BY	PERCENTAGE
1	9	19.1489
2	8	17.0213
3	6	12.766
4	1Ø	21.2766
5	7	14.8936
6	7	14.8936

```
READY
```

13.3 The DIM Statement

A program is to be written that reads 20 values, assigns each to a subscripted variable, and calculates and prints the sum of the 20. For this purpose, consider the following program.

```
250 LET N=Ø
300 FOR I=1 TO 20
350    READ A(I)
400 LET N=N+A(I)
450 NEXT I
500 PRINT "THE SUM IS";N
550 DATA 2,3,4,5,6
```

```
600 DATA 1,3,5,7,9
650 DATA 8,6,4,2,10
700 DATA 9,8,7,6,3
750 END
```

When the program is executed, what would happen is something like

RUN

SUBSCRIPT ERROR AT LINE 350

READY

There seems to be nothing wrong with the program, and yet it results in an error message. We will try to find the problem by using an *echo check*, which is merely a PRINT statement inserted into the program to give some indication of what is happening at that place in the program. Usually an echo check will cause the values of one or more variables to be printed out. To create our echo check we will add the line

```
375 PRINT A(I),
```

This PRINT statement is inserted immediately following line 350 so that we may see the value that has just been read into the array A. Execution of the program with the echo check produces

RUN

2	3	4	5	6
1	3	5	7	9

SUBSCRIPT ERROR AT LINE 350

READY

The echo check shows that the first ten values have been processed and that the error occurred at the eleventh value. The error message indicates that the error was related to a subscript. The error can be eliminated by adding a single line to the program:

```
200 DIM A(20)
```

When this line is added the program will work exactly as expected and produce the desired output, namely,

RUN

THE SUM IS 108

READY

When the program contains an array the computer automatically allows the use of elements of that array (subscripted variables) with subscripts up to and including 10. However, if an array element is to be used that has a subscript greater than 10, the programmer *must* indicate to the computer the largest subscript that will be used. This is done by writing a DIM statement. When we write DIM A(2Ø), we are indicating that the subscripts for the elements of array A might be as large as 20 but will not exceed it. Our program ran into difficulties when the computer tried to read a value into the subscripted variable A(11). The previous values were processed without problems because each of their subscripts was 10 or less. As soon as the subscript reached 11, beyond the largest allowed, the computer terminated the processing, issued an error diagnostic, and stopped. By adding the statement DIM A(2Ø), this problem was overcome and the program was successfully completed.

Another way of viewing the DIM statement is to think of it as a statement that reserves memory locations. If an array is used in a program without a DIM statement, BASIC automatically sets aside or reserves 11 memory locations for the array. The 11 locations are for the 11 subscripted variables whose subscripts range from 0 to 10.[2] If your program is to use more than these 11 array elements, you must reserve enough memory locations for them. This is done with a DIM statement. So DIM A(2Ø) directs the computer to set aside 21 memory locations for the elements of the array A.

None of the programs of the previous section contained a DIM statement and since none of the subscripts used exceeded 10, we may conclude that, in one sense, the programs were correctly written. In another sense, it can be said that the programs were not correctly written. *It is a good programming practice to use a DIM statement whenever the program uses subscripted variables.* In a sense it is part of the program documentation—you are stating that subscripted variables are being used and you are indicating how large the array will be. This practice should be followed even when the largest subscript will not exceed 10. If you specify that a list will have six elements by the statement

```
1ØØ DIM X(6)
```

then the machine will no longer automatically reserve ten locations for your list since you have indicated that you only want six.

DIM is a short version of DIMENSION. You dimension an array when you reserve or DIMENSION memory for it. A single line may be used to dimension more than one array. For instance,

```
1Ø DIM X(5Ø),B(15),C(3Ø)
```

---

[2] Minimal BASIC defines 0 to be the smallest subscript for an array. Many systems do not follow this and, instead, have 1 as the smallest subscript. On those systems, ten memory locations are automatically reserved for an array (subscripts 1 through 10). Many systems also allow the use of a BASE statement that defines the smallest subscript (0 or 1) for all arrays in a particular program. Its form is "line number BASE Ø" or "line number BASE 1" and must be coded prior to any DIM statement in the program.

reserves 51 memory locations for the array X, 16 for B, and 31 for C. In a DIM statement, the value that is in parentheses must always be a constant—never a variable. So, for example, a statement such as

```
100 DIM Y(N)
```

is not allowed. The largest value you can use when dimensioning a list depends upon your computer—you should check it out.[3]

Since the subscript of a subscripted variable tells where in the list the particular variable occurs—$X(4)$ is the fourth value in the list X—the subscript must be an integer. However, it has already been noted that a subscript can be a variable or even an expression. If the value of an expression used as a subscript happens not to be an integer, the computer will automatically round it to become one. (This is another of those aspects of BASIC that depends on the particular computer system. Some computers will truncate the noninteger subscript rather than round it.)

It is a standard programming practice to *overdimension* the subscripted variables you use in a program. To overdimension a list means to dimension the list to a size that would guarantee at least as many subscripted variables as you would need. As an example, suppose that a program were to process the weekly salaries of your employees. You know that the number of your employees will never exceed 50. The beginning of such a program might look like

```
100 DIM S(50)
110 PRINT "HOW MANY EMPLOYEES THIS WEEK";
120 INPUT N
130 PRINT
140 PRINT "ENTER THE";N;"SALARIES,ONE AT A TIME"
150 PRINT
160 FOR I=1 TO N
170    INPUT S(I)
180 NEXT I
```

When running the program, most likely the value of N, which is the *actual* number of employees, will be less than 50, the *maximum* number that could be used with this program without changing line 100. If it did happen that the company expanded so that each week there are certainly more than 50 but, very likely less than 75, line 100 could be changed to

```
100 DIM S(75)
```

Overdimensioning will prevent your program from terminating due to a subscript error like that of the program that started this section. However good sense must be your guide in dimensioning. If you grossly

---

[3] You should also check to see if your computer is one of the few that requires a DIM statement whenever a subscripted variable is used, no matter what the largest subscript is.

overdimension, so much of the computer's memory could be used up as to make the completed execution of your program impossible.

Arrays can be created from other arrays as is shown in the next two examples.

EXAMPLE 13.5. Eight values are to be read into a list. A second list is to be constructed. Each element of the second list is to be the largest integer less than or equal to the corresponding number in the first list. A third list is to be made from the second by taking the absolute value of the corresponding values. After the three lists are completed, they should be printed out, side by side. (Recall that "list" is another name for a one-dimensional array.)

```
10 DIM A(8),B(8),C(8)
15 FOR Z=1 TO 8
20    READ A(Z)
25    LET B(Z)=INT(A(Z))
30    LET C(Z)=ABS(B(Z))
35 NEXT Z
40 PRINT "FIRST","SECOND","THIRD"
45 FOR I=1 TO 8
50    PRINT A(I),B(I),C(I)
55 NEXT I
60 DATA 6.7,-3.4,8,3.33,-5.99,5.99,23.001,45.5
65 END
```

RUN

FIRST	SECOND	THIRD
6.7	6	6
−3.4	−4	4
8	8	8
3.33	3	3
−5.99	−6	6
5.99	5	5
23.001	23	23
45.5	45	45

READY

EXAMPLE 13.6. The annual salaries of the 14 workers in the shipping department are entered into data lines. They are to be read into a list S. The average of the salaries is to be calculated and printed. A new list D is to be created whose elements will contain the difference of the corresponding salary from list S and the average. The two lists S and D will then be printed in two columns, side by side. The numbers in the second column should be printed with no leading minus signs but followed by the phrase "more than average" or "less than average."

The program will contain three loops. The first loop will read salaries into S and sum them (the average salary will be calculated at the end of this loop). The second loop will calculate the difference of a salary and the average and assign this result to an element of the list D. The final loop will generate the output table. The phrases "more than average" and "less than average" will be assigned to string variables and printed according to the value of an element in D. Since negative signs are not to be printed, the absolute value function will be used.

```
200 REM SHIPPING DEPARTMENT SALARIES
210 REM FOURTEEN WORKERS
220 REM
230 REM ANNUAL SALARIES READ INTO LIST S
240 REM A WILL BE AVERAGE ANNUAL SALARY
250 REM DIFFERENCES BETWEEN SALARIES AND AVERAGE INTO LIST D
260 REM
270 DIM S(14),D(14)
280 LET M$="MORE THAN AVERAGE"
290 LET L$="LESS THAN AVERAGE"
300 LET T=0
310 FOR W=1 TO 14
320    READ S(W)
330    LET T=T+S(W)
340 NEXT W
350 LET A=T/14
360 FOR W=1 TO 14
370    LET D(W)=S(W)-A
380 NEXT W
390 PRINT TAB(10);"SHIPPING DEPARTMENT SALARY REPORT"
400 PRINT
410 PRINT
420 PRINT TAB(10);"AVERAGE ANNUAL SALARY IS";A
430 PRINT
440 PRINT
450 PRINT
460 PRINT TAB(10);"SALARY";TAB(25);"DIFFERENCE"
470 PRINT
480 FOR W=1 TO 14
490    PRINT TAB(9);S(W);TAB(24);ABS(D(W));
500    IF D(W)<0 THEN PRINT L$
510    IF D(W)>0 THEN PRINT M$
520 NEXT W
530 DATA 12367.45,11589.66,17246.75,10009.41
540 DATA 14238.25,22679.15,13690.04,11876.50
550 DATA 14020.45,15372.33,16358.99,14532.07
560 DATA 15203.87,11745.00
600 END

RUN


              SHIPPING DEPARTMENT SALARY REPORT


          AVERAGE ANNUAL SALARY IS 14352.1
```

SALARY	DIFFERENCE			
12367.5	1984.69	LESS	THAN	AVERAGE
11589.7	2762.48	LESS	THAN	AVERAGE
17246.8	2894.61	MORE	THAN	AVERAGE
10009.4	4342.73	LESS	THAN	AVERAGE
14238.3	113.887	LESS	THAN	AVERAGE
22679.2	8327.01	MORE	THAN	AVERAGE
13690.	662.097	LESS	THAN	AVERAGE
11876.5	2475.64	LESS	THAN	AVERAGE
14020.5	331.687	LESS	THAN	AVERAGE
15372.3	1020.19	MORE	THAN	AVERAGE
16359.	2006.85	MORE	THAN	AVERAGE
14532.1	179.933	MORE	THAN	AVERAGE
15203.9	851.733	MORE	THAN	AVERAGE
11745	2607.14	LESS	THAN	AVERAGE

READY

Information stored in tables is frequently examined to obtain results or produce additional information. For example, a mileage table might be used to find the distance between two cities. The interest rate that will be used to calculate a mortgage might depend on the amount of the down payment. A table could contain various down payments and interest rates. A life insurance company uses tables showing persons' ages and corresponding premiums. The process of using such tables of data is frequently referred to as table look-up.

EXAMPLE 13.7. Your company stocks eight items coded by the numbers 1 through 8. The quantities on hand for each item are stored in DATA lines. A program is to be written so that the user can type in the code number of an item and be told how many of that item is available. In addition the user should be able to request information about other items if she chooses.

This problem illustrates direct access to the values stored in an array through the array subscripts. The eight values will be read into a table (array) and the user will be asked to enter an item code (1 through 8). The program will then print out the value of the array element whose subscript is the item code.

```
100 REM INVENTORY PROGRAM
110 REM EIGHT ITEMS NUMBERED 1 - 8
120 REM SUPPLY OF ITEMS READ INTO ARRAY S
130 DIM S(8)
140 FOR I=1 TO 8
150    READ S(I)
160 NEXT I
170    PRINT
180    PRINT "ENTER ITEM NUMBER"
190    INPUT N
200    PRINT
210    PRINT "ITEM NUMBER:";N
```

```
220    PRINT S(N);"IN STOCK"
230    PRINT
240    PRINT "ANY MORE REQUESTS?"
250    PRINT "YES OR NO";
260    INPUT A$
270 IF A$="YES" THEN 170
280 PRINT
290 PRINT "END OF PROGRAM"
300 DATA 67,46,9,112,14,32,23,56
310 END

RUN

ENTER ITEM NUMBER
? 7

ITEM NUMBER 7
 23 IN STOCK

ANY MORE REQUESTS?
YES OR NO ? YES

ENTER ITEM NUMBER
? 3

ITEM NUMBER 3
 9 IN STOCK

ANY MORE REQUESTS?
YES OR NO ? NO

END OF PROGRAM

READY
```

The program that follows illustrates the use of a table created by two arrays.

EXAMPLE 13.8. A person who has worked for the Apex Construction Company can retire after 20 or more years employment and receive a pension. The amount of the annual pension is a percentage of the worker's final annual salary. The percentage used to calculate the pension depends upon the number of years worked and is given by the table

Number of Years Employed	Percentage to Use
20–25	65%
26–30	70
31–34	75
35–38	79
39–42	82
43 or more	84

A program is to be written so that an employee's current annual salary and the number of years the employee has worked for the company are entered from the terminal, and then the program will calculate and print the employee's annual pension.

The largest number in each of the first five ranges of the years employed will be read into an array Y. The sixth range ("43 or more") will be considered as a special case if none of the previous ranges is used. The percentages, expressed as decimals, will be read into a six element array P. The variables for INPUT will be N (the number of years worked by the particular employee) and S (the most recent annual salary). The pension will be denoted R. An algorithm is

1. Read five values into array Y.
2. Read six values into array P.
3. Request N and S.
4. As I changes from 1 to 5 do the following:
     if $N \leq Y(I)$ transfer to step 6.
5. Set I=6.
6. Calculate R by S x P(I).
7. Print R.

```
500 REM APEX CONSTRUCTION PENSION PROGRAM
510 REM
520 REM Y: ARRAY WHICH CONTAINS 5 OF 6 EMPLOYMENT RANGES
530 REM P: ARRAY WHICH CONTAINS 6 RETIREMENT PERCENTAGES
540 REM N: NUMBER OF YEARS WORKED BY PARTICULAR EMPLOYEE
550 REM S: EMPLOYEE'S CURRENT ANNUAL SALARY
560 REM R: RETIREMENT SALARY (PENSION)
570 REM I: LOOP INDEX; SUBSCRIPT FOR RETIREMENT PERCENTAGES
580 REM
590 REM N WILL BE CHECKED AGAINST ELEMENT OF Y
600 REM IF N<=Y(I) TRANSFER OUT OF LOOP TO CALCULATE
610 REM R BY S*P(I)
620 REM IF LOOP FINISHED WITHOUT TRANSFER, NUMBER
630 REM OF YEARS EMPLOYED IS 43 OR MORE SO SET I=6
640 REM CALCULATE R AND PRINT R
650 REM
660 DIM Y(5),P(6)
670 FOR I=1 TO 5
680    READ Y(I)
690 NEXT I
700 FOR I=1 TO 6
710    READ P(I)
720 NEXT I
730 PRINT "HOW MANY YEARS EMPLOYED";
740 INPUT N
750 PRINT "WHAT IS CURRENT SALARY";
760 INPUT S
770 FOR I=1 TO 5
780    IF N<=Y(I) THEN 810
790 NEXT I
800 LET I=6
810 LET R=S*P(I)
```

```
820 PRINT "ANNUAL PENSION WILL BE $";R
830 DATA 25,30,34,38,42
840 DATA .65,.70,.75,.79,.82,.84
850 END

RUN

HOW MANY YEARS EMPLOYED? 26
WHAT IS CURRENT SALARY? 15000
ANNUAL PENSION WILL BE $ 10500

READY

RUN

HOW MANY YEARS EMPLOYED? 45
WHAT IS CURRENT SALARY? 20567.25
ANNUAL PENSION WILL BE $ 17276.5

READY

RUN

HOW MANY YEARS EMPLOYED? 34.5
WHAT IS CURRENT SALARY? 18900
ANNUAL PENSION WILL BE $ 14931

READY
```

13.4 Subscripted String Variables

Just as numeric variables can be subscripted, so can string variables. A subscripted string variable is merely a string variable followed by a subscript. So, for example, C$(5) is the name of a subscripted string variable that is the fifth element in the array C$.

The same rules that govern the use of subscripted numeric variables also relate to subscripted string variables.

EXAMPLE 13.9. The program that follows quizzes the user about the original 13 states of the United States. The names of the first 13 states are read into string array S$ in the order in which they were admitted to the Union. The capitals of the states are read into corresponding locations of the string array C$. The user will be asked a question about each state and its capital. If answered incorrectly the correct response will be given. Finally, the program counts and prints the number of correct answers.

```
100 DIM S$(13),C$(13)
110 PRINT "THIS IS A HISTORY QUIZ"
120 PRINT "YOU WILL BE ASKED TWO QUESTIONS ABOUT EACH"
130 PRINT "OF THE FIRST THIRTEEN STATES ADMITTED"
140 PRINT "TO THE UNION"
```

```
150 PRINT "THE FIRST QUESTION WILL BE ABOUT THE ORDER"
160 PRINT "IN WHICH EACH STATE WAS ADMITTED"
170 PRINT "THE SECOND WILL ASK FOR THE STATE'S CAPITAL"
180 PRINT
190 REM C COUNTS CORRECT ANSWERS
200 LET C=0
210 FOR I=1 TO 13
220    READ S$(I),C$(I)
230    PRINT "WHAT WAS STATE NUMBER";I
240    PRINT "ADMITTED TO THE UNION";
250    INPUT A$
260    IF A$=S$(I) THEN 290
270    PRINT "INCORRECT.THE CORRECT ANSWER IS ";S$(I)
280    GO TO 310
290    PRINT "CORRECT"
300    LET C=C+1
310    PRINT "NOW, WHAT IS THE CAPITAL OF ";S$(I);
320    INPUT B$
330    IF B$=C$(I) THEN 360
340    PRINT "INCORRECT.THE CAPITAL IS ";C$(I)
350    GO TO 380
360    PRINT "CORRECT"
370    LET C=C+1
380    PRINT
390 NEXT I
400 PRINT "YOU RESPONDED CORRECTLY";C;"TIMES."
410 DATA DELAWARE,DOVER,PENNSYLVANIA,HARRISBURG
420 DATA NEW JERSEY,TRENTON,GEORGIA,ATLANTA
430 DATA CONNECTICUT,HARTFORD,MASSACHUSETTS,BOSTON
440 DATA MARYLAND,ANNAPOLIS,SOUTH CAROLINA,COLUMBIA
450 DATA NEW HAMPSHIRE,CONCORD,VIRGINIA,RICHMOND
460 DATA NEW YORK,ALBANY,NORTH CAROLINA,RALEIGH
470 DATA RHODE ISLAND,PROVIDENCE
480 END


RUN


THIS IS A HISTORY QUIZ
YOU WILL BE ASKED TWO QUESTIONS ABOUT EACH
OF THE FIRST THIRTEEN STATES ADMITTED
TO THE UNION
THE FIRST QUESTION WILL BE ABOUT THE ORDER
IN WHICH EACH STATE WAS ADMITTED
THE SECOND WILL ASK FOR THE STATE'S CAPITAL

WHAT WAS STATE NUMBER 1
ADMITTED TO THE UNION? VIRGINIA
INCORRECT. THE CORRECT ANSWER IS DELAWARE
NOW, WHAT IS THE CAPITAL OF DELAWARE? WILMINGTON
INCORRECT. THE CAPITAL IS DOVER

WHAT WAS STATE NUMBER 2
ADMITTED TO THE UNION? PENNSYLVANIA
CORRECT
```

NOW, WHAT IS THE CAPITAL OF PENNSYLVANIA? PHILADELPHIA
INCORRECT. THE CAPITAL IS HARRISBURG

WHAT WAS STATE NUMBER 3
ADMITTED TO THE UNION? NEW JERSEY
CORRECT
NOW, WHAT IS THE CAPITAL OF NEW JERSEY? TRENTON
CORRECT

WHAT WAS STATE NUMBER 4
ADMITTED TO THE UNION? GEORGIA
CORRECT
NOW, WHAT IS THE CAPITAL OF GEORGIA? ATLANTA
CORRECT

WHAT WAS STATE NUMBER 5
ADMITTED TO THE UNION? NEW YORK
INCORRECT. THE CORRECT ANSWER IS CONNECTICUT
NOW, WHAT IS THE CAPITAL OF CONNECTICUT? HARTFORD
CORRECT

.
.
.

WHAT WAS STATE NUMBER 12
ADMITTED TO THE UNION? NORTH CAROLINA
CORRECT
NOW, WHAT IS THE CAPITAL OF NORTH CAROLINA? RALEIGH
CORRECT

WHAT WAS STATE NUMBER 13
ADMITTED TO THE UNION? RHODE ISLAND
CORRECT
NOW, WHAT IS THE CAPITAL OF RHODE ISLAND? PROVIDENCE
CORRECT

YOU RESPONDED CORRECTLY 19 TIMES.

READY

Example 13.10 demonstrates a search through a string array until a desired element is found and then information from other arrays printed.

EXAMPLE 13.10. Corrigan Airport is a small airport that handles seven flights daily. The information stored in DATA lines for each of the flights is

airline, flight number, destination, departure time, arrival time

A program is to be written to accept a destination, and if the destination can be reached by one of the seven flights, the information about that flight should be printed. If none of the seven flights is to the destination, an appropriate message should be printed.

Five arrays will be used: A$ for the airline name, F for the flight number, D$ for the destination, and L$ and G$ for departure time and arrival time, respectively. A destination will be entered from the terminal and checked against entries in D$. If a match is found, the corresponding entries from the other arrays will be printed. If there is no match, the message that there is no flight to that destination will be printed.

```
100 REM CORRIGAN AIRPORT FLIGHT DATA
110 REM
120 DIM A$(7),F(7),D$(7),L$(7),G$(7)
130 FOR I=1 TO 7
140    READ A$(I),F(I),D$(I),L$(I),G$(I)
150 NEXT I
160 PRINT "WHERE DO YOU WISH TO FLY";
170 INPUT W$
180 PRINT
190 FOR I=1 TO 7
200    IF W$=D$(I) THEN 240
210 NEXT I
220 PRINT "THERE ARE NO FLIGHTS TO ";W$
230 STOP
240 PRINT "DESTINATION: ";W$
250 PRINT A$(I);" FLIGHT NUMBER";F(I)
260 PRINT "DEPARTS AT ";L$(I)
270 PRINT "ARRIVES AT ";G$(I)
280 DATA WISPER,921,BIRMINGHAM,10:25 A.M.,1:50 P.M.
290 DATA AERO,143,NEW YORK,9:01 A.M.,11:52 A.M.
300 DATA FERGUSON,719,MIAMI,9:45 A.M.,2:23 P.M.
310 DATA TRANSLINE,263,NEWARK,4:15 P.M.,5:42 P.M.
320 DATA AERO,714,TYLER,1:32 P.M.,7:01 P.M.
330 DATA FEATHER,806,NORMAL,8:30 A.M.,11:30 A.M.
340 DATA TRANSLINE,303,KANSAS CITY,10:00 A.M.,1:15 P.M.
350 END


RUN


WHERE DO YOU WISH TO FLY? NORMAL

DESTINATION: NORMAL
FEATHER FLIGHT NUMBER 806
DEPARTS AT 8:30 A.M.
ARRIVES AT 11:30 A.M.

READY

RUN


WHERE DO YOU WISH TO FLY? LONDON

THERE ARE NO FLIGHTS TO LONDON

READY
```

Our final example of the chapter shows elementwise comparison of two arrays.

EXAMPLE 13.11.   The names, positions and batting averages of nine players on the Bears baseball team, entered on DATA lines, are to be read into arrays and the names printed out. The user is then to enter, by name, his choice for a batting order. When this has been done the batting order, as chosen by the user, should be printed out showing the player's position in the batting order, his name, position, and average.

N$ will be the array containing the original list of names, their positions will be stored in an array P$, while their batting averages will be read into the array A. The names entered from the terminal will be stored in the array L$.

After all information has been READ or INPUT, comparisons between elements of L$ and elements of N$ will be made using nested FOR/NEXT loops. Using the index (I) of the outer loop L$(I) will be checked against each of the nine names N$(J) as J changes from 1 to 9. When a match is found, transfer will be made out of the J loop to an output statement printing name, position, and average, and then the I loop will be continued.

```
100 REM BEARS BATTING ORDER
110 REM
120 REM******** VARIABLES ********
130 REM    N$: ORIGINAL LIST OF PLAYERS NAMES
140 REM    P$: POSITIONS OF PLAYERS
150 REM     A: PLAYERS BATTING AVERAGES
160 REM    L$: USER SUPPLIED BATTING ORDER
170 REM  I,J: LOOP INDICES
180 REM**************************
190 REM
200 REM PLAYERS NAMES DISPLAYED TO USER
210 REM BATTING ORDER CHOSEN BY USER BY PLAYER NAME
220 REM FULL INFORMATION ABOUT BATTING ORDER WILL BE DISPLAYED
230 DIM N$(9),P$(9),A(9),L$(9)
240 PRINT "YOUR ROSTER"
250 FOR I=1 TO 9
260    READ N$(I),P$(I),A(I)
270    PRINT N$(I)
280 NEXT I
290 PRINT
300 PRINT
310 PRINT "TYPE IN YOUR BATTING ORDER"
320 PRINT "ONE NAME AT A TIME"
330 FOR I=1 TO 9
340    INPUT L$(I)
350 NEXT I
360 FOR I=1 TO 4
370    PRINT
380 NEXT I
390 PRINT "ORDER","NAME","POSITION","AVERAGE"
400 PRINT
410 REM COMPARING LOOPS
420 FOR I=1 TO 9
430    PRINT I,
```

```
440    FOR J=1 TO 9
450       IF L$(I)=N$(J) THEN 470
460    NEXT J
470    PRINT N$(J),P$(J),A(J)
480 NEXT I
490 DATA PINA,PITCHER,.205
500 DATA FORSE, CATCHER,.298
510 DATA BATORD,1ST BASE,.313
520 DATA BINNEY,2ND BASE,.248
530 DATA COLE,3RD BASE,.278
540 DATA WATT,SHORTSTOP,.302
550 DATA SPENSER,RIGHT FIELD,.263
560 DATA MAREK,CENTER FIELD,.336
570 DATA ZIMMER,LEFT FIELD,.311
580 END

RUN

YOUR ROSTER
PINA
FORSE
BATORD
BINNEY
COLE
WATT
SPENSER
MAREK
ZIMMER


TYPE IN YOUR BATTING ORDER
ONE NAME AT A TIME
? WATT
? COLE
? MAREK
? BATORD
? FORSE
? ZIMMER
? SPENSER
? BINNEY
? PINA
```

ORDER	NAME	POSITION	AVERAGE
1	WATT	SHORTSTOP	.302
2	COLE	3RD BASE	.278
3	MAREK	CENTER FIELD	.336
4	BATORD	1ST BASE	.313
5	FORSE	CATCHER	.298
6	ZIMMER	LEFT FIELD	.311
7	SPENSER	RIGHT FIELD	.263
8	BINNEY	2ND BASE	.248
9	PINA	PITCHER	.205

```
READY
```

1 What is the output of each of the following?

a.

```
10 DIM T(6)
20 FOR I=1 TO 6
30    READ T(I)
40 NEXT I
50 FOR J=6 TO 2 STEP -2
60    PRINT T(J),
70 NEXT J
80 DATA 3,7,4,-1,0,5
90 END
```

b.

```
11 DIM B(6)
21 READ X
31 FOR A=3 TO X
41    READ B(A)
51 NEXT A
61 LET V=4
71 PRINT B(X),B(V+1)
81 DATA 6,2,0,1,8
91 END
```

c.

```
100 DIM D(15)
110 FOR L=1 TO 15
120    LET D(L)=L+3
130 NEXT L
140 READ M,N,R,S
150 FOR P=N TO S
160    PRINT D(P);
170 NEXT P
180 DATA 4,6,15,13
190 END
```

d.

```
200 DIM X(12)
205 FOR Z=1 TO 12
210    READ X(Z)
215 NEXT Z
220 FOR I=1 TO 6
225    LET Y(I)=X(2*I)+I
230 NEXT I
235 FOR T=3 TO 7
240    PRINT X(T+1),Y(T-1)
245 NEXT T
250 DATA 2,7,3,4,9,-3
255 DATA 6,-4,0,5
260 DATA -8,1
265 END
```

e.

```
100 DIM I(5),A(10)
110 FOR N=1 TO 5
120    READ I(N)
130 NEXT N
140 FOR N=I(4) TO J(5)
150    READ A(N)
160 NEXT N
170 FOR N=I(1) TO I(4) STEP - I(2)
180    PRINT A(N),
190 NEXT N
200 DATA 6,1,2,3,8,4
210 DATA -2,0,9,5,7
220 END
```

f.

```
10 DIM A(20)
15 FOR I=1 TO 15
20    LET A(I)=30-2*I
25 NEXT I
30 FOR J=1 TO 20
35    PRINT A(J/3+1),
40 NEXT J
45 END
```

g.

```
100 DIM R(8),S(8)
110 FOR I=1 TO 6
120    READ R(I)
130 NEXT I
140 FOR J=5 TO 1 STEP -1
150    LET S(J)=R(J+1)+R(J)
160 NEXT J
170 FOR I=2 TO 6
180    PRINT S(I-1)
190 NEXT I
200 DATA 3,7,8,-2,0,5
210 END
```

h.

```
190 DIM A(9)
200 FOR J=1 TO 7
210    READ A(J)
220 NEXT J
230 LET I=1
240 FOR J=2 TO 6
250    IF A(J-1)>=A(J) THEN 280
260    LET I=I+1
270 NEXT J
280 FOR V=1 TO I+2
290    PRINT A(V)
300 NEXT V
310 DATA 2,6,7,10,4,3,9
320 END
```

i.

```
200 DIM N$(10)
210 FOR C=1 TO 10
220    READ N$(C)
230 NEXT C
240 FOR J=1 TO 9 STEP 2
250    PRINT N$(J)
260 NEXT J
270 FOR T=2 TO 10 STEP 2
280    PRINT N$(T)
290 NEXT T
300 FOR I=1 TO 5
310    PRINT N$(I),N$(2*I)
320 NEXT I
330 DATA FIRST,SECOND,THEN,AFTER,SECOND
340 DATA FIRST,AND,BEFORE,THIRD,THIRD
350 END
```

j.

```
100 DIM X$(10),Y$(10)
110 FOR N=1 TO 10
120    READ X$(N)
130 NEXT N
140 LET C=0
150 LET K=4
160 FOR N=1 TO 10
170    READ A$
180    IF A$<=X$(K) THEN 210
190    LET C=C+1
200    LET Y$(C)=A$
210 NEXT N
220 PRINT C
230 FOR N=1 TO C
240    PRINT Y$(N)
250 NEXT N
260 DATA CHALK,STAMP,GLUE,PAPER,PEN
270 DATA MARKER,LIGHT,PENCIL,ERASER,PHOTO
280 DATA BLANK,PAPER,FISH,NAIL,HAMMER
290 DATA PHOTO,WALTZ,PEEK,COMMA,SHARP
300 END
```

2 Write a program that puts the first six positive odd integers into a list X. The defining word to use in the program is LET.

3 Read in a list T of 12 values. T should be printed in two rows. The first row should be the odd subscripted elements of T, and underneath, in the second row, the even subscripted elements of T should be printed.

4 Fifteen values are to be read into a list X. The words "original list" are to be printed and the list X is to be printed underneath. Finally the words "reversed list" are to be printed and under them the values of X in reverse order. For your program use the values 7, 9, 1, 0, −3, 0, 5, 6, 10, −1, 0, 4, 2, 8, and 7.

5 Two lists, R and S, each containing 20 values are to be created. The list R is to be read in. The values of S are to be the values of R, only in reverse order; that is, $S(1) = R(20)$, $S(2) = R(19)$, and so on. Then, only the list S should be printed. Use the numbers 1, 3, 5, 7, 9, 2, 8, 6, 4, 0, −1, −2, −3, −4, −5, 10, 20, 30, 99, and 15.

6 Ten values are to be read into a list W. The first value should be assigned to W(1Ø) and W(11), the second value to W(9) and W(12), and so forth until the tenth value is assigned to W(1) and W(2Ø). When this is done, the list W should be printed. For values use 5, 25, 10, −5, 0, 20, −15, 15, −5, and 10.

7 Fifteen positive integers are to be typed by the user into a list L. A second list M is to be defined in the following way: if an element of L is an even integer, set the corresponding element of M equal to that element of L; otherwise set the element of M equal to 0. Print out the lists L and M, side by side. Run your program three times using for data the sets:

Set 1:   4, 9, 0, 8, 3, 12, 14, 9, 1, 5, 8, 20, 11, 15,
Set 2:   2, 4, 6, 8, 10, 12, 20, 18, 16, 14, 12, 10, 30, 40, 50
Set 3:   91, 81, 71, 61, 51, 1, 3, 5, 7, 9, 11, 13, 23, 27, 31

8 Two lists, each with ten elements, are to be read in. A third list is to be created that contains the larger of the two corresponding elements from the original lists. The three lists are to be printed out next to each other. Finally, the average of the numbers in the third list should be calculated and printed. For data use

List 1:   2, 7, 0, 3, 10, −1, 15, 8, 20, 16
List 2:   5, 1, 0, 2, 15, 0, 6, 7, 2, 5

9 Lefty Bendt, a baseball player, first played in the major leagues in 1968 and played for 11 years. Each year he recorded his number of times at bat and his number of hits. Write a program that prints, in column form, Lefty's major league statistics. The column headings should look like

YEAR AT BATS HITS AVG

After the information is printed, Lefty's lifetime batting average should be printed. Also, the program should print his highest yearly batting average and the year it happened and the highest number of hits he got in a single year and the year that happened. (The hits should be read into a list and as each average is calculated, it should be put into a list). The data kept by Lefty are

Number of At Bats	Hits
153	34
185	40
198	55
217	79
228	80
239	84
252	82
265	77
255	87
291	89
276	79

10 Read in two lists A and B, each having 15 values. Create a new list C that *merges* the lists A and B in the following way: C = A_1, B_1, A_2, B_2, . . . , A_{15}, B_{15}. Print out the three lists in adjacent columns. For your lists try

A: 4, 1, 7, 3, −1, −2, 0, 5, 9, 11, −2, 5, 0, −1, 10
B: 3, 0, −6, 1, −2, −3, 4, 7, 9, 15, −1, 0, 10, 1, 6

11 Create a list of 12 values where each value is the square of the subscript: $X(1)=1$, $X(2)=4$, . . . , $X(12)=144$. Print out a two-column table whose first column contains the subscript values and whose second column contains the corresponding entry in the list X. Next type in a number, call it N. If $N<1$ or $N>12$ print OUT OF RANGE. If N^2 equals one of the values in X, print IN THE LIST. Otherwise, print the two-column table again, but insert the value of N in its correct place in the first column and the word HERE in the corresponding place in the second column. For example, if $N=4.1$, you should have

```
     .          .
     .          .
     .          .
     3          9
     4         16
     4.1       HERE
     5         25
     .          .
     .          .
     .          .
```

For values of N try -2, 7.6, 0, 300, 49, 4.9, 2.5, 139.

12 Write a program to create a computerized telephone directory for you. For each of your friends, a DATA line should contain your friend's name and telephone number. The program should request you to enter your friend's name and then it will print his or her telephone number. However, if the name you entered is not found in the data, a message to this effect should be printed.

13 A store carries several items made by different manufacturers. A DATA line will contain four pieces of information:

manufacturer, model number, number in stock, brief description of item.

Write a program to enter a manufacturer's name and then print all the information about all of the items produced by that manufacturer. Use the DATA lines

```
DATA GLOBAL,GW129,9,WALLET
DATA ROTH,X54,23,FILE CABINET
DATA AQUATITE,SS15,2,AQUARIUM
DATA GLOBAL,GK43,15,KEYCASE
DATA ELKER,AM253,5,PORTABLE RADIO
DATA PROLOOK,F8X11,30,PICTURE FRAME
DATA EXECO,PP2,12,PEN AND PENCIL SET
DATA GLOBAL,GC402,18,CHECKBOOK CALCULATOR
DATA ELKER,TR311,6,PERSONAL BEEPER
```

and entering GLOBAL as the manufacturer's name.

14 Write a program to create a list of not more than 25 words. The words are to be entered from the terminal, one at a time, until either the word DISPLAY or DONE is entered. If the word DISPLAY is entered, all the words entered thus far into the list should be printed, and when that has been done, the word entering should continue. If the word DONE is entered, the elements of the list should be printed in reverse order and the program stop.

15 An insurance company charges annual premiums according to certain age ranges. The company will not issue a policy, however, to a person age 75 or older. The age ranges and the corresponding premiums are given in the following table. Write a program to enter the age of an insurance applicant and how many thousand dollars worth of insurance the applicant wishes to purchase; then print the annual premium.

Age Range	Cost per $1000
Up to 25 (not including 25)	$15.35
25 to 40 (not including 40)	17.62
40 to 55 (not including 55)	28.90
55 to 65 (not including 65)	35.27
65 to 75 (not including 75)	41.88

* * *

16   Write a program to read 20 positive integers into a list called A. Then the program should examine the list A, one element at a time. The odd numbers in A should be put into a list named B, while the even numbers should be put into a list called C. Finally, the lists A, B, and C should be printed out next to each other in column form.

17   Read in two integers D and N. D will be the number of digits in N. The output should be a number whose digits are in the reverse order of those in N. (For example, if the values read were 4 and 7,326, the output should be 6237.) For data use 4 and 7,326, 3 and 581, 5 and 20,302, and 6 and 417,930.

18   The *count* of a positive integer is the number of zeroes it contains. For example the count of 73,810,304 is 2. Write a program to read seven numbers and print them out together with their counts. For data in your program use

    DATA 8034, 512, 6006, 5000000, 7, 102, 960

(No additional information concerning the number of digits for a given value should be supplied.)

19   A *numbér palindrome* is a number whose value is the same after its digits have been reversed. For example 303 is a palindrome while 162 is not. Write a program to determine whether or not a number is a palindrome. Try your program using 303, 162, 20,302, 5645, 12,345, and 8,998.

20   Write a program to change a positive integer to its base 2 equivalent. Try your program with 13, 24, 15, 32, and 33.

21   The *standard deviation* of a set of values is a quantity that is used in the area of statistics. To calculate the standard deviation
    a. Find the average of the values.
    b. Calculate the sum of the squares of the differences between the average and each value—that is, if m is the average of the values $x_1, x_2, x_3, \ldots$, the required sum is

$$(x_1 - m)^2 + (x_2 - m)^2 + (x_3 - m)^2 + \cdots$$

    c. Divide the sum obtained in (b) by one less than the number of values there are (for example, if there are 25 values, the sum would be divided by 24).
    d. The square root of the value obtained in (c) is the standard deviation.
    Write a program to calculate the standard deviation of a set of 25 values.

22   A *conjecture* is a statement that has neither been proved nor disproved. A famous mathematics conjecture is called *Goldbach's conjecture*. It claims that every even integer greater than 4 is the sum of two odd primes (for example, 12 = 5 + 7 and 20 = 3 + 17). Enter the first 25 odd primes into a list and use them to check Goldbach's conjecture for the even integers from 6 to 100.

23   The sequence of *Lucas numbers* is 2, 1, 3, 4, 7, 11, . . . , where the first two numbers are 2 and 1, respectively, and each succeeding number is the sum of the previous two (so the pattern, except for the beginning, is the same as that of the Fibonacci numbers, which begins with the numbers 1 and 1).

    a. Generate the first 100 Fibonacci numbers and put them into a list. Into another list put the first 100 Lucas numbers.

b. Print out the first 25 numbers from each list in a two-column table.

c. A *Fibolucas number* is a number that appears in both lists. Obviously 1, 2, and 3 are Fibolucas numbers. If a fourth Fibolucas number is among the first 100 values of each list, find it and print it followed by the word "success." If not, print the word "failure." (Note that your search should begin with the *fourth* value.)

24 Write a program to read in the two 6 × 1 column vectors shown. The sum of the two vectors and a scalar multiple of the first (use 3 as the scalar) should then be calculated. The four vectors should then be printed, next to each other, in column form.

```
  4    −1
  2     4
 −3     8
  5     6
  6    −6
```

25 The following illustrates a correspondence between values in the first row (*x*'s) and values in the second (*y*'s).

```
x:  1    3    4    7    8   10   11   14   17   19   20
y:  3   17   27   69   87  129  153  237  339  417  459
```

For an *x* value, call it *a*, that does not appear in the first row, an approximate *y* value, call it *b*, can be calculated using the formula

$$b = y_1 + \frac{(a - x_1)}{(x_2 - x_1)} \cdot (y_2 - y_1)$$

where x_1 and x_2 are the successive *x* values such that $x_1 < a < x_2$ and y_1 and y_2 are the values that correspond to x_1 and x_2. The formula is called an *interpolation* formula and *b* is an interpolated value. Write a program that reads a value and prints out the value and its corresponding interpolated value. For values, try 2.3, 8.01, 17.5, and 19.23.

26 The following program reads seven values into an array X and checks to see if any two consecutive values, X(J) and X(J+1), are equal.

```
100 FOR I=1 TO 7
110     READ X(I)
120 NEXT I
130 FOR J=1 TO 7
140     IF X(J)=X(J+1) THEN 180
150 NEXT J
160 PRINT "NO TWO CONSECUTIVE NUMBERS ARE EQUAL"
170 STOP
180 PRINT "THERE ARE TWO CONSECUTIVE NUMBERS WHICH ARE EQUAL"
200 END
```

When executed with the DATA line

```
190 DATA 3,7,2,2,1,0,5
```

the output would be

```
THERE ARE TWO CONSECUTIVE NUMBERS WHICH ARE EQUAL
```

and with

```
190 DATA 1,3,6,7,2,0,4
```

the output would be

    NO TWO CONSECUTIVE NUMBERS ARE EQUAL

However the DATA line

    19Ø DATA 4,6,7,Ø,2,3,Ø

produces

    THERE ARE TWO CONSECUTIVE NUMBERS WHICH ARE EQUAL

How did the error occur and what can be done to correct it?

27　The College of Hard Knocks has classes that meet on Mondays, Wednesdays, and Fridays or that meet on Tuesdays and Thursdays. All classes begin on the hour. A program is to be written that reads a student's schedule from a DATA line and prints it out in an easily read form similar to the one shown here. Each line of data shows the student's name and three pieces of information for each course in which the student is enrolled. The first of the three is the time the course starts; the second tells which days the course meets; the third is the abbreviated course name. For instance,

    1ØØØ DATA JOHN SMITH,9,M,MA1ØØ,11,T,PH223

says that John Smith is enrolled in MA100, which meets at 9 o'clock on Monday, Wednesday, and Friday, and also in PH223, which meets at 11 o'clock on Tuesday and Thursday. Each student at the college must enroll in five courses each term. Test your program for the four following students.

```
ROSALIE LOPEZ,8,M,CS101,9,M,EN100,11,T,BI210,12,M,MA105, 2,M,FR101
LEW JAMES,10,M,SO350,12,M,PY272,2,M,EC310,9,T,AN200,12,T,PE110
THOMAS LESS,8,M,MA202,12,M,PY100,10,T,MA301,9,T,CS332,11,M,PE115
MELINDA NELS,11,T,SP400,9,M,HI380,2,M,EN455,3,T,EN470,1,M,AC100
```

The schedule form should look like this:

```
          **COLLEGE  OF  HARD  KNOCKS**
               SCHEDULE  FOR
                student  name
          M       T       W       TH      F
     *************************************************
  8  *                                           *

  9  *                                           *

 1Ø  *                                           *

 11  *                                           *

 12  *                                           *

  1  *                                           *

  2  *                                           *

  3  *                                           *
     *************************************************
```

14

Frequently when writing programs you will find it necessary to have a group of statements executed many times. If this group of statements is to be repeated *at the same place* in the program, this is easily accomplished by putting the group of statements within a FOR/NEXT loop. However, it may happen that the program may require that the group of statements be executed *at different places* within the program. You can already do this by merely rewriting the same statements over again in the various places in the program where they are to be executed. This tedious task need not be done if you code the group of statements once, as a subroutine.

A *subroutine* is a group of statements usually written to perform a single activity that can be referenced (or transferred to) from any part of the program. The important feature of the use of a subroutine is that after transfer has been made to the group of statements that make up the subroutine and after the subroutine has been executed, there is an *automatic transfer back to the statement immediately following the statement that caused the transfer to the subroutine.*

To illustrate this, let's suppose that we write a subroutine that begins at line 500 and that is to be transferred to from lines 50, 180, and 270. Figure 14.1 illustrates this (the lines in the figure indicate programming statements).

The statement that causes transfer to a subroutine is GOSUB.

The *general form of GOSUB* is

line number   GOSUB   line number

where the line number *following* GOSUB is the line number of the first statement in the subroutine. Thus, in the illustration of Figure 14.1,

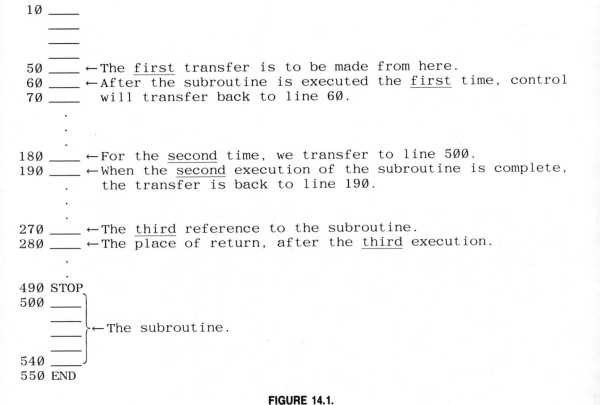

FIGURE 14.1.

we would find 50 GOSUB 500, 180 GOSUB 500, and 270 GOSUB 500. Each of these statements would cause transfer to be made to line 500. But what about this automatic "transfer back" feature?

In each subroutine there must be at least one RETURN statement. Normally, it is the last statement of the subroutine. So our diagram program should include 540 RETURN. When the computer encounters the RETURN statement, it will automatically return to the next statement in sequence after the GOSUB that caused transfer to the subroutine. To illustrate further the sequence of statements executed in our diagram of Figure 14.1, let's look at what happens at the key places in the program.

We first consider line 50. When it is executed, transfer is made to line 500 (the start of the subroutine) and then the usual sequence is followed (that is, 510, 520, 530) until the RETURN statement (line 540) is executed. At this point, transfer is made to line 60 (the line after 50). The normal sequence is followed until line 180 is executed. Then transfer to line 500 and execute it and lines 510, 520 and 530. Execute RETURN and go to line 190. The final sequence that is followed when the subroutine is used for the third time is 270, 500, 510, 520, 530, 540, 280, and so on.

Some other observations should be made about Figure 14.1. The bottom part is shown again (with RETURN entered as line 540).

```
270 ____
280 ____
      .
      .
      .
490 STOP
500 ____
    ____
    ____
540 RETURN
550 END
```

The statement just before the start of the subroutine (line 490) is a
STOP. This statement is necessary to prevent the subroutine from being
entered by other than a GOSUB. Imagine if line 490 were omitted.
The subroutine is referenced for the third time from line 270, the
subroutine is executed, and the RETURN brings us back to line 280.
Line 280 is executed, then 290, and the usual sequence continues. As
control continues down the program, we eventually reach line 500, execute it as well as 510, 520, and 530. Next we encounter line 540—
RETURN. It tells the computer to return to the statement right after
the GOSUB that transferred control to the subroutine. But this time
there was no GOSUB that did this. Lines 500 to 530 were executed
as a result of following the usual sequence of execution. So when line
540 is executed the *fourth* time, an error message[1] like the one shown
would be printed.

```
RETURN WITHOUT GOSUB AT 540
```

So you can see that the STOP statement of line 490 serves the purpose
of isolating the subroutine from the rest of the program and consequently
of preventing the computer from stopping the program due to an error.
    When a program is made up of one or more subroutines, those state-
ments that do not belong to any of the subroutines are together called
the main program.[2] So since subroutines are not considered part of
the main program, they are frequently termed *subprograms*. Subroutines
are *referenced, invoked,* or *called* from the main program or from other
subroutines.
    The second observation is related to the first. Notice where the
subroutine was placed—*after* the main program (and, of course, prior
to the END statement). This is not necessary. Subroutines can be written

---

[1] Similarly, on many systems a GOSUB statement that is not matched with a RETURN
statement would produce

```
GOSUB WITHOUT RETURN AT  some line number
```

[2] Another descriptive term for "main program" is *calling program.* This phrase is derived
from the FORTRAN command CALL, which is used (like GOSUB) to reference subprograms.

anywhere in your programs—however, they must be set off from the main program so that errors of the kind described earlier will not occur. One very easy way of accomplishing this is to use the standard convention of *writing subroutines at the end of programs and to precede them by a STOP statement.*

EXAMPLE 14.1. The following program prints out the heading for the payroll program used by the Simpson Lumber Company. It uses a subroutine that merely prints a row of stars for the heading. The subroutine is used three times.

```
10 GOSUB 200
20 PRINT TAB(24);"PAYROLL REPORT"
30 GOSUB 200
40 PRINT TAB(21);"SIMPSON LUMBER COMPANY"
50 GOSUB 200
60 STOP
200 REM SUBROUTINE TO PRINT LINES OF *'S
210 PRINT TAB(20);"*";
220 FOR I=1 TO 23
230   PRINT "*";
240 NEXT I
250 PRINT
260 RETURN
300 END
```

RUN

```
            * * * * * * * * * * * * * * * * * * * * * * *
                    PAYROLL  REPORT
            * * * * * * * * * * * * * * * * * * * * * * *
                SIMPSON  LUMBER  COMPANY
            * * * * * * * * * * * * * * * * * * * * * * *
```

READY

EXAMPLE 14.2. A subroutine is to be written that reduces a fraction to its lowest terms.

To reduce a fraction to lowest terms, the greatest common divisor (usually referred to as the "gcd") of both numerator and denominator must be found and then numerator and denominator are both divided by the gcd. The resulting fraction is reduced to lowest terms. One way of finding the gcd of two numbers is to start with the smaller of the two. If the smaller divides the larger, the smaller is the gcd. If not, decrease the smaller by 1 and attempt to divide both larger and smaller. Repeat this process until a division is possible. You should note that, if the largest number that divides numerator and denominator is 1, the fraction is already reduced.

We will use this process to reduce a fraction. We will assume that the values of the fraction's numerator, N, and denominator, D, have already been obtained in a main program. The gcd will be found, the

fraction reduced, and the reduced fraction printed. The coding for the
subroutine will begin at line 1000.

```
1000 REM SUBROUTINE TO REDUCE A FRACTION TO LOWEST TERMS
1010 REM N AND D ARE NUMERATOR AND DENOMINATOR
1020 REM REDUCED FRACTION WILL BE PRINTED
1030 REM S IS SMALLER OF N AND D, L IS LARGER
1040 REM G IS THE GCD
1050 IF N<D THEN 1090
1060 LET S=D
1070 LET L=N
1080 GOTO 1110
1090 LET S=N
1100 LET L=D
1110 REM CHECK TO SEE IF SMALL DIVIDES LARGE
1120 IF L/S<>INT(L/S) THEN 1150
1130 LET G=S
1140 GOTO 1220
1150 FOR I=S-1 TO 1 STEP -1
1160    REM CHECK IF I DIVIDES NUMERATOR
1170    IF N/I<>INT(N/I) THEN 1200
1180    REM CHECK IF I DIVIDES DENOMINATOR
1190    IF D/I=INT(D/I) THEN 1210
1200 NEXT I
1210 LET G=I
1220 REM CHECK IF FRACTION ALREADY REDUCED
1230 IF G>1 THEN 1260
1240 PRINT "YOUR FRACTION ";N;"/";D;" IS ALREADY REDUCED"
1250 RETURN
1260 REM REDUCE AND PRINT FRACTION
1270 LET N0=N/G
1280 LET D0=D/G
1290 PRINT "THE FRACTION ";N;"/";D;"REDUCES TO ";N0;"/";D0
1300 RETURN
```

It was previously stated that a subroutine must have at least one
RETURN—this one has two, which is certainly permissible since the
logic of the problem requires a return to the main program at two
different points in the subroutine.

EXAMPLE 14.3. A program is to be written that inputs the numerator
and denominator of two fractions, one fraction at a time. After each
fraction is entered, it should be reduced to lowest terms and printed
out. Then the original fractions should be added, the answer printed,
and the answer reduced to lowest terms should also be printed.

The main program will call the subroutine of Example 14.2 three
times. If the numerator and denominator of the first fraction are N1
and D1, respectively, and the second fraction's terms are N2 and D2,
the sum of the two fractions is found using the formula

$$\frac{N1}{D1} + \frac{N2}{D2} = \frac{N1 \times D2 + D1 \times N2}{D1 \times D2}$$

The variables used for numerators and denominators in the main program are different from those used in the subroutine, so before the subroutine is called, N and D (the terms in the subroutine) must be given the correct values.

```
100 REM ADDITION OF FRACTIONS AND REDUCING TO LOWEST TERMS
110 REM
120 REM FIRST FRACTION: N1-NUMERATOR;D1-DENOMINATOR
130 REM SECOND FRACTION: N2 AND D2
140 REM SUM FRACTION: T-NUMERATOR;B-DENOMINATOR
150 PRINT "ENTER NUMERATOR AND DENOMINATOR OF FIRST FRACTION"
160 INPUT N1,D1
170 LET N=N1
180 LET D=D1
190 GOSUB 1000
200 PRINT "ENTER NUMERATOR AND DENOMINATOR OF SECOND FRACTION"
210 INPUT N2,D2
220 LET N=N2
230 LET D=D2
240 GOSUB 1000
250 PRINT
260 LET T=N1*D2+D1*N2
270 LET B=D1*D2
280 PRINT "THE SUM IS ";T;"/";B
290 LET N=T
300 LET D=B
310 GOSUB 1000
320 STOP
1000 REM SUBROUTINE TO REDUCE A FRACTION TO LOWEST TERMS
  —
  —      (rest of subroutine goes here)
  —
1300 RETURN
1310 END

RUN

ENTER NUMERATOR AND DENOMINATOR OF FIRST FRACTION
? 8,12
THE FRACTION 8 / 12 REDUCES TO 2 / 3
ENTER NUMERATOR AND DENOMINATOR OF SECOND FRACTION
? 1,12
YOUR FRACTION 1 / 12 IS ALREADY REDUCED

THE SUM IS 108 / 144
THE FRACTION 108 / 144 REDUCES TO 3 / 4

READY

RUN

ENTER NUMERATOR AND DENOMINATOR OF FIRST FRACTION
? 7,20
```

YOUR FRACTION 7 / 20 IS ALREADY REDUCED
ENTER NUMERATOR AND DENOMINATOR OF SECOND FRACTION
? 3,8
YOUR FRACTION 3 / 8 IS ALREADY REDUCED

THE SUM IS 116 / 160
THE FRACTION 116 / 160 REDUCES TO 29 / 40

READY

Before the first call to the subroutine at line 190, N and D must be given the values of the numerator and denominator to be reduced in the subroutine. This is done in lines 170 and 180. Similar assignments, for the same reason, occur in lines 220 and 230 as well as in lines 290 and 300.

14.2 The Flowcharting Symbols

When flowcharting a subroutine, two symbols are used. The first symbol is [ ] and is used in the main program to indicate that transfer to the subroutine is to take place. It corresponds to the GOSUB statement.

The other symbol used with subroutines is the oval (the terminal symbol). Like a main program, it is used to indicate the beginning (or entry) and the end of a subprogram.

The first line number of the subroutine is written in the top part of the symbol corresponding to GOSUB, [1000], and inside the oval that begins the subroutine, (1000). The oval depicting an exit from a subroutine will be drawn (RETURN)

When drawing a detailed flowchart, both of the symbols [ ] and (RETURN) will be assigned line numbers, but the oval at the beginning (for example, the (START) at the beginning of the main program) will not.

The use of the new flowcharting symbols will be illustrated by flowcharting the program of Example 14.1, which printed out a heading for the Simpson Lumber Company. Since main programs and subprograms are considered separate entities, their flowcharts are drawn sepa-

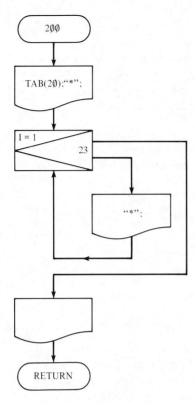

FIGURE 14.2.

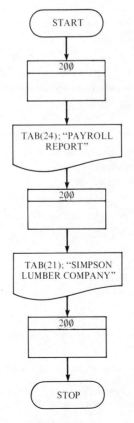

FIGURE 14.3.

rately. The flowchart for the subroutine to print the *'s is shown in Figure 14.2.

The number in the $\left(2\varnothing\varnothing\right)$ symbol is the starting line number

of the subroutine. The number is entered solely for identification purposes in case a program contained several subroutines. In fact it is a common practice to code the first line of a subroutine as a REM briefly describing what the subroutine does.

The flowchart for the main program is shown in Figure 14.3.

Here in the main program the symbol ⎡2ØØ⎤ means "transfer

to the subroutine starting at line 200."

14.3 Modules and Top-Down Programming

Example 10.13 presented a program that calculated the average of a collection of savings account balances and then counted how many of the accounts contained greater than the average amount. We will now consider this problem and include subroutines in its solution.

There is another significant use of subroutines in addition to making a collection of programming statements accessible from various parts of a program. Frequently, the solution to a problem involves solving several smaller problems. These "smaller problems" may be coded as subroutines, and the main program will then consist mostly of GOSUBs. This technique is a common one (especially useful for large, complicated problems): break the large problem into several smaller ones, solve the smaller ones in subroutines, and unify the entire solution through the main program.[3] We illustrate this approach, in a simplified way, by solving the problem discussed earlier.

The set of values needs to be read in, summed, and averaged. This will be done in one subroutine (or module). Next the data need to be restored; since this is simply done in one instruction, it will occur in the main program. Now each data element needs to be compared with the average and the counter possibly increased. A second module will do this. Finally, the printing of the average and the value of the counter will be done in the main program.[4]

```
1ØØ REM PROGRAM TO AVERAGE ACCOUNTS AND
11Ø REM COUNT NUMBER OF ACCOUNTS ABOVE AVERAGE
12Ø GOSUB 5ØØ
13Ø RESTORE
14Ø GOSUB 6ØØ
```

---

[3] These smaller parts of the large problem are called *modules,* and the process of breaking a problem into modules to achieve problem solution is called *modular programming.*

[4] Thus the problem will be solved by using three modules: the main program; the reading, summing, and averaging subroutine; and the counting subroutine.

```
150 PRINT "ACCOUNT AVERAGE IS $";A
160 PRINT "NUMBER OF ACCOUNTS ABOVE AVERAGE IS";N
170 DATA
  –
  –
  –
    STOP
500 REM SUBROUTINE TO READ,SUM,AVERAGE
510 REM S IS SUM; Z ACCOUNT VALUE; A AVERAGE
520 LET S=0
530 FOR I=1 TO 20
540   READ Z
550    LET S=S+Z
560 NEXT I
570 LET A=S/20
580 RETURN
600 REM COUNTING SUBROUTINE
610 REM N COUNTS ACCOUNT ABOVE AVERAGE
620 LET N=0
630 FOR I=1 TO 20
640   READ Z
650   IF Z<=A THEN 670
660   LET N=N+1
670 NEXT I
680 RETURN
1000 END
```

We now consider another problem that will be solved along the same lines as the previous one, namely, that the problem will be broken down into modules and the modules solved and put back together to make the total solution.

EXAMPLE 14.4. The Long Real Estate Company wants a program written that will produce a quarterly report on all its salespeople. The information for each salesperson will be typed into DATA lines and will contain the salesperson's number, the number of weeks the salesperson has worked during this quarter, the selling price of each property sold by the salesperson during this quarter, and an eod tag at the end of each salesperson's set of data. In addition, an eod tag (different from the first kind) will be used to indicate the end of *all* the data. The output, for each salesperson, should show the salesperson's number, the number of weeks worked, the number of sales made, each individual sale, the total sales, the average sale, and the number of sales per week.

The problem is somewhat complex, and so the approach to its solution will be to try to break the problem into smaller, more simple tasks. The tasks that must be performed are

1. Reading the data
2. Counting the number of sales
3. Summing the sales
4. First averaging (total/number of sales)

5. Second averaging (count/weeks)
6. Output

In addition, a heading for the report will be printed.

Next we decide how to group these tasks into subprograms. The following breakdown will be used:

1. The main program will print the heading, read and print the first two data items (salesperson's number and weeks worked), and call the two subroutines. Also, after all the data have been processed, the main program will print that the report is finished.
2. A subprogram will count the number of sales and sum all sales giving a total sales. The subprogram will output these values.
3. A subprogram will calculate and print both averages.

Having identified the tasks that are to be done and assigning these tasks to various program parts, we next decide on what variables will be used and what they will stand for. This is important because, in BASIC, variables are *global*—that is, a variable stands for the same quantity wherever the variable is used—whether in the main program or one or more subprograms.[5] Our choices are

N will be the salesperson's number
W will be the number of weeks worked
A will be a sale
C will count the number of sales
T will be the total sales
M1 will be the first average (total sales/number of sales)
M2 will be the second average (number of sales/number of weeks)

The program is now broken down into its various parts, and the necessary variables have been chosen. The next step is to return to the modules and examine each of them. Our ultimate aim is to produce the BASIC code that will solve the problem. Does the description of the first module (the main program) lead to code? From the first part of the breakdown described, the activities for the main program are

1. Print report heading.
2. Read N.
3. As long as there is a salesperson left, repeat steps 4 through 8.
4. Read W.
5. Print N.
6. Print W.
7. Transfer to counting and summing subroutine.
8. Transfer to averaging routine.
9. Print that the report is done.

[5] If two subprograms are prepared by two different people each using the same variable, say, X, for totally different purposes, when the entire program, including subprograms, is unified, the result could be disastrous. It would be wise to draw up a table of all variables used throughout the program and check the table for possible problems before execution.

Each of the statements can be translated into BASIC code with the exception of the looping statement, number 3. We create the loop by changing 3 to a step, call it 3a, which will start the loop:

3a. If N is the eod tag (for all data), transfer to step 9; otherwise, execute steps 4 through 8.

and by adding a step 8a:

8a. Transfer to step 2.

With this change and addition we are ready to go to code. The process of taking general program statements and writing more detailed statements is called *top-down programming*. The idea is that we start at the top with a general statement that describes an action to be performed by the computer, and if that statement cannot be translated into code, the statement is broken down into additional, more specific statements that can be coded. The process of top-down programming is also called *stepwise refinement* since each step is refined until code can be written.

To illustrate this idea further, consider the tasks to be performed by the second module:

2. A subprogram will count the number of sales and sum all sales giving a total sales. The subprogram will output these values.

This module can be generally described as

1. Initialize C and T.
2. Read, print, count, and total all sales, A.
3. Print C and T.

Step 1 leads immediately to code (LET C=0 and LET T=0) and so needs no further refinement. Step 2, however, is too general and so must be refined. Since step 2 uses a loop depending on an eod tag, the refinement might be

2a. Read A.
2b. If A is eod tag, transfer to step 3.
2c. Print A.
2d. Increase C by 1.
2e. Add A to T.
2f. Transfer to step 2a.

Since code can be written directly from step 3, the second module is complete.

Once the top-down approach has been applied to all modules, the final job is the choice of line numbers for the various modules. Since the individual parts may be coded separately, we must be certain that no two parts use the same line numbers. The allocation of line numbers will be

100–199:	main program
200–299:	counting and summing subroutine
300–399:	averaging subroutine
400–999:	DATA lines
1000:	END

The entire program and a RUN follow.

```
100 PRINT TAB(25);"**** LONG REAL ESTATE ****"
105 REM READ SALESPERSON NUMBER
110 READ N
115 REM CHECK FOR END OF ALL DATA
120 IF N=9999 THEN 195
125 REM W IS NO. OF WEEKS WORKED THIS QUARTER
130 READ W
135 FOR I=1 TO 4
140 PRINT
145 NEXT I
150 PRINT "NUMBER:";N;TAB(40);"WEEKS WORKED:";W
155 PRINT
160 PRINT
165 GOSUB 200
170 GOSUB 300
175 GOTO 110
195 PRINT
196 PRINT
197 PRINT TAB(35);"*** END OF REPORT ***"
199 STOP
200 REM.................... COUNTING AND SUMMING SUBROUTINE ..........
205 REM C COUNTS NUMBER OF SALES
210 LET C=0
215 REM T TOTALS SALES
220 LET T=0
225 PRINT TAB(28);"** SALES **"
230 REM A IS AMOUNT OF A SALE
235 READ A
240 REM -1 IS EOD FOR INDIVIDUAL SALESPERSON
245 IF A=-1 THEN 285
250 PRINT A,
255 LET C=C+1
260 LET T=T+A
265 GO TO 235
285 PRINT
290 PRINT
295 PRINT "NUMBER OF SALES:";C;TAB(40);"TOTAL SALES: $";T
299 RETURN
300 REM.................... AVERAGING SUBROUTINE ...............
310 REM M1 IS TOTAL SALES / NUMBER OF SALES
320 LET M1=T/C
330 REM M2 IS NUMBER OF SALES / NUMBER OF WEEKS
340 LET M2=C/W
350 PRINT "AVERAGE SALE: $";M1;TAB(40);M2;"SALES PER WEEK"
399 RETURN
400 REM....................... DATA....................
405 REM DATA SHOULD BE ENTERED IN THE FOLLOWING FORM
410 REM SALESPERSON NUMBER,NUMBER OF WEEKS WORKED
415 REM EACH SALE MADE IN QUARTER
420 REM LAST DATA ITEM FOR EACH PERSON SHOULD BE -1(EOD)
425 REM.............................................
430 DATA 123,10
```

```
435 DATA 43000,39900,54500,35000,40000
440 DATA 62500,85000,42400,63500
445 DATA 72000,60000,38200,-1
450 DATA 734,5
455 DATA 24500,45000,37500,88000,73000
460 DATA 55900,68400,72500,-1
465 DATA 349,8
470 DATA 95000,76500,102000,63900
475 DATA 89200,68900,-1
998 REM 9999 IS EOD FOR ALL DATA
999 DATA 9999
1000 END
```

RUN

```
                    ****  LONG  REAL  ESTATE  ****

NUMBER:  123                               WEEKS  WORKED:  10

                          **  SALES  **
43000              39900        54500            35000             40000
62500              85000        42400            63500             72000
60000              38200

NUMBER  OF  SALES:  12                     TOTAL  SALES:  $  636000
AVERAGE  SALE:  $  53000                     1.2  SALES  PER  WEEK

NUMBER:  734                               WEEKS  WORKED:  5

                          **  SALES  **
24500              45000        37500            88000             73000
55900              68400        72500

NUMBER  OF  SALES:  8                      TOTAL  SALES:  $  464800
AVERAGE  SALE:  $  58100                     1.6  SALES  PER  WEEK

NUMBER:  349                               WEEKS  WORKED:  8

                          **  SALES  **
95000              76500        102000           63900             89200
68900

NUMBER  OF  SALES:  6                      TOTAL  SALES:  $  495500
AVERAGE  SALE:  $  82583.3                    .75  SALES  PER  WEEK

                    ***  END  OF  REPORT  ***

READY
```

Frequently interactive programs are written that perform several distinct tasks, and the choice of which task is to be performed is left to the user.

EXAMPLE 14.5. Fourteen states border the Atlantic Ocean. The names of the states are to be entered into one array and their abbreviations into another. The program should give the user five options:

1. Print the states.
2. Print their abbreviations.
3. Enter a state and have its abbreviation printed.
4. Enter an abbreviation and have the full name printed.
5. End the program.

The first four options will be made into modules. The last option will merely cause the program to halt. Another module will be constructed that will display the options to the user. Such a display is frequently called a *menu,* and programs using a menu are called *menu programs* or *menu-driven programs.* The execution of our program will follow the order

1. Print the menu.
2. Request user's choice
3. If choice is to end the program, stop; otherwise,
4. Transfer to appropriate subroutine.
5. Transfer to step 1.

The user's options will be numbered 1 through 5, and transfer to the appropriate subroutine will be made by the ON-GOSUB statement, which works like the ON-GOTO statement (see Section 9.11).

The *general form of ON-GOSUB* is

line number   ON X GOSUB $ln_1, ln_2, \ldots, ln_k$

where the line numbers following GOSUB are the starting lines of subroutines.

The main program is listed next, followed by each of the subprograms it uses and finally by sample RUNs.

```
1000 REM MENU DRIVEN PROGRAM
1010 REM ATLANTIC COAST STATES AND THEIR ABBREVIATIONS
1020 REM
1030 REM N$ CONTAINS NAMES OF STATES
1040 REM A$ CONTAINS THEIR ABBREVIATIONS
1050 REM
1060 REM FIVE MODULES:
1070 REM     1.PRINT NAMES OF STATES(LINE 2000)
1080 REM     2.PRINT ABBREVIATIONS(LINE 3000)
1090 REM     3.NAMESUPPLIED,ABBREVIATION PRINTED(LINE 4000)
1100 REM     4.ABBREVIATION SUPPLIED,NAME PRINTED(LINE 5000)
1110 REM     5.MENUPRINTED(LINE 6000)
1120 REM
1130 DIM N$(14),A$(14)
1140 FOR I=1 TO 14
1150    READ N$(I),A$(I)
1160 NEXT I
1170    GOSUB 6000
1180    PRINT "ENTER YOUR CHOICE(1-5)"
1190    INPUT C
```

```
1200    IF  C=5  THEN  9999
1210    ON  C  GOSUB  2000,3000,4000,5000
1220 GOTO  1170
1230 DATA  MAINE,ME
1240 DATA  NEW  HAMPSHIRE,NH
1250 DATA  MASSACHUSETTS,MA
1260 DATA  RHODE  ISLAND,RI
1270 DATA  CONNECTICUT,CT
1280 DATA  NEW  YORK,NY
1290 DATA  NEW  JERSEY,NJ
1300 DATA  DELAWARE,DEL
1310 DATA  MARYLAND,MD
1320 DATA  VIRGINIA,VA
1330 DATA  NORTH  CAROLINA,NC
1340 DATA  SOUTH  CAROLINA,SC
1350 DATA  GEORGIA,GA
1360 DATA  FLORIDA,FL
9999 END


2000 REM****************************
2010 REM SUBROUTINE  TO  PRINT  NAMES  OF  STATES
2020 PRINT
2030 PRINT
2040 PRINT  TAB(20);"THE  STATES  ARE:"
2050 PRINT
2060 FOR  I=1  TO  14
2070    PRINT  TAB(22);N$(I)
2080 NEXT  I
2090 FOR  I=1  TO  3
2100    PRINT
2110 NEXT  I
2120 RETURN


3000 REM****************************
3010 REM SUBROUTINE  TO  PRINT  ABBREVIATIONS
3020 PRINT
3030 PRINT
3040 PRINT  TAB(20);"ABBREVIATIONS"
3050 PRINT
3060 FOR  I=1  TO  14
3070    PRINT  TAB(24);A$(I)
3080 NEXT  I
3090 FOR  I=1  TO  3
3100    PRINT
3110 NEXT  I
3120 RETURN


4000 REM****************************
4010 REM SUBROUTINE  TO  FIND  AND  PRINT  ABBREVIATION
4020 REM GIVEN  NAME  OF  STATE  BY  USER
4030 PRINT
```

```
4040 PRINT
4050 PRINT "ENTER NAME OF STATE"
4060 INPUT S$
4070 PRINT
4080 FOR I=1 TO 14
4090    IF S$=N$(I) THEN 4140
4100 NEXT I
4110 PRINT S$;" IS NOT THE NAME OF"
4120 PRINT "AN ATLANTIC COASTAL STATE"
4130 GOTO 4150
4140 PRINT "THE ABBREVIATION FOR ";S$;" IS ";A$(I)
4150 FOR I=1 TO 3
4160    PRINT
4170 NEXT I
4180 RETURN


5000 REM****************************
5010 REM SUBROUTINE TO REQUEST STATE ABBREVIATION
5020 REM AND PRINT FULL STATE NAME
5030 PRINT
5040 PRINT
5050 PRINT "ENTER ABBREVIATION FOR STATE"
5060 INPUT T$
5070 PRINT
5080 FOR I=1 TO 14
5090    IF T$=A$(I) THEN 5140
5100 NEXT I
5110 PRINT "THERE IS NO ATLANTIC COASTAL STATE"
5120 PRINT "WHOSE ABBREVIATION IS ";T$
5130 GOTO 5150
5140 PRINT "THE FULL NAME IS ";N$(I)
5150 FOR I=1 TO 3
5160    PRINT
5170 NEXT I
5180 RETURN


6000 REM****************************
6010 REM MENU SUBROUTINE
6020 REM
6030 PRINT "NAMES AND ABBREVIATIONS OF STATES"
6040 PRINT "THAT BORDER THE ATLANTIC OCEAN"
6050 PRINT
6060 PRINT "YOU HAVE FIVE OPTIONS. THEY ARE"
6070 FOR I=1 TO 3
6080    PRINT
6090 NEXT I
6100 PRINT "OPTION";TAB(20);"DESCRIPTION"
6110 PRINT "   1";TAB(15);"PRINT NAMES OF STATES"
6120 PRINT
6130 PRINT "   2";TAB(15);"PRINT STATE ABBREVIATIONS"
6140 PRINT
```

```
6150 PRINT "   3";TAB(15);"GET AN ABBREVIATION FOR A"
6160 PRINT TAB(15);"STATE YOU ENTER"
6170 PRINT
6180 PRINT "   4";TAB(15);"GET THE STATE'S NAME FOR THE"
6190 PRINT TAB(15);"ABBREVIATION YOU ENTER"
6200 PRINT
6210 PRINT "   5";TAB(15);"END THE PROGRAM"
6220 PRINT
6230 RETURN


RUN

NAMES AND ABBREVIATIONS OF STATES
THAT BORDER THE ATLANTIC OCEAN


YOU HAVE FIVE OPTIONS.  THEY ARE

OPTION                 DESCRIPTION
   1            PRINT NAMES OF STATES

   2            PRINT STATE ABBREVIATIONS

   3            GET AN ABBREVIATION FOR A
                STATE YOU ENTER

   4            GET THE STATE'S NAME FOR THE
                ABBREVIATION YOU ENTER

   5            END THE PROGRAM

ENTER YOUR CHOICE(1-5)
? 3


ENTER NAME OF STATE
? VIRGINIA

THE ABBREVIATION FOR VIRGINIA IS VA


NAMES AND ABBREVIATIONS OF STATES
THAT BORDER THE ATLANTIC OCEAN


YOU HAVE FIVE OPTIONS.  THEY ARE
```

```
OPTION                    DESCRIPTION
    1              PRINT NAMES OF STATES

    2              PRINT STATE ABBREVIATIONS

    3              GET AN ABBREVIATION FOR A
                   STATE YOU ENTER

    4              GET THE STATE'S NAME FOR THE
                   ABBREVIATION YOU ENTER

    5              END THE PROGRAM
```

ENTER YOUR CHOICE(1-5)
? 5

READY

RUN

NAMES AND ABBREVIATIONS OF STATES
THAT BORDER THE ATLANTIC OCEAN

YOU HAVE FIVE OPTIONS. THEY ARE

```
OPTION                    DESCRIPTION
    1              PRINT NAMES OF STATES

    2              PRINT STATE ABBREVIATIONS

    3              GET AN ABBREVIATION FOR A
                   STATE YOU ENTER

    4              GET THE STATE'S NAME FOR THE
                   ABBREVIATION YOU ENTER

    5              END THE PROGRAM
```

ENTER YOUR CHOICE(1-5)
? 1

                    THE STATES ARE

                    MAINE
                    NEW HAMPSHIRE
                    MASSACHUSETTS
                    RHODE ISLAND
                    CONNECTICUT
                    NEW YORK
                    NEW JERSEY

```
                    DELAWARE
                    MARYLAND
                    VIRGINIA
                    NORTH  CAROLINA
                    SOUTH  CAROLINA
                    GEORGIA
                    FLORIDA
```

NAMES AND ABBREVIATIONS OF STATES
THAT BORDER THE ATLANTIC OCEAN

YOU HAVE FIVE OPTIONS. THEY ARE

```
OPTION                  DESCRIPTION
   1                PRINT NAMES OF STATES

   2                PRINT STATE ABBREVIATIONS

   3                GET AN ABBREVIATION FOR A
                    STATE YOU ENTER

   4                GET THE STATE'S NAME FOR THE
                    ABBREVIATION YOU ENTER

   5                END THE PROGRAM
```
ENTER YOUR CHOICE(1-5)
?4

ENTER ABBREVIATION FOR STATE
? CA

THERE IS NO ATLANTIC COASTAL STATE
WHOSE ABBREVIATION IS CA

NAMES AND ABBREVIATIONS OF STATES
THAT BORDER THE ATLANTIC OCEAN

YOU HAVE FIVE OPTIONS. THEY ARE

```
OPTION                  DESCRIPTION
   1                PRINT NAMES OF STATES

   2                PRINT STATE ABBREVIATIONS
```

3	GET AN ABBREVIATION FOR A STATE YOU ENTER
4	GET THE STATE'S NAME FOR THE ABBREVIATION YOU ENTER
5	END THE PROGRAM

ENTER YOUR CHOICE(1-5)
? 5

READY

You should note that modular programming and top-down programming are related approaches to the writing of good programs. Your problem should be broken into modules and perhaps one or more of these modules into other, smaller modules. The modules are refined by the top-down approach until you are ready to write BASIC code.

We conclude this chapter with a simple program that shows that *subroutines can be nested*—that is, a subroutine can cause a transfer to another subroutine. Hence, we can have one subroutine "within" another.

EXAMPLE 14.6. The following is a program using nested subroutines.

```
100 REM MAIN PROGRAM
110 PRINT "STARTING"
120 PRINT "GOING TO SUBROUTINES"
130 PRINT
140 GOSUB 200
150 PRINT
160 PRINT "RETURNED FROM SUBROUTINES"
170 PRINT "FINISHING"
180 STOP
200 REM FIRST SUBROUTINE
210 PRINT TAB(5);"IN SUB 1"
220 PRINT TAB(5);"GOING TO SUB 2"
230 PRINT
240 GOSUB 300
250 PRINT
260 PRINT TAB(5);"BACK IN SUB 1"
270 PRINT TAB(5);"GOING BACK TO MAIN PROGRAM"
280 RETURN
300 REM SECOND SUBROUTINE
310 PRINT TAB(10);"IN SUB 2"
320 PRINT TAB(10);"GOING BACK TO SUB 1"
330 RETURN
400 END

RUN

STARTING
```

GOING TO SUBROUTINES

    IN SUB 1
    GOING TO SUB 2

       IN SUB 2
       GOING BACK TO SUB 1

    BACK IN SUB 1
    GOING BACK TO MAIN PROGRAM

RETURNED FROM SUBROUTINES
FINISHING

READY

---

1 What is the output of each program?

a.

```
11 READ X
16 GOSUB 77
21 IF T<X+10 THEN 11
26 PRINT "DONE"
31 STOP
77 LET T=X↑2
79 PRINT T-1
81 RETURN
89 DATA -2,3,0,4
91 DATA -3,1
93 END
```

c.

```
10 FOR M=1 TO 3
20    ON M GOSUB 50,90,70
30 NEXT M
40 STOP
50 PRINT "THIRD"
60 RETURN
70 PRINT "SECOND"
80 RETURN
90 PRINT "FIRST"
95 RETURN
99 END
```

b.

```
100 READ A,B
110 GOSUB 200
120 GOSUB 400
130 STOP
200 LET C=A
210 LET A=B
220 LET B=C
230 GOSUB 400
240 READ C
250 GOSUB 400
260 RETURN
400 PRINT A,B,C
410 RETURN
450 DATA 4,7,2
500 END
```

d.

```
100 READ X
110 GOSUB 200
120 PRINT "Y=";Y
130 IF Y>10 THEN 110
140 STOP
200 READ Y
210 IF X<Y THEN GOSUB 300
220 PRINT X
230 RETURN
300 LET X=X+1
310 RETURN
400 DATA 17,22,15,18,10
499 END
```

2 Write a subroutine (which starts at line 500) that prints out a line of N #'s. The value of N is supplied in the main program.

3 Write a program to print out a solid rectangle made of #'s. The program should ask the user how wide and how high the rectangle should be. The subroutine of Exercise 2 should be used.

4 Write a subroutine that calculates $1 + 3 + 5 + \cdots + N$ if N is odd or $2 + 4 + 6 + \cdots + N$ if N is even. N is a value that comes from the main program.

5 If A, B, and C are the sides of a triangle then its area can be calculated by the expression $\sqrt{S(S - A)(S - B)(S - C)}$ where $S = (A + B + C)/2$. (This is called *Heron's formula*.) Write a subroutine to calculate the area of a triangle using this formula.

6 Write a program that reads three values and uses the subroutine of Exercise 5 to calculate the area of a triangle having the three values as lengths of its sides. You could use

A	B	C
2	9	10
5	4	8
7	3	6
2	11	10

7 Write a subroutine (beginning at line 1000) that calculates the sum, S, of W and X, which have been defined in the main program. If S is positive, return to the main program; if S is zero, transfer to a subroutine which begins at line 2000; if S is negative, square it and return to the main program.

8 The least common multiple (lcm) of two positive integers M and N is an integer (a) that is a multiple of M, (b) that is a multiple of N, and (c) that is the smallest such number. A subroutine is to be written which calculates the lcm of M and N that are defined in the main program. (One approach that can be used is to first determine which of M and N is larger—if $M = N$, then the lcm is either value. Once larger is determined, if smaller divides larger, the larger is the lcm. Otherwise, starting with two times the larger, construct consecutive multiples of the larger. The first one of these that the smaller number divides evenly is the lcm.)

9 The subroutine of Exercise 8 is to be used in a program to subtract fractions. A pair of fractions is to be typed in, one at a time, by entering numerators and denominators. For the two fractions a least common denominator is to be found. The least common denominator for two fractions is the lcm of the denominators. Convert each of the fractions into two new fractions each having the lcm as their denominator and print them out. Finally perform the subtraction by using the formula

$$\frac{A}{C} - \frac{B}{C} = \frac{A - B}{C}$$

and print the result. Try the problems $\frac{5}{6} - \frac{1}{3}$, $\frac{11}{12} - \frac{7}{8}$, and $\frac{7}{9} - \frac{1}{2}$.

10 Five values are to be read. Four subroutines are to be written. The first calculates the sum of the five values, the second the average of the five, the third the product of the five, and the fourth is to print out all five values. A menu program, using the subroutines, is to be written that allows the user to obtain the results of one of the subprograms.

11 Modify the program of Example 14.5 so that the menu is printed only at the start of the program unless the user wants to see it again (this means that an additional option needs to be added to the menu—option 6: look at menu).

12 Each line in a collection of DATA lines contains the following information.

item, manufacturer, number in stock, retail price per item

A menu program that uses this data is to be written. The user's options should include

a. Enter a manufacturer's name and have all items made by that manufacturer listed together with the number of each item in stock.

b. Enter an item name and print out each manufacturer that produces the item followed by the item price as well as the number in stock.

c. Print out the entire inventory in a five-column table, the first four columns showing the data from the data lines and the fifth column displaying the total stock retail value for that item. In addition, at the bottom of the table, the total number of all items in stock should be printed and the total retail value of the entire inventory.

* * *

13 a. Write a subroutine that calculates the distance between two points in the plane whose coordinates are (X1,Y1) and (X2,Y2).

b. Write a program that uses the subroutine of part (a) to solve the following problem. The user is to type in the coordinates of three points, one point at a time. The program should determine whether or not the three points are colinear. If not, since they must then form a triangle, the program should determine if the triangle is equilateral, isosceles, or scalene. Of course, some appropriate output is required.

14 a. If n is a positive integer the product

$$n \times (n - 1) \times (n - 2) \times \cdots \times 2 \times 1$$

is called n factorial and is written $n!$. If $n = 0$, $0!$ is defined to be 1. Write a subprogram to calculate and print $n!$.

b. Write a short main program to have the user enter a positive integer and then its factorial will be printed by the subroutine of part (a).

15 Change the subroutine of Exercise 14(a) so that the value of $n!$ is not printed and write a program to calculate and print a *binomial* coefficient. To calculate a binomial coefficient, the user will supply two nonnegative integers k and r where $r \leq k$. The symbol for a binomial coefficient is $\binom{k}{r}$ and is defined by

$$\binom{k}{r} = \frac{k!}{r!(k - r)!}$$

16 The value of the irrational number e can be obtained by printing the value of EXP(1). It can also be calculated by the sum

$$e = 1 + \frac{1}{1!} + \frac{1}{2!} + \frac{1}{3!} + \cdots$$

Use the subprogram for $n!$ to approximate e by this sum. The last term in the sum should be $\frac{1}{10!}$.

17 Calculate e^x for $x = 2, 3, 4,$ and 5 using $e^x = 1 + x + \frac{x^2}{2!} + \frac{x^3}{3!} + \cdots$. The last term in the sum should be $\frac{x^{10}}{10!}$. With each sum, the value of EXP(X) should be printed, for visual comparison.

18 sin x (x in radians) can be calculated by

$$\sin x = x - \frac{x^3}{3!} + \frac{x^5}{5!} - \frac{x^7}{7!} + \cdots$$

Write a program in which the value of x (in degrees) is supplied from the terminal and then is changed to radians. Two values should be printed—the value of sin x using the built-in function and the value of sin x using the formula above. Use only 10 terms in the formula. For values of x you might try 1, 1.57, 3.14, 6.28, and 1.05.

19 Suppose that political data have been collected about all the registered voters in a small town. The data are of the form

    name, political affiliation, precinct

where political affiliation is D for democrat, R for republican, or I for independent and precinct is a 1, 2, 3, or 4. Write a menu-driven program to perform the tasks

   a. User enters a precinct number and program lists names and political affiliation of all people in that precinct counting the number of people of the various affiliations and the percentage of each.

   b. User enters a political affiliation and program lists names and precincts.

   c. User enters a single name and program prints political affiliation and precinct.

   d. User requests a total, by precinct, of all people according to political affiliation.

Two-Dimensional Arrays

This chapter continues and expands the discussion of arrays that was begun in Chapter 13.

15.1 Warehouse Inventory

Suppose that you own three warehouses, for convenience denoted A, B, and C, and that each warehouse stocks terminals, paper, pencils, and flowcharting templates. At present, your inventory status can be described as

	Warehouse A	Warehouse B	Warehouse C
Terminals	15	7	11
Paper	22	9	18
Pencils	75	40	50
Templates	32	0	26

Of course, an interpretation can be given to the numbers in the table to give a sense of reality. For example, a number that refers to pencils might mean "hundreds of boxes."

It is easy to read from the table that the number of pencils in Warehouse B is 40. It is just as easy to see that the total number of templates in stock is 58.

Tables such as this are frequently used to present and analyze data. The significant part of the table is not the labeling (although for an applied problem we should know what the numbers stand for) but rather the rectangular configuration of numbers.

A rectangular configuration of numbers is called a *matrix,* a *two-dimensional array,* or a *table.* As long as no confusion results both one-dimensional and two-dimensional arrays are sometimes merely called arrays. A horizontal line of numbers in an array is called a *row.* So the first (top) row of our inventory array

15	7	11
22	9	18
75	40	50
32	0	26

is

15 7 11

A vertical arrangement of numbers is called a *column.* The third column of our array is

11
18
50
26

The inventory array has 4 rows and 3 columns. For this reason we refer to it as a *4 by 3* array and we sometimes write 4×3. When describing an array in this way, remember to mention the rows first and columns second. Thus it would be incorrect to describe the inventory array as a 3×4 array.

15.2 Double-Subscripted Variables in Mathematics and BASIC

It has already been noted that the number of pencils in Warehouse B is 40. The number 40 is the value that appears, at the same time, in the third row and the second column. Generally, any value of the array is specifically determined by telling in which row and in which column the value lies. For example, the value in the fourth row and first column is 32.

As do lists, tables are given letter names. Suppose that the table that described the inventory status was named M. Then M contains 12 values or elements, and each element is identified by the number of the row and number of the column in which it is found. As noted, 32 is the element of M found in the fourth row and first column. The notation used to indicate this is

$$M_{4,1} = 32$$

$M_{4,1}$ is read "M sub four comma one" or more frequently "M sub four one."

The pair "4,1" forms a *double subscript.* The first number of a double subscript always refers to the row in which the element is found and the second subscript refers to the column.

Similar to what was done with single subscripts, in BASIC double subscripts will be written after the array name, enclosed within parentheses and a comma between the subscripts. So

$M_{4,1}$ in BASIC is   M(4,1)

Also as with lists, you should note that a 4 × 3 array M is actually made up of the 12 distinct, double subscripted variables M(1,1), M(1,2), M(1,3), M(2,1), . . . , M(4,2), M(4,3). In addition, double subscripts may also be expressions, and rounding will be done to the subscripts if necessary.

A sequence of examples will be used to bring us to the point where we can write a program to construct the entire array.

EXAMPLE 15.1. We will write a sequence of statements to assign to double subscripted variables the first row of values of the inventory array.

The problem is merely to assign the proper values to the correct variables. The variables that appear in the first row are M(1,1), M(1,2), and M(1,3). So one way of assigning the first row is

```
10 LET M( 1 , 1 )=15
20 LET M( 1 , 2 )=7
30 LET M( 1 , 3 )=11
```

For a 12-element array, this method of using LETs is tiresome at least. If the array under consideration contained significantly more elements, the use of LETs to assign values to it would be prohibitive. Thus we will use the READ statement as a convenient way of assigning the values of the first row.

When we examine the subscripts of the elements in the first row, we can detect a pattern. The first subscript is always the same—it is a 1. The second subscript changes from 1 to 3 in increments of 1. So the second subscript can be a variable that changes as the index of a FOR/NEXT loop changes. So the statements that follow handle the first row of the array.

```
10 FOR J=1 TO 3
20    READ M( 1 , J )
30 NEXT J
40 DATA 15 , 7 , 11
```

EXAMPLE 15.2. Assign values to the second row of the array using a READ statement.

Again examining the pattern of subscripts of the elements in the second row, we see the first subscript is the constant 2 while the second subscript changes, as before, from 1 to 3. The following statements work for the second row.

```
10 FOR J=1 TO 3
20    READ M( 2 , J )
30 NEXT J
40 DATA 22 , 9 , 18
```

EXAMPLE 15.3. Assign the third and fourth rows of the inventory array M. The third row is given by

```
10 FOR J=1 TO 3
20    READ M(3,J)
30 NEXT J
40 DATA 75,40,50
```

and the fourth row by

```
10 FOR J=1 TO 3
20    READ M(4,J)
30 NEXT J
40 DATA 32,0,26
```

To assign values to the entire array M, we note a pattern that runs through the previous three examples. As we go across a row, the first subscript is a constant—it does not change. However, the second subscript changes from 1 to 3. Notice that as we go from example to example—that is, as we go from one row to the next—the *first* subscript is also changing. Our inventory array has four rows and the first subscript is changing from 1 to 4. So to get the entire array M we need to use nested loops. The inner (J) loop will go from 1 to 3, while the outer one (we will use I) will go from 1 to 4. Putting all these together, we get

```
100 FOR I=1 TO 4
150    FOR J=1 TO 3
200        READ M(I,J)
250    NEXT J
300 NEXT I
350 DATA 15,7,11
400 DATA 22,9,18
450 DATA 75,40,50
500 DATA 32,0,26
550 END
```

In addition to assigning values to the array M, we would like to have M printed out. So right after line 200, where an element has been read in, a PRINT statement will be inserted. Since we will want the output to look like an array, the PRINT statement will be ended with a comma. So we insert

```
225        PRINT M(I,J),
```

With this, the output is

```
RUN

15            7            11           22           9
18            75           40           50           32
0             26

READY
```

Clearly this is not the form we want. We wish to have three values printed per line. Thus after three values have been printed on the same line (the use of the comma at the end of line 225), we wish to begin printing on the next line. So we want to cancel the effect of the comma. This is done by inserting a simple PRINT statement immediately after the J loop (which is executed three times). As the J loop is executed three times, three values will be printed on the same line. When the J loop is done and we are about to increment the I loop, this PRINT statement will be executed. But what does a PRINT do? It prints a blank—in fact, this blank will "appear" on the same line as the previous three values. But since this PRINT statement does not end with a comma, the next value to be output (which is the first of the next trio of values) will begin on a new line. The completed program and RUN are now given.

```
100 FOR I=1 TO 4
150    FOR J=1 TO 3
200       READ M(I,J)
225       PRINT M(I,J),
250    NEXT J
275    PRINT
300 NEXT I
350 DATA 15,7,11
400 DATA 22,9,18
450 DATA 75,40,50
500 DATA 32,0,26
550 END

RUN

15              7              11
22              9              18
75             40              50
32              0              26

READY
```

The inventory array is said to have been assigned *rowwise;* that is, the array has been assigned its values by going across an entire row before going on to the next row (starting, of course, with the first row). It is conventional to assign values to an array this way; however, it is clearly not the only way. An array could be assigned *columnwise;* that is, by going down the columns. This will be illustrated in Example 15.11.

We will now show how totals may be computed for a specified row or column of an array.

EXAMPLE 15.4. Write a subroutine to calculate the total number of teletypes in stock.

We assume that the inventory array has been read in and that the main program will take care of any output. The writing of the subroutine deals with summing and discovering a subscript pattern (which we have already looked at). Thus

```
1000 REM TTY TOTAL SUBROUTINE
1010 LET S=0
1020 FOR T=1 TO 3
1030    LET S=S+M(1,T)
1040 NEXT T
1050 RETURN
```

EXAMPLE 15.5. Write a subroutine that allows the user to indicate any one of the three warehouses. The total number of items in stock in the indicated warehouse should be calculated and printed.

```
1100 REM SELECT SUBROUTINE
1110 REM DIRECTIONS
1120 FOR I=1 TO 3
1130    READ W$
1140    PRINT "FOR WAREHOUSE ";W$;" ENTER A";I
1150 NEXT I
1160 PRINT
1170 INPUT H
1180 LET T=0
1190 FOR I=1 TO 4
1200    LET T=T+M(I,H)
1210 NEXT I
1220 PRINT "TOTAL IS";T
1230 DATA A,B,C
1240 RETURN
```

The execution of this subroutine (as part of a complete program) would display

```
FOR WAREHOUSE A ENTER A 1
FOR WAREHOUSE B ENTER A 2
FOR WAREHOUSE C ENTER A 3

? 2
TOTAL IS 56
```

15.3 The DIM Statement Used with Two Subscripts

As with lists, the DIM statement is used with tables to reserve space in memory for variables. *The DIM statement must be used as long as at least one of the subscripts exceeds 10.*

EXAMPLE 15.6. A 12 × 15 array T must be dimensioned and would be by such a statement as

```
10 DIM T(12,15)
```

EXAMPLE 15.7. A matrix B having 7 rows and 20 columns would be dimensioned by

```
5 DIM B(7,20)
```

It should be repeated that, as with one-dimensional arrays, even though a two-dimensional array need not be dimensioned in a program if it is small enough, it is always a good practice to do so. Thus the inventory array M did not have to be dimensioned but nevertheless the line

```
90 DIM M(4,3)
```

should be included.

EXAMPLE 15.8. An 8×8 array is to be read from DATA lines. The largest value on the minor diagonal is to be found and printed.

The main purpose of this example is the investigation of subscripts. The *minor diagonal* of an array (it must be a *square* array—that is, it must have the same number of rows as columns) is the line of elements from the upper right-hand corner of the array to the lower left-hand corner.

Suppose that we call the array A. Then the elements on the minor diagonal are

A(1,8), A(2,7), A(3,6), A(4,5), A(5,4), A(6,3), A(7,2), and A(8,1)

Looking at the subscripts of these variables, we see that the subscripts of each variable add to 9. So if A(I,J) represents any element on the minor diagonal, then it must be that I+J=9. But if I+J=9, this means that J=9−I. So a variable on the minor diagonal must be of the form A(I,9−I).

The program and RUN follow.

```
190 DIM A(8,8)
200 REM READ IN 8×8 ARRAY
210 FOR R=1 TO 8
220    FOR S=1 TO 8
230       READ A(R,S)
240    NEXT S
250 NEXT R
260 REM FIND LARGEST VALUE ON MINOR DIAGONAL
270 REM TO START, ASSUME LARGEST,L, IS A(1,8)
280 LET L=A(1,8)
290 REM COMPARE LOOP
300 FOR I=2 TO 8
310    IF L>=A(I,9-I) THEN 330
320    LET L=A(I,9-I)
330 NEXT I
340 PRINT "LARGEST VALUE ON MINOR DIAGONAL IS";L
350 DATA 2,7,9,5,12,-6,0,4
360 DATA 4,11,0,-3,2,-1,7,4
370 DATA 1,3,5,2,10,5,-2,0
380 DATA 15,-6,5,-2,8,1,1,3
```

```
390 DATA 12,-9,5,3,0,0,5,1
400 DATA 7,7,-4,8,6,5,2,6
410 DATA 34,9,18,-41,17,20,3,8
420 DATA 5,7,11,9,2,0,13,17
430 END

RUN

LARGEST VALUE ON MINOR DIAGONAL IS 9

READY
```

Obviously, if we wanted the array A to be printed out, the use of the comma with a PRINT statement would not be sufficient. A TAB would have to be used to get a neat output. So we could insert

```
235      PRINT TAB(5*S);A(R,S);
245   PRINT
```

and get the output

```
RUN

    2    7    9    5   12   -6    0    4
    4   11    0   -3    2   -1    7    4
    1    3    5    2   10    5   -2    0
   15   -6    5   -2    8    1    1    3
   12   -9    5    3    0    0    5    1
    7    7   -4    8    6    5    2    6
   34    9   18  -41   17   20    3    8
    5    7   11    9    2    0   13   17
LARGEST VALUE ON MINOR DIAGONAL IS 9

READY
```

Example 15.9 shows a table containing strings.

EXAMPLE 15.9. At Midton College, each class elects four officers: president, vice president, secretary, and treasurer. This year the officers of the senior class are Bill Chase (president), Peg Moran (vice president), Ron Gault (secretary), and Sheila Tarpy (treasurer). The junior class officers are Meredith Lee, Judy Fabio, Bonie Saltz, and Ron Garth. Marge Foster, Than Ton, Gladys Page, and Alan Dale were elected by the sophomores, and Luke Jones, Cheryl Smith, John Brown, and Tom Johnson serve the freshman class. For each class, if the officers are listed according to their office, across a row we get the following rectangular configuration of names:

```
BILL CHASE      PEG MORAN       RON GAULT       SHEILA TARPY
MEREDITH LEE    JUDY FABIO      BONNIE SALTZ    ROY GARTH
MARGE FOSTER    THAN TON        GLADYS PAGE     ALAN DALE
LUKE JONES      CHERYL SMITH    JOHN BROWN      TOM JOHNSON
```

Since the table is made up of strings and has four rows and four columns, we would dimension it by

```
100 DIM N$(4,4)
```

Entering the names rowwise into DATA lines enables them to be read into N$ with nested loops similar to what we have already seen.

```
110 FOR I=1 TO 4
120    FOR J=1 TO 4
130        READ N$(I,J)
140    NEXT J
150 NEXT I
```

In addition to printing the table of names, we wish to add more identifying information to the table. To do this we will print the abbreviations PRES., V.P., SEC., and TREAS. over the columns, and at the left of the top row we will print SENIOR; at the left of the second row, JUNIOR; third row, SOPHOMORE; and bottom row, FRESHMAN. Before they are printed the abbreviations will be read into a four-element list A$ and the class descriptions into a four-element list C$. Line 100 would have to be changed to

```
100 DIM N$(4,4),A$(4),C$(4)
```

and the additional necessary code would be

```
160 FOR I=1 TO 4
170    READ A$(I)
180 NEXT I
190 FOR I=1 TO 4
200    READ C$(I)
210 NEXT I
```

There will be five output columns (we will use the print zones) but only four column headings so a blank will be printed in the first zone and then a loop will be used to print out the headings

```
220 PRINT " ",
230 FOR I=1 TO 4
240    PRINT A$(I),
250 NEXT I
260 PRINT
```

The rest of the table will be displayed by using nested loops, the outer index being I, the inner J. For each value of I, we will print C$(I) (the class description) and then, on the same line, the names of the class officers; that is, we will print N$(I,J) as J ranges from 1 to 4.

```
270 FOR I=1 TO 4
280    PRINT C$(I),
```

```
290    FOR J=1 TO 4
300       PRINT N$(I,J),
310    NEXT J
320    PRINT
330 NEXT I
```

When executed all these lines (and the necessary DATA lines) would produce

	PRES.	V.P.	SEC.	TREAS.
SENIOR	BILL CHASE	PEG MORAN	RON GAULT	SHEILA TARPY
JUNIOR	MEREDITH LEE	JUDY FABIO	BONNIE SALTZ	ROY GARTH
SOPHOMORE	MARGE FOSTER	THAN TON	GLADYS PAGE	ALAN DALE
FRESHMAN	LUKE JONES	CHERYL SMITH	JOHN BROWN	TOM JOHNSON

The next example shows one more table manipulation by use of the subscripts of the table elements.

EXAMPLE 15.10. A company records the total volume of sales made by each of its five salespersons. The records are categorized by the four seasons, winter, spring, summer, and fall. The last names of the sales staff are Terry, Alves, Mee, Oban, and Clark. The sales report is displayed by the table

	WINTER	SPRING	SUMMER	FALL
TERRY	14790	15500	18920	16880
ALVES	13820	16000	21475	20905
MEE	15540	15200	22840	22900
OBAN	17620	14385	19500	20100
CLARK	19210	16380	24810	22005

A program will be written that will enable the user to enter a salesperson's name and a season and that will then print out the sales figure for that person in that season. Finally, the user will be given the opportunity to obtain more data.

The program will be written in two modules: the first (starting at line 1000) will read in the seasons and then the names and sales amounts for each name; the second (starting at 2000) will ask the user for a name and season, search the table until the requested value is found, and then print it out. The main program will call the first subprogram and then the second and then will ask the user if any more searching is to be done.

The main program is simply

```
100 REM TABLE SEARCH
110 REM
120 REM N$: NAMES OF SALES STAFF
130 REM Q$: FOUR SEASONS
140 REM   V: SALES AMOUNTS
150 REM
160 REM SUB 1000 READS DATA
170 REM SUB 2000 FINDS AND PRINTS SPECIFIED DATA ITEM
```

```
180 REM
190 DIM N$(5),Q$(4),V(5,4)
200 GOSUB 1000
210   GOSUB 2000
220   PRINT "MORE SEARCHING? YES OR NO";
230   INPUT R$
240 IF R$="YES" THEN 210
250 PRINT "SEARCH COMPLETE"
260 STOP
9999 END
```

The first module is

```
1000 REM READING SUBROUTINE
1010 FOR I=1 TO 4
1020   READ Q$(I)
1030 NEXT I
1040 FOR I=1 TO 5
1050   READ N$(I)
1060   FOR J=1 TO 4
1070     READ V(I,J)
1080   NEXT J
1090 NEXT I
1100 DATA WINTER,SPRING,SUMMER,FALL
1110 DATA TERRY,14790,15500,18920,16880
1120 DATA ALVES,13820,16000,21475,20905
1130 DATA MEE,15540,15200,22840,22900
1140 DATA OBAN,17620,14385,19500,20100
1150 DATA CLARK,19210,16380,24810,22005
1160 RETURN
```

The other module is

```
2000 REM SEARCH SUBROUTINE
2010 PRINT
2020 PRINT "ENTER NAME OF SALESPERSON"
2030 INPUT A$
2040 PRINT
2050 FOR I=1 TO 5
2060   IF A$=N$(I) THEN 2110
2070 NEXT I
2080 PRINT A$;" IS NOT A MEMBER OF THE SALES STAFF"
2090 PRINT
2100 RETURN
2110 PRINT "WHAT SEASON IS TO BE CONSIDERED";
2120 INPUT B$
2130 PRINT
2140 FOR J=1 TO 4
2150   IF B$=Q$(J) THEN 2210
2160 NEXT J
2170 PRINT "YOUR RESPONSE ";B$;" CANNOT BE PROCESSED"
2180 PRINT "ENTER WINTER,SPRING,SUMMER OR FALL"
2190 PRINT
```

```
2200 GOTO 2110
2210 PRINT "DURING THE ";B$;" SEASON"
2220 PRINT "THE SALES VOLUME FOR ";A$
2230 PRINT "WAS";V(I,J)
2240 PRINT
2250 RETURN
```

When the transfer is made at line 2060, the value of I is the subscript of the name of the salesperson under consideration and is also the number of the row where the sales amount is found. The transfer in line 2150 determines a value of J that is the column number of the sales amount. Thus I and J are the subscripts of the table element that is printed in line 2230.

```
RUN

ENTER NAME OF SALESPERSON
? ALVES

WHAT SEASON IS TO BE CONSIDERED? FIRST

YOUR RESPONSE FIRST CANNOT BE PROCESSED
ENTER WINTER, SPRING, SUMMER OR FALL

WHAT SEASON IS TO BE CONSIDERED? SPRING

DURING THE SPRING SEASON
THE SALES VOLUME FOR ALVES
WAS 16000

MORE SEARCHING? YES OR NO? YES

ENTER NAME OF SALESPERSON
? SMITH

SMITH IS NOT A MEMBER OF THE SALES STAFF

MORE SEARCHING? YES OR NO? YES

ENTER NAME OF SALESPERSON
? OBAN

WHAT SEASON IS TO BE CONSIDERED? FALL

DURING THE FALL SEASON
THE SALES VOLUME FOR OBAN
WAS 20100

MORE SEARCHING? YES OR NO? NO
SEARCH COMPLETE

READY
```

EXAMPLE 15.11. The Farr Savings Bank has three branches: Uphams Corner, Broadway, and Hobart Square. Each Friday afternoon the three branch managers send a report to the home office that indicates the total amount of all transactions for each day during that week. A program at the home office then processes that data to produce a report that looks like this:

```
           UPHAMS  CORNER      BROADWAY      HOBART  SQUARE

MON              —                —                —
TUES             —                —                —
WED              —                —                —
THUR             —                —                —
FRI              —                —                —


DAILY  TOTALS
MON              —
TUES             —
WED              —
THUR             —
FRI              —


BRANCH  WEEKLY  TOTALS
UPHAMS  CORNER      —
BROADWAY            —
HOBART  SQUARE      —


GRAND  TOTAL        —
```

The program will use three DATA lines, one for each branch bank, showing the five daily totals. The first data line will correspond to the Uphams Corner branch, the second to the Broadway branch, and the third to Hobart Square. This means that the data will have to be read *columnwise*, that is, down the first column, then the second column, and finally the third.

We will approach the problem by breaking it down into four modules:

Reading the data and printing the data table
Finding and printing the daily totals
Finding and printing the weekly totals for each branch
Finding and printing the grand total

The variables used will include

B$ = a three-element array containing the names of the three branches

D$ = a five-element array containing the days of the week

M   = a 5×3 array containing the data from the DATA lines

T   = the variable for a daily total

W   = the variable for a weekly total

G   = the grand total

The first subroutine, starting at line 1000, will read all data and print
the table. The data must be read in columnwise and printed out rowwise.

```
1000 REM READ AND PRINT
1010 FOR I=1 TO 3
1020    READ B$(J)
1030 NEXT I
1040 FOR I=1 TO 5
1050    READ D$(I)
1060 NEXT I
1070 FOR I=1 TO 3
1080    FOR J=1 TO 5
1090       READ M(J,I)
1100    NEXT J
1110 NEXT I
1120 PRINT " ",
1130 FOR I=1 TO 3
1140    PRINT B$(I),
1150 NEXT I
1160 PRINT
1170 FOR I=1 TO 5
1180    PRINT D$(J),
1190    FOR J=1 TO 3
1200       PRINT M(I,J),
1210    NEXT J
1220    PRINT
1230 NEXT I
1240 PRINT
1250 PRINT
1260 RETURN
```

The daily totals will be calculated in the subroutine starting at line
1500. A single daily total will be found by adding the values in one
row. This will be repeated five times.

```
1500 REM DAILY TOTALS
1510 PRINT "DAILY TOTALS"
1520 FOR I=1 TO 5
1530    LET T=0
1540    PRINT D$(I);
1550    FOR J=1 TO 3
1560       LET T=T+M(I,J)
1570    NEXT J
1580    PRINT TAB(10);T
1590 NEXT I
1600 PRINT
1610 PRINT
1620 RETURN
```

To find the weekly total for a branch, a column sum must be calculated.
This will be done three times.

```
2000 REM BRANCH TOTALS
2010 PRINT "BRANCH WEEKLY TOTALS"
```

```
2020 FOR I=1 TO 3
2030    LET W=0
2040    PRINT B$(I),
2050    FOR J=1 TO 5
2060       LET W=W+M(J,I)
2070    NEXT J
2080    PRINT W
2090 NEXT I
2100 PRINT
2110 PRINT
2120 RETURN
```

Finally, the grand total G is calculated by summing all array elements.

```
2500 REM GRAND TOTAL
2510 LET G=0
2520 FOR I=1 TO 5
2530    FOR J=1 TO 3
2540       LET G=G+M(I,J)
2550    NEXT J
2560 NEXT I
2570 PRINT "GRAND TOTAL",G
2580 RETURN
```

The problem is solved by writing the main program.

```
100 REM FARR SAVINGS
110 DIM B$(3),D$(5),M(5,3)
120 GOSUB 1000
130 GOSUB 1500
140 GOSUB 2000
150 GOSUB 2500
160 GOTO 9999
170 DATA UPHAMS CORNER,BROADWAY,HOBART SQUARE
180 DATA MON,TUES,WED,THUR,FRI
190 DATA (data from Uphams Corner)
200 DATA (data from Broadway)
210 DATA (data from Hobart Square)
9999 END
```

EXAMPLE 15.12. A certain type of commercial airplane uses a seating arrangement made up of 15 rows. In each row there are 4 seats. So the arrangement looks like

```
                      SEAT NUMBERS

              1:   1    2    3    4
              2:   1    2    3    4
              3:   1    2    3    4
                   .    .    .    .
ROW NUMBERS        .    .    .    .
                   .    .    .    .
             14:   1    2    3    4
             15:   1    2    3    4
```

A program is to be written to process requests for seats. A request, entered from the terminal, should specify row number and seat number. The response to the request should take one of three forms:

1. If the seat is available, the request should be confirmed.
2. If the seat has already been reserved but there is an available seat in the specified row, the first such available seat in that row should be reserved.
3. If the seat has already been reserved and if there are no more seats available in the specified row, a message to that effect should be printed.

After any of the three possible responses, the program should inquire if there is another request to be made. Depending on the response, suitable action should be taken.

The plane's seating arrangement is a 15×4 array, which will be named S.

How shall we determine whether or not a seat is available? Since there are only two possibilities—seat available or already taken—we shall use two numbers, say, 0 and 1, to stand for these two possible conditions. If the value of a seat is 0, it will mean that the seat is available; if it is 1, the seat has been taken.

The program will begin by reading in the 60 values of the array S. For purposes of illustration, we will assume that certain seats have already been reserved. Thus the data to be assigned to S will be a collection of 0's and 1's. Let's suppose that after this data has been read into S, S looks like

```
0  1  0  0
0  0  0  1
1  1  0  0
0  0  0  0
0  1  0  0
0  0  0  0
0  0  1  0
1  1  1  1
1  0  0  0
1  0  0  0
0  1  1  0
0  0  0  0
0  1  1  1
1  0  1  0
1  0  0  0
```

From the picture of S we can see, for example, that the first two seats of row 3—seats $S(3,1)$ and $S(3,2)$—are already taken and that all the seats in the sixth row—$S(6,1)$ through $S(6,4)$—are available.

Note that once an available seat has been reserved from the terminal, its code must be changed from 0 to 1, thus making it unavailable.

The program begins by reading in the array S.

```
100 REM AIRLINE RESERVATIONS
110 DIM S(15,4)
```

```
120 REM READ ARRAY S
130 FOR I=1 TO 15
140    FOR J=1 TO 4
150        READ S(I,J)
160    NEXT J
170 NEXT I
```

Next the request for a certain seat is made from the terminal.

```
180 REM REQUEST SEAT
190 PRINT "WHAT SEAT IS REQUESTED?"
200 PRINT "ENTER ROW NUMBER,SEAT NUMBER."
210 INPUT N1,N2
```

We will investigate the rest of the program, in parts, by looking at pieces of a flowchart. If the seat requested is available, a message that the request for the seat is confirmed should be printed, then the status of the seat should be changed and finally the question asked whether there is another request. This is shown by the chart in Figure 15.1.

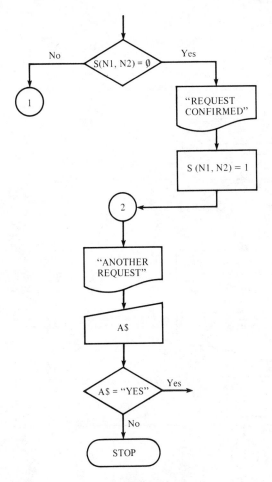

FIGURE 15.1.

Connector (1) leads to the activity that must take place if the seat is already taken. This will be shown in a moment. After the activities along the "no" branch are concluded the user will be asked if there is another request. The "no" branch leads into connector (2). The "yes" branch leading out of the bottom decision box would lead back to a part of the flowchart that corresponds to line 19Ø of the program.

Let's now take up the discussion following (1). We want to assign the first available seat in the specified row. That row is N1. So we wish to examine each of the seats (there are four of them) in row N1 to see if one is empty. This means we want to check seat number S(N1,I) for each I going from 1 to 4. If we find an empty seat, we print out its location (the two subscripts), change its code to "occupied," and transfer to the question (connector (2)). The flowchart for this much is shown in Figure 15.2.

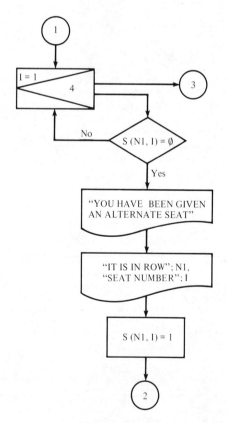

FIGURE 15.2.

Finally we consider what happens if no alternate seat is available. This will occur if the loop is gone through all four times and so is exited from along the branch which leads to 3. This option is simply that shown in Figure 15.3.

FIGURE 15.3.

Using the logic developed in flowchart form, we would code the complete program as follows.

```
100 REM AIRLINE RESERVATIONS
110 DIM S(15,4)
120 REM READ ARRAY S
130 FOR I=1 TO 15
140    FOR J=1 TO 4
150       READ S(I,J)
160    NEXT J
170 NEXT I
180 REM REQUEST SEAT
190    PRINT "WHAT SEAT IS REQUESTED?"
200    PRINT "ENTER ROW NUMBER,SEAT NUMBER."
210    INPUT N1,N2
220    PRINT
230    REM SEE IF SEAT EMPTY
240    REM CODE FOR EMPTY=0,FULL=1
250    IF S(N1,N2)=0 THEN 420
260    REM CHECK SEATS IN ROW N1
270    FOR I=1 TO 4
280       REM IF EMPTY SEAT FOUND, ASSIGN IT
290       IF S(N1,I)=0 THEN 360
300       REM IF NOT, CONTINUE LOOP
310    NEXT I
320    REM NO EMPTY SEAT FOUND IN ROW
330    PRINT "REQUEST UNABLE TO BE FILLED."
340    REM SEE IF ANOTHER REQUEST
350    GOTO 470
360    REM ASSIGN ALTERNATE SEAT
370    PRINT "YOU HAVE BEEN GIVEN AN ALTERNATE SEAT."
380    PRINT "IT IS IN ROW";N1,"SEAT NUMBER";I
390    REM CHANGE CODE TO FULL
400    LET S(N1,I)=1
```

```
410    GOTO 460
420    REM ASSIGN REQUESTED SEAT
430    PRINT "REQUEST CONFIRMED"
440    REM CHANGE CODE TO FULL
450    LET S(N1,N2)=1
460    REM SEE IF ANOTHER REQUEST
470    PRINT
480    PRINT "IS THERE ANOTHER REQUEST?"
490    INPUT A$
500 IF A$="YES" THEN 190
510 REM CODED DATA FOR SEATS
520 DATA . . .
525 DATA . . .
 —
 —
 —
599 END
```

Referring to the coded seating arrangement shown earlier, a RUN
is now shown.

RUN

WHAT SEAT IS REQUESTED?
ENTER ROW NUMBER, SEAT NUMBER.
? 3,4 ————————an empty seat

REQUEST CONFIRMED

IS THERE ANOTHER REQUEST?
? YES
WHAT SEAT IS REQUESTED?
ENTER ROW NUMBER, SEAT NUMBER.
? 14,3————— a seat already taken

YOU HAVE BEEN GIVEN AN ALTERNATE SEAT
IT IS IN ROW 14   SEAT NUMBER 2

IS THERE ANOTHER REQUEST?
? YES
WHAT SEAT IS REQUESTED?
ENTER ROW NUMBER, SEAT NUMBER.
? 8,1————— seat in full row

REQUEST UNABLE TO BE FILLED.

IS THERE ANOTHER REQUEST?
? YES
WHAT SEAT IS REQUESTED?

ENTER ROW NUMBER, SEAT NUMBER.
? 3,4 ————— seat already taken, by first request

YOU HAVE BEEN GIVEN AN ALTERNATE SEAT
IT IS IN ROW 3   SEAT NUMBER 3

IS THERE ANOTHER REQUEST?
? NO

READY

---

1 What is the output of each of the following programs?   **EXERCISES**

a.

```
100 DIM G(2,4)
110 FOR I=1 TO 2
120   FOR J=1 TO 4
130     READ G(I,J)
140     PRINT G(I,J),
150   NEXT J
160 NEXT I
170 DATA 4,6,8,3
180 DATA 2,0,9,1
190 END
```

b.

```
100 DIM W(7,4)
110 FOR T=1 TO 7
120   FOR V=1 TO 4
130     LET W(T,V)=T-V
140   NEXT V
150 NEXT T
160 FOR A=1 TO 5
170   FOR B=2 TO 3
180     PRINT W(A,B),
190   NEXT B
200   PRINT
210 NEXT A
220 END
```

c.

```
200 DIM Y(3,12)
210 FOR X=1 TO 3
220   FOR Z=1 TO 12
230     LET Y(X,Z)=X*Z+1
240   NEXT Z
250 NEXT X
260 FOR C=1 TO 3
270   FOR D=3 TO 11 STEP 3
280     PRINT C,D,Y(C,D)
290   NEXT D
300 NEXT C
310 END
```

d.

```
1000 DIM A(5,5)
1100 FOR I=1 TO 2
1110   FOR J=1 TO 3
1120     LET A(I,J)=I+J
1130   NEXT J
1140 NEXT I
1150 FOR I=1 TO 2
1160   PRINT
1170   FOR J=1 TO 3
1180     PRINT A(I,J),
1190   NEXT J
1200 NEXT I
1210 PRINT
1220 PRINT
1230 FOR L=1 TO 2
1240   PRINT
1250   FOR K=1 TO 3
1260     PRINT A(K,L),
1270   NEXT K
1280 NEXT L
1290 PRINT
1300 PRINT
1310 FOR T=1 TO 3
1320   PRINT
1330   FOR S=1 TO 2
1340     PRINT A(S,T),
1350   NEXT S
1360 NEXT T
1370 END
```

e.

```
500 DIM A$(2,5),B$(2,5),C$(4,5)
510 FOR I=1 TO 2
520   FOR J=1 TO 5
530     READ A$(I,J)
540   NEXT J
550 NEXT I
560 FOR J=1 TO 2
570   FOR I=1 TO 5
580     READ B$(J,I)
590   NEXT I
600 NEXT J
610 FOR X=1 TO 4
```

```
620    FOR Y=1 TO 5
630      ON X GOTO 640,660,680,700
640      LET C$(X,Y)=A$(X,Y)
650      GOTO 710
660      LET C$(X,Y)=B$(X,Y)
670      GOTO 710
680      LET C$(X,Y)=A$(X-1,Y)
690      GOTO 710
700      LET C$(X,Y)=B$(X-2,Y)
710    NEXT Y
720 NEXT X
730 FOR I=1 TO 4
740    FOR J=1 TO 5
750      PRINT C$(I,J),
760    NEXT J
770    PRINT
780 NEXT I
790 DATA PHILIP,MARY,DAVID,JOHN,JEANNE,BETTY
800 DATA THOMAS,AGATHA,SOPHIA,PAT,MARLOWE
810 DATA STUART,GOLIATH,KEMENY,D'ARC
820 DATA CROCKER,KURTZ,CHRISTIE,LOREN,SHEA
830 END
```

2   Write a sequence of steps that will read in an array Q that has eight rows and five columns.

3   Write a program that reads in the inventory array columnwise. (You might have to rearrange your data.)

4   Suppose that the items stored in the warehouses have the following values: teletypes, $1300 each; paper, $55 each; pencils, $12.75 each; templates, $3.60 each. Write a program that reads in the inventory, reads in each item value, and calculates and prints the values from each item in each warehouse. Your output should be in the form of an array with the labeling at the top and left of the array as indicated at the start of the chapter.

5   Exercise 4 so that after the array is printed the total value of all items in all warehouses is calculated and printed.

6   The *main* (or *major*) *diagonal* of a square matrix is the line of elements from the upper left corner to the lower right corner. Write a program that creates a 4 × 4 array with 1's in each location on the main diagonal and 2's everywhere else. Have the array printed out.

7   Write a program to create and print a 5 × 5 array that contains only 2's on the main diagonal, only 1's above the main diagonal, and only 3's below the main diagonal.

8   Write a program that will read in the array

```
2 7 0 3 4
6 2 9 8 1
3 5 1 6 5
```

and print it out as

```
2 6 3
7 2 5
0 9 1
3 8 6
4 1 5
```

9 Write a program to read and print the first array of Exercise 8. When this is done, two different numbers should be entered from the terminal. The numbers indicate the columns of the array that are to be switched. Print out the changed matrix.

10 A 5 × 6 array T is to be initialized to all zeroes. Then a sequence of numbers should be assigned to it in the following way (the numbers are to be entered, one at a time from the terminal). The first number will go into position T(1,1).

The position of each following number will depend on its relation to the previous number. If a number is greater than or equal to the previous, the position of that number will be to the immediate right of the previous one. Otherwise its position will be immediately below the previous one. The array will be considered completed when the number from the terminal cannot be placed in the array.

Finally, if the number entered from the terminal is a zero, it should be rejected and another number requested. Try your program with the following sequences.

Sequence 1: 3, 4, 2, 6, 5, 1, 1, 0, 2, 3

Sequence 2: 10, 9, 8, 7, 6, 7, 8, 9, 10, 11

Sequence 3: 7, 4, 8, 9, 1, 10, 9, 8, 7, 6, 5, 9, 1, 10, 12

11 Given the array

```
4  7  -2   3   8
0  5   9  -4   3
1  1   5   6  -1
7  5  -1   0   2
```

write a program that finds the sum of the interior elements (that is, the elements that are not on the outside of the array).

12 Two arrays are shown next. Write a program that reads both from DATA lines and then prints out all elements that the two arrays have in common. A common element should be printed only once.

```
7   9  11   2   5        3   4   6
3   8   8   1   6       19  10   4
10  1   5  13  14       16  20   2
2   9   8   5  12        9  10   8
```

13 Read in the 4 × 5 array shown, print it out, and then define a 20-element list from the array elements. Print the list.

```
-4   6   2  11   1
 3  -1   5  -2   5
 7   0  -3   7  10
 8   4   2   0   3
```

14 Four candidates ran for a single position on the town council. The candidates names are Jenson, Ortega, Plauss, and Graham. The votes were tallied by political affiliation (Democrat, Republican, and Independent). These results are

```
121 Democrats voted for Jenson
104 Democrats voted for Ortega
 91 Democrats voted for Plauss
115 Democrats voted for Graham
118 Republicans voted for Jenson
 52 Republicans voted for Ortega
134 Republicans voted for Plauss
 65 Republicans voted for Graham
```

        62 Independents voted for Jenson
       110 Independents voted for Ortega
       121 Independents voted for Plauss
       106 Independents voted for Graham

Write a program to
    a. Display the results of the voting in table form with labels for each row
    b. Print out the name of the winner (the winner is the candidate with the most votes) and the number of votes received by the winner
    c. Print the total number of votes cast by each political group

15 A mileage chart for the distances between five cities is shown.

	Boston	Chicago	Dallas	Los Angeles	Miami
Boston	0	975	1819	3052	1542
Chicago	975	0	936	2095	1360
Dallas	1819	936	0	1403	1309
Los Angeles	3052	2095	1403	0	2712
Miami	1542	1360	1309	2712	0

Write a program to read the data and then ask the user to supply the city of origin and the destination; the program should print the distance between them.

16 Modify the program of Exercise 15 so that the user can enter an average speed (in miles per hour); the program should then print a table of travel times between each of the cities.

17 A teacher has a class in a room that contains six rows. Each row contains five seats. Write a program that will assign a seat to each student and, when this is done, will print out a seating chart. The assignment is to be done from the terminal. The student's name should be entered and then the row and seat number assigned to the student. If a seat has already been assigned, the teacher should be told so and another seat for that student should be requested. An eod tag should be supplied from the terminal after all the students have been entered. (A commonly used eod tag for names is ZZZ.)

    Try the program with the following data.

Name	Row	Seat
Jenny	2	3
Matthew	6	4
Sara	1	3
Jessica	3	4
Jeffrey	1	1
Bridget	4	2
Andrew	1	2
Amy	1	4
Eileen	2	1
Joseph	3	4

(this will have to be done again—to row 5, seat 2)

| Michael | 5 | 4 |
| Duncan | 1 | 1 |

(first try 1, 2 then 2, 3 then 6, 3)

Louise	2	2
Laura	3	3
Angus	4	3
Heather	5	1
Alison	3	4

(then 4, 4)

| Matt | 4 | 5 |

18 Modify the airplane reservation program of Example 15.12 so that the first six rows are considered the "no smoking" section while smoking is allowed in the remaining rows. A request for a seat should be first made by section: smoking, no-smoking, or either. A check should be made to determine whether the row and seat requested is in the proper section.

* * *

19 A square matrix is called a "magic square" if all its row sums and all its column sums and both its diagonal sums are equal. Write programs for the matrices given that will determine whether or not they are magic. The matrix should be read in and printed. Its row, column, and diagonal sums should be stored as subscripted variables. All these sums should be printed, clearly labeled. Finally, the program should determine whether or not the square is magic and print an appropriate message.

a.

17	24	1	8	15
23	5	7	14	16
4	6	13	20	21
10	12	19	22	3
11	18	25	2	9

b.

20	27	4	11	18
26	8	10	17	19
7	9	16	23	25
13	15	22	24	6
14	21	28	5	12

20 Write a subroutine that interchanges the Ith and Jth rows of an M $\times$ N array A. Use the subroutine in a program that
    a. Creates a 6 $\times$ 8 array whose values are the absolute value of the row number minus the column number
    b. Prints the array
    c. Skips several lines
    d. Interchanges the first and sixth rows, the second and fifth rows, and the third and fourth rows
    e. Prints the new matrix

21 An element of an array is called "strong" if it is the largest element in its row and in its column. Of course, there may be more than one strong element in an array. Write one program to find and print the strong elements of the two arrays shown. The first array should be printed and under it the information about its strong elements. Then a similar activity should take place for the second array.

First Array				**Second Array**		
9	4	7	10	1	3	2
5	15	12	8	8	2	6
9	13	4	6	7	5	4
6	0	7	12	9	10	9
				4	8	4
				6	2	5

22 Write a program that reads 42 values into a 7 $\times$ 6 array. The rest of the program should
    a. Print the array.
    b. Find the largest element in the array.
    c. Tell where the largest element is found in the array.
    d. If the largest element occurs more than once, tell how many times it occurs and where each occurrence is located.

Use the arrays given.

1	2	3	4	5	6		7	4	−1	3	2	5
2	4	6	8	0	2		15	0	2	4	6	8
9	7	5	3	1	9		3	8	9	−2	7	1
4	10	8	−1	0	2		1	1	2	2	3	3
5	5	1	1	5	1		1	2	3	5	8	13
2	3	5	7	−1	0		2	3	5	15	1	0
6	7	1	0	5	2		6	6	8	9	−1	2

16

The Random Number Generator

In Chapter 11, we considered several built-in functions. There is another built-in function, called the *random number generator,* that can be used for a number of interesting, and even amusing, applications.

16.1 The Built-in Function, RND

The name of the random number generating function is RND. Each time it is used, RND *randomly* chooses a number between 0 and 1, possibly including 0 but not including 1; that is,

$$0 \leq RND(X) < 1$$

The choice of the argument for the RND function is highly dependent upon the computer that is used to execute the program. Minimal BASIC presents RND with no argument; that is, RND alone is used. Some machines require 0 as the argument: you must use RND(Ø). Others require 1 as the argument; others demand −1; still others allow any value as the argument, and some require the presence of an additional statement in the program. (This will be discussed following Example 16.1.) You should be sure that you know what the particular requirement of your computer is before you begin your program. So that RND will resemble other functions presented in this text, we shall write RND with an argument and will use −1 as an argument.

EXAMPLE 16.1. The following program shows the results of using the RND function.

```
100 REM RANDOM NUMBER ILLUSTRATION
110 FOR I=1 TO 10
120   PRINT RND(-1),
130 NEXT I
140 END
```

RUN

| .140775 | .143441 | .602157 | .995925 | .331023 |
| .659462 | .150346 | .145793 | .205776 | .255753 |

READY

RUN

| .140779 | .305836 | 3.77681E-2 | .351009 | .28577 |
| .800785 | 4.96389E-2 | .379334 | .927283 | .974313 |

READY

RUN

| .140783 | .46823 | .473379 | .706093 | .240517 |
| .942108 | .948932 | .612876 | .648789 | .692873 |

READY

As you scan the 30 values printed from three runs, notice that each number lies between 0 and 1, that some of the numbers are printed using E-notation, and that 10 different values are generated for each run. (Some computers use a version of BASIC that, if this program were executed, would give 10 numbers but the *same* 10 numbers would be printed each time the program is run. Such a version of BASIC requires that the statement RANDOMIZE be included at the start of the program. So if a line 9Ø RANDOMIZE were added to the program, 10 different values would be printed for each run.)

16.2 Random Numbers over Any Range

Recall from the first section that the range of the RND function is from 0 to 1; that is, $0 \leq \text{RND}(-1) < 1$. Let's consider $0 \leq \text{RND}(-1) < 1$ as a mathematics inequality with three parts:

Left-Hand Side		Middle		Right-Hand Side
0	$\leq$	RND(-1)	$<$	1

Let's multiply each of the three parts by 7. If we do, we get

Left-Hand Side		Middle		Right-Hand Side
0	$\leq$	$7*\text{RND}(-1)$	$<$	7

Now let's add 2 to the three parts, giving

Left-Hand Side		Middle		Right-Hand Side
2	$\leq$	$7*RND(-1)+2$	$<$	9

What does this show? It shows that calculations can be performed using the random number generator that will generate random numbers over a range different than 0 to 1. In particular, this shows that the expression $7*RND(-1)+2$ will generate a random number from 2 to 9.

We will now generalize this result to generate random numbers over *any* range. To do this suppose that A and B are two different numbers and that $A < B$.

	Left		Middle		Right
We already know that	0	$\leq$	$RND(-1)$	$<$	1
Multiply the three parts by the positive quantity					
$B-A$	0	$\leq$	$(B-A)*RND(-1)$	$<$	$B-A$
Add A to the three parts	A	$\leq$	$(B-A)*RND(-1)+A$	$<$	B

So we see that the expression $(B-A)*RND(-1)+A$ gives a random number between A and B for *any* values of A and B (where, as stipulated, $A<B$).

EXAMPLE 16.2. The following program generates and prints random numbers from 3 to 12.

Here $A = 3$ and $B = 12$ so we simply plug these values into the expression that we just derived.

```
10 REM RANDOM NUMBERS FROM 3 TO 12
20 REM 12-3 IN LINE 40 SHOULD BE WRITTEN AS 9
30 FOR J= TO 10
40    PRINT (12-3)*RND(-1)+3,
50 NEXT J
60 END

RUN

 3.10845        9.90827        11.0863        6.72948        9.98867
10.8576         8.624          10.2518        8.3084         9.41208

READY
```

RUN

| 3.00145 | 11.3698 | 6.00685 | 9.92524 | 9.5814 |
| 3.12949 | 7.71764 | 3.35364 | 5.80196 | 6.87912 |

READY

RUN

| 7.62954 | 4.1583 | 4.98737 | 9.28336 | 8.88014 |
| 5.8474 | 6.5017 | 8.8962 | 8.27969 | 5.39201 |

READY

The REM in line 20 merely indicates that if you were writing a program that needed to use a random number between 3 and 12, the expression that should be used is 9*RND(−1)+3—the "12−3" is used in the program for purposes of illustration only. In the expression 9*RND(−1)+3, the number 9, which is multiplying RND(−1), is sometimes called a *scaling factor* and the number 3, which is being added, is sometimes called the *displacement* or *starting value*. Scaling factors and displacements are especially useful when dealing with random integers.

16.3 Random Integers

Consider the expression 10*RND(−1)+1. It generates a random number between 1 and 11, namely,

$$1 \leqslant 10*RND(-1)+1 < 11$$

A few of the numbers that might be generated by the expression at the lower or smaller end of the range are 1.8, 1.1, and 1.002.

If we apply the INT function to these values, we get, in each case, the number 1. Now 10.1, 10.9, and 10.996 are three values that could be generated at the upper or larger end of the range. When INT is applied to them, the result is the same number, 10. So if we consider the expression

$$INT(10*RND(-1)+1)$$

we know that (1) the value will be an integer, (2) the smallest possible value is 1, and (3) the largest possible value is 10. We conclude that *INT(10*RND(−1)+1) will generate a random **integer** from 1 to 10 **inclusive**.*

EXAMPLE 16.3. The following program prints randomly generated integers from 1 to 6 inclusive.

Paralleling the development just outlined, the expression that must be used is INT(6*RND(−1)+1).

```
10 REM RANDOM INTEGERS 1-6
20 FOR R=1 TO 10
```

```
30    PRINT INT(6*RND(-1)+1),
40 NEXT R
50 END
```

RUN

| 5 | 2 | 1 | 3 | 4 |
| 6 | 1 | 5 | 2 | 3 |

READY

RUN

| 3 | 4 | 6 | 1 | 4 |
| 5 | 3 | 5 | 5 | 4 |

READY

RUN

| 5 | 5 | 1 | 3 | 2 |
| 3 | 5 | 4 | 3 | 4 |

READY

EXAMPLE 16.4. What are the possible values generated by the expression INT(6*RND(−1)+4)?

To answer the question, we begin by examining RND(−1) and its range and construct the expression involved, INT(6*RND(−1)+4), step by step, noting the derived ranges that each step in the construction produces.

Expression	Operation	Range
1. RND(−1)	none	0 to 1, decimal
2. 6*RND(−1)	multiply by 6	0 to 6, decimal
3. 6*RND(−1)+4	add 4	4 to 10, decimal
4. INT(6*RND(−1)+4)	greatest integer function	4 to 9, integer

So INT(6*RND(−1)+4) randomly generates integers over the range from 4 to 9, inclusive; that is, INT(6*RND(−1)+4) will generate one of the numbers 4, 5, 6, 7, 8, 9. What should be noted is that the displacement is 4 and the smallest value of the integers generated is 4. Also, there are six possible integers that can be generated and 6 is the scaling factor.

When generating random integers,

1. *The displacement tells the smallest value that can be generated*
2. *The scaling factor tells how many values will be generated*

EXAMPLE 16.5. Write an expression that generates a random integer from 3 to 11.

The smallest value is 3, so 3 will be the displacement. The number of values to be generated is 9[1] (that is, 3, 4, 5, 6, 7, 8, 9, 10, 11) so the scaling factor is 9. So the desired expression is

INT(9*RND(-1)+3)

16.4 Simulation and Games

We have devoted the last three sections to the development of random numbers, integer or otherwise, that can be produced over any range. A question that might naturally be asked at this time is, "How can this be used?" One area to which random numbers may be applied is that of *simulation*. One definition reads "to simulate a situation is to mimic or imitate some or all of the behavior found in the situation by a system which is dissimilar to the original situation." In our case, the system referred to in the definition is the computer we are using.

Computer simulation may be described less technically as a program that causes the computer to apparently perform activities that are usually attributed to people or other objects.

To illustrate, recall that the expression INT(6*RND(-1)+1) randomly generates an integer from 1 to 6. How can this be used for simulation? To answer this question, try to think of a noncomputer activity that involves the use of the integers 1 through 6. The rolling of a single die is one such activity. When a person rolls a die, the upturned face of the die shows 1, 2, 3, 4, 5, and 6 spots. Thus the expression INT(6*RND(-1)+1) can be used to simulate the rolling of a die as is shown in the following program.

EXAMPLE 16.6. A program simulating the rolling of a single die.

```
10 REM SIMULATION PROGRAM
20 REM ROLLING A DIE
30 REM GENERATE RANDOM INTEGER FROM 1 TO 6
40 LET R=INT(6*RND(-1)+1)
50 PRINT "A";R;"WAS ROLLED"
60 END

RUN

A 4 WAS ROLLED

READY

RUN

A 5 WAS ROLLED

READY
```

[1] The number of values to be generated can be calculated as follows. If an integer is to be generated from X to Y ($X < Y$), that number is $Y - X + 1$. The example generates 9 values from 3 to 11 and $11 - 3 + 1 = 9$.

RUN

A 1 WAS ROLLED

READY

Once you know how to make the computer "roll a die" it is an easy task to simulate the rolling of a pair of dice, which is an ingredient in many games of chance.

EXAMPLE 16.7. The following involves rolling a pair of dice ten times.

```
100 REM 10 ROLLS OF A PAIR OF DICE
110 REM SHOWING EACH DIE AS WELL AS TOTAL
120 PRINT "ROLL","1ST DIE","2ND DIE","TOTAL"
130 FOR J=1 TO 10
140    LET R1=INT(6*RND(-1)+1)
150    LET R2=INT(6*RND(-1)+1)
160    LET T=R1+R2
170    PRINT J,R1,R2,T
180 NEXT J
190 END
```

RUN

ROLL	1ST DIE	2ND DIE	TOTAL
1	3	4	7
2	5	4	9
3	1	5	6
4	3	2	5
5	6	5	11
6	2	6	8
7	6	6	12
8	1	3	4
9	4	4	8
10	3	5	8

READY

Why does the expression INT(6*RND(−1)+1) correctly simulate the rolling of a die? Perhaps the easy explanation is that the only possible numbers that can be rolled with a die are 1, 2, 3, 4, 5, and 6 and that these are the only possible numbers that can be generated by the expression. However, this explanation is incomplete. If a die is rolled, the *chance* that a 1 will show up is the same as the chance that a 2 will show up, which is the same as the chance that a 3, 4, 5, or a 6 will show up. The *chance* that INT(6*RND(−1)+1) will generate a 1 is the same as the chance that it will generate a 2 and so on. Since the possible outcomes of the real event (rolling a die) correspond precisely to the possible outcomes of a computer activity (the random generation of a 1, 2, 3, 4, 5, or 6), we can say that the computer activity simulates the real event.

It is important to note that it is the programmer who determines in what way the computer simulation will correspond to the real event. For example, the programmer could have used the expression INT(6*RND(−1)+21) instead of INT(6*RND(−1)+1). The expression INT(6*RND(−1)+21) generates a random integer from 21 to 26; that is, it generates a 21, 22, 23, 24, 25, or 26, and the chance that one of these numbers is generated is the same as the chance of any other. Therefore, the expression INT(6*RND(−1)+21) can be used to simulate the rolling of a die. The programmer merely *interprets* the results of the random number generator and applies the results to the real problem, the rolling of a die. For example, the programmer could interpret the generation of 21 as meaning that a 1 was rolled, a 22 as the rolling of a 2 and so on. It should be clear, however, that the choice of INT(6*RND(−1)+1) is better, since it corresponds exactly to the real situation of rolling a die. The idea of interpretation is further illustrated in the next example.

EXAMPLE 16.8. A program is to be written that simulates the tossing of a coin ten times. If a head is tossed, the word "head" should be printed, otherwise the word "tail."

First you should notice that there are only two possible outcomes: heads or tails. Next note that the chance of one accurring is the same as the chance of the other. However, in contrast to the earlier situation where the computer could generate the 1, 2, 3, 4, 5, or 6 that corresponded to the roll of a die, the computer does not toss coins or generate "heads" or "tails"—it can only generate *numbers*. So it is the job of the programmer to interpret what the computer can do (generate numbers) and make that simulate the actual activity (the tossing of a coin). Since there are only two possible outcomes when a coin is tossed and since these two outcomes are equally likely to happen, *the action of tossing a coin can be simulated by an expression that generates two random integers.* We will decide to use the expression INT(2*RND(−1)), which generates either the number 0 or the number 1. We then give the following interpretations:

1. If a 0 is generated, it will mean a "head" has been tossed.
2. A 1 means a "tail."

(You should again notice that the choice of the particular numbers that are generated and the interpretations given to them is the choice of the programmer. So the programmer could have generated the numbers 16 and 17 and decided to call 17 "heads" and 16 "tails.") The program follows.

```
100 REM SIMULATION COIN TOSS
110 REM TEN TOSSES
120 FOR A=1 TO 10
130    REM GENERATE A 0 OR 1
140    LET T=INT(2*RND(-1))
150    REM T=0 MEANS HEADS
160    IF T=0 THEN 190
```

```
170    PRINT "TAILS"
180    GOTO 200
190    PRINT "HEADS"
200 NEXT A
210 END
```

RUN

```
HEADS
TAILS
TAILS
HEADS
TAILS
HEADS
HEADS
HEADS
TAILS
HEADS
```

READY

The next program performs the same simulation as the previous one but does not use integers.

EXAMPLE 16.9.   This problem involves tossing a coin ten times.

The approach here is that a "head" should be tossed half the time and the other half a "tail" should be tossed. The range of RND is from 0 to 1. So half this range will be called the "heads" range and the other half the "tails" range. We will interpret the first half of the numbers from 0 to 1 to be "heads" numbers. So if the random number generated by RND is less than .5, we will interpret this as a "heads" being tossed, otherwise a "tails." The program with this interpretation follows.

```
100 REM SIMULATION COIN TOSS
110 REM TEN TOSSES
120 FOR A=1 TO 10
130    REM GENERATE RANDOM TOSS
140    LET T=RND(-1)
150    REM T<.5 MEANS HEADS
160    IF T<.5 THEN 190
170    PRINT "TAILS"
180    GOTO 200
190    PRINT "HEADS"
200 NEXT A
210 END
```

EXAMPLE 16.10.   A baseball player for a semiprofessional team had a batting average of .317 last year. Usually this player comes to the plate four times each game. Write a program to simulate the player's activities during 12 games. The information sought is how many hits (0 to 4) he can expect in each of the 12 games.

For our purposes, either of two things will happen when the batter comes to the plate: he will get a hit or not. However, these two possibilities are not equally likely. The .317 batting average says that the player is more likely not to get a hit than he is to get one. (A batting average of .500 would imply that the batter is just as likely to get a hit as not). To simulate the player's appearance at the plate, we will use simply RND(−1), which generates a number between 0 and 1. If the number generated is less than or equal to .317, the interpretation will be that the player got a hit. However, if the number is greater than .317 then there was no hit.

A part of the program, the simulation of one game, is as follows. (We will later put this into a loop that is executed 12 times to complete the simulation for the required 12 games.)

```
170 REM C COUNTS HITS IN A GAME
180 LET C=0
190 REM FOUR AT BATS EACH GAME
200 FOR B=1 TO 4
210 REM GENERATE RANDOM NUMBER
220 LET A=RND(-1)
230 REM IF A>.317, NO HIT
240 IF A>.317 THEN 270
250 REM HIT, SO INCREASE COUNTER
260 LET C=C+1
270 NEXT B
```

To finish the program we include the preceding statement in a loop that will include the output.

```
110 REM BASEBALL SIMULATION
120 REM BATTING AVERAGE IS .317
130 REM SIMULATE TWELVE GAMES
140 PRINT "GAME","HITS"
150 PRINT
160 FOR G=1 TO 12
170    REM C COUNTS HITS IN A GAME
180    LET C=0
190    REM FOUR AT BATS EACH GAME
200    FOR B=1 TO 14
210      REM GENERATE RANDOM NUMBER
220      LET A=RND(-1)
230      REM IF A>.317, NO HIT
240      IF A>.317 THEN 270
250      REM HIT, SO INCREASE COUNTER
260      LET C=C+1
270    NEXT B
280    PRINT G,C
290 NEXT G
300 END

RUN

GAME                HITS
 1                   1
 2                   1
 3                   2
```

4	2
5	Ø
6	1
7	3
8	1
9	2
1Ø	2
11	1
12	1

READY

One of the traditional problems of calculus is to find the area under a curve. For example,

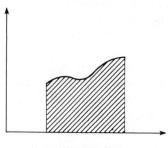

FIGURE 16.1.

we would like to calculate the area of the shaded region in Figure 16.1. This will be done using random numbers, in the following example.

EXAMPLE 16.11. Calculate the area under a curve.

The curve must be the graph of some function. For this example, we shall use $f(x) = -x^2 + 1$.

The graph of the function and the region whose area we seek is shown in Figure 16.2. In terms of the x values, the area lies between $x = 0$ and $x = 1$.

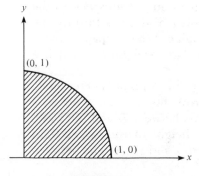

FIGURE 16.2.

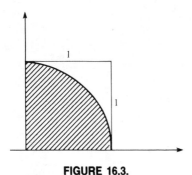

FIGURE 16.3.

The technique is to program a sort of computer game—dart throwing. We first "build" a target by considering the shaded area to be contained within some square or rectangle. For this example, a square with one unit on each side will be sufficient. This is shown in Figure 16.3.

We now *randomly* "throw darts" at this target. We will assume that all the darts land somewhere on the target. Some of the darts will land in the shaded region; others will not.

Let A stand for the target's area (for us, $A = 1$). Let D stand for the area of the shaded region (this is what we want.) Let N be the total number of darts thrown at the target and H the number of darts that land in the shaded region. The result that will be used to approximate the area of the shaded region is an approximate equality between two ratios. The first ratio is the ratio of the area of the shaded region to the total area of the target (D/A); the second is the ratio of the number of darts that lands in the shaded region to the total number of darts thrown (H/N). That is,

$$\frac{D}{A} \doteq \frac{H}{N}$$

Solving for D, we get

$$D \doteq \frac{H}{N} \cdot A$$

You might observe that this technique gives an *approximation* to the area. However, it is true that if a large number of darts is thrown, the approximation is quite close to the actual value. What remains now is to determine how to randomly throw the darts and how to tell if a dart lands in the shaded region.

When a dart hits the target, it hits it at a point. A point is determined by a pair of coordinates (x, y). Thus to throw the dart, we generate a random pair of numbers, x and y, where x is between 0 and the width of the target and y is between 0 and the height of the target. This means that for our example the values of both x and y are to be between 0 and 1.

Suppose that r and s are the values that were generated for x and

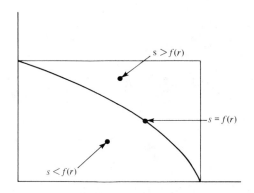

FIGURE 16.4.

y, respectively. If $s = f(r)$, the point (r, s) is *on* the curve. If $s > f(r)$, the point is *above* the curve, and if $s < f(r)$, the point is *below* the curve. (This is illustrated in Figure 16.4.) The points that we wish to count, then, are those points (r, s) for which $s < f(r)$.

The program will ask the user how many darts are to be thrown and then, using the procedure described, approximate the area under the curve. (Using calculus, the actual value of the area is 2/3.)

```
110 REM AREA BY RANDOM NUMBERS- DARTS
120 REM DEFINE FUNCTION
130 DEF FNY(X)=-X↑2+1
140 REM H COUNTS DARTS IN SHADED AREA
150 LET H=∅
160 REM A IS TOTAL AREA OF TARGET
170 LET A=1
180 PRINT "HOW MANY DARTS DO YOU WISH TO THROW";
190 INPUT N
200 PRINT
210 REM SIMULATE THROWING N DARTS
220 FOR I=1 TO N
230    REM R IS ABSCISSA, S IS ORDINATE
240    LET R=RND(-1)
250    LET S=RND(-1)
260    REM CHECK WHERE DART LANDS
270    REM IF S>=FNY(R), DART OUTSIDE SHADED AREA
280    IF S>=FNY(R) THEN 31∅
290    REM COUNT DART
300    LET H=H+1
310 NEXT I
320 REM D IS AREA WE WANT
330 LET D=H/N*A
340 PRINT "APPROXIMATE AREA IS";D
350 END

RUN

HOW MANY DARTS DO YOU WISH TO THROW? 1∅∅
APPROXIMATE AREA IS  .66
```

```
READY

RUN

HOW MANY DARTS DO YOU WISH TO THROW? 100
APPROXIMATE AREA IS .65

READY

RUN

HOW MANY DARTS DO YOU WISH TO THROW? 1000
APPROXIMATE AREA IS .662

READY

RUN

HOW MANY DARTS DO YOU WISH TO THROW? 50000
APPROXIMATE AREA IS .6723

READY

RUN

HOW MANY DARTS DO YOU WISH TO THROW? 50000
APPROXIMATE AREA IS .6655

READY
```

The simulation examples that have been presented so far have all used random numbers. However, it is not always necessary to use random numbers in simulation. After all, computer simulation merely means that the computer is imitating some other real situation. We finish the chapter with an example to illustrate this.

EXAMPLE 16.12. The population of Centerville is presently 18,789. The following information has been gathered about the annual population change of Centerville.

1. There are 17.2 births per 1000 population.
2. There are 11.7 deaths per 1000.
3. Each year (on the average) 43 people move into town.
4. Each year 37 people move out of town.

We wish to find the approximate population of Centerville for the next 20 years.

The population P will be initialized to 18,789. The program will use a loop that will be executed 20 times. The net population change due to people moving in and moving out of Centerville is +6. This will be added (in the loop) before the calculations due to births and deaths. The increase due to births is calculated by dividing the current population by 1000 and then multiplying by 17.2. A similar activity will find the decrease due to deaths. The new population will be rounded to the nearest integer and printed.

```
100 REM CENTERVILLE POPULATION SIMULATION
110 REM POPULATION P IS CURRENTLY 18789
120 REM POPULATION CHANGE DUE TO MOVING, M, IS INCREASE OF 6
130 REM BIRTH RATE B IS 17.2 PER 1000
140 REM DEATH RATE D IS 11.7 PER 1000
150 REM SIMULATION IS FOR 20 YEARS
160 REM
170 LET P=18789
180 LET M=6
190 LET B=17.2
200 LET D=11.7
210 PRINT TAB(3);"CURRENT POPULATION IS";P
220 PRINT
230 PRINT "YEARS FROM NOW";TAB(20);"POPULATION"
240 FOR Y=1 TO 20
250    LET P=P+M
260    LET B1=P/1000*B
270    LET D1=P/1000*D
280    LET P=P+(B1-D1)
290    LET P=INT(P+.5)
300    PRINT TAB(8);Y;TAB(22);P
310 NEXT Y
320 END

RUN

    CURRENT POPULATION IS 18789

YEARS FROM NOW       POPULATION
            1           18898
            2           19008
            3           19119
            4           19230
            5           19342
            6           19454
            7           19567
            8           19681
            9           19795
           10           19910
           11           20026
           12           20142
           13           20259
           14           20376
           15           20494
           16           20613
           17           20732
           18           20852
           19           20973
           20           21094

READY
```

1 Write a BASIC expression to randomly generate
  a. A number between 0 and 8
  b. A number between 7 and 15
  c. A number between 2.6 and 11.1
  d. A number between −3 and 4
  e. A number between −4.7 and 0
  f. A number between −12 and −5
  g. An integer from 1 to 9
  h. An integer from 2 to 12
  i. An integer from 0 to 7
  j. An integer from 4 to 13
  k. An integer from −2 to 6
  l. One of the integers 2, 4, 6, or 8
  m. One of the integers 4, 9, 16, 25, or 36

2 Determine what numbers are generated by the following expressions.
  a. 6*RND(−1)   g. INT(8*RND(−1)+1)
  b. RND(−1)+5   h. INT(14*RND(−1)+3)
  c. 4*RND(−1)+3   i. INT(11*RND(−1)−2)
  d. 8*RND(−1)−2   j. INT(−5*RND(−1)+1)
  e. −7*RND(−1)+1   k. INT(−6*RND(−1)−5)
  f. 2*RND(−1)+2   l. 15*(INT(RND(−1))+1)

3 Write a program to generate 1000 random integers from 1 to 8 and count how many are 5's.

4 Write a program that prints out N lines of asterisks. Each line should have M asterisks in it. N is to be a random integer from 3 to 10 and M a random integer from 15 to 50.

5 Generate 100 random integers from 5 to 200, print them ten to a line, and find the largest one.

6 Write a program to simulate tossing two coins 30 times. The output for each toss should be printed as HH, HT, TH, or TT.

7 Write a program to simulate tossing two coins 500 times. The output should tell how many tosses produced a match (both heads or both tails) and how many produced no match.

8 The expression INT(11*RND(−1)+2) generates a random integer from 2 to 12. Why would it be incorrect to use this expression to simulate rolling a pair of dice?

9 A single die is to be rolled 10,000 times. Count how many times a 1 is rolled, how many times a 2 is rolled, . . . , how many times a 6 is rolled.

10 Roll a pair of dice 1000 times. Count how many times a 2 was rolled, a 3 was rolled, . . . , how many times a 12 was rolled. The values of the counts should be printed.

11 A pair of dice are to be rolled 1000 times. Three counts are to be kept: how many times the sum of the two dice was an odd number; how many times "snake eyes" (a pair of ones) were rolled; how many times "box cars" (a pair of sixes) were rolled.

12 A list X, which will contain 100 values, is to be created using the random number generator. The first 25 values in X should be randomly generated integers from 1 to 4, the next 25 from 3 to 5, and the remaining 50 from 4 to 8. The program should then count how many times the integers from 1 to 8 appeared in the list X. The results of the counting should be printed.

13 Create a 10 × 10 array whose entries are randomly generated integers from −4 to 7 inclusive. Print out the array. Calculate and print the average of the elements on the main diagonal.

14 Write a program that generates and prints a 9 × 6 array whose elements are randomly generated integers from 16 to 124 inclusive. Then the program should find and print the largest value in the array and the subscripts of that value.

15 Write a program to generate a 20 × 25 string array according to the following instructions. For each of the 25 columns, generate a random integer from 0 to 20 inclusive. Call this random integer *N*. Fill each of the *bottom N* positions of the column with the alphanumeric character #. Print out the array using a semicolon as the print control character. (Note: The string array should be initialized to blanks.)

16 Write a program that generates 200 random integers over the range from 1 to 13 inclusive. Count how many l's, how many 2's, and so on were generated. Create a 20 × 25 string matrix similar to the one in the previous exercise. However, the columns of the matrix should be filled in with #'s in the following way.

In the first column, the number of #'s should be the same as the number of l's that were generated. The second column should be left blank.

The third column should contain the same number of #'s as there were 2's generated. The fourth column should be left blank. The fifth column should contain the same number of #'s as therewere 3's generated.

.

.

.

The twenty-fourthcolumn should be left blank. The twenty-fifth column should contain the same number of #'s as there were 13's generated. Print out the matrix.

17 An inebriate is standing in the exact middle of a bridge that is 14 feet long. When the drunk walks, he takes only one step at a time and then stops, preparing for the next step. Each step is exactly 1 foot long. The drunk cannot fall off the bridge and, in fact, can only take a step toward one end of the bridge or the other. He is just as likely to step one way as the other. Write a program to simulate the drunk's meanderings. The output should tell which end of the bridge (right or left) the drunk finally reached and the total number of steps he took before reaching there. (This problem is usually referred to as a *one-dimensional random walk.*)

18 Modify the program of Exercise 17 so that the drunk walks the bridge each night for a month (30 days). The output should tell the average number of steps taken each night before he gets off the bridge and how many nights he reached the right end and how many nights he reached the left end.

19 Sonya, Helene, and Patricia are soccer players. Statistics collected on the three show that Sonya averages 7 shots on goal per game and that her scoring average is .257; Helene gets 5 shots per game for a .198 average; and Patricia gets 9 shots and averages .299. Write a program that simulates a 20-game season. The output should be in table form. The first column should list the game number; the second should show the number of Sonya's goals in that game; the third should show the number of Helene's goals; the fourth Patricia's goals; and the last column should show the total goals by all three players.

20 Murray and Hugo had eliminated all other contestants in the stationary target shooting contest. Thus they met for the championship. Over the course of the contest, it was calculated that Murray could hit the target once out of every six shots whereas Hugo could hit it twice in seven shots. The rules say that the worse shot shoots first. Thus Murray will shoot first. They will alternate shots until one of them hits the target. The first to hit the target is the champion. Write a program to simulate the shooting contest. The output should show, for each shot, the name of the shooter and whether the shot was a hit or a miss. Finally, the champion's name should be printed out. Run the program several times.

21 A simple board game is played by moving pieces around the board according to the outcome of a spinner. The spinner is divided into five equal parts. These parts are labeled

Move back one square.
Lose turn.
Move ahead one square.
Move ahead two squares.
Move ahead three squares.

The game is played by three players. The board contains 50 squares so that the first player to move ahead 50 squares is the winner. Write a program that simulates this game. The output should show the result of each player's turn. It should show what each player spun and then the block to which the player has moved because of the spin. The winning player should be clearly identified. The program should include the use of subroutines.

22 Calculate the area under the curve for
  a. $y = 3x + 1$ from 1 to 3 (use 11 as the height of the "box").
  b. $y = x^2$ from .5 to 2 (use 4.5 as height).
  c. $y = -x^2 + 2x + 3$ from 1 to 2.5 (use 5 as height).
Each program should be run several times using successively larger numbers of "darts."

23 The I-P-S Mining Company wants to set up a sampling and exploration camp near a small pond. At the end of winter, when the water in the pond is at its maximum, it contains 110,000 gallons of water. Each week, due to a number of factors, including evaporation, the amount of water decreases by 850 gallons. The exploration camp's weekly usage of the water would amount to 2200 gallons. However a small stream leading into the pond adds 375 gallons every two weeks. A program is to be written that simulates water consumption at the pond. The output should be in the form of a three-column table. The first column should show the week number, the second the total amount of water consumed, and the third the amount of water left. The program should end when the amount of water left is insufficient for another week's use by the camp's personnel.

24 Refer to the airplane seating arrangement of Example 15.12. The program will begin with an empty plane. Generate a random integer N from 45 to 55 inclusive. N is the number of people who will be requesting seats on the plane. The program should process each of the N requests. A request should be a random choice of a row number and seat number. The output of the program should tell how many people made requests for the flight, how many people were given their first choice, and how many people were turned away because their requests could not be filled. Finally, the seating arrangement, showing empty and filled seats, should be printed. Run the program several times.

* * *

25 The nine starting players for a baseball team have batting averages of .298, .304, .336, .313, .278, .248, .212, .263, and .205. Assume the line-up order is the same order as the averages listed. Write a program that would show, for ten games, the inning-by-inning hit production of the team. The output should show 11 columns. The first column contains the game number; columns 2 through 10 should show how many hits were gotten in each of nine innings and the eleventh column should show the total number of hits in the game.

26 Using "darts," find the area under the curve $y = 4x^2 + 3x + 2$ from 1 to 5. For the height of the box, find the largest y value as x goes from 1 to 5 in steps of .1. The height of the box should be .5 more than the largest y value.

27 Calculate the area under $y = \sin(x)$ from 0 to π.

28 Calculate the area under $y = 4x - x^3$ from 0 to 2.

29 Calculate the area under $y = e^x$ from .1 to 1.8.

30 The area of a circle of radius 1 is π. Thus the area of a quarter-circle of radius 1 is $\pi/4$. This area can be found using the "dart" method by using the equation $y = \sqrt{1 - x^2}$ from 0 to 1. The height of the box should be 1. Use these facts to obtain an approximation for π by writing a program that calculates the area of the quarter-circle and multiplies it by 4.

31 Generate 1500 random integers from 1 to 50 and count how many of them are between 1 and 10, 11 and 20, 21 and 30, 31 and 40 and 41 and 50.

32 Program the following coin-match game that is to be played by the computer and the user. Each player starts with $10. The game ends when the user doesn't want to continue or when either player is broke. Two coins are tossed by the machine and the user is asked if he thinks the coins match or not. After the user answers, the machine prints the outcome of the toss, tells the user whether he (the user) won or lost, and prints the current amount of money now held by each player. The bet on each toss is always $1.

33 The Dicky-Doo Club is running a raffle. It will sell 200 tickets numbered 1 to 200. There are 2 prizes of $20, 3 prizes of $10, and 15 prizes of $2. Each ticket can win only 1 prize. The winning numbers will be determined by a random number generator. Write the program that prints out the list of prize winners. The output should look something like

```
TICKET NUMBER n WINS $x
```

where n is the random number generated (1 to 200) and x is the amount of the prize. Prizes will be awarded in the order listed. In case the same number is drawn more than once, each time it is drawn (after the first) a message like

```
NUMBER n HAS BEEN DRAWN AGAIN. NO ADDITIONAL PRIZE
```

should be printed.

34 A probability result that generally does not appeal to one's intuition is that from a random group of 25 people the probability that at least two of them will have the same birthday (month and day only) is approximately 50%. Write a simulation program to test this probability claim. Simulate giving 100 parties. Invite 25 people at random to each party. The only item of interest about each person is the date of birth. Put these into a list. If any two are the same, the party was a success. The output should show the percentage of successful parties.

35 One of the interesting claims of probability concerns monkeys that bang away at the keys of typewriters. (Clearly the method by which a monkey presses a key is random.) The claim is that if an infinite number of monkeys were typing at an infinite number of typewriters, eventually all the works of literature would be typed. This problem is similar but not quite so ambitious. Suppose that a monkey were typing on a typewriter that had only five keys: A, B, C, I, S. How long would it take before the monkey typed the word BASIC? What is to be written is a program that simulates the monkey's random typing and that checks the results. One approach is to assign numeric values to the letters, say A = 1, B = 2, C = 3, I = 4, and S = 5. Then the word BASIC could be thought of as the number 21,543. The program should randomly generate five-digit numbers consisting only of the digits 1, 2, 3, 4, and 5 until the number 21,543 is generated. In addition, the program should count how many "words" have been generated before BASIC was. The output should be something like

```
THE MONKEY TYPED 'BASIC' AS WORD n
```

where n is the value of the counter. Since it is likely that a large number of attempts will be made before BASIC is generated, you might want to include some intermediate output that tells you how many words have been generated. For example, you could have the value of the counter printed each time it is a multiple of 100.

36 The first annual drunkards' convention is about to take place. Twenty drunks have reserved all the rooms of a small 20-room hotel. That night they return totally inebriated to the hotel lobby where one by one they head for their rooms. Each drunk opens a door to a room at random. If he finds the room vacant he immediately goes to bed and falls asleep. If he finds the room occupied (by a sleeping drunk), he selects another room at random and repeats the procedure (note that it is possible for a drunk to open the same door randomly many times). The problem is to find out how many doors were opened before all 20 drunks are settled in for the night. To make the problem more meaningful, suppose that the situation is repeated every night for two weeks. Have your program, then, calculate, *on the average*, how many doors might be expected to be opened before everyone is asleep.

37 The line-up and batting average of a baseball team was given in Exercise 25. The batting averages should be entered into a list A. Thus $A(1) = .298$ and so on. Write a program in which the user can indicate the batting order and then perform ten game simulations with this line-up. The output should be the same as that for Exercise 25.

This appendix will acquaint you with the procedures to initiate connection between the terminal and the computer, store a program within the computer, access a program that has already been stored, change a stored program, and end the session at the terminal. In addition, several other features and commands that may be available on your computer will be mentioned.

It should be pointed out that the actual commands used are highly machine dependent—that is, although many computer systems include the features that follow, the actual commands that must be used will likely differ from one computer to the next, and so you should be sure to check the manual for your own system.

A.1 Log-in

The term "log-in" means opening communication between the terminal and the computer. It will usually include the following steps.

1. Beginning the process will require turning a knob, depressing a switch or button, or perhaps dialing a number from a telephone or a dial that is part of the terminal. When this has been done,[1] the computer will identify itself by printing a heading (which usually describes the computer system being used) and may also print the date and the time of day. For example, you might see

```
TIMELAG COMPUTER SYSTEM-VERSION 6
JUNE 24, 1983    10:45:23 A.M.
```

2. At this point the computer will request you to identify yourself as a valid user. This is done by typing in two items of identifying informa-

[1] Several computer systems require that the user type in a word such as HELLO or LOGIN.

tion in response to requests by the computer. First the computer
will print

USER NUMBER:

stop and wait for you to type in your number[2] and then press the
RETURN key.[3] Next, the computer will request that you enter a password. It does this by typing

PASSWORD:
■■■■■

You type in your password, *which will not be seen,* since it will be typed
into the black boxes. Some computers do not print the black boxes.
Instead, to keep the password secret, as you type in your password,
the computer prevents it from being typed on the paper or shown
on the screen. If your computer works this way, you should take
extra care that you do not make an error entering your password.
(Again, remember to press ® at the end of your password.)

When entering your user number and/or password if you make
a typing error and enter the error, the computer will respond with
something like

LOG-IN ERROR, TRY AGAIN

and request again that you identify yourself. Many computers consider
blanks to be significant in the log-in process. On such systems, special
care should be taken that unneeded blanks are not typed in—even
if it might make the typing easier to read. Suppose, for example,
that your user number is 16Ø4X. The way it should be entered is

USER NUMBER:16Ø4X ®

not

USER NUMBER:ƀ16Ø4X ®

(where ƀ means that you have typed a blank). The latter response
will cause the log-in error shown.
3. If your system uses several computer languages, next will be typed

SYSTEM:

and you respond BASIC ®.
At this point some computers skip steps 4 and 5 and go directly to
6. Otherwise,

---

[2] Actually the user number and password are likely to be combinations of numbers
and letters. This is perfectly allowable.
[3] ® means that the RETURN key is pressed.

4. The computer then types

OLD OR NEW:

and you type NEW ®.
5. Now the computer prints

PROGRAM NAME:

and you type in the name you are giving to your program. On computer systems such as the one we are describing, each program must be given a name. In general, the program name must be some combination of letters and numbers. Normally the program name must begin with a letter. The number of characters allowed in a program name varies from computer to computer. PROG1, RFS9, A793X, and SALES are examples of names that can be used on most systems.
6. Finally, the log-in procedure ends by the computer printing

READY

to indicate that it is awaiting your next action. At this point you will enter one or more BASIC statements or system commands.

EXAMPLE A.1.   The following is a sample log-in, together with a short program. Note: items that are underlined are those that are printed by the computer.

TIMELAG COMPUTER SYSTEM—VERSION 6
JUNE 24, 1983   10:45:23 A.M.

USER NUMBER:16Ø4X®
PASSWORD:
■■■■■   The password ® was entered here.
SYSTEM: BASIC ®
OLD OR NEW: NEW ®
PROGRAM NAME: P1 ®
READY

1Ø LET A=4 ®
2Ø LET B=7 ®
3Ø LET C=A+B ®
4Ø PRINT C ®
5Ø END ®
RUN ®

JUNE 24, 1983   10:48:07 A.M.
PROGRAM P1

  11

READY

(The first one or two lines, which show the date, time, and program name, are called a "heading." Many, but not all, computers print a heading as part of RUN or LIST.)

LIST ®

JUNE 24, 1983   10:49:32 A.M.
PROGRAM P1

10 LET A=4
20 LET B=7
30 LET C=A+B
40 PRINT C
50 END

READY

LISTNH ®

10 LET A=4
20 LET B=7
30 LET C=A+B
40 PRINT C
50 END

READY

(Usually there are commands, such as LISTNH and RUNNH, that allow you to LIST or RUN your program with no heading.)

In Chapter 1 a diagram of a central processing unit was given. It is reproduced here as Figure A.1.

A.2 Storing a Program

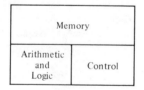

FIGURE A.1

The diagram can be modified to show another memory unit as displayed in Figure A.2.

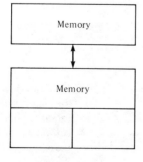

FIGURE A.2

The first memory unit, shown in the bottom part of the diagram, can be called *central memory*. In it are stored instructions and data that are to be momentarily used (you probably will LIST or RUN your program). When you enter a program from a terminal, it goes into central memory. The second memory unit (shown at the top) is referred to as *peripheral memory*. Peripheral memory can be used to store part or all of a program.

To cause a program, which has been entered into central memory, to be permanently stored in peripheral memory, you merely type

SAVE ®

When this is done, the computer makes a copy of the program in central memory and stores that copy in peripheral memory. The computer tells you that it has saved your program by typing

READY

A program that is located in central memory is temporary. For example, when you log off (break connection with the computer), anything in central memory vanished. Programs in central memory are often referred to as *local* programs. Although temporary, it is only your local program that is affected by such commands as LIST and RUN. A program that has been saved is called a *permanent* program.

A.3 Accessing a Stored Program

Suppose that you have saved a program named RM2 and at some later date you wish to use it. *A program that you have stored is considered to be an "old" program.* So when you log in, you type OLD ® in response to the query

NEW OR OLD:

and when the computer asks

PROGRAM NAME:

you type RM2 ®

The OLD command (used with the name of the permanent program) causes a copy of the permanent program to be brought into central memory. So now a version of RM2 is a local program and hence may be listed or executed.

We see that both the NEW and the OLD commands create local programs. NEW is used when the program is to be first entered from the terminal. OLD is used when the program is to be entered from peripheral memory (that is, when it has already been typed in and SAVEd).

It should be pointed out that, in addition to log in, the command

NEW or OLD may be typed in at any time during a session at the terminal. The computer will respond with

    PROGRAM NAME:

and you then enter the name of the program you wish to use next. When OLD ® or NEW ® is typed in, whatever program is in central memory will be erased from central memory.

To eliminate a program from peripheral memory, a command like UNSAVE is used. Often there are two different methods to use with this command. They are equivalent.

1. Access the program with the OLD command and then type UNSAVE ®.
2. Once logged-in, type

    UNSAVE, permanent program name

EXAMPLE A.2. The two methods to UNSAVE a program are shown now. The permanent program to be unsaved is named PROG1.

Method 1	Method 2
OLD ®	UNSAVE, PROG1 ®
PROGRAM NAME: PROG1 ®	
	READY
READY	
UNSAVE ®	
READY	

A.4 Changing a Permanent Program

One or more statements are to be changed, added, or deleted to a program that has been saved. The changing, adding, or deleting can only be done from the terminal, so first the OLD command is used to bring a copy of the permanent program into central memory. The modifications are then made. It is important to note that the modifications have only been made to the local version of the program. Generally, a computer will not accept a SAVE command that refers to a local program that has the same name as a permanent program (as it does in this case). So, to make the changes permanent, type

    RESAVE ®

and the computer will answer READY.

A.5 Log-off

When your session with the computer is over, you must break the connection between the terminal and the computer. To do this, type

BYE ®

and the computer will type something like

1604X LOG-OFF   11:27:15 A.M.

Finally, you manually turn your terminal off.

A.6 Some Extras

Your computer may also have other features that can be very helpful. Some are briefly described in the paragraphs that follow. For more detailed information, consult your computer system's manual or someone who is knowledgeable about your computer.

Your computer may contain a *library*. A library is a collection of programs, stored in peripheral memory, that is available to all the users of your system. A computer library could include programs that solve various kinds of mathematics and statistics problems. There are some that can be used to provide financial information such as the amount of each monthly payment needed to pay back a loan. Frequently, programs are available that play games with the user. Some computers even include programs that teach you how to use the computer!

Many computers contain an EDIT command. With EDIT it is possible to insert an omitted character into its proper place in a BASIC statement. Or with the single use of an EDIT command, it would be possible to change all the misspelled PRUNT statements in a program to PRINT. A use of EDIT could be to delete from your program one or several unwanted lines. The EDIT command permits relatively easy modification of your program.

CATALOG may be entered to show you a listing of all the names of your permanent programs.

The RESEQ (for resequence) command can be a very helpful aid. When the computer executes RESEQ, it automatically changes the numbers that you have used in your program (including transfer statements). Usually, the new line numbers that are assigned will begin with 100 and change by 10's. So if you find yourself adding lines between other lines already in your program and feel that more room between the lines is necessary, type RESEQ (and after the computer types READY, type LIST to see what you have). (The command RENUM, found on several systems, is equivalent to RESEQ.)

There are numerous other system commands that you have available. Check your computer manual for them.

B

It frequently happens that a collection of data must be used by several programs. Obviously one way to do this would be to type the same set of DATA lines in these several programs. Many computers will allow this rather tiresome task to be made significantly easier.

Also it is a frequent occurrence that the output of one program is to be used as the input of another program. If the quantity of such values is very small, you could take a copy of the output and from this copy enter the data into the second program as DATA lines or by responding to INPUT statements. This method is certainly not feasible if the amount of data is not insignificant. This situation can also be easily handled by many computers.

The situations described in the preceding paragraphs can be accomplished if data can be stored within the computer and accessed from the computer independent of the program that processes that data. This collection of data is called a *data file* or simply a *file*. A BASIC data file is a collection of data that can be referenced by a BASIC program and that is external to the program. Most files are named by *file names*.

This appendix deals with procedures to create and access files. It must be noted that the procedures needed on your particular computer may differ from those presented here. You should confer with your instructor or consult the computer manufacturer's manual for your system to get the precise methods that will work for you.

A generalized procedure to be followed when using files can be described by the following steps.

1. Inform the computer that a data file will be used and to name the data file.
2. Retrieve data from the file or store data on it.
3. Inform the computer that the use of the data file has been completed.

These steps are illustrated and explained in the examples that follow.

EXAMPLE B.1.   This program requests the user to enter a worker identification number and an hourly wage for each of five workers. After the
information has been typed from the terminal, it will be entered on a
data file (so this program creates a data file).

```
1Ø OPEN 1, "RATES"
2Ø LET I=1
3Ø    PRINT "ENTER I.D. NUMBER AND HOURLY PAY RATE"
4Ø    INPUT N,R
5Ø    PRINT #1,N,R
6Ø    LET I=I+1
7Ø IF I<=5 THEN 3Ø
8Ø CLOSE 1
9Ø END
```

Line 1Ø declares that the file named RATES will be used as a data
file by the program. Associated with each BASIC data file is a file number
or *file ordinal* that is used by any input or output statement that references
the data file. The file number is chosen by the programmer and the
range of numbers that can be used as file ordinals depends on the particular BASIC system. In line 1Ø the number "1" that follows the word
OPEN is the ordinal associated with the data file RATES. Line 1Ø is
said to "open" RATES.

After each pair of numbers is entered from the terminal (at line 4Ø),
they are output to the data file RATES by the statement in line 5Ø.
The statement is PRINT followed by a #, which is then followed by a
file number and comma. After this are listed the variables (separated
by a comma) whose values are to be stored in the data file.

Line 8Ø "closes" the data file—that is, it informs the computer that
the action on the file has been completed. Note that the CLOSE statement includes the file ordinal.

A RUN of this program would look like

```
RUN

ENTER I.D. NUMBER AND HOURLY PAY RATE
? 11Ø4,3.75
ENTER I.D. NUMBER AND HOURLY PAY RATE
? 1234,5.ØØ
ENTER I.D. NUMBER AND HOURLY PAY RATE
? 32Ø3,4.5Ø
ENTER I.D. NUMBER AND HOURLY PAY RATE
? 77Ø7,1Ø
ENTER I.D. NUMBER AND HOURLY PAY RATE
? 9876,4.ØØ

READY
```

At completion of execution the data file RATES contains five pairs
of numbers. You can now view the contents of RATES by typing

LIST, RATES[1]

and the computer would display

```
1104        3.75
1234        5.00
3203        4.50
7707        10
9876        4.00
```

The file RATES has been created in *central memory* and assuming that it is to be made permanent, you would type

SAVE, RATES[2]

and the computer would make a copy of RATES and store it in peripheral memory.

There are two additional comments to be made about the previous program.

1. Because of the comma between N and R in line 50, the values of the variables will be stored on the RATES with quite a bit of unused space between them (like the output print zones). To use the storage space more efficiently, a semicolon can be used between the variables (i.e., 50 PRINT #1,N;R). If RATES had been created this way, when you LIST it, you would see

```
1104    3.75
1234    5.00
3203    4.50
7707    10
9876    4.00
```

2. Although many computers will automatically close a data file at the end of a program's execution, you should not assume this but rather close the file with a statement in your program.

We now present a program that accesses and uses the data on RATES.

EXAMPLE B.2.   This program prints the weekly wage for each of the five workers whose information is stored on RATES.

```
100 OPEN 7,"RATES"
110 LET J=1
120     INPUT #7,X,Y
130     PRINT "ENTER HOURS WORKED FOR WORKER NUMBER";X
140     INPUT H
150     LET S=H*Y
```

---

[1] Note that if you typed LIST alone, it would mean to list the program that created RATES.

[2] SAVE alone means to save the program, not the data file.

```
160    PRINT "WEEKLY SALARY IS";S
170    LET  J=J+1
180 IF  J<=5 THEN 120
190 CLOSE 7
200 END
```

RATES is identified in this program by the file ordinal 7 (the choice is the programmer's). Data are transferred from the file to the program by line 120

```
120 INPUT #7,X,Y
```

identifying the data file by number and then using the variables to hold the data. Finally, when the loop is done, the data file is closed.

There are also two comments about this program.

1. Whether the data were entered onto RATES by a statement such as

```
PRINT #1,N,R
```

or

```
PRINT #1,N;R
```

when reading data *from* a file, the variables are *always* separated by a comma.
2. There is a pointer associated with a data file that is similar to the pointer associated with a data stack. As data are printed on the file, the pointer moves down the file indicating the next line of the file that is available for printing data. As data are being input from a file, the pointer moves down the file indicating the next available data to be input (just as it does with a data stack). Because of this, it is a good practice to be certain that the pointer is at the beginning of the data file as the program begins. This can be done by using the RESTORE# statement whose general form is

```
line number   RESTORE#   file ordinal
```

Similar to the RESTORE statement, the RESTORE# statement, upon execution, will cause the pointer to return to the top of the data file.

On some systems special consideration must be given when a program creates a data file on which string data are to be printed. It may be that if a PRINT# statement is to print several variables, at least one of which is a string variable, then a comma must be *printed* between the string variable and any other variable(s) next to it. This is illustrated in the next example.

EXAMPLE B.3. A person's last name and age are to be entered from the terminal and then printed on a data file.

Two similar programs to accomplish this task are shown.

```
100 OPEN 3,"INFO"              100 OPEN 3,"INFO"
110 PRINT "TYPE IN LAST NAME"  110 PRINT "TYPE IN LAST NAME"
120 INPUT L$                   120 INPUT L$
130 PRINT "TYPE IN AGE"        130 PRINT "TYPE IN AGE"
140 INPUT A                    140 INPUT A
150 PRINT#3,L$,A               150 PRINT#3,L$,",",A
160 CLOSE 3                    160 CLOSE 3
170 END                        170 END
```

The program on the right explicitly prints a comma between the string variable L$ and the numeric variable A. Whether your system requires this or not, the manner in which the data are read from such a file is the same—imagine that the comma is not there.

EXAMPLE B.4. The following program reads a last name and an age.

```
10 OPEN 4,"INFO"
20 INPUT#4,R$,V
30 PRINT R$;"'S AGE IS";V
40 CLOSE 4
50 END
```

The files illustrated in this appendix are known as *BCD* (binary coded decimal) *files*. Information stored on BCD files is written by the computer in a form that we can read when we LIST the file. Some BASIC systems allow you to create a BCD file from your terminal (in contrast to the creation of data files by programs). Such files are called *terminal files*.

Suppose that you wish to create a file named "PAIRS" that is to contain the five pairs of numbers 2 and 3, 6 and −1, 5 and 4, 11 and 9, and 7 and 6. At your terminal you type

```
100,2,3®
150,6,-1®
200,5,4®
250,11,9®
300,7,6®
```

The second and third numbers on each line are our data pairs. The first number of each line is a line number, just like the line numbers of the program you have written. You have now created the file. It can now be saved and used with programs such as the one that follows.

EXAMPLE B.5. This program uses the file PAIRS.

```
10 OPEN 1,"PAIRS"
20 RESTORE#1
30 PRINT "1ST NO.","2ND NO.","SUM"
```

```
40 FOR N=1 TO 5
50    INPUT#1,L,A,B
60    PRINT A,B,A+B
70 NEXT N
80 CLOSE 1
90 END
```

As mentioned earlier, the data file pointer should be positioned at the beginning of the file—this is done in line 20.

Line 50 causes three values to be input from file #1 (the file PAIRS) and assigned to the variables L, A, and B. The value of L is not used. It was only the value of a "dummy" line number that was necessary when we created the file PAIRS. However, the values of A and B are used—they, and their sum, are printed.

When the program is executed, the output will be

RUN

1ST NO.	2ND NO.	SUM
2	3	5
6	−1	5
5	4	9
11	9	20
7	6	13

READY

Eod tags are frequently used with data files. This is illustrated in the following example.

EXAMPLE B.6. A collection of positive and negative numbers is to be entered, one at a time, from the terminal. The positive values are to be stored on a file POS and the negatives on a file NEG. The eod tag 0 will be entered from the terminal to indicate that no more numbers will be typed in. At that point, 0 will be printed at the end of each data file as an eod tag.

```
100 OPEN 1,"POS"
110 OPEN 2,"NEG"
120 PRINT "IN RESPONSE TO EACH QUESTION MARK"
130 PRINT "TYPE IN A NUMBER"
140 PRINT "TYPE A 0 TO STOP"
150 INPUT X
160 IF X=0 THEN 230
170    IF X>0 THEN 200
180    PRINT#2,X
190    GOTO 210
200    PRINT#1,X
210    INPUT X
220 GOTO 160
230 PRINT#1,X
240 PRINT#2,X
```

```
250 CLOSE 1
260 CLOSE 2
270 END
```

EXAMPLE B.7. The values on POS can be input and printed at the terminal by

```
100 OPEN 1,"POS"
110 RESTORE#1
120 INPUT#1,A
130 IF A=0 THEN 170
140    PRINT A
150    INPUT#1,A
160 GOTO 130
170 END
```

From time to time, the contents of a data file may need to be changed. This is referred to as *updating a file*.

EXAMPLE B.8. The auditorium at the Civic Center is divided into sections numbered 1 through 5, and the price for a seat for an event differs from one section to another. The number of seats in each section and the ticket price for a seat in the various sections is shown in a table:

Section	Number of Seats	Ticket Price
1	100	$9.50
2	150	$7.50
3	150	$7.50
4	250	$6.50
5	350	$5.00

The program reads the information displayed above and enters it onto a data file called SEATS.

```
100 OPEN 5,"SEATS"
110 LET I=1
120    READ A,B
130    PRINT#5,A;B
140    LET I=I+1
150 IF I<=5 THEN 120
160 PRINT "DATA HAS BEEN ENTERED ON FILE"
170 CLOSE 5
180 DATA 100,9.00
190 DATA 150,7.50
200 DATA 150,7.50
210 DATA 250,6.50
220 DATA 350,5.00
230 END
```

The next program is written for the ticket office at the Civic Center. It will do the following tasks:

1. Input the data into two one-dimensional arrays N and P, where N contains the number of seats in each section and P contains the five prices.
2. Allow the ticket seller to enter a request for ticket sales. The seller will enter the number of tickets to be purchased and the section requested. If there are enough tickets in that section, the total cost will be printed and the number of seats available in that section will be decreased by the number just sold. If there are not enough seats left, a message to that effect will be printed. In either case the seller will be given the opportunity to enter additional requests.
3. When the ticket seller indicates that no more requests will be made, the current information (the number of seats now left in each section) as well as the ticket prices will be printed on file SEATS.

```
100 REM CIVIC CENTER TICKET SALES
110 REM N CONTAINS THE NUMBER OF SEATS
120 REM LEFT IN EACH OF THE 5 SECTIONS
130 REM P CONTAINS THE TICKET PRICES FOR
140 REM THE 5 SECTIONS
150 REM
160 REM INPUT DATA FROM FILE 'SEATS'
170 DIM N(5),P(5)
180 OPEN 1,"SEATS"
190 RESTORE#1
200 LET I=1
210    INPUT#1,N(I),P(I)
220    LET I=I+1
230 IF I<=5 THEN 210
240 REM
250 REM PROCESS REQUESTS FOR TICKETS
260    PRINT "HOW MANY TICKETS";
270    INPUT T
280    PRINT "FOR WHAT SECTION";
290    INPUT S
300    PRINT
310    IF T<=N(S) THEN 350
320    PRINT "REQUEST IMPOSSIBLE"
330    PRINT "ONLY";N(S);"TICKETS LEFT FOR SECTION";S
340    GOTO 370
350    PRINT "PRICE FOR";T;"TICKETS IS";T*P(S)
360    LET N(S)=N(S)-T
370    PRINT
380    PRINT "IS THERE ANOTHER REQUEST?"
390    PRINT "YES OR NO";
400    INPUT A$
410    PRINT
420 IF A$="YES" THEN 260
430 REM
440 REM UP-DATE FILE 'SEATS'
450 RESTORE#1
460 LET I=1
470    PRINT#1,N(I);P(I)
480    LET I=I+1
```

```
490 IF I<=5 THEN 470
500 CLOSE 1
510 END
```

At the end of the input loop (lines 210 through 230), the data from SEATS are stored in the arrays N and P, and the file pointer has moved down the file beyond all the data. When the ticket seller indicates that there are no more requests (line 400), SEATS must be prepared to receive new data. The file pointer is moved to the start of the file (line 450) so that the new, current data are written over the old data.

A RUN of the program might be

```
RUN

HOW MANY TICKETS? 75
FOR WHAT SECTION? 1

PRICE FOR 75 TICKETS IS 675

IS THERE ANOTHER REQUEST?
YES OR NO? YES

HOW MANY TICKETS? 10
FOR WHAT SECTION? 4

PRICE FOR 10 TICKETS IS 65

IS THERE ANOTHER REQUEST?
YES OR NO? YES

HOW MANY TICKETS? 30
FOR WHAT SECTION? 1

REQUEST IMPOSSIBLE
ONLY 25 TICKETS LEFT FOR SECTION 1

IS THERE ANOTHER REQUEST?
YES OR NO? YES

HOW MANY TICKETS? 2
FOR WHAT SECTION? 3

PRICE FOR 2 TICKETS IS 15

IS THERE ANOTHER REQUEST?
YES OR NO? NO

READY
```

At the end of this RUN, the contents of SEATS are

```
25      9.00
150     7.50
```

```
148    7.5Ø
24Ø    6.5Ø
35Ø    5.ØØ
```

A second RUN of the program would use this data, modify it, and then print the modified results on SEATS.

This appendix has shown one way of

1. Opening a file.
2. Processing file data (input and output).
3. Closing a file.

The particular statements needed for the BASIC system you are working with will be found in your system's manual.

To *sort* a collection of data means to arrange it into some predetermined configuration. Usually numeric data are sorted from largest to smallest or from smallest to largest, whereas alphabetic data are sorted from A to Z. In this appendix we shall consider two different techniques for sorting lists.

C.1 A Simple Sorting Algorithm

The first technique we consider to be an easily understood process. We begin by supposing that we have read in a list of N values, the list being named A. We wish to sort A from high to low. An important part of this algorithm is finding the largest value in a collection of data. You should be familiar with this by now, but if you are not, it would be best if you went back and reviewed it before proceeding any farther.

The sorting algorithm may be described in the following steps.

1. Find the largest value in A, call it B. In addition, keep track of the position in A where B was found.
2. Put B into the first position of a new list C; that is, set C(1) = B.
3. Go back to list A, to the position where B was found, and put into this position a very small number (one that is smaller than any value in A).
4. Now repeat the search through A for the largest element (this is actually the second largest value in A). It goes into C(2) and is replaced by that small value. Continue the process, putting the next largest value into C(3) and so on, until all the original N values of list A are put into list C. List C now contains the sorted values of list A.

A few observations should be made about this algorithm, but before doing so, let's consider an example.

Suppose the list A contains the five values 6, 7, 2, 3, and 4. So

A(1)=6 A(2)=7 A(3)=2 A(4)=3 A(5)=4

The first time, we find the largest value in list A is 7, and it occurs in the second location of A. So we set C(1)=7 and A(2)=0, where 0 is the value we will use since it is smaller than any of the values in A. Therefore, now we have

C(1)=7
A(1)=6 A(2)=0 A(3)=2 A(4)=3 A(5)=4

The largest *now* in A is 6, which is found in the first location of A. We set C(2)=6 and A(1)=0 giving

C(1)=7 C(2)=6
A(1)=0 A(2)=0 A(3)=2 A(4)=3 A(5)=4

The next search produces

C(1)=7 C(2)=6 C(3)=4
A(1)=0 A(2)=0 A(3)=2 A(4)=3 A(5)=0

The fourth time we get

C(1)=7 C(2)=6 C(3)=4 C(4)=3
A(1)=0 A(2)=0 A(3)=2 A(4)=0 A(5)=0

The fifth and final time through gives

C(1)=7 C(2)=6 C(3)=4 C(4)=3 C(5)=2
A(1)=0 A(2)=0 A(3)=0 A(4)=0 A(5)=0

The first observation can be quickly seen from the example. In the example, A contains five elements, and the sequence of steps must be executed five times. More generally, if list A contains N values, then N passes through A will have to be made.

Second, it was pointed out in the example that we used 0 as the replacement since it was smaller than any of the original values in A. It should be clear why we do this. Once we have found the largest value and have stored it in list C, we want to guarantee that it will never show up as a largest value in any upcoming search. This is accomplished by using a replacement value that will be smaller than anything that could be in our list. One way of guaranteeing this is to *make the replacement value approximately equal to the smallest value that your computer can handle.*

The final point to observe refers to the statement in the algorithm that says to keep track of the place where the largest value in the list was found. But the subscript of an element in a list tells us where the element is in the list. So each time the largest value, B, is defined or redefined, another variable, which will equal the current subscript of the element in A, will be defined or redefined.

A flowchart of the algorithm and a LIST and RUN of the program follow. Since the flowchart is rather long, it will be presented in three parts.

First the list A, of N values, is read in. (See Figure C.1.)

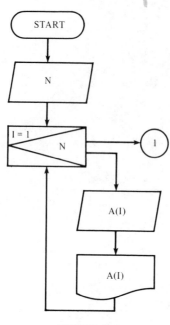

FIGURE C.1

The next activity the flowchart describes is the sorting of the list A into the list C. This is seen in Figure C.2.

What remains is to print out the sorted list. This is depicted in Figure C.3.

From the flowchart, adding REMs and two PRINTs, the program is written.

```
100 REM SORTING PROGRAM
110 DIM A(25),C(25)
120 PRINT "ORIGINAL LIST"
130 REM N IS NO. OF DATA VALUES
140 READ N
150 REM READ AND PRINT LIST A
160 FOR I=1 TO N
170    READ A(I)
180    PRINT A(I)
190 NEXT I
200 PRINT
210 REM BEGIN SORTING
220 FOR I=1 TO N
230    REM B IS MAX
240    LET B=A(1)
250    REM K KEEPS TRACK WHERE B FOUND
```

```
260    LET K=1
270    FOR J=2 TO N
280      IF B>=A(J) THEN 320
290      REM REDEFINE B AND K
300      LET B=A(J)
310      LET K=J
320    NEXT J
330    REM DEFINE LIST C
340    LET C(I)=B
350    REM REPLACE MAX WITH SMALL VALUE
360    LET A(K)=-1.0E+10
370 NEXT I
380 PRINT "SORTED LIST"
390 FOR L=1 TO N
400    PRINT C(L)
410 NEXT L
420 DATA 15
430 DATA 7,5,11,-4,16.3,-3.1
440 DATA 18,9.62,0,-1.7,13.2
450 DATA 2.54,-6,8,11
460 END

RUN

ORIGINAL LIST
 7
 5
 11
-4
 16.3
-3.1
 18
 9.62
 0
-1.7
 13.2
 2.54
-6
 8
 11

SORTED LIST
 18
 16.3
 13.2
 11
 11
 9.62
 8
 7
 5
 2.54
 0
-1.7
-3.1
-4
-6

READY
```

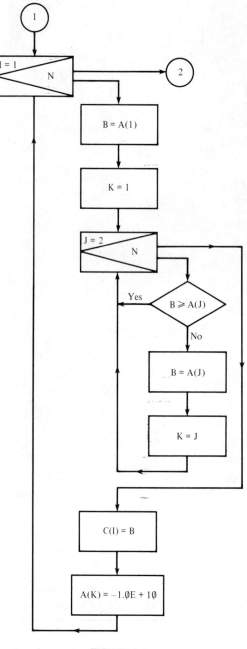

FIGURE C.2

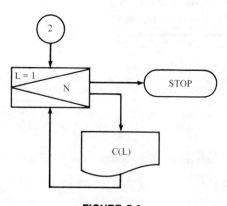

FIGURE C.3

Notice that the program could have been nicely broken into subroutines. One subroutine could read and print the original list. A second subroutine could sort the list. A final subroutine could print the sorted list.

C.2 The Bubble Sort

This sorting technique will be illustrated by an example and then the more general result given in a program. Suppose that we have the list L containing 3, 4, 6, 2, 8, and 7. L will be sorted by the *bubble sort*. The bubble sort compares a pair of consecutive elements. If they are

in the correct order (for us, the correct order means that the first one is greater than the second one), move on and compare the next pair; if not, switch the elements around. This procedure is repeated over and over until the list is sorted. This simplified explanation is illustrated by sorting L.

The original list: 3 4 6 2 8 7

The first comparison is between 3 and 4. Since they are not in the correct order, they are switched.

After one comparison: 4 3 6 2 8 7

Next 3 and 6 are compared. They also are not in the correct order and so must be switched.

After two comparisons: 4 6 3 2 8 7

The 3 and the 2 are now compared and are found to be in correct order. They are left alone.

After three comparisons: 4 6 3 2 8 7

Next 2 and 8 are compared and switched.

After four comparisons: 4 6 3 8 2 7

Finally, 2 and 7 are compared and switched.

After five comparisons: 4 6 3 8 7 2

Clearly L is not yet sorted. But the significant thing that happened is that the smallest element in L (the number 2) was moved to the last position in the list, L(6). The bubble sort continues by repeating the process on the other five elements of L, namely, L(1) through L(5). This is shown in the following.

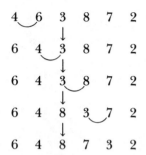

Now the second smallest value in L is found in the second to last position of L, L(5). Also notice that four comparisons were made—one less than the time before. The pattern continues, only now comparing just L(1) through L(4).

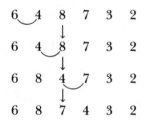

The process is repeated once again, still decreasing the size of the list to be compared, this time only L(1) through L(3).

```
6   8   7   4   3   2
    ↓
8   6   7   4   3   2
        ↓
8   7   6   4   3   2
```

Even though the list is now sorted, the last step in the bubble sort is to compare the current first two values.

```
8   7   6   4   3   2
    ↓
8   7   6   4   3   2
```

It is at this point that the bubble sort is done, and our list L is guaranteed to be sorted. With this example as motivation, we will move on to the program. However one last item needs to be discussed. The bubble sort requires that two elements be switched. Suppose that the values to be switched are the values of the variables R and S. It would not be sufficient to merely write

```
120 LET R=S
130 LET S=R
```

Why not? A third variable is needed to temporarily hold one of the values to be switched. This will be seen shortly. Instead of writing the bubble sort as a program we will present it as a subroutine. It is assumed that the list A, of N values, has been read in by the main program and that the main program will handle any output that is required.

```
1000 REM SORTING SUBROUTINE-BUBBLE SORT
1010 FOR I=1 TO N-1
1020  FOR J=1 TO N-I
1030   IF A(J)>=A(J+1) THEN 1080
1040   REM SWITCH-H IS TEMPORARY VALUE
1050   LET H=A(J)
1060   LET A(J)=A(J+1)
1070   LET A(J+1)=H
1080  NEXT J
1090 NEXT I
1100 RETURN
```

We finish the appendix with three observations. The first is that if you are going to continue to study computers and especially computer programming, you will discover several more sorting techniques—sorting is an important and frequently used computer activity. Second, you may still be wondering why this sorting method is called a bubble sort. Consider the following set of data, written in a vertical configuration. We will begin the bubble sort at the bottom of the *column* and interchange two values if the top one is greater than the one beneath it. Watch what happens to the number 3, the smallest value, which is circled as the action of the sort takes place.

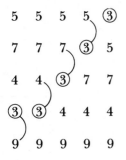

The ③ makes its way to the top of the list—just like a bubble rising in the water. Finally, since strings can be ordered by their number codes, a list of strings can be sorted. You will be directed to do this in Exercise 8.

1 How would you change the first sorting technique so that the data are sorted from low to high?

2 Write a main program that reads in a list of values, sorts them by the bubble sort subroutine, and then prints the sorted list.

3 How would you change the bubble sort so that the data are sorted from low to high?

4 Read in a list of 30 values. Sort the first 15 from low to high and the last 15 from high to low. Print out the sorted list.

5 Read a list X of 50 values. Separate X into two other lists Y and Z, where Y contains the positive values of X and Z contains the negative values of X. Sort and print the lists Y and Z.

6 Read in a list A of 30 values. A is to be separated into three lists B, C, and D. B should contain the values A(1), A(4), A(7), . . . , A(28); C should contain A(2), A(5), . . . , and D contain A(3), A(6), ... Lists B, C, and D should be sorted and printed.

7 Create a list L of 1000 values (if your computer allows this many—if not, use as large a number as possible) that are randomly generated integers from −20 to 30. Sort the list L and print out every tenth value of the sorted list.

8 Alphabetically sort the words: COMPUTER, PROGRAM, INPUT, OUTPUT, TERMINAL, FLOWCHART, TERMINATE, BOOK, SOFTWARE, TEXT, TEXTBOOK, SORT, BUBBLE, DATA, NAME, SORTED, ALPHA, DATE, COMPUTE.

9 Two lists, R and S, of equal length are to be read in. The sorting is to be done on the list R, but whenever an element of R is moved in the sort (either put into another list or interchanged with another element in R), the corresponding element of S must also be moved—namely, whatever is done to R(J) must also be done to S(J). Print out R and S, side by side, in their original configuration and then after they have been sorted.

10 Write a program for the M & M Oriental Rug Company. The data to be used are given. Each line shows a salesperson's name, amount of sales so far this year, and the number of years in the employ of the company. The program should request of the user one of the words: name, sales, service. If "name" is supplied, the data should be sorted by the names of the salespeople; if "sales", the sort should be by amount of sales; if "service", sort by number of years in service. Whatever option is used, the sorted list should be printed out.

Randall Levit	$10,042	14.5
Harold DiArko	8433	5
Prudence Sullivan	9100	7.2
Roberta Selta	12,450	9.4
Raoul Beniques	11,500	14.5
Henri Mayo	15,255	17
Darlene Sampson	10,112	11.8
Mary Adams	9520	12.2
Ralph Questly	8975	7.8
Terri Miles	7505	9.3
Glenda Sanchez	11,408	3.8
Winifred Grant	13,945	13.8
Francis Leary	12,375	11.5
Manuel Mannerly	14,333	12

(You might want to use a string function or enter the first and last names as separate data items.)

11 A list X of not more than 25 values and a list Y of not more than 20 values are to be read in and sorted. A *sorted* list Z is to be created by merging the sorted lists X and Y. The three lists should be printed in three adjoining columns.

12 A program is to be written for the Tri-Town Baseball League. The league has eight teams. The program concerns the best fielders from each team. A player's fielding percentage is given by the fraction $\dfrac{P + A}{P + A + E}$ where P is putouts, A is assists, and E is errors. Each team will supply the relevant information about its best fielder. This information should be entered from the terminal in the order team name, player name, number of putouts, number of assists, number of errors. A table should then be printed that displays, in order of fielding percentage (high to low), the player, the team and the fielding percentage. The information you should enter is

Team	Player	Putouts	Assists	Errors
Bombers	Gig Gray	115	131	15
Imports	Ben James	112	128	18
Strokers	Lenny Wong	119	136	16
Lemons	Pat Vucci	127	116	5
Profs	Clay Donson	116	117	23
Stripes	Chic O'Reilly	123	124	3
Woodies	Lefty Richardson	118	124	7
Diggers	Sparky Faucette	128	115	6

D.1 Structured Programming

The primary objective in writing computer programs is to solve the problem for which they are written. A secondary but major objective is to write programs that are easy to read, test, maintain, and modify. A structured program will do all of these. *Structured programming* is the process of organizing and writing programs that adhere to certain constructs or structures. These constructs are called *control structures* and are of three types:

1. Sequence.
2. Selection.
3. Repetition.

D.2 Sequence

The sequence construct is a sequence of instructions executed in order. It is like the "straight-line" programs mentioned at the beginning of Chapter 8. A sequence structure has the form shown in Figure D.1. All the programs in the first seven chapters have had this structure.

D.3 Selection

The selection construct is used when one of several alternative actions is to be taken. *Two-way selection* occurs when two possible choices are present. The form of two-way selection is given in Figure D.2.

Suppose that part of a problem stated that if the value of X is bigger than the value of Y the word "affirmative" should be printed; otherwise, the word "negative." The flowchart for this is displayed in Figure D.3.

The required code for this has already been examined and would be

```
 ─
 ─
 ─
400 IF X>Y THEN 430
```

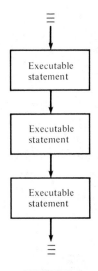

FIGURE D.1

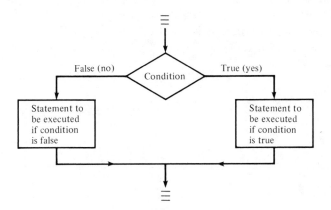

FIGURE D.2

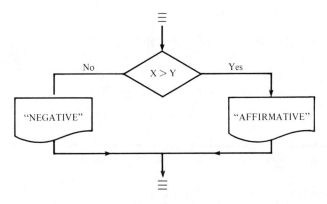

FIGURE D.3

```
410 PRINT "NEGATIVE"
420 GOTO 440
430 PRINT "AFFIRMATIVE"
440 (continuation of program)
  _
  _
  _
```

A structured algorithm (an algorithm written in accordance with the three constructs mentioned earlier) for this last situation would be

If X>Y then
  print "affirmative"
otherwise
  print "negative"

and would call for the printing of the word AFFIRMATIVE to be coded first (since it corresponds to the condition being true) and afterward NEGATIVE. This does not correspond to our BASIC code because when the condition in the IF-THEN is true, a transfer is made (in this case to the printing of AFFIRMATIVE). However, it is possible to parallel the algorithm if the *opposite relation* (see Chapter 9) is used in the IF-THEN. Thus we could code

```
  _
  _
  _
400 IF X<=Y THEN 430
410 PRINT "AFFIRMATIVE"
420 GOTO 440
430 PRINT "NEGATIVE"
440 (continuation of program)
  _
  _
  _
```

The important thing is not the way you code the two-way selection but rather that you recognize the need for a two-way selection and code it in a readable and understandable way.

Some BASICs include a two-way selection statement: the IF-THEN-ELSE. Its *general form* is

line number IF condition THEN statement$_1$ ELSE statement$_2$

If the condition is true, statement$_1$ is executed; if false, statement$_2$. In either case after one of the statements is executed, control continues to the next statement after the IF-THEN-ELSE (unless statement$_1$ or statement$_2$ is a GOTO).

The restriction on this statement occurs if either the true branch or the false branch requires more than a *single* statement to be executed.

If multiple statements are to be executed, then the coding must be done similar to the explanation given in Chapter 9, or statement₁ or statement₂ must be a GOSUB.

One-way selection takes place when a condition requires that either nothing be done or a single statement (or sequence of statements) be executed. One-way selection is actually a special case of two-way selection—when nothing is to be done if the condition is false. One-way selection looks like the diagram of Figure D.4.

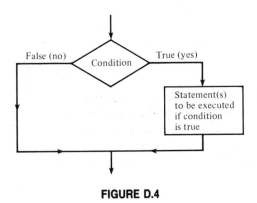

FIGURE D.4

But it is frequently described by Figure D.5.

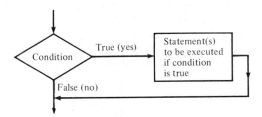

FIGURE D.5

Section 9.6 illustrated this situation where only a single statement is to be executed if the condition is true. The form of the BASIC statement is

line number   IF condition   THEN statement

Part of the program of Example 9.10 that uses one of these statements is shown next. (Example 9.10 dealt with admitting a student to a school's honor society if the student's average on three tests was greater than 90, the value of the variable R.)

```
14Ø INPUT X,Y,Z
15Ø LET A=(X+Y+Z)/3
```

```
160 IF A>R THEN PRINT "ADMIT THIS STUDENT"
170 PRINT
```

The statement from a structured algorithm that describes one-way
selection is

—
—
—

if condition then
    statement(s)

—
—
—

As long as there is only one statement to be executed, the selection
can be easily handled as was just done. Again the difficulty arises if
more than one statement is to be executed when the condition is true.
One option for the programmer is to make the set of statements into
a subroutine and use a statement such as

IF condition   THEN   GOSUB

If this option is not used, an alternate approach is described in the
example that follows.

EXAMPLE D.1.   In a program, a number is entered from the terminal.
If the number is negative the message "correction made" should be
printed, the number changed to positive, and the program continued;
otherwise the program should merely continue. The BASIC code for
this would be

```
260 INPUT C
270 IF C<0 THEN 290
280 GOTO 310
290 PRINT "CORRECTION MADE"
300 LET C=-C
310 (program continues)
```

There are two problems with this program segment: first, the activities
to be performed when the condition is true (lines 290 and 300) do
not occur immediately after the condition (which is what the one-way
selection structure requires); second, there is a GOTO statement that
can be eliminated. Both problems can be corrected if the opposite relation is used in line 270. If this is done the code would be

```
260 INPUT C
270 IF C>=0 THEN 300
280 PRINT "CORRECTION MADE"
290 LET C=-C
300 (program continues)
```

Thus the BASIC structure for one-way selection involving more than one statement may be better described by the diagram in Figure D.6.

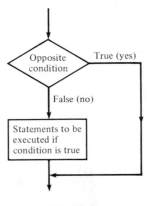

FIGURE D.6

Multiple selection occurs when more than one condition must be tested before a statement can be selected for execution. Generally multiple selection can be covered by a series of IF-THENs. However, if the expression on which the selection depends takes on, as its only values, a consecutive set of integers, then the ON-GOTO or ON-GOSUB statements can be used.

D.4 Repetition

Repetition is looping. Looping structures are shown in Figure D.7 (which is sometimes called a "prechecked" loop because the condition appears at the start of the loop) and in Figure D.8 (which is called a "postchecked" loop because the condition is at the bottom of the loop).

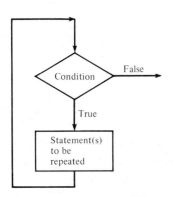

FIGURE D.7. Prechecked loop.

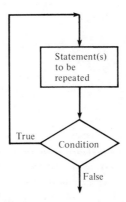

FIGURE D.8. Postchecked loop.

An example of each type of loop is shown in the paragraphs that follow.

EXAMPLE D.2. Numbers are to be entered one at a time from the terminal and added. This is to be done as long as the number entered is not 0. When 0 is entered, the sum should be printed.

```
100 REM PRE-CHECKED LOOP
110 LET S=0
120 INPUT X
130 IF X=0 THEN 170
140    LET S=S+X
150    INPUT X
160 GOTO 130
170 PRINT "SUM IS";S
180 END
```

Note once again that the opposite relation (X=0 instead of X<>0) is used in the conditional statement. Also note that lines 120 and 150 are duplicate statements. This is necessary if the exact form of the pre-checked loop is to be followed. However frequently BASIC programs are written that produce the same result but without the duplication by transferring from the bottom of the loop to the statement prior to the IF-THEN.

```
120    INPUT X
130    IF X=0 THEN 160
140    LET S=S+X
150 GOTO 120
160 PRINT "SUM IS";S
```

This repetition, which is close to the prechecked loop structure, is often used by people programming in BASIC.

EXAMPLE D.3. Eight numbers are to be entered from the terminal. After each has been entered, its square is to be calculated and printed.

```
100 REM POST-CHECKED LOOP
110 LET I=1
120    PRINT "ENTER A NUMBER"
130    INPUT N
140    LET S=N↑2
150    PRINT "IT'S SQUARE IS";S
160    LET I=I+1
170 IF I<=8 THEN 120
180 END
```

This loop precisely parallels the form of a postchecked loop.

The importance of structured programming lies in the fact that the logic to solve any programming problem can be completely described by the three structured programming constructs. Thus, as you develop your algorithm or flowchart to solve a problem, frequently ask yourself whether your logic displays one or more of these constructs.

With few exceptions, the BASIC statements presented in this text follow the guidelines of the American National Standards Institute (ANSI) for minimal BASIC, a collection of BASIC statements that should be part of every BASIC system, and the proposed guidelines for an expanded version of BASIC. Most manufacturers of BASIC systems will include these statements as a subset of their BASIC and include several additional features. BASIC systems including additional features may be described as "enhanced BASICs" and one vendor's enhanced BASIC may be considerably different from another's. The remainder of this appendix will briefly examine some of these enhancements. You should check which, if any, are available on your system.

The use of the word LET is optional in many BASICs. The statements 120 LET A=7 and 120 A=7 would be equivalent.

A multiple assignment allows several variables to be assigned the same value with a single statement such as

```
100 LET S=C=T=N=0
```

This is particularly convenient with initializations.

Longer, and thus more descriptive, variable names are permitted. COUNT could be used as a counter variable and NAME$ a string variable used to store a name.

Several statements can be entered on a single line as long as they are separated by some special symbol such as a backslash (\) or a colon (:). For example,

```
100 LET S=0\PRINT "ENTER NUMBER"\INPUT X
```

A quoted string may follow an INPUT and would be equivalent to a PRINT with the string and then the INPUT statement. The statement

```
80 INPUT "TYPE A POSITIVE VALUE";X
```

would be the same as

```
80 PRINT "TYPE A POSITIVE VALUE";
85 INPUT X
```

The TAB feature has been used to produce output that was neat and orderly looking. Columns of numbers were printed whose first digits were all aligned. The alignments were made at the left-hand end of the numbers, and the printing of these numbers is sometimes described as being *left-justified*. Sometimes we will want our output to be printed *right-justified*, that is, the numbers printed so that the digits at their right ends are aligned. We might want monetary output printed so that the decimal points align. These requirements can be met by using BASIC's PRINT USING statement.

The PRINT USING statement does two things: it causes the values of variables to be displayed (just as with a PRINT statement), and it also specifies the *format* for the output. (By format we mean a precise description of the appearance of the output.)

To specify an output format means to use a group of special characters (we will use #) to describe how the output is to appear. The specifications differ according to the kind of number that will be printed. If an integer is to be printed, the specification is merely a collection of consecutive #'s. To illustrate PRINT USING with integers, we will look at a program that reads and prints six integers one under the other. Then we will change the program to include a PRINT USING statement and see the difference in the appearance of the output.

EXAMPLE D.4

```
100 REM PRINT COLUMN OF SIX INTEGERS
110 REM USUAL OUTPUT APPEARANCE
120 REM COLUMN HEADINGS FOR REFERENCE
130 PRINT "1234567890"
140 LET J=1
150    READ N
160    PRINT N
170    LET J=J+1
180 IF J<=6 THEN 150
190 DATA 34,7,-1,159,-6666,98765
200 END

RUN

1234567890
 34
 7
-1
 159
-6666
 98765

READY
```

We now change line 160 to

```
160 PRINT USING 185,N
```

add line 185

```
185 :#####
```

and the output is

```
RUN

1234567890
    34
     7
```

```
  -1
 159
-6666
98765
```

READY

Line 160 directs the computer to print the value of the variable N according to the specification shown in line 185. Line 185 begins with the line number and a colon. Immediately following the colon are five #'s. These #'s are said to describe the *output field*—the amount of space that will be used to print the value of the variable. The output field is five characters wide and the numbers are printed right-justified in the field. Any spaces not used in the printing will be left blank. If the value to be printed is larger than the field, the number will not be printed, but instead each position of the field will be filled with an error symbol. For example, if we attempted to print the number 234567 in the field described by line 185, our output would show

```
*****
```

The programmer must take care that the field is large enough to handle the output (including possible minus signs).

Line 185, which gives the appearance of the output field, is usually called an "image" statement and is a nonexecutable statement. For ease of reference, all image statements are usually put near the end of a program.

Numbers that include a decimal point are handled slightly differently. The descriptions of their output fields must show (1) the number of spaces to the left of the decimal point, (2) the decimal point, and (3) the number of places to the right of the decimal point. To the left of the decimal point, any unfilled printing spaces will be left blank, while to the right of the decimal point, excess spaces will be filled with 0's. If the number of digits to the right of the decimal point exceeds the number of spaces indicated in the field specification, the number will be rounded to fit into the field. The next example illustrates these points.

EXAMPLE D.5

```
100 REM PRINT USING WITH DECIMAL NUMBERS
110 LET R1=345.276
120 PRINT "1234567890"
130 PRINT R1
140 PRINT USING 180,R1
150 PRINT USING 190,R1
160 PRINT USING 200,R1
170 PRINT USING 210,R1
180 :#####.###
190 :###.##
200 :###.#
210 :###.####
220 END
```

```
RUN

1234567890
 345.276
   345.276
345.28
345.3
345.2760
```

READY

Commas may also be included in a field specification to aid the readability of output. This is shown in Example D.6.

EXAMPLE D.6

```
100 REM COMMA IN IMAGE STATEMENT
110 LET R=62794.35
120 PRINT USING 130,R
130 :##,###.##
140 END

RUN

62,794.35
```

READY

If it happens that due to the size of the number no digit would appear to the left of the comma, the comma will not be printed. For example, if the value of R, in Example D.6, were 142.91, the output would be

```
RUN

   142.91
```

READY

The next example illustrates two additional features that can be used in image statements: (1) an output field specification can begin with a $ (to be used for monetary output) and (2) several field specifications can be displayed in a single image statement.

EXAMPLE D.7. A salesperson is paid \$650.00 per month plus a commission of 10% of sales. For each of six salespeople, a DATA line contains a three-digit identification code and the amount of sales for that salesperson. The program should read the data and print a sales report that shows

1. For each salesperson, the identification code, the amount of sales, the amount of commission, and the monthly salary
2. The total sales, total commissions, and total salaries

As with the writing of programs, advanced planning is needed to produce polished-looking output. There will be four types of output lines: a heading line, an item line (to be repeated six times) displaying the output mentioned earlier, a line to print sequences of dashes under the money columns, and a line to print the totals. A piece of graph paper can be helpful with the planning. A plan is shown in Figure D.9.

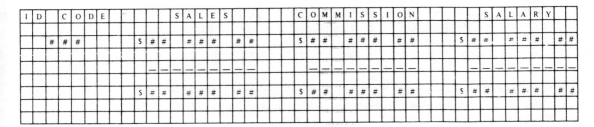

FIGURE D.9.

The program is

```
100 PRINT "ID CODE";TAB(13);"SALES";TAB(23);"COMMISSION";TAB(38);"SALARY"
110 PRINT
120 LET T1=0
130 LET T2=0
140 LET T3=0
150 LET I=1
160    READ N,S
170    LET C=.10*S
180    LET P=650+C
190    PRINT USING 270,N,S,C,P
200    LET T1=T1+S
210    LET T2=T2+C
220    LET T3=T3+P
230    LET I=I+1
240 IF I<=6 THEN 160
250 PRINT USING 280
260 PRINT USING 290,T1,T2,T3
270 :   ###      $##,###.##    $##,###.##    $##,###.##
280 :           ---------    ---------    ---------
290 :            $##,###.##    $##,###.##    $##,###.##
300 DATA 329,14782.65
310 DATA 107,9267.75
320 DATA 994,783.20
330 DATA 272,0
340 DATA 816,46897.95
350 DATA 475,19806.00
360 END
```

Note that line 280 prints an image statement that contains no numeric fields, merely the dashes for the bottoms of the three columns to be summed.

RUN

ID CODE	SALES	COMMISSION	SALARY
329	$14,782.65	$ 1,478.27	$ 2,128.27
107	$ 9,267.75	$ 926.77	$ 1,576.77
994	$ 783.20	$ 78.32	$ 728.32
272	$ .00	$ .00	$ 650.00
816	$46,897.95	$ 4,689.79	$ 5,339.79
475	$19,806.00	$ 1,980.60	$ 2,630.60
	---------	---------	---------
	$91,537.55	$ 9,153.75	$13,053.75

Finally, it should be noticed that a PRINT USING can be used to print the values of string variables. The output field is just a group of #'s and the string will be printed *left-justified* in the field.

Conditional statements can be written that use the *logical operators* NOT, AND, and OR to form *compound logical statements.*

If NOT precedes a condition, the result has the opposite truth value. For example, if X=3 and Y=8 then X<Y is true and so NOT(X<Y) is false. Similarly 2*X=Y is false and NOT(2*X=Y) is true. Generally, if *p* is any condition, then *p* can be classified as true or false. If *p* is true, NOT(*p*) is false, and if *p* is false, NOT(*p*) is true. These results can be displayed in a tabular form called a *truth table.*

p	NOT(*p*)
true	false
false	true

If p and q are two conditions, the truth table for p AND q is

p	*q*	*p* AND *q*
true	true	true
true	false	false
false	true	false
false	false	false

In words, *p* AND *q* is true only when both parts (*p* and *q*) are true at the same time. Thus if the value of X is 6 and the value of Y is 0,

(X > Y) AND (Y >= 0) is true
(Y <= X) AND (X > 10) is false
(Y > 5) AND (X <> Y) is false
(X < 4) AND (X = Y) is false

The OR operator is defined by the truth table

p	*q*	*p* OR *q*
true	true	true
true	false	true
false	true	true
false	false	false

so *p* OR *q* is false only when both parts (*p* and *q*) are false.

With compound logical statements, IF-THENs like the following can be written.

```
210 IF (X↑2>7.2) OR (Y=5) THEN 500
```

End of data tags can be eliminated from data stacks and data files if a statement such as NODATA is available on your system. When executed, the computer automatically will check to see if any more data remain to be read from the stack (file). If not, transfer will be made to the line number following NODATA. To illustrate,

```
100 REM SUMMING WITH NODATA
110 LET S=0
120 NO DATA,160
130    READ X
140    LET S=S+X
150 GOTO 120
160 PRINT "SUM IS";S
170 DATA 8,3,9,2
180 DATA 4,2
190 END
```

An equivalent statement for data files would be

```
450 NODATA#1,530
```

where 1 is the data file ordinal.

The various built-in functions differ from system to system. Those mentioned in Chapter 11 will be found in all BASICs, and yours will probably include more.

User-defined functions of more than one variable are frequently available. The function FNZ is a function of the two variables X and Y that calculates the hypotenuse of a right triangle with sides X and Y.

```
FNZ(X,Y) = SQR(X↑2+Y↑2)
```

You may find that your system supports additional string functions and even includes user-defined string functions.

Three-dimensional arrays are found in some BASIC systems. If you owned three warehouses in each of five cities and each warehouse stocked the items illustrated at the beginning of Chapter 15, you would have a three-dimensional array M(I,J,K) where I refers to the item stocked (pencils, etc.), J the particular warehouse (A, B, or C), and K the city where the warehouse is located.

Input and output of two-dimensional arrays can be simplified by certain MAT statements.

EXAMPLE D.8.   Read in the values of a 3 × 2 matrix A and then print A.

```
100 BASE 1
110 DIM A(3,2)
120 MAT READ A
130 MAT PRINT A
140 DATA 7,3,4,2,0,1
150 END
```

RUN

```
7                   3

4                   2

0                   1
```

READY

Line 100 is necessary only on systems where the smallest subscript used is 0 (on such systems, without line 100, A would be a 4 × 3 array). Whenever a MAT statement is used, each array *must* be dimensioned. The array A is declared to be 3 × 2 and so will contain six values. The six numbers in the DATA line are automatically read into A in a rowwise fashion. So line 120 is equivalent to

```
116 FOR I=1 TO 3
118    FOR J=1 TO 2
120        READ A(I,J)
122    NEXT J
124 NEXT I
```

and line 130 is equivalent to

```
126 FOR I=1 TO 3
128    FOR J=1 TO 2
130        PRINT A(I,J),
132    NEXT J
134    PRINT
136 NEXT I
```

If line 130 in the program were changed to

```
130 MAT PRINT A;
```

the output would be

RUN

    7   3

    4   2

    Ø   1

READY

You have some degree of control over the way the matrix is printed by following the matrix by a semicolon to print the entries close together or followed by nothing, which acts like a comma and prints the entries in successive print zones. We shall shortly see the comma explicitly used to determine the appearance of the output.

Values can be entered into a matrix from the terminal by using the MAT INPUT statement as shown.

EXAMPLE D.9

```
100 BASE 1
110 DIM B(2,4)
120 MAT INPUT B
130 MAT PRINT B;
140 END

RUN
? 7,Ø,9,1
? 2,6,1,4

    7    Ø    9    1

    2    6    1    4

READY
```

As with MAT READ, values should be entered by rows.

Several matrices may be used with MAT READ or MAT PRINT. The matrices are listed in the MAT PRINT followed by a comma or semicolon (or no character after the final matrix if print zones are to be used).

EXAMPLE D.10

```
100 BASE 1
110 DIM G(2,3),H(2,2)
120 MAT READ G,H
130 MAT PRINT G,H;
140 DATA 7,1,4,Ø,5
150 DATA 6,2,8,3,9
160 END
```

Six values are read into G and then four into H. G is printed with its elements printed in zones and then H is printed with its elements close together.

RUN

```
7                    1              4

Ø                    5              6

 2    8

 3    9
```

READY

Several matrix operations and functions are included with the MAT statements.

If A and B are two matrices that are of the same size (that is, have the same number of rows and same number of columns), the statement

```
MAT  C=A+B
```

will add A and B and assign their sum to the matrix C (which also must have the same size as A and B). Similarly,

```
MAT  C=A-B
```

will calculate the matrix C as the difference of A and B.

EXAMPLE D.11.   This program illustrates the addition and subtraction of two matrices.

```
100 DIM A(3,2),B(3,2),S(3,2),D(3,2)
110 MAT READ A
120 MAT READ B
130 PRINT "MATRIX A"
140 MAT PRINT A;
150 PRINT "MATRIX B"
160 MAT PRINT B;
170 MAT S=A+B
180 PRINT "THEIR SUM"
190 MAT PRINT S;
200 MAT D=A-B
210 PRINT "THE DIFFERENCE"
220 MAT PRINT D;
230 DATA 1,7,4,3,Ø,5
240 DATA Ø,3,5,1,6,4
250 END
```

RUN

MATRIX A
  1   7

  4   3

  Ø   5

MATRIX B
  Ø   3

  5   1

  6   4

THEIR SUM
  1   1Ø

  9   4

  6   9

THE DIFFERENCE
  1   4

 -1   2

 -6   1

READY

Multiplication of a matrix by a scalar (number) and multiplication of two matrices is also possible. Scalar multiplication is done by the statement

MAT C=(N)*A

where A is a matrix and N is the scalar. (Note that the scalar must be enclosed within parentheses.) To multiply two matrices, the number of columns of the first matrix must be the same as the number of rows of the second matrix. The number of rows of the product matrix will be the same as the number of rows of the first matrix and will have as many columns as does the second matrix. The multiplication is done by the statement

MAT D=A*B

For example, if A is a 2 × 3 matrix and B is a 3 × 4 matrix, then D will be a 2 × 4 matrix.

EXAMPLE D.12. The following involves multiplication with matrices.

```
100 DIM A(2,3),B(3,4),C(2,3),D(2,4)
110 MAT READ A
120 MAT READ B
130 LET N=5
140 MAT C=(N)*A
150 MAT D=A*B
160 MAT PRINT C
170 PRINT
180 MAT PRINT D
190 DATA 1,0,4,2,8,3
200 DATA 1,4,3,9,0,1,2,6,4,5,0,2.
210 END
```

RUN

```
  5            0            20
 10           40            15


 17           24            3            17

 14           31            22           72
```

READY

Some of the matrix functions included in enhanced versions of BASIC are ZER, CON, and IDN. The ZER function produces a matrix all of whose entries are zeroes. A matrix that is the result of the CON function contains all 1's as its entries. The IDN function is used to produce a square matrix (same number of rows as columns) whose entries are all 0's except for values on the diagonal from the upper left corner to the lower right corner. Elements on this diagonal will be 1's.

EXAMPLE D.13. This program illustrates the ZER, CON, and IDN matrix functions.

```
100 DIM A(2,3),B(3,2),C(3,3)
110 MAT A=ZER(2,3)
120 MAT B=CON(3,2)
130 MAT C=IDN(3,3)
140 PRINT "ZER FUNCTION"
150 MAT PRINT A;
160 PRINT "CON FUNCTION"
170 MAT PRINT B;
180 PRINT "IDN FUNCTION"
190 MAT PRINT C;
200 END
```

RUN

ZER FUNCTION
  Ø   Ø   Ø

  Ø   Ø   Ø

CON FUNCTION
  1   1

  1   1

  1   1

IDN FUNCTION
  1   Ø   Ø

  Ø   1   Ø

  Ø   Ø   1

READY

Two other matrix functions that are sometimes used to solve problems involving matrices are TRN and INV. If A is a matrix, then TRN(A) will return the *transpose* of A (the transpose of A is that matrix whose rows are the columns of A and whose columns are A's rows.)

EXAMPLE D.14. This program illustrates the TRN function. A 3×4 matrix A is read and printed, and then its 4×3 transpose B is calculated and printed.

```
100 DIM A(3,4),B(4,3)
110 MAT READ A
120 PRINT "MATRIX"
130 MAT PRINT A;
140 PRINT
150 MAT B=TRN(A)
160 MAT PRINT B;
170 DATA 1,2,3,4,5,6
180 DATA 2,3,7,8,9,4
190 END
```

RUN

MATRIX
  1   2   3   4

  5   6   2   3

  7   8   9   4

```
1   5   7

2   6   8

3   2   9

4   3   4
```

READY

If A is a square matrix, the inverse of A is the square matrix (which is the same size as A) that, when multiplied by A, gives the identity matrix of the same size. (It should be noted that not all square matrices have inverses.) If A is a square matrix that has an inverse, that inverse is found by using the INV function.

EXAMPLE D.15. This program illustrates the INV function.

```
100 DIM A(2,2),B(2,2)
110 MAT READ A
120 PRINT "MATRIX A"
130 MAT PRINT A;
140 PRINT
150 MAT B=INV(A)
160 PRINT "INVERSE OF A"
170 MAT PRINT B;
180 DATA 1,1,0,1
190 END

RUN

MATRIX A
 1   1

 0   1

INVERSE OF A
 1  -1

 0   1

READY
```

Chapter 2

1 Assign 5.34 to R.
Assign 37.5 to H.
Calculate P by P=R×H.
Print P.

2

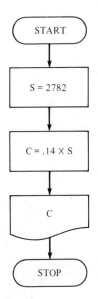

START

S = 2782

C = .14 × S

C

STOP

3 Assign 6 to L.
Assign 5.2 to W.
Calculate A by L×W.
Print "area."
Print A.
Calculate C by A×12.95.
Print "cost."
Print C.

4

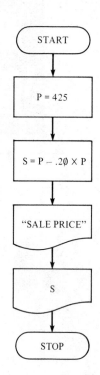

5 Assign 16.50 to R1.
Assign 1.25 to R2.
Assign 9 to H.
Assign 23 to M.
Calculate C by (R1×H) + (R2×M).
Print "total cost."
Print C.

9 FIRST VALUE
　6
SECOND VALUE
　7

11

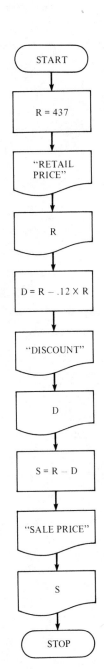

12

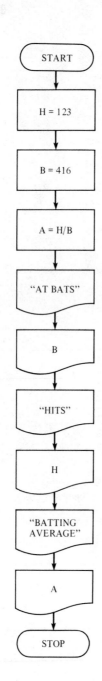

13

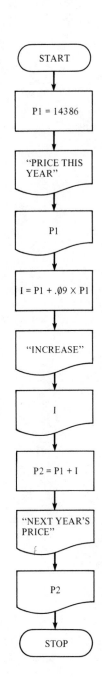

15

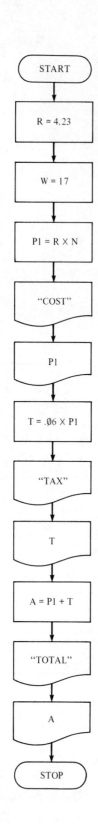

Chapter 3

1 a. c. d. h.
2 Valid except for
  b. 7*X+1
  f. A+(−4)
  g. C*(D+E)
  h. 3*Y↑2
  i. 6↑(−2)
3 a. 23   c. −6   e. −49   g. 9
  i. 2   k. 1   m. 1
4 a. −5   c. −10   e. 6.5
5 a. R*T   c. P*R↑2   e. X/(Y+Z)
  g. X/Y+Z   i. B↑2−4*A*C   k. P/Q*R/S
  m. (A+B)/(C+D)
6 286 (26 letters and 260 letters
  followed by digits)

Chapter 4

1 a. 1Ø LET X=7
  c. 1Ø LET Q=3*M+3*N
  e. 9Ø LET M=(Y2−Y1)/(X2−X1)
2 a. 2Ø PRINT Y
  b. 4Ø PRINT "YOUR RESULT IS"
  c. 9Ø PRINT "VOLUME";V
  d. 5Ø PRINT "THE SURFACE AREA IS",S
4 a. Missing line number.
  b. A MESSAGE should be quoted.
  d. There should be a * between 2 and
    X (i.e., 2*X).

6

```
1Ø LET T=14572
2Ø LET X=T+.12*T
3Ø PRINT "POPULATION WILL BE"
4Ø PRINT X
5Ø END
```

7

```
1Ø LET L=6
2Ø LET W=5.2
3Ø LET A=L*W
4Ø PRINT "AREA"
5Ø PRINT A
6Ø LET C=A*12.95
7Ø PRINT "COST"
8Ø PRINT C
9Ø END
```

10

```
1Ø LET R=4.23
2Ø LET N=17
3Ø LET P1=R*N
4Ø PRINT "COST"
5Ø PRINT P1
6Ø LET T=.Ø6*P1
7Ø PRINT "TAX"
```

```
80 PRINT T
90 LET A=P1+T
100 PRINT "TOTAL"
110 PRINT A
120 END
```

Chapter 5

2

```
10 PRINT "NOT"
20 PRINT "OVER"
30 PRINT "YET"
40 END
```

3

```
10 LET X=Ø
20 LET A=4
30 LET G=X+A
40 PRINT F
50 END
```

4

```
15 PRINT "START"
25 LET R=2.7
45 LET W=3*R
55 LET T=3
65 PRINT "FINISH"
75 PRINT T,W
85 END
```

Chapter 6

1

```
100 PRINT "DOUBLE TROUBLE"
114 PRINT "ENTER AN INTEGER"
119 INPUT Z
125 PRINT "THANK YOU"
140 INPUT Y,X
150 LET Z2=2*Z
160 LET Y2=2*Y
204 PRINT Z2,Y2,X
210 PRINT "AND MORE"
226 INPUT J
233 PRINT J
240 END
```

3

```
10 PRINT "TYPE IN LENGTH, IN FEET"
20 INPUT F
30 LET I=12*F
40 PRINT "LENGTH, IN INCHES, IS";I
50 END
```

5

```
10 PRINT "HOW MANY LITERS"
20 INPUT L
30 LET Q=1.06*L
40 PRINT L;"LITERS IS";Q;"QUARTS"
50 END
```

7

```
10 PRINT "HOW DEEP IS THE WATER"
20 INPUT D
30 LET P=62.4*D
40 PRINT "THE PRESSURE IS";P
50 END
```

8

```
10 LET R1=12.95
20 LET R2=.16
30 PRINT "HOW MANY DAYS RENTED"
40 INPUT D
50 PRINT "HOW MANY MILES DRIVEN"
60 INPUT M
70 LET A=(R1*D)+(R2*M)
80 PRINT "AMOUNT DUE IS";A
90 END
```

10

```
10 PRINT "ENTER ANNUAL NUMBER OF MILES"
20 INPUT M
30 PRINT "ENTER MILES PER GALLON RATE"
40 INPUT R
50 LET G=M/R
60 PRINT "GALLONS USED IS";G
70 END
```

11

```
10 PRINT "WHAT IS PRICE"
20 INPUT P
30 PRINT "WHAT IS TAX RATE"
40 INPUT R
50 LET T=P*R
60 LET A=P+T
70 PRINT "TOTAL PRICE IS";A
80 END
```

12

```
10 PRINT "ENTER SALES AND COSTS"
20 INPUT S,C
30 LET P=S-C
40 PRINT "PROFIT"; P
50 END
```

14

```
10 PRINT "ENTER THREE TEST GRADES"
20 INPUT T1,T2,T3
30 PRINT "ENTER EXAM GRADE"
40 INPUT E
50 LET A=(T1+T2+T3+E)/4
60 PRINT "AVERAGE IS";A
70 END
```

15

```
10 PRINT "ENTER THREE TEST GRADES"
20 INPUT T1,T2,T3
30 LET A1=(T1+T2+T3)/3
40 PRINT "ENTER EXAM GRADE"
50 INPUT E
60 LET A2=(A1+E)/2
70 PRINT "AVERAGE IS";A2
80 END
```

17

```
100 PRINT "WHAT GRADE IN SCHOOL HAVE YOU COMPLETED"
110 INPUT G
120 LET D=180*G
130 LET H=5.25*D
140 PRINT "YOU HAVE SPENT";H;"HOURS IN SCHOOL"
150 END
```

19

```
100 PRINT "ENTER AMOUNT OF LOAN"
110 INPUT P
120 PRINT "ENTER INTEREST RATE"
130 INPUT R
140 PRINT "ENTER NUMBER OF DAYS"
150 INPUT T
160 LET T1=T/360
170 LET T2=T/365
180 LET I1=P*R*T1
190 LET I2=P*R*T2
200 PRINT "ORDINARY","EXACT"
210 PRINT "INTEREST","INTEREST"
220 PRINT I1,I2
230 END
```

23

```
100 PRINT "LINEAR EQUATION AX+B=C"
110 PRINT "ENTER VALUES FOR A,B AND C"
120 INPUT A,B,C
130 LET X=(C-B)/A
140 PRINT "X=";X
150 END
```

Chapter 7

1

   13

2

  7   11
    11   17

4

  11

5

3Ø3Ø3Ø3Ø3Ø3Ø3Ø
VALUE
  5
   VALUE
      5
  5   5

6

          START
      BACKING
UP

7

ROMEO   AND   JULIET
JULIET
    AND
         ROMEO

8 a. Missing line number and *expression* following LET.
   c. Missing line number and what follows PRINT must be expression.
   d. No semicolon after PRINT.
   e. TAB(1Ø) is *not* in second print zone.
   f. Numeric constant (43) assigned to string variable.
   g. String variable assigned to numeric variable.

9

	N1	N2	N3	output
1Ø2 LET N1=1	1	?	?	
1Ø4 LET N2=3	1	3	?	
1Ø6 PRINT "FIRST","SECOND"	1	3	?	"FIRST","SECOND"
1Ø8 PRINT N1,N2	1	3	?	1,3
11Ø LET N3=4*(N1+N2)	1	3	16	
112 PRINT "NEXT"	1	3	16	"NEXT"
114 PRINT N3	1	3	16	16
116 PRINT "ALL",N1;N2;N3	1	3	16	"ALL",1;3;16

118 END

Output is

FIRST	SECOND
1	3
NEXT	
16	
ALL	1 3 16

11

	X	Y	Z	output
1Ø LET X=Ø	Ø	?	?	
2Ø LET X=X+1	1	?	?	
3Ø LET Y=X+1	1	2	?	
4Ø LET X=X+Y	3	2	?	
5Ø LET Y=Y*X	3	6	?	
6Ø LET Z=(X+1)*(Y−1)	3	6	2Ø	
7Ø PRINT X,Y,Z	3	6	2Ø	3,6,2Ø

8Ø END

Output is

3   6   2Ø

14

```
1Ø PRINT (7+2+3+5)/4
2Ø END
```

3 a. IS EQUAL TO should be =
b. N+6 is not a condition
c. Missing line number
e. ≠ should be <>
g. EXIT should be "EXIT"

4 a. 775   c. 1,5ØØ   e. 1,Ø75   g. 1,575

5 a. B and Y are control variables
Transfer condition is B+Y<M

```
14Ø LET M=11
15Ø LET B=5
16Ø LET Y=2
17Ø    PRINT B,Y
18Ø    LET B=B+1
19Ø    LET Y=Y+2
2ØØ IF B+Y<M THEN 17Ø
```

b. F is control variable
Transfer condition is F<=7
Counting loop

6 a.

```
RECORDING
ERROR   1
ERROR   2
ERROR   3
ERROR   4
ERROR   5
```

c.

```
N1                 N2
  5                 6
  7                 6
  9                 6
 11                 6
 13                 6
 15                16
```

7

```
ENTER  A  NUMBER
?  4
ENTER  A  NUMBER
?  -1
ENTER  A  NUMBER
?  Ø
ENTER  A  NUMBER
?  3
ENTER  A  NUMBER
?  6
ENTER  A  NUMBER
?  9
ENTER  A  NUMBER
?  -2
ENTER  A  NUMBER
?  6
ENTER  A  NUMBER
?  7
DONE  7
```

8

```
?  BASE
BASEBALL
?  BALL
?  GUM
GUMBALL
?  FOOT
FOOTBALL
?  BALL
?  BASKET
BASKETBALL
```

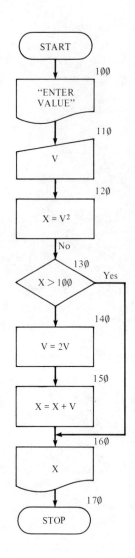

10 a.

```
100 PRINT "ENTER VALUE"
110 INPUT V
120 LET X=V↑2
130 IF X>100 THEN 160
140 LET V=2*V
150 LET X=X+V
160 PRINT X
170 END
```

11

```
10 PRINT "ENTER PRINCIPAL"
20 INPUT P
30 PRINT "ENTER INTEREST RATE AS A DECIMAL"
40 INPUT R
50 PRINT "HOW MANY YEARS SHOULD MONEY BE LEFT IN ACCOUNT"
60 INPUT Y
70 PRINT "END OF YEAR", "AMOUNT"
```

```
80 LET N=1
90   LET C=P*(1+R)↑N
100   PRINT N,C
110   LET N=N+1
120 IF N<=Y THEN 90
130 END
```

12

```
10 PRINT "WHAT YEAR IS IT"
20 INPUT Y
30 LET N=Y-1626
40 LET P=24
50 LET R=.045
60 LET C=P*(1+R)↑N
70 PRINT
80 PRINT "IN";Y;"THE AMOUNT IS";C
90 END
```

14 a.

```
100 REM ASSUME INITIAL POPULATION IS 16483
110 LET P=16483
120 LET R=.041
130 PRINT "AFTER YEAR","POPULATION"
140 LET Y=1
150   LET P=P+P*R
160   PRINT Y,P
170   LET Y=Y+1
180 IF Y<=25 THEN 150
190 END
```

1 a. A line number must follow GOTO (or change statement to 175 STOP)
   b. Missing line number
   c. Infinite loop (though syntactically correct)
   d. Only correct when X=0
   e. ANSWER should be in quotes; PRINT should follow THEN
   f. Variable must be numeric, not string (T$)

2 a. 110   b. 80   c. 700   d. 370

4

```
100 REM YORKVILLE POPULATION
110 REM Y IS ORIGINAL POPULATION
120 LET Y=14326
130 REM N COUNTS YEARS UNTIL POPULATION DOUBLED; INITIALIZE
140 LET N=0
150 REM P IS POPULATION AFTER N YEARS
160 REM AT START P IS THE SAME AS Y
170 LET P=Y
180 REM POPULATION INCREASES 3.2 PCT. EACH YEAR
190   LET P=P+.032*P
200   LET N=N+1
210   REM COMPARE CURRENT AND ORIGINAL POPULATIONS
220 IF P<2*Y THEN 190
230 REM POPULATION HAS NOW AT LEAST DOUBLED
```

```
240 PRINT "POPULATION DOUBLED BY";N;"YEARS"
250 END
```

6

```
150 PRINT "MONTH","PAYMENT","BALANCE","INTEREST"
195     LET I=.0125*L
310       PRINT M,P,L,I
350 PRINT M,L,0,I
```

7

```
100 PRINT "HOW MUCH MONEY WILL YOU INVEST"
110 INPUT P
120 LET N=10
130 LET R=.06
140 LET C=P*(1+R)↑N
150 IF C<=2*P THEN 190
160   LET R=R+.0001
170   LET C=P*(1+R)↑N
180 GOTO 150
190 PRINT "THE NECESSARY RATE IS";100*R;"PERCENT"
200 END
```

8

```
100    PRINT "ENTER A NUMBER"
110    INPUT N
120    PRINT "DO YOU WANT THE SQUARE OR CUBE OF";N
130    INPUT A$
140    IF A$="SQUARE" THEN 180
150    LET C=N↑3
160    PRINT "THE CUBE OF";N;"IS";C
170    GOTO 200
180    LET S=N↑2
190    PRINT "THE SQUARE OF";N;"IS";S
200    PRINT
210    PRINT "ANOTHER NUMBER? YES OR NO?"
220    INPUT R$
230 IF R$="YES" THEN 100
240 END
```

9

```
200 REM BABY-SITTER PAY PROGRAM
210 REM RATE: 1.25 UP TO MIDNIGHT : 1.75 AFTER
220 REM 24 HOUR CLOCK IS USED
230 REM EX. 5 A.M. IS HOUR 5; 3 P.M. IS 15; MIDNIGHT IS 24
240 REM P1 IS BEFORE MIDNIGHT PAY
250 REM P2 IS AFTER MIDNIGHT PAY
260 LET P1=0
270 LET P2=0
280 PRINT "WHAT TIME DID SITTER ARRIVE";
290 INPUT S
300 PRINT "WHAT TIME DID SITTER LEAVE";
310 INPUT E
320 REM CHECK FOR TIME, IF ANY, AFTER MIDNIGHT
330 REM IF S<E, NO AFTER MIDNIGHT PAY
```

```
340 IF S<E THEN 430
350 REM CALCULATE UP TO MIDNIGHT PAY
360 LET P1=(24-S)*1.25
370 REM AFTER MIDNIGHT PAY
380 LET P2=E*1.75
390 REM P IS TOTAL PAY
400 LET P=P1+P2
410 PRINT "AMOUNT DUE: $";P
420 STOP
430 LET P1=(E-S)*1.25
440 PRINT "AMOUNT DUE: $";P1
450 END
```

10

```
300 REM PUBLISHING ROYALTIES
310 REM 12 PCT ON 1ST 5000
320 REM PLUS 14 PCT ON ANY SOLD OVER 5000
330 PRINT "WHAT IS THE COST OF THE BOOK";
340 INPUT C
350 PRINT "HOW MANY COPIES HAVE BEEN SOLD";
360 INPUT N
370 PRINT
380 REM CHECK NUMBER OF COPIES SOLD
390 IF N<=5000 THEN 440
400 REM ROYALTIES FOR SALES OF MORE THAN 5000 COPIES
410 LET R=5000*.12*C+(N-5000)*.14*C
420 PRINT "ROYALTIES DUE AUTHOR: $";R
430 STOP
440 REM ROYALTIES FOR SALES OF 5000 OR LESS
450 LET R=.12*N*C
460 PRINT "ROYALTIES DUE AUTHOR: $";R
470 END
```

12

```
100 REM BUILDING SUPPLY BILL-POSSIBLE DISCOUNTS
110    PRINT "HOW MUCH IS BILL";
120    INPUT B
130    REM NO DISCOUNT FOR BILL<$50
140    IF B<50 THEN 210
150    REM DISCOUNT: 7 PCT FOR >=$50 BUT LESS THAN $200
160    REM 11 PCT FOR >=$200
170    IF B<200 THEN 200
180    LET B=B-.11*B
190    GOTO 210
200    LET B=B-.07*B
210    PRINT "CUSTOMER CHARGE IS";B
220    PRINT
230    PRINT "ANOTHER CUSTOMER BILL? YES OR NO?"
240    INPUT A$
250 IF A$="YES" THEN 110
260 PRINT "FINISHED"
270 END
```

15

```
100 REM BRAINTREE PAINTING COMPANY TAX
110 PRINT "WHAT WAS ANNUAL INCOME";
```

```
120 INPUT I
130 PRINT "HOW MUCH WERE EXPENSES";
140 INPUT E
150 REM PROFIT=INCOME-EXPENSES
160 LET P=I-E
170 PRINT
180 PRINT "PROFIT:";P
190 IF P>0 THEN 230
200 REM IF LOSS OR NO PROFIT, NO TAX
210 PRINT "NO TAXES DUE"
220 STOP
230 REM TAX MUST BE PAID; FIND OUT HOW MUCH
240 IF P>15000 THEN 290
250 REM FOR PROFIT <= 15000 TAX IS 20 PCT.
260 LET T=.2*P
270 PRINT "TAX DUE:";T
280 STOP
290 IF P>40000 THEN 350
300 REM FOR PROFIT BETWEEN 15000 AND 40000
310 REM TAX IS 20 PCT. OF 15000 PLUS 35 PCT. OF AMT. OVER 15000
320 LET T=.2*15000+.35*(P-15000)
330 PRINT "TAX DUE:";T
340 STOP
350 REM IF PROFIT>40000 TAX IS
360 REM T=.2*15000+.35*25000+50 PCT. OF ANYTHING ELSE
370 LET T=.2*15000+.35*25000+.5*(P-40000)
380 PRINT "TAX DUE:";T
390 END
```

16 a.

```
10 LET S=0
20 LET X=2
30    LET S=S+X
40    LET X=X+2
50 IF X<=100 THEN 30
60 PRINT "SUM IS";S
70 END
```

Parts (b), (c), and (d) can be coded from (a) by the following modifications:

b.

```
20 LET X=10
40    LET X=X+10
50 IF X<=1000 THEN 30
```

c.

```
20 LET X=-7
50 IF X<=121 THEN 30
```

d.

```
20 LET X=1
30    LET S=S+X↑2
40    LET X=X+1
50 IF X<=10 THEN 30
```

17

```
100 LET  C=0
120 LET  S=0
130     PRINT "TYPE IN A VALUE"
140     INPUT X
150     IF X=0 THEN 210
160     IF X<0 THEN 190
170     LET S=S+X
180     GOTO 130
190     LET C=C+1
200 GOTO 130
210 PRINT C;"NEGATIVE NUMBERS"
220 PRINT S;"IS POSITIVE SUM"
230 END
```

18 a. 728.34   f. .4832
   c. 81011   g. .0000000200304
   d. .0003091

19 a. 3.4095E+4   f. 6.34829E−3
   c. 7.63512E+2   g. 1.0E+6
   d. 4.38621E−2

20

```
100 REM BOUNCING BALL;20 BOUNCES
110 REM INITIAL HEIGHT OF BALL TO BE INPUT
120 REM EACH BOUNCE HALF AS HIGH AS PREVIOUS BOUNCE
130 PRINT "AT WHAT HEIGHT SHALL WE START";
140 INPUT H
150 LET B=1
160     LET H=H/2
170     PRINT "AFTER BOUNCE";B;"HEIGHT IS";H
180     LET B=B+1
190 IF B<=20 THEN 160
200 END
```

22 a. 280
   b. 35
   c. Depending on the machine you are using, either an error will be printed and the program will halt or the line immediately following 220 will be executed.

24

```
100 PRINT "ENTER A NUMBER"
110 INPUT N
120 PRINT "TO GET THE DOUBLE OF";N;"TYPE 1"
130 PRINT "TO GET THE TRIPLE OF";N;"TYPE 2"
140 PRINT "TO GET THE SQUARE OF";N;"TYPE 3"
150 PRINT "TO GET THE CUBE OF";N;"TYPE 4"
160 PRINT
170 PRINT "WHAT IS YOUR CHOICE (1-4)";
180 INPUT C
190 ON C GOTO 200,220,240,260
200 PRINT 2*N
210 STOP
220 PRINT 3*N
230 STOP
240 PRINT N↑2
```

```
250 STOP
260 PRINT N↑3
270 END
```

25

```
100 PRINT "ENTER  THREE  SIDES"
110 INPUT A,B,C
120 IF C↑2=A↑2+B↑2 THEN 150
130 PRINT "NOT  A  RIGHT  TRIANGLE"
140 STOP
150 PRINT "RIGHT  TRIANGLE"
160 END
```

27

```
100 PRINT "ENTER  AN  ANGLE  BETWEEN  0  AND  180  DEGREES"
110 INPUT X
120 IF X>0 THEN 150
130 PRINT "OUT  OF  RANGE"
140 STOP
150 IF X>=90 THEN 180
160 PRINT "ACUTE"
170 STOP
180 IF X>90 THEN 210
190 PRINT "RIGHT"
200 STOP
210 IF X>=180 THEN 240
220 PRINT "OBTUSE"
230 STOP
240 PRINT "OUT  OF  RANGE"
250 END
```

28

```
200 PRINT "TERMS","RATIO"
210 PRINT "-----","-----"
220 PRINT
230 REM N COUNTS LINES OF OUTPUT
240 LET N=0
250 LET A=1
260 LET B=1
270 LET R=B/A
280 PRINT A;"AND";B,R
290 LET N=N+1
300 REM 30 TERMS IS THE SAME AS 29 LINES OF OUTPUT
310 IF N=29 THEN 360
320 LET C=A+B
330 LET A=B
340 LET B=C
350 GO TO 270
360 END
```

31

```
100 PRINT "SUPPLY  COEFFICIENTS  FOR  AX+B<C"
110 INPUT A,B,C
120 LET X=(C-B)/A
130 IF A<0 THEN 160
```

```
140 PRINT "X<";X
150 STOP
160 PRINT "X>";X
170 END
```

32

```
300 PRINT "ENTER DIVIDEND"
310 INPUT A
320 PRINT "INPUT DIVISOR"
330 INPUT B
340 REM C COUNTS NUMBER OF SUBTRACTIONS
350 REM C WILL BE QUOTIENT
360 LET C=0
370 REM DO SUBTRACTION, INCREASE COUNTER
380    LET A=A-B
390    LET C=C+1
400    REM CHECK FOR END OF DIVISION PROCESS
410    REM IF DIVIDEND>=DIVISOR ANOTHER SUBTRACTION CAN TAKE PLACE
420 IF A>=B THEN 380
430 REM DIVISION DONE, SO CALCULATE REMAINDER R
440 LET R=A
450 REM CHECK FOR 0 REMAINDER
460 IF R=0 THEN 490
470 PRINT "QUOTIENT=";C,"REMAINDER=";R
480 STOP
490 PRINT "QUOTIENT=";C
500 END
```

It should be noted that this program does not take care of the case where the divisor is initially larger than the dividend. For example, this program would not work for $5 \div 8$. The reader might want to modify the program to take care of this special case.

33

```
100 PRINT "ENTER X-COORDINATE OF POINT"
110 INPUT X
120 PRINT "AND NOW THE Y-COORDINATE"
130 INPUT Y
140 PRINT
150 PRINT "THE POINT (";X;",";Y;") IS ";
160 IF X<>0 THEN 190
170 PRINT "ON AN AXIS"
180 STOP
190 IF Y<>0 THEN 220
200 PRINT "ON AN AXIS"
210 STOP
220 IF X>0 THEN 260
230 IF Y>0 THEN PRINT "IN QUADRANT 2"
240 IF Y<0 THEN PRINT "IN QUADRANT 3"
250 STOP
260 IF Y>0 THEN PRINT "IN QUADRANT 1"
270 IF Y<0 THEN PRINT "IN QUADRANT 4"
280 END
```

35

```
100 PRINT "ENTER LEFT HAND ENDPOINT OF INTERVAL"
125 INPUT L
```

```
150 PRINT "ENTER RIGHT END POINT"
175 INPUT R
200 PRINT "HOW MANY SUBINTERVALS DO YOU WANT";
225 INPUT N
250 REM CALCULATE LENGTH OF A SUBINTERVAL
275 LET S=(R-L)/N
300 REM EACH ENDPOINT LOOKS LIKE L+I*S
325 REM WHERE I=0,1,2,...,N
350 LET I=0
375 PRINT "THE ENDPOINTS ARE"
400    PRINT L+I*S
425    LET I=I+1
450 IF I<=N THEN 400
475 END
```

36

```
100 REM RICK'S RETIREMENT
110 REM RICK IS NOW 35 YEARS OLD
120 LET A=35
130 REM INTEREST RATE IS 6.5 PCT
140 LET R=.065
150 REM ANNUAL INVESTMENT IS 250
160 LET I=250
170 REM M WILL BE MONEY ACCUMULATED TO DATE
180 LET M=0
190 PRINT "AGE","MONEY"
200 PRINT
210 REM THE NEW AMOUNT M WILL EQUAL THE FORMER AMOUNT M PLUS
220 REM THE INVESTMENT PLUS INTEREST EARNED ON BOTH
230    LET M=M+I+(M+I)*R
240    PRINT A,M
250    LET A=A+1
260 REM RICK WILL RETIRE AT AGE 65
270 IF A<=65 THEN 230
280 END
```

37

```
100 LET P=5.00
110 LET F1=.08
120 LET F2=.18
130 LET C=.15
140 LET B=0
150    LET B=B+1
160    LET R1=B*P*F1
170    LET R2=B*P*C
180    IF B<=4000 THEN 210
190    LET N=B-4000
200    LET R1=4000*P*F1+N*P*F2
210 IF R1<=R2 THEN 150
220 PRINT "AT";B;"BOOKS"
230 PRINT "FIRST METHOD: $";R1
240 PRINT "SECOND METHOD: $";R2
250 END
```

38

```
100 PRINT "ENTER FIRST WORD"
110 INPUT F$
```

```
120 PRINT "AFTER EACH ?"
130 PRINT "ENTER ANOTHER WORD"
140 INPUT N$
150 IF N$<F$ THEN 190
160    LET F$=N$
170    INPUT N$
180 GOTO 150
190 PRINT "OUT OF SEQUENCE"
200 END
```

39

```
100 LET T=.04
110 PRINT "WHAT IS WINDOW STICKER";
120 INPUT W
130 IF W>=3500 THEN 170
140 PRINT "PRICE TOO LOW"
150 PRINT "RE-CHECK AND ENTER AGAIN"
160 GOTO 110
170 PRINT "WHAT IS DISCOUNT RATE";
180 INPUT R
190 IF R<=12 THEN 230
200 PRINT "ERROR-RATE TOO HIGH"
210 PRINT "RE-ENTER"
220 GOTO 170
230 LET R=R/100
240 PRINT "FROM DETROIT OR HARRISBURG";
250 INPUT A$
260 IF A$="DETROIT" THEN LET C=42.87
270 IF A$="HARRISBURG" THEN LET C=36.05
280 PRINT
290 PRINT
300 PRINT
310 PRINT "STICKER PRICE:";TAB(25);"$";W
320 PRINT "DISCOUNT RATE:";TAB(26);R*100;"%"
330 LET D=W*R
340 PRINT "DISCOUNT:";TAB(25);"$";D
350 LET P=W-D
360 PRINT "SELLING PRICE:";TAB(25);"$";P
370 LET S=P*T
380 PRINT "SALES TAX:";TAB(25);"$";S
390 PRINT "SHIPPING:";TAB(25);"$";C
400 PRINT
410 PRINT
420 PRINT "***TOTAL PRICE***";TAB(25);"$";P+S+C
430 END
```

Chapter 10

1 b. $B should be B$
   c. No comma after READ
   d. Comma between X and Y
   e. Semicolon should be comma
   f. Commas instead of semicolons
   i. 22/7 denotes *operation,* not constant
   j. No line number following RESTORE
   k. No variables following RESTORE

2 a.   2   4
     −3   9
      Ø   Ø
      4   16
      1   1

c. AMERICA   BIRTHDAY
    1776
   HAPPY   BIRTHDAY
    1776
   AMERICA

d. −1 2
    5
    1
   OUT OF DATA AT 4Ø

e.   2 3
  −6 8
   1 2

g. −6
    20
    44
  −99
    12
    24
   SQUARE 36

h. CRAB
   SMYTH
   MAN
   WOMAN
   FLEECE

3 Change line 14Ø to 14Ø IF C$="DONE" THEN 195 and add the following lines

```
123 LET I=Ø
126 LET T=Ø
155 LET I=I+N
165 LET T=T+V
195 PRINT " "," ","------","-----"
197 PRINT" "," ",I,T
```

4

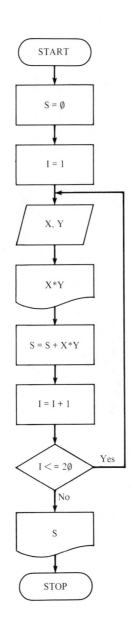

5

```
10 LET S=0
20 LET I=1
30   READ X,Y
40   PRINT X*Y
50   LET S=S+X*Y
60   LET I=I+1
70 IF I<=20 THEN 30
80 PRINT S
90 DATA...
  _
  _
  _
99 END
```

6

```
200 LET P=Ø
210 LET S=Ø
220 LET I=1
230    READ X
240    IF X<=Ø THEN 270
250    LET P=P+1
260    LET S=S+X
270    LET I=I+1
280 IF I<=3Ø THEN 230
290 LET A=S/P
300 PRINT P;"POSITIVE NUMBERS WERE READ"
310 PRINT "THEIR SUM IS";S
320 PRINT "THE AVERAGE IS";A
330 DATA ...
 −
 −
 −
400 END
```

9

```
100 LET C=Ø
110 PRINT "FANS TO BE INVITED"
120 PRINT
130 READ N$,Y
140 REM "ZZZ" IS EODTAG FOR NAMES
150 IF N$="ZZZ" THEN 210
160    IF Y<1Ø THEN 190
170    LET C=C+1
180    PRINT N$
190    READ N$,Y
200 GOTO 150
210 PRINT C; "FANS WILL BE INVITED"
220 DATA ...
 −
 −
 −
300 END
```

11

```
100 PRINT "ENTER CUSTOMER NUMBER"
110 INPUT N
120 PRINT "ENTER AMOUNT TO BE CHARGED"
130 INPUT A
140 LET I=1
150    READ C
160    LET I=I+1
170 IF I<=N THEN 150
180 PRINT
190 IF A>C THEN 240
200 PRINT "SUFFICIENT CREDIT"
210 LET C=C-A
220 PRINT "CREDIT REMAINING IS";C
230 STOP
240 PRINT "CHARGE REJECTED"
```

```
250 PRINT "MAXIMUM CREDIT IS";C
260 DATA ...
 ─
 ─
 ─
300 END
```

13

```
100 PRINT "  ","MORE PICTUREFRAME COMPANY"
110 PRINT
120 PRINT TAB(5);"NAME";TAB(25);"NUMBER";TAB(35);"SALARY"
130 LET B=40
140 LET W=1
150    READ N$,F
160    LET S=B+8*F
170    PRINT N$;TAB(26);F;TAB(36);S
180    LET W=W+1
190 IF W<=12 THEN 150
200 DATA ...
 ─
 ─
 ─
300 END
```

14

```
100 REM DEPRECIATION PROBLEM
110 REM SIX ITEMS TO BE DEPRECIATED
120 REM K COUNTS THE ITEMS
130 LET K=1
140 REM DATA IS A TRIPLE OF VALUES N$,L,C
150 REM N$ IS ITEM DESCRIPTION, L LIFE OF ITEM, C INITIAL COST
160    READ N$,L,C
170    PRINT "  ",N$
180    PRINT
190    PRINT "YEAR","DEPRECIATION","CURRENT VALUE"
200    REM Y COUNTS YEARS THROUGH LIFE OF ITEM
210    LET Y=1
220    REM DEPRECIATION FORMULA: D=2/L*W
230    REM W IS ITEM'S WORTH AT START OF EACH YEAR
240    REM TO BEGIN, W IS SAME AS C
250    LET W=C
260      LET D=2/L*W
270      REM CURRENT VALUE IS OLD VALUE - DEPRECIATION
280      LET W=W-D
290      PRINT Y,D,W
300      LET Y=Y+1
310    IF Y<=L THEN 260
320    PRINT
330    LET K=K+1
340 IF K<=6 THEN 160
350 DATA ...
 ─
 ─
 ─
400 END
```

15

```
10 LET C=1
20    READ W$
30     IF W$<"D" THEN 60
40     IF W$>="T" THEN 60
50     PRINT W$
60     LET C=C+1
70 IF C<=20 THEN 20
80 DATA ...
—
—
—
99 END
```

16

```
100 READ W$
110 LET F$=W$
120 LET L$=W$
130 LET C=2
140    READ W$
150     IF W$<F$ THEN LET F$=W$
160     IF W$>L$ THEN LET L$=W$
170     LET C=C+1
180 IF C<=20 THEN 140
190 PRINT "FIRST","LAST"
200 PRINT F$,L$
210 DATA ...
—
—
—
250 END
```

20

```
100 REM INSURANCE CLAIMS
110 PRINT "ENTER POLICY NUMBER"
120 INPUT N1
130 REM READ DATA: POLICY NUMBER, CATEGORY
140 READ N2,C
150 REM CHECK FOR EOD: 0
160 IF N2=0 THEN 430
170 REM SINCE NOT END OF DATA, CHECK FOR MATCH
180 IF N1<>N2 THEN 140
190 PRINT "ENTER AMOUNT OF CLAIM"
200 INPUT A
210 REM TRANSFER TO DEDUCTIBLE
220 ON C GOTO 230, 280, 330, 380
230 REM C=1 IS 25 DEDUCTIBLE
240 PRINT "POLICY HAS $25 DEDUCTIBLE"
250 LET A=A-25
260 PRINT "AMOUNT TO BE PAID IS $";A
270 STOP
280 REM C=2 IS 50 DEDUCTIBLE
290 PRINT "POLICY HAS $50 DEDUCTIBLE"
300 LET A=A-50
310 PRINT "AMOUNT TO BE PAID IS $";A
```

```
320 STOP
330 REM C=3 IS 100 DEDUCTIBLE
340 PRINT "POLICY HAS A $100 DEDUCTIBLE"
350 LET A=A-100
360 PRINT "AMOUNT TO BE PAID IS $";A
370 STOP
380 REM C=4 IS 200 DEDUCTIBLE
390 PRINT "POLICY HAS A $200 DEDUCTIBLE"
400 LET A=A-200
410 PRINT "AMOUNT TO BE PAID IS $";A
420 STOP
430 PRINT "POLICY NUMBER ENTERED DOES NOT MATCH WITH DATA"
440 DATA 354,1,628,1,533,4,609,3
450 DATA 588,2,634,4,123,3,901,2
460 DATA 981,2,419,4,512,3
470 DATA 0,0
480 END
```

Chapter 11

1 a. -16 b. 2 c. 7 d. 5
    e. 34 f. 8 g. -2

2

```
10 PRINT "ENTER TWO SIDES OF RIGHT TRIANGLE"
20 INPUT R,S
30 LET H=SQR(R↑2+S↑2)
40 PRINT "HYPOTENUSE IS";H
50 END
```

3

```
100    PRINT "ENTER A POSITIVE INTEGER"
110    INPUT N
120    REM CHECK FOR POSITIVE INTEGER
130    IF N<=0 THEN 100
140    IF N<>INT(N) THEN 100
150    REM CHECK DIVISIBILITY BY 2
160    IF N/2=INT(N/2) THEN 190
170    PRINT N;"IS NOT DIVISIBLE BY 2"
180    GOTO 210
190    PRINT N;"IS DIVISIBLE BY 2"
200    REM CHECK DIVISIBILITY BY 3
210    IF N/3=INT(N/3) THEN 240
220    PRINT N;"IS NOT DIVISIBLE BY 3"
230    GOTO 260
240    PRINT N;"IS DIVISIBLE BY 3"
250    REM CHECK DIVISIBILITY BY 6
260    IF N/6=INT(N/6) THEN 290
270    PRINT N;"IS NOT DIVISIBLE BY 6"
280    GOTO 300
290    PRINT N;"IS DIVISIBLE BY 6"
300    PRINT
310    PRINT "ANOTHER NUMBER TO ENTER?"
320    PRINT "YES OR NO"
330    INPUT A$
340 IF A$="YES" THEN 100
350 END
```

4

```
10 PRINT "WHAT IS DISTANCE TO SUBJECT";
20 INPUT D
30 PRINT
40 PRINT "CLARITY WILL BE ";
50 IF ABS(D-12)<2.5 THEN 80
60 PRINT "BAD"
70 STOP
80 PRINT "GOOD"
90 END
```

5

```
110 PRINT "ENTER DIVISOR AND DIVIDEND"
120 INPUT F,D
130 REM CALCULATE QUOTIENT
140 LET Q=INT(D/F)
150 REM CALCULATE REMAINDER
160 LET R=D-Q*F
170 REM CHECK TO SEE IF REMAINDER
180 IF R=0 THEN 210
190 PRINT "QUOTIENT=";Q,"REMAINDER=";R
200 STOP
210 PRINT "QUOTIENT=";Q,"NO REMAINDER"
220 END
```

7

```
100 REM 1ST 30 PRIMES
110 REM C IS COUNTER, P WILL BE PRIME
120 REM D IS TRIAL DIVISOR
130 LET C=1
140 LET P=2
150 LET D=2
160 IF D<=SQR(P) THEN 220
170 PRINT P
180 LET P=P+1
190 LET C=C+1
200 IF C<=30 THEN 150
210 STOP
220 IF P/D=INT(P/D) THEN 250
230 LET D=D+1
240 GOTO 160
250 LET P=P+1
260 GOTO 150
270 END
```

9

```
90 REM P IS PREVIOUS BALANCE
92 READ P
94 PRINT "PREVIOUS BALANCE IS $";P
100 PRINT "DEPOSIT","WITHDRAWAL","PRESENT BALANCE"
111 REM D IS NO. OF DEPOSITS
113 REM W IS NO. OF WITHDRAWALS
115 LET D=0
117 LET W=0
```

```
160 PRINT,ABS(B),
165 LET W=W+1
180 PRINT B,,
185 LET D=D+1
193 LET P=P+B
195 PRINT P
223 PRINT "THE NUMBER OF DEPOSITS IS";D
226 PRINT "THE NUMBER OF WITHDRAWALS IS";W
235 DATA the previous balance
```

12

```
100 PRINT "TYPE IN NUMBER OF SECONDS"
110 INPUT S
120 LET M=INT(S/60)
130 LET S=S-M*60
140 LET H=INT(M/60)
150 LET M=M-H*60
160 PRINT H;"HOURS";M;"MINUTES";S;"SECONDS"
170 END
```

13

```
200 PRINT "ENTER ANNUAL SALARY"
210 INPUT S
220 LET I=2.5*S
230 LET I=I+100
240 LET I=INT(I/100)
250 LET I=I*100
260 PRINT "INSURANCE IS $";I
270 END
```

14

```
10 DEF FND(X)=16*X↑2
15 PRINT "TIME(SEC.)","DISTANCE(FT.)"
20 LET T=0
25    PRINT T,FND(T)
30    LET T=T+5
35 IF T<=60 THEN 25
40 END
```

15 a) DEF FNM(X)=INT(1000*X+.5)/1000

16

```
241 REM 5 GRADE COUNTERS
242 LET N1=0
243 LET N2=0
244 LET N3=0
245 LET N4=0
246 LET N5=0
247 REM T IS NO. OF STUDENTS
248 LET T=0
249 DEF FNC(X)=INT(10*X+.5)/10
250 IF N$="EOD" THEN 441
325    LET N5=N5+1
345    LET N4=N4+1
365    LET N3=N3+1
```

```
385    LET N2=N2+1
405    LET N1=N1+1
441 LET T=N1+N2+N3+N4+N5
442 PRINT N1;"A'S",FNC(N1/T*100);"PERCENT"
443 PRINT N2;"B'S",FNC(N2/T*100);"PERCENT"
444 PRINT N3;"C'S",FNC(N3/T*100);"PERCENT"
445 PRINT N4;"D'S",FNC(N4/T*100);"PERCENT"
446 PRINT N5;"F'S",FNC(N5/T*100);"PERCENT"
```

17

```
100 PRINT "ITEM","ABBREVIATION"
110 READ I$
120 IF I$="DONE" THEN 210
130    LET A$=LEFT$ (I$,3)
140    PRINT I$,A$
150    READ I$
160 GOTO 120
170 DATA LAMP,...
180 DATA LIGHT,...
190 DATA TENT,...
200 DATA DONE
210 END
```

19

```
100 LET I=1
110    READ N$
120    LET I$=LEFT$(N$,1)
130    LET P=2
140    IF MID$(N$,P,1)=" " THEN 170
150      LET P=P+1
160    GOTO 140
170    LET K=LEN(N$)-P
180    LET L$=RIGHT$(N$,K)
190    PRINT L$;" ";I$
200    LET I=I+1
210 IF I<=7 THEN 110
220 DATA...
-
-
-
260 END
```

22

```
10 LET W=0
20 READ D$
30 LET L=LEN(D$)
40 LET C=1
50 IF MID$(D$,C,1)=" " THEN LET W=W+1
60    LET C=C+1
70 IF C<=L THEN 50
80 PRINT W+1;"WORDS"
90 DATA THE TROPHY WAS PRESENTED TO THE TWO MEN FROM TAY
99 END
```

23

```
10 LET C=0
20 LET N=1
30    PRINT "TYPE IN A NUMBER"
40    INPUT V
50    IF V/10=INT(V/10) THEN LET C=C+1
60    LET N=N+1
70 IF N<45 THEN 30
80 PRINT C;"NUMBERS ENDED IN A 0"
90 END
```

24

```
100 LET D=1
110 PRINT "ENTER A POSITIVE INTEGER"
120 INPUT N
130 IF INT(N/10)=0 THEN 170
140    LET D=D+1
150    LET N=INT(N/10)
160 GOTO 130
170 PRINT "IT IS A";D;"DIGIT NUMBER"
180 END
```

29

```
10 LET N=1
20    PRINT N, SQR(N),N↑.5,SQR(N)-N↑.5
30    LET N=N+1
40 IF N<=25 THEN 20
50 END
```

30

```
10 DEF FNR(D)=D*3.14159/180
20 PRINT "DEGREES","RADIANS"
30 LET A=0
40    PRINT A,FNR(A)
50    LET A=A+10
60 IF A<=360 THEN 40
70 END
```

Chapter 12

1 a. The dash between the 1 and 5
c. "Oh" and "zero" should be interchanged
d. Nothing
f. Needs a negative STEP value
h. Improperly nested loops

2   i: a. J;   b. 2;   c. 7;   d. 2, 3, 4, 5, 6, 7;   e. 6
      iii: a. T;   b. 5;   c. 15;   d. 5, 6, 7, 8, 9, 10, 11, 12, 13, 14, 15;   e. 11
      vi: a. D2;   b. 8;   c. 3;   d. 8, 7, 6, 5, 4, 3;   e. 6
      viii: a. M;   b. −2;   c. −33;   d. −2, −7, −12, −17, −22, −27, −32;   e. 7

3   i: a: Y;   b. 3;   c. −4;   d. 3, 2, 1, 0, −1, −2, −3, −4;   e. 8
      iii: a. I;   b. −4;   c. 12;   d. −4, −2, 0, 2, 4, 6, 8, 10, 12;   e. 9

4 a. FOR A=1 TO 5
    c. FOR C=7 TO 19 STEP 2
    f. FOR F=-11 TO 17 STEP 4
    g. FOR G=16 TO 1 STEP -3
    h. FOR H=150 TO 60 STEP -10
    j. FOR J=-5 TO -59 STEP -6

5 a. 1   b. 3   6   3   c. 1
          4   4   8   5   -1
          9   5   10   7   -3
       16   6   12   9
                 7   14   11
                 8   16   13

5 e. GOING   f. 6
       GOING   8
       GONE   10
                      12

6 a. 110   b. 20, 30, 40   c. 20   d. 10, 15
    e. 20, 30   f. 30, 40   g. 25, 30, 35, 40

7

```
10 PRINT "NUMBER","SQUARE"
20 FOR N=6 TO 22 STEP 2
30    PRINT N,N↑2
40 NEXT N
50 END
```

8 a.

```
10 LET S=0
20 FOR X=1 TO 11 STEP 2
30    LET S=S+X
40 NEXT X
50 PRINT S
60 END
```

b.

```
10 LET T=0
20 FOR N=17 TO -11 STEP -4
30    LET T=T+N
40 NEXT N
50 PRINT T
60 END
```

9 Yes. The programs in (b) and (d) do. In (a) seven values are entered. In (c) the dividing needs to be done after the loop.

10

```
100 REM 1MPH=1.467 FPS
110 PRINT "MPH","FPS"
120 FOR M=0 TO 60 STEP 5
130    LET F=M*1.467
140    PRINT M,F
150 NEXT M
160 END
```

11

```
10 PRINT "ENTER NUMBER"
20 INPUT X
30 LET P=1
40 FOR I=1 TO 10
50    LET P=P*X
60 NEXT I
70 PRINT X;"TO THE TENTH POWER IS";P
80 END
```

12

```
131 REM M WILL BE MAX PROFIT
132 REM N1 IS NO. OF SEMI-SKILLED
133 REM N2 IS NO. OF SKILLED
134 REM NEEDED TO PRODUCE M
135 LET M=0
136 LET N1=0
137 LET N2=0
181 IF P<M THEN 190
182 LET M=P
183 LET N1=X
184 LET N2=Y
220 PRINT "MAXIMUM PROFIT WITH"
230 PRINT N1;"SEMI-SKILLED WORKERS AND"
240 PRINT N2;"SKILLED WORKERS"
250 END
```

14

```
100 REM COMPOUND INTEREST
110 REM P IS PRINCIPAL, R INTEREST RATE
120 LET P=500
130 LET R=.055
140 REM COMPOUNDING DONE SEVERAL TIMES
150 REM CHECK AMOUNT FOR SEVERAL DIFFERENT YEARS
160 REM COLUMN HEADINGS-HOW MANY YEARS AND VARIOUS COMPOUNDINGS
170 PRINT "YEARS";
180 PRINT TAB(10);"1X";TAB(20);"2X";TAB(30);"3X";TAB(40);"4X";
190 PRINT TAB(50);"6X";TAB(60);"12X"
200 PRINT
210 REM N IS NUMBER OF YEARS
220 FOR N=1 TO 25 STEP 3
230    PRINT N;
240    REM T IS NUMBER OF COMPOUNDS
250    FOR J=1 TO 6
260      READ T
270      LET C=P*(1+R/T)↑(N*T)
280      PRINT TAB(10*J);C;
290    NEXT J
300    PRINT
310    RESTORE
320    PRINT
330 NEXT N
340 DATA 1,2,3,4,6,12
350 END
```

15

```
100 PRINT "DAY","JACKPOT"
110 LET A=.50
120 FOR D=1 TO 30
130    PRINT D,A
140    LET A=2*A
150 NEXT D
160 END
```

16

```
100 PRINT "DIGIT","SUM OF DIGITS"
110 FOR T=1 TO 9
120    FOR U=0 TO 9
130       LET S=T+U
140       PRINT T;U,S
150    NEXT U
160 NEXT T
170 END
```

17

```
100 LET D=1200
110 LET T=0
120 LET S=.01
130 PRINT " ","NUMBERCRUNCH","J & A","J & A"
140 PRINT "DAY","TOTAL","DAILY","TOTAL"
150 FOR I=1 TO 30
160    LET T=T+S
170    PRINT I,D*I,S,T
180    LET S=2*S
190 NEXT I
200 END
```

18

```
100 LET T=.01
110 PRINT "FOLD","THICKNESS"
120 FOR F=1 TO 15
130    LET T=2*T
140    IF T<12 THEN 170
150    PRINT F,T;"FEET"
160    GOTO 180
170    PRINT F,T;"INCHES"
180 NEXT F
190 END
```

20

```
10 PRINT TAB(15);"X";
20 FOR I=1 TO 14
30    PRINT "X";
40 NEXT I
50 END
```

22 b.

```
10 FOR I=1 TO 5
15   PRINT "*";
20 NEXT I
25 PRINT
30 FOR I=2 TO 4
35   PRINT TAB(I);"*"
40 NEXT I
45 FOR I=3 TO 2 STEP -1
50   PRINT TAB(I);"*"
55 NEXT I
60 FOR I=1 TO 5
65   PRINT "*";
70 NEXT I
75 END
```

c.

```
10 FOR I=1 TO 9
20   PRINT "X";
30 NEXT I
40 PRINT
50 FOR I=5 TO 1 STEP -1
60   PRINT TAB(I);"SHIFT"
70 NEXT I
80 END
```

23

```
100 REM VOLUNTEER BAND AIRLINE PROGRAM
110 PRINT "PEOPLE","EMPTY","PRICE PER"
120 PRINT "ON FLIGHT","SEATS","PERSON"
130 PRINT
140 REM S IS THE NUMBER OF SEATS ON PLANE
150 LET S=175
160 REM C IS COST OF TRIP IF PLANE IS FULL
170 LET C=165
180 REM U IS NUMBER OF UNFILLED SEATS
190 FOR U=80 TO 0 STEP-1
200    REM EXTRA CHARGE IS $98 PER UNFILLED SEAT
210    REM T IS TOTAL CHARGE
220    LET T=U*98
230    REM F IS NUMBER OF PEOPLE ON FLIGHT
240    LET F=S-U
250    REM A IS CHARGE FOR EACH PASSENGER
260    LET A=C+T/F
270    PRINT F,U,A
280 NEXT U
290 END
```

24

```
100 REM FERNDALE REPORT
110 REM ROUND TO HUNDREDTH
120 DEF FNR(X)=INT(1000*X+.5)/1000
130 REM EOD TAG IS "FINISH"
```

```
140 PRINT "SUBJECT","NO. OF GRADES","PERCENT PASSING"
150 READ N$,P,F
160 IF N$="FINISH" THEN 270
170    LET S=P+F
180    LET C=P/S
190    PRINT N$,S,FNR(C)
200    READ N$,P,F
210 GOTO 160
220 DATA GENERAL MATH,95,65
  ─
  ─
  ─
265 DATA FINISH,0,0
270 END
```

25

```
100 PRINT "MONTH","AVG. TEMP."
110 FOR J=1 TO 12
120    READ M$
130    READ W
140    LET S=0
150    FOR I=1 TO W
160      READ T
170      LET S=S+T
180    NEXT I
190    LET A=S/W
200    PRINT M$,A
210 NEXT J
400 DATA MARCH,5,36.7,40.1,33.8,43.9,48.7
  ─
  ─
  ─
510 DATA MAY ...
520 END
```

27

```
10 FOR I=1 TO 5
20    READ L$
30    FOR J=1 TO I
40      PRINT L$;
50    NEXT J
60    PRINT
70 NEXT I
80 DATA A,B,C,D,E
90 END
```

29

```
200 REM PI APPROXIMATION
210 REM P IS PRODUCT; INITIALIZE TO 1
220 LET P=1
230 REM 15 TERM APPROXIMATION
240 REM 1ST 7 PAIRS HAVE EQUAL NUMERATORS
250 FOR I=1 TO 7
260    REM 1ST DENOMINATOR IS ONE LESS THAN NUMERATOR
270    REM 2ND IS ONE MORE
```

```
280    REM N IS NUMERATOR
290    LET N=2*I
300    REM D1 AND D2 ARE DENOMINATORS
310    LET D1=N-1
320    LET D2=N+1
330    LET P=P*(N/D1)*(N/D2)
340 NEXT I
350 REM 15TH TERM
360 LET P=P*(16/15)
370 PRINT 2*P
380 END
```

31

```
100 PRINT "HOW MANY FOLDS";
150 INPUT N
200 PRINT
250 LET T=.01
300 PRINT "FOLD","THICKNESS"
350 FOR F=1 TO N
400    LET T=2*T
450    IF T>=12*5280 THEN 650
500    IF T>=12 THEN 750
550    PRINT F,T;"INCHES"
600    GOTO 800
650    PRINT F,T/(12*5280);"MILES"
700    GOTO 800
750    PRINT F,T/12;"FEET"
800 NEXT F
850 END
```

33 a.

```
100 PRINT "ENTER INTEREST"
110 INPUT I
120 PRINT
130 PRINT "PAYMENT","INTEREST"
140 FOR M=1 TO 12
150    REM D IS NUMERATOR OF FRACTION
160    LET D=13-M
170    PRINT M,D/78*I
180 NEXT M
190 END
```

b.

```
100 PRINT "ENTER INTEREST"
110 INPUT I
120 PRINT "ENTER NUMBER OF PAYMENTS"
130 INPUT N
140 PRINT
150 LET S=N*(N+1)/2
160 PRINT "PAYMENT","INTEREST"
170 FOR M=1 TO N
180    LET D=N+1-M
190    PRINT M,D/S*I
200 NEXT M
210 END
```

34

```
110 REM PUT FUNCTION ON NEXT LINE
120 DEF FNA(X)=4*X↑2-8*X-21
130 REM X1 IS INITIAL X VALUE
140 LET X1=-5
150 REM LOOP THROUGH REMAINING X VALUES
160 FOR X=-4 TO 5
170    REM CALCULATE FUNCTION VALUE
180    LET Y1=FNA(X1)
190    REM CALCULATE NEXT FUNCTION VALUE
200    LET X2=X
210    LET Y2=FNA(X2)
220    REM CHECK SIGNS OF CONSECUTIVE FUNCTION VALUES
230    IF Y1*Y2>0 THEN 260
240    PRINT "GRAPH CROSSES X-AXIS"
250    PRINT "BETWEEN";X1;"AND";X2
260    REM RESET LEFT HAND X VALUE
270    LET X1=X2
280 NEXT X
290 END
```

Chapter 13

1 a. 5   −1   7
   b. 8   1
   c. 9 10 11 12 13 14 15 16
   e. 9 0 −2 4
   g. 10
      15
       6
      −2
       5
   i. FIRST
      THEN
      SECOND
      AND
      THIRD
      SECOND
      AFTER
      FIRST
      BEFORE
      THIRD
      FIRST   SECOND
      SECOND   AFTER
      THEN   FIRST
      AFTER   BEFORE
      SECOND   THIRD

2

```
10 DIM X(6)
20 FOR I=1 TO 6
30    LET X(I)=2*I-1
40 NEXT I
50 END
```

3

```
100 DIM T(12)
110 FOR J=1 TO 12
120    READ T(J)
130 NEXT J
140 FOR I=1 TO 6
150    PRINT TAB(10*I);T(2*I-1);
160 NEXT I
170 PRINT
180 FOR I=1 TO 6
190    PRINT TAB(10*I);T(2*I);
200 NEXT I
210 DATA ...
 _
 _
 _
250 END
```

5

```
200 DIM R(20),S(20)
210 FOR N=1 TO 20
220    READ R(N)
230 NEXT N
240 FOR N=1 TO 20
250    LET S(N)=R(21-N)
260 NEXT N
270 FOR N=1 TO 20
280    PRINT S(N)
290 NEXT N
300 DATA ...
 _
 _
 _
350 END
```

7

```
100 DIM L(15),M(15)
110 FOR J=1 TO 15
120    READ L(J)
130 NEXT J
140 FOR J=1 TO 15
150    IF (L(J)/2=INT(L(J)/2)) THEN 180
160    LET M(J)=0
170    GOTO 190
180    LET M(J)=L(J)
190    PRINT L(J),M(J)
200 NEXT J
210 DATA ...
 _
 _
 _
250 END
```

9

```
100 DIM Y(11),B(11),H(11),A(11)
110 PRINT "YEAR","AT BATS","HITS","AVG"
120 FOR I=1 TO 11
130    LET Y(I)=1967+I
140    READ B(I),H(I)
150    LET A(I)=H(I)/B(I)
160    PRINT Y(I),B(I),H(I),A(I)
170 NEXT I
180 REM M IS HIGHEST BATTING AVERAGE
190 REM J IS SUBSCRIPT WHERE M FOUND
200 LET M=A(1)
210 LET J=1
220 FOR I=2 TO 11
230    IF M>A(I) THEN 260
240    LET M=A(I)
250    LET J=I
260 NEXT I
270 PRINT
280 PRINT "HIGH AVERAGE WAS";M
290 PRINT "EARNED IN";Y(J)
300 REM L IS LARGEST NUMBER OF HITS
310 REM K IS SUBSCRIPT WHERE L FOUND
320 LET L=H(1)
330 LET K=1
340 FOR I=2 TO 11
350    IF L>H(I) THEN 380
360    LET L=H(I)
370    LET K=I
380 NEXT I
390 PRINT
400 PRINT L;"WAS LARGEST NUMBER OF HITS"
410 PRINT "OCCURRING IN";Y(K)
420 DATA ...
 _
 _
 _
500 END
```

10

```
500 DIM A(15),B(15),C(30)
510 FOR I=1 TO 15
520    READ A(I)
530 NEXT I
540 FOR I=1 TO 15
550    READ B(I)
560 NEXT I
570 FOR I=1 TO 29 STEP 2
580    LET C(I)=A(I)
590    LET C(I+1)=B(I)
600 NEXT I
610 FOR I=1 TO 15
620    PRINT A(I),B(I),C(I)
630 NEXT I
640 FOR I=16 TO 30
650    PRINT " "," ",C(I)
660 NEXT I
```

```
670 DATA ...
  —
  —
700 END
```

12

```
100 REM ASSUME 20 ENTRIES
110 REM IF DIFFERENT CHANGE DIM
120 REM AND VALUE OF F
130 DIM N$(20),T$(20)
140 LET F=20
150 FOR I=1 TO F
160    READ N$(I),T$(I)
170 NEXT I
180 PRINT "TELEPHONE DIRECTORY"
190 PRINT
200 PRINT "ENTER NAME OF PERSON"
210 PRINT "WHOSE NUMBER YOU WANT"
220 INPUT A$
230 FOR I=1 TO F
240    IF A$=N$(I) THEN 290
250 NEXT I
260 PRINT A$;" IS NOT LISTED"
270 PRINT "IN THIS DIRECTORY"
280 STOP
290 PRINT A$;"'S NUMBER IS ";T$
300 DATA JANE ROSS,555-0238
  —
  —
500 END
```

13

```
100 DIM M$(9),N$(9),Q(9),D$(9)
110 FOR I=1 TO 9
120    READ M$(I),N$(I),Q(I),D$(I)
130 NEXT I
140 PRINT "ENTER NAME OF MANUFACTURER"
150 INPUT X$
160 FOR I=1 TO 9
170    IF X$<>M$(I) THEN 230
180    PRINT "MODEL NUMBER:";N$(I)
190    PRINT "QUANTITY IN STOCK:";Q(I)
200    PRINT "DESCRIPTION:";D$(I)
210    PRINT
220    PRINT
230 NEXT I
240 DATA ...
  —
  —
300 END
```

15

```
200 DIM A(5),C(5)
210 FOR J=1 TO 5
```

```
220    READ A(J),C(J)
230 NEXT I
240 PRINT "HOW OLD IS APPLICANT";
250 INPUT Y
260 PRINT
270 IF Y>=75 THEN 400
280 PRINT "HOW MANY THOUSAND DOLLARS"
290 PRINT "WORTH OF INSURANCE IS TO"
300 PRINT "BE PURCHASED";
310 INPUT T
320 LET T=INT(T/1000)
340 FOR J=1 TO 5
350    IF Y<A(J) THEN 370
360 NEXT J
370 LET P=T*C(J)
380 PRINT "ANNUAL PREMIUM IS $";P
390 STOP
400 PRINT "APPLICANT'S AGE EXCEEDS"
410 PRINT "COMPANY MAXIMUM"
420 PRINT "NO INSURANCE CAN BE SOLD"
430 DATA 25,15.35,40,17.62,55,28.90,65,35.27,75,41.88
440 END
```

16

```
100 DIM A(20),B(20),C(20)
110 REM SET B AND C TO 0
120 REM TO USE AS CHECK IN PRINTING
130 FOR I=1 TO 20
140    LET B(I)=0
150    LET C(I)=0
160 NEXT I
170 REM N1 SUBSCRIPT OF NON-ZERO B ENTRIES
180 REM N2 SUBSCRIPT OF NON-ZERO C ENTRIES
190 LET N1=0
200 LET N2=0
210 FOR I=1 TO 20
220    READ A(I)
230    IF A(I)/2=INT(A(I)/2) THEN 270
240    LET N1=N1+1
250    LET B(N1)=A(I)
260    GOTO 290
270    LET N2=N2+1
280    LET B(N2)=A(I)
290 NEXT I
300 REM OUTPUT
310 REM PRINT ELEMENT OF B OR C
320 REM ONLY IF NOT ZERO
330 FOR I=1 TO 20
340    PRINT A(I),
350    IF B(I)=0 THEN 380
360    PRINT B(I),
370    GOTO 390
380    PRINT " ",
390    IF C(I)=0 THEN 420
400    PRINT C(I)
410    GOTO 430
420    PRINT
430 NEXT I
```

```
440 DATA ...
  —
  —
  —
500 END
```

17

```
100 DIM X(10)
110 REM ASSUME MAX. OF 10 DIGITS
120 PRINT "NUMBER","REVERSED"
130 FOR I=1 TO 4
140    READ D,N
150    PRINT N,
160    FOR J=1 TO D
170      LET Y=INT(N/10)
180      LET Z=N-10*Y
190      LET X(J)=Z
200      LET N=INT(N/10)
210    NEXT J
220    LET R=0
230    FOR J=D TO 1 STEP -1
240      LET R=R+X(J)↑(D-1)
250    NEXT J
260    PRINT R
270 NEXT I
280 DATA 4,7326
290 DATA 3,581
300 DATA 5,20302
310 DATA 6,417930
320 END
```

20

```
100 DIM B(20)
110 PRINT "ENTER POSITIVE INTEGER"
120 INPUT X
130 LET S=1
140 LET D=X-2*INT(X/2)
150 LET B(S)=D
160 LET S=S+1
170 LET X=INT(X/2)
180 IF X<>0 THEN 140
190 LET S=S-1
200 PRINT "THE BASE TWO EQUIVALENT IS"
210 FOR I=S TO 1 STEP -1
220    PRINT B(I);
230 NEXT I
240 END
```

21

```
100 REM STANDARD DEVIATION
110 DIM X(25)
120 REM FIND AVERAGE M
130 LET S=0
140 FOR I=1 TO 25
150    READ X(I)
```

```
160    LET S=S+X(I)
170 NEXT I
180 LET M=S/25
190 REM SUM OF SQUARES OF DIFFERENCES
200 LET T=0
210 FOR I=1 TO 25
220    LET T=T+(X(I)-M)↑2
230 NEXT I
240 LET Q=T/24
250 LET D=SQR(Q)
260 PRINT "STANDARD DEVIATION IS";D
270 DATA . . .
  −
  −
  −
300 END
```

22

```
100 REM GOLDBACH'S CONJECTURE
110 DIM P(25)
120 FOR I=1 TO 25
130    READ P(I)
140 NEXT I
150 PRINT "EVEN NUMBER","PRIMES"
160 FOR N=6 TO 100 STEP 2
170    FOR I=1 TO 25
180       FOR J=1 TO 25
190          IF N<>P(I)+P(J) THEN 220
200          PRINT N,P(I);"+";P(J)
210          GOTO 240
220       NEXT J
230    NEXT I
240 NEXT N
250 DATA 2,3,5,7,11
260 DATA 13,17,19,23,29
270 DATA 31,37,41,43,47
280 DATA 53,59,61,67,71
290 DATA 73,79,83,87,89
300 END
```

24

```
100 DIM V(6),W(6),S(6),P(6)
110 FOR I=1 TO 6
120    READ V(I),W(I)
130 NEXT I
140 LET M=3
150 FOR I=1 TO 6
160    LET S(I)=V(I)+W(I)
170    LET P(I)=3*V(I)
180 NEXT I
190 FOR I=1 TO 6
200    PRINT V(I),W(I),S(I),P(I)
210 NEXT I
220 DATA 4,-1
  −
  −
  −
270 END
```

Chapter 14

1

a.   b.   c.

```
3          7          4          4          THIRD
8          7          4          2          FIRST
-1                                          SECOND
15
DONE
```

2

```
500 REM PRINT N #S
510 FOR I=1 TO N
520    PRINT "#";
530 NEXT I
540 PRINT
550 RETURN
```

3

```
100 PRINT "HOW WIDE";
110 INPUT W
120 PRINT "HOW HIGH";
130 INPUT H
140 LET N=W
150 FOR I=1 TO H
160    REM SUBROUTINE OF EXERCISE 2
170    GOSUB 500
180 NEXT I
190 STOP
500 REM PRINT N #S
  -
  -
  -
550 RETURN
600 END
```

5

```
500 REM HERON'S FORMULA
510 LET S=(A+B+C)/2
520 LET T=SQR(S*(S-A)*(S-B)*(S-C))
530 RETURN
```

6

```
100 PRINT "SIDE","SIDE","SIDE","AREA"
110 FOR X=1 TO 4
120    READ A,B,C
130    REM EXERCISE 5 SUBROUTINE
140    GOSUB 500
150    PRINT A,B,C,T
160 NEXT X
170 DATA . . .
  -
  -
  -
```

```
210 STOP
500 . . .
  _
  _
  _
530 RETURN
540 END
```

8

```
500 REM LCM SUBROUTINE
510 REM M AND N FROM MAIN PROGRAM
520 REM X WILL BE LCM
530 IF M<>N THEN 560
540 LET X=M
550 RETURN
560 REM DETERMINE LARGER
570 IF M>N THEN 650
580 REM SEE IF M DIVIDES N
590 IF N/M<>INT (N/M) THEN 620
600 LET X=M
610 RETURN
620 LET S=M
630 LET B=N
640 GOTO 710
650 REM SEE IF N DIVIDES M
660 IF M/N<>INT(M/N) THEN 690
670 LET X=N
680 RETURN
690 LET S=N
700 LET B=M
710 REM MULTIPLES OF LARGER
720 LET Z=2
730 IF Z*B/S<>INT(Z*B/S) THEN 760
740    LET X=Z*B
750    RETURN
760    LET Z=Z+1
770 GOTO 730
```

10

```
100 REM MENU PROGRAM
110 DIM N(5)
120 FOR I=1 TO 5
130    READ N(I)
140 NEXT I
150 GOSUB 300
160 PRINT "ENTER YOUR CHOICE (1-4)"
170 INPUT C
180 ON C GOSUB 400,500,600,700
190 ON C GOTO 200,220,240,250
200 PRINT "THE SUM IS";S
210 STOP
220 PRINT "THE AVERAGE IS";A
230 STOP
240 PRINT "THE PRODUCT IS";P
250 STOP
300 REM *** MENU ***
310 PRINT "YOUR CHOICES, NUMBERED 1-4 ARE"
```

```
320 PRINT
330 PRINT 1;TAB(5);"FIND THE SUM"
340 PRINT 2;TAB(5);"FIND THE AVERAGE"
350 PRINT 3;TAB(5);"FIND THE PRODUCT"
360 PRINT 4;TAB(5);"PRINT THE NUMBERS"
370 PRINT
380 RETURN
400 REM *** SUM ***
410 LET S=0
420 FOR I=1 TO 5
430    LET S=S+N(I)
440 NEXT I
450 RETURN
500 REM *** AVERAGE ***
510 REM FIRST FIND SUM
520 GOSUB 400
530 LET A=S/5
540 RETURN
600 REM *** PRODUCT ***
610 LET P=1
620 FOR I=1 TO 5
630    LET P=P*N(I)
640 NEXT P
650 RETURN
700 REM *** PRINT ***
710 FOR I=1 TO 5
720    PRINT N(I)
730 NEXT I
740 RETURN
800 DATA . . .
999 END
```

12

```
100 DIM I$(100),M$(100),N(100),P(100)
110 REM FIVE SUBROUTINES
120 REM READ AND COUNT DATA
130 REM MENU
140 REM THREE MENU OPTIONS
150 GOSUB 200
160 GOSUB 400
170 PRINT "ENTER NUMBER (1-3) OF YOUR CHOICE"
180 ON C GOSUB 600,750,800
190 STOP

200 REM READ AND COUNT SUBROUTINE
210 REM EODTAG IS "NO MORE"
220 REM C IS COUNTER
230 LET C=0
240 READ D$,E$,F,G
250 IF D$="NO MORE" THEN RETURN
260    LET C=C+1
270    LET I$(C)=D$
280    LET M$(C)=E$
290    LET N(C)=F
300    LET P(C)=G
310    READ D$,E$,F,G
320 GOTO 250
```

```
400 REM MENU
410 PRINT TAB(10);"YOUR OPTIONS"
420 PRINT
430 PRINT 1,"ENTER MANUFACTURER'S NAME."
440 PRINT " ","ITEMS AND QUANTITIES LISTED."
450 PRINT
460 PRINT 2,"ENTER ITEM NAME."
470 PRINT " ","MANUFACTURERS' NAMES,PRICES"
480 PRINT " ","AND QUANTITIES LISTED."
490 PRINT
500 PRINT 3,"ENTIRE INVENTORY AND TOTAL"
510 PRINT " ","RETAIL VALUES DISPLAYED"
520 PRINT
530 RETURN

600 REM OPTION 1
610 PRINT "TYPE IN MANUFACTURER'S NAME"
620 INPUT T$
630 PRINT
640 PRINT TAB(3);"ITEM","QUANTITY"
650 PRINT
660 FOR J=1 TO C
670    IF T$<>M$(J) THEN 690
680      PRINT I$(J),N(J)
690 NEXT J
700 RETURN

750 REM OPTION 2
755 PRINT "ENTER ITEM NAME"
760 INPUT V$
765 PRINT
770 PRINT "MANUFACTURER","PRICE","QUANTITY"
775 FOR J=1 TO C
780    IF V$<>I$(J) THEN 790
785      PRINT M$(J),P(J),N(J)
790 NEXT J
795 RETURN

800 REM OPTION 3
805 REM T1: TOTAL ITEMS IN STOCK
810 REM T2: TOTAL RETAIL VALUE
820 LET T1=0
825 LET T2=0
830 PRINT "ITEM","MANUFACTURER","QUANTITY","ITEM PRICE","TOTAL VALUE"
835 FOR J=1 TO C
840    PRINT I$(J),M$(J),N(J),P(J),N(J)*P(J)
845    LET T1=T1+N(J)
850    LET T2=T2+N(J)*P(J)
855 NEXT J
860 PRINT
865 PRINT
870 PRINT "TOTAL ITEMS ON HAND:";T1
875 PRINT "INVENTORY RETAIL VALUE: $";T2
880 RETURN
890 DATA . . .
  ─
  ─
  ─
990 DATA NO MORE,X,0,0
999END
```

13

```
100 PRINT "ENTER COORDINATES OF FIRST POINT"
110 INPUT A1,B1
120 PRINT "OF THE SECOND POINT"
130 INPUT A2,B2
140 PRINT "AND OF THE THIRD"
150 INPUT A3,B3
160 PRINT
170 LET X1=A1
180 LET Y1=B1
190 LET X2=A2
200 LET Y2=B2
210 GOSUB 600
220 LET D1=D
230 LET X1=A2
240 LET Y1=B2
250 LET X2=A3
260 LET Y2=B3
270 GOSUB 600
280 LET D2=D
290 LET X1=A1
300 LET Y1=B1
310 LET X2=A3
320 LET Y2=B3
330 GOSUB 600
340 LET D3=D
350 REM COLLINEAR IF ONE DISTANCE IS
360 REM SUM OF OTHER TWO
370 IF D1=D2+D3 THEN 500
380 IF D2=D1+D3 THEN 500
390 IF D3=D1+D2 THEN 500
400 REM DETERMINE KIND OF TRIANGLE
410 IF D1=D2 THEN 450
420 IF D1=D3 THEN 460
430 IF D2=D3 THEN 460
440 PRINT "SCALENE"
450 STOP
460 IF D2=D3 THEN 490
470 PRINT "ISOSCELES"
480 STOP
490 PRINT "EQUILATERAL"
495 STOP
500 PRINT "THE THREE POINTS ARE COLLINEAR"
510 STOP
600 REM SOLUTION TO PART A
610 LET D=SQR((X2-X1)↑2+(Y2-Y1)↑2)
620 RETURN
700 END
```

19

```
100 REM POLITICAL DATA PROCESSING
110 REM SIX SUBROUTINES:
120 REM READING AND COUNTING
130 REM MENU
140 REM FOUR MENU OPTIONS
150 DIM N$(100),A$(100),P(100)
160 GOSUB 300
```

```
170 GOSUB 400
180 PRINT "TO INDICATE YOUR CHOICE"
190 PRINT "TYPE IN A NUMBER FROM 1-4"
200 INPUT X
210 ON X GOSUB 600,900,1000,1500
220 STOP

300 REM READ AND COUNT
310 REM EODTAG IS "JOHN BARLEYCORN"
320 LET J=1
330 READ N$(J),A$(J),P(J)
340 IF N$(J)="JOHN BARLEYCORN" THEN 380
350    LET J=J+1
360    READ N$(J),A$(J),P(J)
370 GOTO 340
380 LET J=J-1
390 RETURN

400 REM MENU
410 PRINT "THIS PROGRAM ALLOWS YOU TO"
420 PRINT "CHOOSE ONE OF FOUR OPTIONS"
430 PRINT "THEY ARE:"
440 PRINT
450 PRINT 1,"DISPLAY INFORMATION FOR"
460 PRINT " ","PARTICULAR PRECINCT"
470 PRINT
480 PRINT 2,"DISPLAY INFORMATION FOR A"
490 PRINT " ","PARTICULAR POLITICAL AFFILIATION"
500 PRINT
510 PRINT 3,"DISPLAY INFORMATION FOR"
520 PRINT " ","A PARTICULAR INDIVIDUAL"
530 PRINT
540 PRINT 4,"DISPLAY SUMMARY TABLE BY"
550 PRINT " ","PRECINCT AND AFFILIATION"
560 PRINT
570 RETURN

600 REM PROCESS BY PRECINCT
610 REM THREE COUNTERS D,R,I
620 LET D=0
630 LET R=0
640 LET I=0
650 PRINT "ENTER PRECINCT NUMBER"
660 INPUT Z
670 FOR L=1 TO J
680    IF Z<>P(L) THEN 730
690    PRINT N$(L),A$(L)
700    IF A$(L)="D" THEN LET D=D+1
710    IF A$(L)="R" THEN LET R=R+1
720    IF A$(L)="I" THEN LET I=I+1
730 NEXT L
740 PRINT
750 PRINT
760 LET T=D+R+I
770 PRINT " ","DEMOCRAT","REPUBLICAN","INDEPENDENT"
780 PRINT
790 PRINT "NUMBER:",D,R,I
800 PRINT "PERCENT:",D/T*100,R/T*100,I/T*100
810 PRINT
820 RETURN
```

```
900 REM PROCESS BY AFFILIATION
910 PRINT "ENTER AFFILIATION (D,R, OR I)"
920 INPUT F$
930 PRINT
940 FOR L=1 TO J
950    IF F$<>A$(L) THEN 970
960    PRINT N$(L),P(L)
970 NEXT L
980 RETURN


1000 REM PROCESS INDIVIDUAL
1010 PRINT "TYPE IN PERSON'S NAME"
1020 INPUT G$
1030 PRINT
1040 FOR L=1 TO J
1050    IF G$=N$(L) THEN 1090
1060 NEXT L
1070 PRINT N$;" IS NOT RECORDED"
1080 RETURN
1090 PRINT G$,A$(L),P(L)
1100 RETURN


1500 REM SUMMARY SUBROUTINE
1510 REM COUNTERS D0,R0,I0
1520 FOR L=1 TO 4
1530    LET D0(L)=0
1540    LET R0(L)=0
1550    LET I0(L)=0
1560 NEXT L
1570 FOR L=1 TO J
1580    IF A$(L)="D" THEN LET D0(P(L))=D0(P(L))+1
1590    IF A$(L)="R" THEN LET R0(P(L))=R0(P(L))+1
1600    IF A$(L)="I" THEN LET I0(P(L))=I0(P(L))+1
1610 NEXT L
1620 PRINT TAB(20);"SUMMARY"
1630 PRINT
1640 PRINT "PRECINCT","DEMOCRAT","REPUBLICAN","INDEPENDENT"
1650 FOR L=1 TO J
1660    PRINT L,D0(L),R0(L),I0(L)
1670 NEXT L
1680 RETURN
1690 DATA . . .
  —
  —
  —
1999 DATA JOHN BARLEYCORN,N,5
2000 END
```

Chapter 15

1

a.

4	6	8	3	2
0	9	1		

b.

-1	-2
Ø	-1
1	Ø
2	1
3	2

d.

2	3	4
3	4	5
2	3	Ø
3	4	Ø
2	3	
3	4	
4	5	

2

```
100 DIM Q(8,5)
110 FOR M=1 TO 8
120    FOR N=1 TO 5
130       READ Q(M,N)
140    NEXT N
150 NEXT M
```

3

```
100 FOR B=1 TO 3
110    FOR A=1 TO 4
120       READ M(A,B)
130    NEXT A
140 NEXT B
150 DATA 15,22,75,32
155 DATA 7,9,40,Ø
160 DATA 11,18,50,26
```

4

```
100 DIM M(4,3),P(4)
110 FOR I=1 TO 4
120    FOR J=1 TO 3
130       READ M(I,J)
140    NEXT J
150 NEXT I
160 FOR I=1 TO 4
170    READ P(I)
180 NEXT I
190 FOR I=1 TO 4
200    READ D$(I)
210 NEXT I
220 PRINT " ","WAREHOUSE A","WAREHOUSE B","WAREHOUSE C"
230 PRINT
240 FOR I=1 TO 4
250    PRINT D$(I),
260    FOR J=1 TO 3
270       PRINT P(I)*M(I,J),
280    NEXT J
290    PRINT
300 NEXT I
310 DATA 15,7,11
320 DATA 22,9,18
330 DATA 75,40,50
340 DATA 32,Ø,26
```

```
350 DATA 1300,55,12.75,3.60
360 DATA TERMINALS,PAPER,PENCILS,TEMPLATES
370 END
```

6

```
200 DIM A(4,4)
210 FOR X=1 TO 4
220   FOR Y=1 TO 4
230     LET A(X,Y)=2
240   NEXT Y
250 NEXT X
260 FOR X=1 TO 4
270   LET A(X,X)=1
280 NEXT X
290 FOR X=1 TO 4
300   FOR Y=1 TO 4
310     PRINT A(X,Y),
320   NEXT Y
330   PRINT
340 NEXT X
350 END
```

7

```
500 DIM F(5,5)
510 FOR J=1 TO 5
520   FOR K=1 TO 5
530     IF J=K THEN LET F(J,K)=2
540     IF J<K THEN LET F(J,K)=1
550     IF J>K THEN LET F(J,K)=3
560   NEXT K
570 NEXT J
580 FOR J=1 TO 5
590   FOR K=1 TO 5
600     PRINT F(J,K),
610   NEXT K
620   PRINT
630 NEXT J
640 END
```

8

```
100 DIM A(3,5)
110 FOR I=1 TO 3
120   FOR J=1 TO 5
130     READ A(I,J)
140   NEXT J
150 NEXT I
160 FOR I=1 TO 5
170   FOR J=1 TO 3
180     PRINT A(J,I),
190   NEXT J
200   PRINT
210 NEXT I
220 DATA 2,7,0,3,4
225 DATA 6,2,9,8,1
230 DATA 3,5,1,6,5
240 END
```

10

```
100 DIM T(5,6)
110 FOR I=1 TO 5
120    FOR J=1 TO 6
130       LET T(I,J)=0
140    NEXT J
150 NEXT I
160 LET R=1
170 LET C=1
180 PRINT "ENTER FIRST NUMBER"
190 INPUT T(R,C)
200 IF T(R,C)=0 THEN 180
210 LET L=T(R,C)
220 REM T FILLED IF R+C=11
230 IF R+C=11 THEN 370
240    PRINT "ENTER NEXT NUMBER"
250        INPUT N
260         IF N>=L THEN 320
270      IF R=5 THEN 240
280      LET R=R+1
290      LET T(R,C)=N
300      LET L=N
310     GOTO 230
320    IF C=6 THEN 240
330    LET C=C+1
340    LET T(R,C)=N
350    LET L=N
360 GOTO 230
370 PRINT
380 FOR I=1 TO 5
390    FOR J=1 TO 6
400       PRINT TAB(6*J);T(I,J);
410    NEXT J
420    PRINT
430 NEXT I
440 END
```

11

```
100 DIM X(4,5)
110 LET R=4
120 LET C=5
130 FOR I=1 TO R
140    FOR J=1 TO C
150       READ X(I,J)
160    NEXT J
170 NEXT I
180 LET S=0
190 FOR I=2 TO R-1
200    FOR J=2 TO C-1
210       LET S=S+X(I,J)
220    NEXT J
230 NEXT I
240 PRINT "INTERIOR SUM IS";S
250 DATA . . .
  —
  —
  —
260 END
```

13

```
400 DIM T(4,5),L(20)
410 FOR I=1 TO 4
420   FOR J=1 TO 5
430     READ T(I,J)
440      PRINT T(I,J),
450   NEXT J
460   PRINT
470 NEXT I
480 LET C=0
490 FOR I=1 TO 4
500   FOR J=1 TO 5
510     LET C=C+1
520     LET L(C)=T(I,J)
530   NEXT J
540 NEXT I
550 FOR C=1 TO 20
560   PRINT L(C)
570 NEXT C
580 DATA . . .
  _
  _
  _
600 END
```

14

```
100 DIM V(3,4),A$(3),N$(4),T(4)
110 REM VOTE TALLY IN TABLE FORM
120 REM ROWS: DEMOCRAT,REPUBLICAN,INDEPENDENT
130 REM COLUMNS: JENSON,ORTEGA,PLAUSS,GRAHAM
140 FOR X=1 TO 3
150   FOR Y=1 TO 4
160     READ V(X,Y)
170   NEXT Y
180 NEXT X
190 REM READ POLITICAL AFFILIATION
200 FOR X=1 TO 3
210   READ A$(X)
220 NEXT X
230 REM READ CANDIDATE'S NAMES
240 FOR Y=1 TO 4
250   READ N$(Y)
260 NEXT Y
270 REM PRINT TABLE
280 PRINT " ",
290 FOR Y=1 TO 4
300   PRINT N$(Y),
310 NEXT Y
320 PRINT
330 FOR X=1 TO 3
340   PRINT A$(X),
350   FOR Y=1 TO 4
360     PRINT V(X,Y),
370   NEXT Y
380   PRINT
390 NEXT X
400 PRINT
```

```
410 PRINT
420 REM FIND WINNER
430 FOR Y=1 TO 4
440   LET T(Y)=Ø
450   FOR X=1 TO 3
460     LET T(Y)=T(Y)+V(X,Y)
470   NEXT X
480 NEXT Y
490 LET W=T(1)
500 LET S=1
510 FOR X=2 TO 4
520   IF W>T(X) THEN 550
530   LET W=T(X)
540   LET S=X
550 NEXT X
560 PRINT N$(S);" IS THE WINNER"
570 PRINT
580 PRINT " ","VOTES CAST"
590 FOR X=1 TO 3
600   PRINT A$(X),
610 NEXT X
620 PRINT
630 FOR X=1 TO 3
640   LET G=Ø
650   FOR Y=1 TO 4
660     LET G=G+V(X,Y)
670   NEXT Y
680   PRINT G,
690 NEXT X
700 DATA 121,104,91,115
710 DATA 118,52,134,65
720 DATA 62,110,121,106
730 DATA DEMOCRAT,REPUBLICAN,INDEPENDENT
740 DATA JENSON,ORTEGA,PLAUSS,GRAHAM
750 END
```

15

```
100 DIM C$(5),D(5,5)
110 FOR I=1 TO 5
120   READ C$(I)
130 NEXT I
140 FOR I=1 TO 5
150   FOR J=1 TO 5
160     READ D(I,J)
170   NEXT J
180 NEXT I
190 PRINT "ENTER CITY OF ORIGIN"
200 INPUT B$
210 PRINT "ENTER DESTINATION"
220 INPUT E$
230 FOR I=1 TO 5
240   IF B$=C$(I) THEN LET X=I
250   IF E$=C$(I) THEN LET Y=I
260 NEXT I
270 PRINT
280 PRINT "THE DISTANCE BETWEEN ";B$
290 PRINT "AND ";E$;" IS";D(X,Y);"MILES."
```

```
300 DATA BOSTON,CHICAGO. . .
310 DATA 0,975, . . .
320 DATA 975,0. . .
  —
  —
  —
360 DATA 1542,1360, . . .
370 END
```

17

```
100 DIM C$(6,5)
110 REM INITIALIZE ARRAY WITH BLANKS
120 FOR R=1 TO 6
130    FOR S=1 TO 5
140       LET C$(R,S)=" "
150    NEXT S
160 NEXT R
170 PRINT "TO SEE THE SEATING CHART"
180 PRINT "AND THEN END THE PROGRAM"
190 PRINT "ENTER 'ZZZ' AS STUDENT NAME."
200 PRINT
210 PRINT "ENTER STUDENT NAME"
220 INPUT N$
230 IF N$="ZZZ" THEN 370
240    PRINT "ENTER SEAT BY ROW AND SEAT NUMBER"
250    PRINT "WHICH ROW";
260    INPUT R
270    PRINT "WHICH SEAT IN ROW";R;
280    INPUT S
290    IF C$(R,S)=" " THEN 330
300    PRINT C$(R,S);" IS ALREADY IN THAT SEAT."
310    PRINT "ENTER ANOTHER SEAT"
320    GOTO 250
330    LET C$(R,S)=N$
340    PRINT "ENTER NEXT NAME"
350    INPUT N$
360 GOTO 230
370 FOR R=1 TO 6
380    FOR S=1 TO 5
390       PRINT C$(R,S),
400    NEXT S
410    PRINT
420 NEXT R
430 END
```

18

```
171 REM SECTION CHOICE
172 PRINT "CHOOSE 'NO SMOKING'(1),'SMOKING'(2)"
173 PRINT "OR EITHER (3)."
174 PRINT "ENTER 1,2, OR 3 AS CHOICE."
175 INPUT C
211 IF C=3 THEN 230
212 IF C=1 THEN 217
213 IF N1>=7 THEN 230
214 PRINT "WRONG SEAT FOR SMOKING SECTION"
215 PRINT "CHOOSE ANOTHER SEAT"
```

```
216 GOTO 200
217 IF N1<=6 THEN 230
218 PRINT "WRONG SEAT FOR NON-SMOKING SECTION"
219 PRINT "CHOOSE ANOTHER SEAT"
220 GOTO 200
225 PRINT
```

20

```
1000 REM SUBROUTINE TO SWITCH ROWS
1010 REM M AND N COME FROM MAIN PROGRAM
1020 REM I AND J COME FROM MAIN PROGRAM
1030 FOR L=1 TO N
1040    LET T=A(I,L)
1050    LET A(I,L)=A(J,L)
1060    LET A(J,L)=T
1070 NEXT L
1080 RETURN

100 REM PART A: CREATE MATRIX A
110 DIM A(6,8)
120 LET M=6
130 LET N=8
140 FOR X=1 TO M
150    FOR Y=1 TO N
160       LET A(X,Y)=ABS(X-Y)
170    NEXT Y
180 NEXT X
190 REM PART B: PRINT ARRAY A
200 FOR X=1 TO M
210    FOR Y=1 TO N
220       PRINT TAB(5*Y);A(X,Y);
230    NEXT Y
240    PRINT
250 NEXT X
260 REM PART C
270 FOR X=1 TO 4
280    PRINT
290 NEXT X
300 REM PART D: SWITCHING
310 LET I=1
320 LET J=6
330 GOSUB 1000
340 LET I=2
350 LET J=5
360 GOSUB 1000
370 LET I=3
380 LET J=4
390 GOSUB 1000
400 REM PART E: PRINT NEW ARRAY
410 FOR X=1 TO M
420    FOR Y=1 TO N
430       PRINT TAB(5*Y);A(X,Y);
440    NEXT Y
450    PRINT
460 NEXT X
470 STOP
2000 END
```

22

```
100 DIM M(7,6)
110 FOR I=1 TO 7
120    FOR J=1 TO 6
130       READ M(I,J)
140       PRINT TAB(5*J);M(I,J);
150    NEXT J
160    PRINT
170 NEXT I
180 PRINT
190 LET L=M(1,1)
200 LET R=1
210 LET C=1
220 FOR I=1 TO 7
230    FOR J=1 TO 6
240       IF L>=M(I,J) THEN 280
250       LET L=M(I,J)
260       LET R=I
270       LET C=J
280    NEXT J
290 NEXT I
300 PRINT "THE LARGEST ELEMENT IS";L
310 PRINT "IT IS FOUND IN"
320 PRINT "     ROW";R;" COLUMN";C
330 LET K=1
340 FOR I=1 TO 7
350    FOR J=1 TO 6
360       IF L<>M(I,J) THEN 420
370       IF R<>I THEN 400
380       IF C<>J THEN 400
390       GOTO 420
400       PRINT "AND ROW";I;" COLUMN";J
410       LET K=K+1
420    NEXT J
430 NEXT I
440 PRINT "NUMBER OF OCCURENCES OF";L;":";K
450 DATA . . .
   .
   .
   .
500 END
```

Chapter 16

1 a. 8*RND(−1)   g. INT(9*RND(−1))+1
   b. 8*RND(−1)+7   h. INT(11*RND(−1)+2)
   d. 7*RND(−1)−3   i. INT(8*RND(−1))
   f. 7*RND(−1)−12   l. 2*INT(4*RND(−1)+1)

2 a. A number between 0 and 6
   b. A number between 5 and 6
   d. A number between −2 and 6
   e. A number between −6 and 1
   g. An integer from 1 to 8
   h. An integer from 3 to 16
   i. An integer from −2 to 8
   l. The integer 15

3

```
110 REM C IS COUNTER
120 LET C=0
130 FOR I=1 TO 1000
140    LET N=INT(8*RND(-1)+1)
150    IF N/5<>INT(N/5) THEN 170
160    LET C=C+1
170 NEXT I
180 PRINT C;"FIVES WERE GENERATED"
190 END
```

5

```
100 LET L=0
110 FOR I=1 TO 10
120    FOR J=1 TO 10
130       LET N=INT(196*RND(-1)+5)
140       PRINT N;
150       IF L>=N THEN 170
160       LET L=N
170    NEXT J
180    PRINT
190 NEXT I
200 PRINT "LARGEST IS";L
210 END
```

6

```
110 REM TWO COINS,THIRTY TIMES
120 FOR I=1 TO 30
130    LET T1=INT(2*RND(-1))
140    LET T2=INT(2*RND(-1))
150    REM T1+T2=0,1 OR 2
160    ON T1+T2+1 GOTO 170,230,200
170    REM T1+T2=0 SO BOTH TAILS
180    PRINT "TT"
190    GOTO 290
200    REM T1+T2=2 SO BOTH HEADS
210    PRINT "HH"
220    GOTO 290
230    REM T1+T2=1 SO COINS DIFFER
240    REM FIND WHICH COIN WAS HEADS
250    IF T1=1 THEN 280
260    PRINT "TH"
270    GOTO 290
280    PRINT "HT"
290 NEXT I
300 END
```

10

```
200 REM ROLL DIE 10000 TIMES
210 REM COUNT OCCURENCES OF EACH FACE
220 DIM F(6)
230 FOR I=1 TO 6
240    LET F(I)=0
250 NEXT I
```

```
260 FOR I=1 TO 10000
270    LET R=INT(6*RND(-1)+1)
280    LET F(R)=F(R)+1
290 NEXT I
300 PRINT "FACE","OCCURENCES"
310 FOR I=1 TO 6
320    PRINT I,F(I)
330 NEXT I
340 END
```

13

```
100 DIM X(100),C(8)
110 FOR I=1 TO 25
120    LET X(I)=INT(4*RND(-1)+1)
130 NEXT I
140 FOR I=26 TO 50
150    LET X(I)=INT(3*RND(-1)+3)
160 NEXT I
170 FOR I=51 TO 100
180    LET X(I)=INT(5*RND(-1)+4)
190 NEXT I
200 FOR I=1 TO 8
210    LET C(I)=0
220 NEXT I
230 FOR I=1 TO 100
240    LET C(X(I))=C(X(I))+1
250 NEXT I
260 FOR I=1 TO 8
270    PRINT I,C(I)
280 NEXT I
290 END
```

14

```
500 REM 10X10 RANDOM ARRAY
510 DIM R(10,10)
520 REM GENERATE AND PRINT
530 FOR I=1 TO 10
540    FOR J=1 TO 10
550      LET R(I,J)=INT(12*RND(-1)-4)
560      PRINT TAB(4*J);R(I,J);
570    NEXT J
580    PRINT
590 NEXT I
600 PRINT
610 REM AVG ON MAIN DIAGONAL
620 LET S=0
630 FOR I=1 TO 10
640    LET S=S+R(I,I)
650 NEXT I
660 LET A=S/10
670 PRINT "AVERAGE IS";A
680 END
```

16

```
100 DIM A$(20,25)
110 REM INITIALIZE TO BLANKS
```

```
120 FOR I=1 TO 20
130   FOR J=1 TO 25
140     LET A$(I,J)=" "
150   NEXT J
160 NEXT I
170 FOR J=1 TO 25
180   LET N=INT(21*RND(-1))
190   IF N=0 THEN 230
200   FOR I=20 TO 21-N STEP -1
210     LET A$(I,J)="#"
220   NEXT I
230 NEXT J
240 FOR I=1 TO 20
250   FOR J=1 TO 25
260     PRINT A$(I,J);
270   NEXT J
280   PRINT
290 NEXT I
300 END
```

18

```
100 REM 1-DIM RANDOM WALK
110 REM C IS TOTAL STEPS
120 LET C=0
130 REM P IS POSITION ON BRIDGE
140 REM BRIDGE IS 14 FEET
150 REM SO 7 IS MIDDLE
160 LET P=7
170 REM SIMULATE STEP
180 LET S=INT(2*RND(-1)+1)
190 LET C=C+1
200 REM S=1 MEANS STEP LEFT
210 REM S=2 MEANS STEP RIGHT
220 IF S=1 THEN 250
230 LET P=P+1
240 GOTO 260
250 LET P=P-1
260 REM CHECK FOR END OF BRIDGE
270 REM P=0, LEFT END OF BRIDGE
280 REM P=14, RIGHT END OF BRIDGE
290 IF P=0 THEN 330
300 IF P=14 THEN 350
310 REM TAKE NEXT STEP
320 GOTO 180
330 PRINT "LEFT BANK REACHED AFTER";C;"STEPS"
340 STOP
350 PRINT "RIGHT BANK REACHED AFTER";C;"STEPS"
360 END
```

20

```
110 REM THREE SOCCER PLAYERS
120 PRINT "GAME","SONYA","HELENE","PATRICIA","TOTAL"
130 PRINT
140 FOR G=1 TO 20
150 LET S=0
160 LET H=0
170 LET P=0
```

```
180    REM SIMULATE SONYA'S GAME
190    FOR I=1 TO 7
200      LET X=RND(-1)
210      IF X>.257 THEN 230
220      LET S=S+1
230    NEXT I
240    REM SIMULATE HELENE'S GAME
250    FOR I=1 TO 5
260      LET X=RND(-1)
270      IF X>.198 THEN 290
280      LET H=H+1
290    NEXT I
300    REM SIMULATE PATRICIA'S GAME
310    FOR I=1 TO 9
320      LET X=RND(-1)
330      IF X>.299 THEN 350
340      LET P=P+1
350    NEXT I
360    PRINT G,S,H,P,S+H+P
370 NEXT G
380 END
```

21

```
110 REM MURRAY AND HUGO SHOOTOUT
120 REM MURRAY SHOOTS FIRST
130 REM MURRAY HITS TARGET ON AVG. 1 OF 6 TRIES
140 REM GENERATE RANDOM INTEGER FROM 1 TO 6
150 LET M=INT(6*RND(-1)+1)
160 REM DECIDE THAT M=6 MEANS HIT
170 IF M<6 THEN 220
180 REM MURRAY WINS
190 PRINT "MURRAY SHOOTS AND HITS THE TARGET"
200 PRINT "HE IS THE CHAMPION TARGET SHOOTER"
210 STOP
220 REM MURRAY MISSES TARGET
230 PRINT "MURRAY SHOOTS AND MISSES"
240 PRINT
250 REM NOW IT IS HUGO'S TURN TO SHOOT
260 REM HUGO HITS ON AVG. 2 OF 7 TRIES
270 REM GENERATE RANDOM INTEGER FROM 1 TO 7
280 LET H=INT(7*RND(-1)+1)
290 REM DECIDE THAT H=1,2 MEANS HIT
300 IF H>2 THEN 350
310 REM HUGO WINS
320 PRINT "HUGO SHOOTS. HE HITS THE TARGET."
330 PRINT "HUGO IS THE WINNER"
340 STOP
350 REM HUGO MISSES
360 PRINT "HUGO'S SHOT MISSES"
370 PRINT
380 REM CONTINUE CONTEST WITH MURRAY SHOOTING
390 GO TO 150
400 END
```

22

```
110 REM 3 PLAYER BOARD GAME
120 REM VARIABLE A WILL BE SQUARE WHERE 1ST PLAYER IS
```

```
130 REM B IS FOR 2ND PLAYER AND C FOR 3RD
140 LET A=0
150 LET B=0
160 LET C=0
170 REM 1ST PLAYERS TURN
180    GOSUB 580
190    REM CHECK IF A IS NOT ON BOARD
200    IF A>0 THEN 250
210    REM A=0 SO CHECK FOR S=-1
220    REM IF S=-1, SET S=0, SO NO MOVE
230    IF S<>-1 THEN 250
240    LET S=0
250    LET A=A+S
260    REM CHECK FOR WIN
270    IF A<50 THEN 300
280    PRINT "1ST PLAYER SPINS A";S;"AND WINS"
290    STOP
300    PRINT "1ST PLAYER IS ON SQUARE";A
310    REM 2ND PLAYERS TURN
320    GOSUB 580
330    REM CHECK IF B IS NOT ON BOARD
340    IF B>0 THEN 370
350    IF S<>-1 THEN 370
360    LET S=0
370    LET B=B+S
380    REM CHECK FOR WIN
390    IF B<50 THEN 420
400    PRINT "2ND PLAYER SPINS A";S;"AND WINS"
410    STOP
420    PRINT "2ND PLAYER IS ON SQUARE";B
430    REM 3RD PLAYERS TURN
440    GOSUB 580
450    REM CHECK IF C IS NOT ON BOARD
460    IF C>0 THEN 490
470    IF S<>-1 THEN 490
480    LET S=0
490    LET C=C+S
500    REM CHECK FOR WIN
510    IF C<50 THEN 540
520    PRINT "3RD PLAYER SPINS A";S;"AND WINS"
530    STOP
540    PRINT "3RD PLAYER IS ON SQUARE";C
550    PRINT
560    REM NOW IT IS 1ST PLAYERS TURN AGAIN
570 GO TO 180
580 REM SUBROUTINE TO SIMULATE SPINNER
590 REM GENERATE -1,0,1,2 OR 3
600 LET S=INT(5*RND(-1)-1)
610 RETURN
620 END
```

24

```
100 REM I-P-S MINING
110 REM G IS WATER LEFT
120 LET G=110000
130 REM C IS TOTAL CONSUMED
140 LET C=0
150 REM NATURAL DECREASE
```

```
160 LET D1=850
170 REM CAMP USE DECREASE
180 LET D2=2200
190 REM STREAM INCREASE
200 LET I=375
210 LET W=1
220 PRINT "WEEK","AMT. CONSUMED","AMT. LEFT"
230 LET C=C+(D1+D2)
240 LET G=G-(D1+D2)
250 PRINT W,C,G
260 LET W=W+1
270 IF G>=D1+D2 THEN 230
280 END
```

26

```
110 REM BASEBALL SIMULATION
120 REM COLUMN HEADINGS
130 PRINT "GAME";
140 FOR I=1 TO 9
150    PRINT TAB(6*I+3);I;
160 NEXT I
170 PRINT TAB(63);"TOTAL"
180 PRINT
190 REM 10 GAMES
200 FOR G=1 TO 10
210    PRINT G;
220    REM T IS TOTAL HITS FOR 9 INNINGS
230    LET T=0
240    REM I IS INNING NUMBER
250    FOR I=1 TO 9
260      REM H IS HITS IN AN INNING, P IS OUTS
270      LET H=0
280      LET P=0
290      REM READ A BATTING AVERAGE
300      READ A
310      REM IF A=-1(EOD) MUST RESTORE
320      REM TO CONTINUE BATTING ROTATION
330      IF A<>-1 THEN 350
340      RESTORE
350      LET X=RND(-1)
360      REM CHECK FOR HIT
370      IF X>A THEN 410
380      LET H=H+1
390      REM NEXT BATTER'S TURN
400      GO TO 300
410      LET P=P+1
420      REM CHECK FOR END OF INNING
430      IF P<3 THEN 300
440      PRINT TAB(6*I+3);H;
450      LET T=T+H
460    NEXT I
470    PRINT TAB(63);T
480    REM ON TO NEXT GAME
490 NEXT G
500 DATA .298,.304,.336,.313,.278
510 DATA .248,.212,.263,.205,-1
520 END
```

27

```
100 REM RANDOM NUMBER AREA
110 REM HEIGHT OF BOX TO BE CALCULATED
120 REM DEFINE FUNCTION
130 DEF FNY(X)=4*X↑2+3*X+2
140 REM H COUNTS DARTS IN SHADED AREA
150 LET H=Ø
160 REM USER SUPPLIES BOTH ENDPOINTS
170 PRINT "ENTER LEFT AND RIGHT ENDPOINTS"
180 INPUT L,E
190 PRINT
200 REM GET HEIGHT,B,OF BOX FROM SUBROUTINE
210 GOSUB 500
220 REM A IS TOTAL AREA OF TARGET
230 LET A=B*(E-L)
240 PRINT "HOW MANY DARTS DO YOU WISH TO THROW";
250 INPUT N
260 PRINT
270 REM SIMULATE THROWING N DARTS
280 FOR I=1 TO N
290    REM R IS ABSCISSA, BETWEEN E AND L
300    LET R=(E-L)*RND(-1)+L
310    REM S IS ORDINATE, BETWEEN Ø AND B
320    LET S=B*RND(-1)
330    REM CHECK WHERE DART LANDS
340    IF S>=FNY(R) THEN 360
350    LET H=H+1
360 NEXT I
370 LET S=H/N*A
380 PRINT "APPROXIMATE AREA IS";S
390 STOP
500 REM MAX VALUE SUBROUTINE
510 LET X=L
520 LET M=FNY(X)
530 LET X=X+.1
540 IF X>E THEN 590
550 LET Y=FNY(X)
560 IF M>=Y THEN 530
570 LET M=Y
580 GO TO 530
590 REM B IS MAX - IT IS TO BE .5 LARGER
600 REM THAN MAX FUNCTION VALUE
610 LET B=M+.5
620 RETURN
700 END
```

33

```
100 REM COIN MATCH GAME
110 REM C IS COMPUTER'S MONEY; H IS HUMAN'S
120 REM BOTH START AT $1Ø
130 LET C=10
140 LET H=10
150 REM INTRODUCTION
160 PRINT "HELLO,HUMAN. I WILL TOSS TWO COINS."
170 PRINT "YOU WILL BET WHETHER OR NOT THE COINS MATCH."
180 PRINT "WE EACH BEGIN WITH $10 AND EACH BET IS $1."
190 PRINT "LET'S BEGIN."
```

```
200 PRINT
210 PRINT
220 GOSUB 1000
230 GOSUB 1100
240 GOSUB 1200
250 GOSUB 1300
260 GOSUB 1500
270 REM SEE IF USER WANTS TO CONTINUE
280 PRINT
290 PRINT "DO YOU WISH TO CONTINUE PLAYING?"
300 PRINT "IF YES, TYPE IN A 1. IF NO, TYPE A 2."
310 INPUT A
320 IF A=1 THEN 210
330 IF A=2 THEN 370
340 PRINT "THE NUMBER";A;"IS NOT A CORRECT RESPONSE"
350 PRINT "TRY AGAIN."
360 GOTO 290
370 PRINT "OH, WELL. PERHAPS ANOTHER DAY."
380 STOP
1000 REM SUBROUTINE WHICH TOSSES TWO COINS
1010 LET T1=INT(2*RND(-1))
1020 LET T2=INT(2*RND(-1))
1030 PRINT "THE TWO COINS HAVE BEEN TOSSED."
1040 RETURN
1100 REM SUBROUTINE TO GET HUMAN'S GUESS
1105 PRINT "DO YOU THINK THE COINS MATCH OR NOT?"
1110 PRINT "IF YOU THINK THEY MATCH, TYPE IN THE NUMBER 50."
1115 PRINT "IF YOU THINK THE COINS DON'T MATCH, TYPE IN A 100."
1120 PRINT "WHAT IS YOUR GUESS: 50 OR 100";
1125 INPUT G
1130 PRINT
1135 IF G<>50 THEN 1145
1140 RETURN
1145 IF G<>100 THEN 1155
1150 RETURN
1155 PRINT "ONLY THE NUMBERS 50 OR 100 ARE MEANINGFUL."
1160 PRINT "TRY AGAIN."
1165 GOTO 1120
1200 REM SUBROUTINE FOR SHOWING RESULTS OF TOSS
1205 PRINT
1210 REM VARIABLE=0 MEANS HEADS; =1 MEANS TAILS
1215 PRINT "THE COINS COME UP A"
1220 IF T1<>0 THEN 1235
1225 PRINT "HEAD",
1230 GOTO 1240
1235 PRINT "TAIL",
1240 PRINT "AND A",
1245 IF T2<>0 THEN 1260
1250 PRINT "HEAD"
1255 RETURN
1260 PRINT "TAIL"
1265 RETURN
1300 REM SUBROUTINE CHECKS FOR CORRECT GUESS
1310 REM AND ADJUSTS MONIES
1320 REM FROM SUB 1000 IF MATCH, T1+T2=0 OR 2
1330 REM VARIABLE T WILL BE SET =50 IF COINS MATCH
1340 REM T=100 IF COINS DON'T MATCH
1350 LET T=50
1360 IF T1+T2<>1 THEN 1380
1370 LET T=100
```

```
1380 REM CHECK HUMAN'S GUESS,G, WITH MATCH INDICATOR,T
1390 IF G=T THEN 1450
1400 REM GUESS WAS INCORRECT
1410 PRINT "TOO BAD. YOU GUESSED WRONG."
1420 LET C=C+1
1430 LET H=H-1
1440 RETURN
1450 REM GUESS WAS CORRECT
1460 PRINT "GOOD GUESS."
1470 LET H=H+1
1480 LET C=C-1
1490 RETURN
1500 REM SUBROUTINE TO PRINT CURRENT AMOUNTS
1510 REM AND CHECK IF MONEY LEFT TO BET
1520 PRINT "YOU NOW HAVE $";H,"AND I HAVE $";C
1530 IF H=20 THEN 1560
1540 IF C=20 THEN 1580
1550 RETURN
1560 PRINT "THE GAME IS OVER. YOU WIN."
1570 STOP
1580 PRINT "THE GAME ENDS. ANOTHER VICTORY FOR COMPUTERS."
1590 STOP
1600 END
```

36

```
110 REM MONKEY TYPING
120 LET N=0
130 REM GENERATE LETTERS
140 LET A=INT(5*RND(-1)+1)
150 LET B=INT(5*RND(-1)+1)
160 LET C=INT(5*RND(-1)+1)
170 LET I=INT(5*RND(-1)+1)
180 LET S=INT(5*RND(-1)+1)
190 REM GENERATE WORD
200 LET W=10↑4*B+10↑3*A+10↑2*S+10*I+C
210 LET N=N+1
220 IF W<>21543 THEN 250
230 PRINT "THE MONKEY TYPED 'BASIC' AS WORD";N
240 STOP
250 REM CHECK COUNTER
260 IF N/100<>INT(N/100) THEN 140
270 PRINT N;"'WORDS' TYPED SO FAR"
280 GO TO 140
290 END
```

38   See Example 13.10.

INDEX

abacus, 1
ABS, 171
absolute value function, 171
addition, 26
algorithm, 15
alphabetic ordering, 122
alphanumeric, 67
American National Standards Institute, viii, 359
analog computer, 2
analysis of the problem, 14
AND, 364
ANSI, viii, 359
area under curve, 315
argument of a function, 169
arithmetic and logic unit, 5
arithmetic operations, 26
array
  matrix, 279
  one-dimensional, 228
  string, 241
  two-dimensional, 279
array element, 228

BACKSPACE key, 43
BASE, 234
BASIC, 1, 25
BCD file, 336
binary, 11
binary-coded decimal file, 336
binary number system, 11
branch, 77
BREAK key, 82
bubble sort, 347
bug, 15
built-in function, 169

call of a subprogram, 256
card reader, 1

CATALOG, 331
cathode ray tube, 1
central memory, 329
central processing unit, 5
chance in simulation, 311
chip, 8
CLOSE, 333
COBOL, 12
coding, 15
column, 280
columnwise entry into array, 283
comma used with PRINT, 37
command, 36
comparison of strings, 121
compiler, 12
complementary relations, 112
compound logical statements, 364
computer, 7
  home, 8
  mainframe, 7
  micro, 8
  mini, 8
  personal, 8
computer program, 12, 14
computer system, 7
CON function, 370
concatenation, 187
conditional transfer, 74
control structure
  repetition, 357
  selection, 352
  sequence, 352
control unit, 5
control variable, 88
CONTROL/T keys, 82
conversational language, 95
correcting errors, 40
counter, 123, 192
counting loop, 88

counting with subscripted variables, 231
CPU, 5
CRT, 1

data file, 332
data pointer, 143
data set, 13
data stack, 143
debugging, 15
decision flowcharting symbol, 76
DEF FN, 182
designs, 217
detailed flowchart, 72
digital computer, 2
DIM, 233, 284
DIMENSION, 234
displacement, 308
divisibility, 175
division, 26
double subscript, 280

E-numbers, 131
echo check, 233
EDIT, 331
editing, 40
element of an array, 228
END, 33
end of data indicator, 155
enhanced BASICs, 359
ENIAC, 7
entering a program, 15, 31
eod tag, 155
ERASE key, 43
error message, 44, 145, 170, 233, 256
ESC key, 82
evaluating an expression, 27
executing a program, 15
execution errors, 45
exponentiation, 26
expression, 27

file, 332
file name, 332
file number, 333
file ordinal, 333
file statement
  CLOSE, 333
  INPUT#, 335
  OPEN, 333
  PRINT#, 333
  RESTORE#, 335
final value, 196
flow arrow, 15
flow line, 15
flowchart, 14, 15
flowcharting symbol
  decision, 76
  diamond, 76

flowcharting symbol—*Continued*
  flowline, 15, 104, 205
  FOR, 204
  GOSUB, 260
  GOTO, 104
  IF–THEN, 70
  INPUT, 52
  NEXT, 205
  output, 15
  oval, 15, 260
  parallelogram, 146
  process, 16
  READ, 146
  rectangle, 15
  REM, 85
  RETURN, 260
  terminal, 15
flowcharting template, 16
format for output, 360
FOR/NEXT, 193
FOR/NEXT loops (observations), 206
FORTRAN, 12
function, 169
  ABS, 171
  ATN, 182
  COS, 182
  DEF FN, 182
  EXP, 182
  INT, 173
  LEFT$, 186
  LEN, 185
  LOG, 182
  MID$, 186
  RIGHT$, 186
  RND, 305
  SGN, 182
  SIN, 182
  SQR, 169
  TAN, 182
functions
  built-in, 169
  matrix, 370
  string, 185
  table, 182
  user-defined, 182, 365

general form
  DATA, 145
  FOR–NEXT, 195
  GOSUB, 254
  GOTO, 103
  IF–THEN, 120
  IF–THEN, 75
  IF–THEN–ELSE, 354
  INPUT, 51
  LEFT$, 186
  LET, 34

general form—*Continued*
  MID$, 186
  ON–GOSUB, 268
  ON–GOTO, 134
  READ, 145
  REM, 83
  RESTORE, 159
  RIGHT$, 186
  STOP, 114
global variable, 264
GOTO, 103
greatest integer function, 173

hardware, 12
high-level language, 12
home computer, 8

IDN function, 370
IF–THEN, 74
IF–THEN (a second form), 120
IF–THEN–ELSE, 354
image statement, 361
increment value, 196
indenting a loop, 88, 193
index, 192
ingredients of a loop, 88
initial value, 195
initializing, 88
INPUT, 48
INPUT (flowcharting symbol), 52
INPUT#, 335
input device, 2
INT, 173
interpretation with random numbers, 312
interpreter, 12
INV function, 372
inverse of a matrix, 372
invoke a subprogram, 256

Kemeny, John, vii
keyboard, 1, 31
Kurtz, Thomas, vii

language independent, 16
LEFT$, 186
LEN, 185
length of a string, 185
LET, 34
library, 331
line numbers, 33, 41
line printer, 6
LIST, 35
list (array), 228
local program, 329
log-in, 325
log-off, 330
logical operators, 364
loop, 79
loop configurations, 213

machine language, 11
main program, 256
mainframe, 7
maintainable program, 82
MAT difference, 368
MAT function
  CON, 370
  IDN, 370
  INV, 372
  TRN, 371
  ZER, 370
MAT INPUT, 367
MAT multiplication of matrices, 369
MAT PRINT, 366
MAT READ, 366
MAT scalar multiplication, 369
MAT statements, 366
MAT sum, 368
matrix, 279
memory diagram for loop, 92
memory diagrams, 64
memory unit, 5
menu, 268
menu-driven programs, 268
message (output), 20
microcomputer, 8
microprocessor, 8
MID$, 186
minicomputer, 8
minimal BASIC, viii
minor diagonal, 285
modem, 13
modular programming, 262
module, 262
multiple assignment, 359
multiple branch transfer, 134
multiple selection, 357
multiplication, 26

name of an array, 228
nested FOR loops, 211
nested IFs, 115
nested subroutines, 274
network, 13
NEW, 329
NODATA, 365
NOT, 364
numeric variables, 67

object program, 12
OCR, 4
OLD, 329
ON–GOSUB, 268
ON–GOTO, 134
on-line, 32
one-dimensional array, 228
one-way selection, 355
OPEN, 333
operating command, 36

opposite relations, 112
optical character recognition, 4
OR, 365
order of evaluation, 27
output device, 5
output field, 361
output symbol, 15, 16
overdimension, 235

paper printing unit, 4
parallelogram, 146
peripheral memory, 329
permanent program, 329
personal computer, 8
plotter, 6
pointer, 143
postchecked loop, 357
prechecked loop, 357
PRINT, 35, 56
PRINT#, 333
print control characters, 57
print positions, 57
PRINT USING, 359
PRINT with INPUT, 49
print zones, 57
problem definition, 14
problem solving, 14
program, 14

quotation marks, 20
quoted text, 67

raising to a power, 26
random integers, 308
RANDOMIZE, 306
random number generator, 305
random numbers over any range, 306
READ, 142
readable program, 82
READY, 36
rectangle (flowchart symbol), 15
reference a subprogram, 256
relation, 75
REM, 83
RENUM, 331
repetition construct, 357
RESAVE, 330
RESEQ, 331
RESTORE, 159
RESTORE#, 335
RETURN, 255
RETURN key, 31
RIGHT$, 186
rounding to nearest hundredth, 177
row, 279
rowwise entry into array, 283
RUBOUT key, 43
RUN, 35
run-time errors, 45

SAVE, 329
scaling factor, 308
scientific notation, 131
selection construct, 352
semicolon used with PRINT, 38
sequence construct, 352
serial printer, 6
simple variable, 226
simulation, 310
software, 12
sort, 342
source program, 12
spacing, 37, 38
SQR, 169
square array, 285
square root function, 169
stack, 143
STEP, 196
stepwise refinement, 265
STOP, 114
stopping a program, 81
storing a program, 328
straight-line programs, 72
string array, 241
string constant, 67
string functions, 185
string variable, 67
strings with
    IF–THEN, 94
    INPUT, 68
    LET, 68
structured programming, 352
subprogram, 256
subroutine, 254
subscript, 227
subscripted string variable, 241
subscripted variable, 227
substring, 186
subtraction, 26
summing, 127
syntax errors, 45
system, 7
system command, 36

TAB, 59
TAB with variable argument, 216
table, 279
table look-up, 238
template, 16
terminal, 4
terminal file, 336
terminal symbol, 15, 260
testing, 15
time-sharing, 12
top-down programming, 265
tracing, 66
transfer statement
    GOTO, 103
    IF–THEN, 74

transfer statement—*Continued*
  ON–GOSUB, 268
  ON–GOTO, 134
transpose of matrix, 371
TRN function, 371
two-dimensional array, 279
two-way selection, 108, 352

UNSAVE, 330
UPC codes, 4
updating a file, 338
user-defined function, 182, 365

variable
  control, 88
  description of, 25, 26
  doubly subscripted, 280
  numeric, 67
  simple, 226
  singly subscripted, 227
  string, 67
variable names (enhanced), 359
visual display unit, 1

ZER function, 370